The Developing Person
Through Childhood

Christian Pierre. *Reading to Me* **(front cover),** *Festival Bandita* **(back cover).**
The luminous colors and figures in *Reading to Me* and *Festival Bandita* reflect the hope
and discovery apparent in all Pierre's paintings—of adults, animals, plants, landscapes,
and children. Pierre has lived in several cultures, under many life circumstances, but she
says she could never make herself paint anything depressing. Instead, by combining
colors, shapes, and composition in ways that reflect fantasy and reality, she allows us to
recognize human development. Note that the mother in *Reading to Me* focuses on the
big book, while her child snuggles against her cheek and looks outward with a wide-
eyed, happy expression. This is a metaphor for this textbook: The grownups read it
carefully to help the next generation of children develop an eager and secure outlook on
the world.

About the Author

Kathleen Stassen Berger received her undergraduate education at Stanford University and Radcliffe College, earned an M.A.T. from Harvard University and an M.S. and Ph.D from Yeshiva University. Her broad experience as an educator includes directing a preschool, teaching philosophy and humanities at the United Nations International School, teaching child and adolescent development to graduate students at Fordham University, and teaching social psychology to inmates earning a paralegal degree at Sing Sing Prison.

For the past 30 years Berger has taught at Bronx Community College of the City University of New York, recently as the elected chair of the Social Science Department. She has taught introduction to psychology, child and adolescent development, adulthood and aging, social psychology, abnormal psychology, and human motivation. Her students—who come from many ethnic, economic, and educational backgrounds and who have a wide range of interests—consistently honor her with the highest teaching evaluations. Her own four children attended New York City public schools, one reason that she was elected as president of the Community School Board in District Two.

Berger is also the author of *The Developing Person Through the Life Span* and *The Developing Person Through Childhood*. Her three developmental texts are currently being used at nearly 700 colleges and universities worldwide. Her research interests include adolescent identity, sibling relationships, and bullying, and she has contributed articles on developmental topics to the *Wiley Encyclopedia of Psychology*. Berger's interest in college education is manifest in articles published in 2002 by the American Association for Higher Education and the National Education Association for Higher Education. She continues to teach and learn with every semester and every edition of her books.

Brief Contents

Contents

Part III
The Play Years

Part IV
The School Years

Preface

Like so many people, I was profoundly affected by the events of September 11, 2001. From my home in New York City, I could smell the smoke from the World Trade Center site until almost Thanksgiving. Beyond deep gratitude that my family and students were unharmed, I felt renewed commitment to what we all do—teach the future professionals and parents who will raise the next cohort of children, or learn as much as we can to become a person who really helps children. As you know, education occurs not just in one memorable moment but cumulatively, in every day and every hour, and I was very grateful that I saw my students many times after that September morning. I realized again why I love teaching and why I put so much time and effort into revising every paragraph of this book.

In my own classroom, I start with high standards and clear expectations. But I'm aware that learning does not occur throughout the term unless I follow through with enthusiasm, humor, and intellectual honesty. I try to apply this insight to textbook writing as well.

The best developmental textbooks integrate theory and practice with such powerful clarity that students think deeply about the long-term implications of what they are learning. There should be no gap between theory and practice; the two inform each other. If my personal standards and experiences are evident in this text, I thank my heroes and mentors: not only my own gifted professors who studied directly with Erikson, Piaget, and Skinner, and not only the researchers whom I admire from the cool distance of the printed page—Ainsworth, Baltes, Bem, the Coles, Dweck, Garbarino, Gardner, the Gibsons, Lightfoot, Olweus, Plomin, Rogoff, Rutter, Schaie, Vygotsky, Whitborne, Zigler, and many more (which explains why the bibliography is longer than any comparable book's)—but also the thousands of peers and students who continue to teach me.

New Features

A number of aspects of this edition may be singled out for special mention:

- **Even stronger integration of theory and practice**   The five theories introduced in Chapter 2—psychoanalytic, behavioral, cognitive, sociocultural, and epigenetic—are applied repeatedly and in new ways, from explanations of how babies learn language to how children develop sexual identity. I want students to become accustomed to thinking from alternate perspectives. Nothing is quite so practical as a good theory, and nothing about child development is a mere abstraction. In this new edition, more than ever, theoretical insights are connected to practical issues. This linkage occurs in many ways, including the "Especially For . . ." questions in the margins as well as through a new series of features called "A Case to Study" that helps readers see how the experience of one developing person can illustrate a universal truth.

- **Up-to-date research citations**   Every year brings new concepts and research about human development. The best of these are integrated into the text, including hundreds of new references on many topics—challenges to Piaget's theories, infant language, emotional regulation, theory of mind, psychoactive drugs, and social conflicts in childhood among them.

■ **New material on schooling**   Education is a crucial foundation of childhood, and many who study this book will be educators. Accordingly, this edition highlights up-to-date, international research on education-related issues: the effects of infant day care, phonics versus whole language, standardized testing, multiple intelligences, special education, bilingual instruction, group problem solving, teacher–student ratios, and many more. The goal is twofold: to provide information (through new material on such topics as special-education laws and categories, family income and day care) and to encourage student readers to think critically, scientifically, and analytically about those issues.

■ **New learning features**   With every edition, changes in the narrative are made to enhance readers' understanding of what scientists who study children actually do. Readers are offered many opportunities to test their observational and analytical skills by applying what they have learned to actual children. A series of new features, called "Thinking Like a Scientist," illuminates the thinking and research process. I have also increased the number of observational quizzes for photographs and have added some for graphs and tables so that quantitative data will be examined more carefully and will be better understood.

Ongoing Features

Many characteristics of this text have been acclaimed since the first edition and have been retained in this revision:

■ **Language that communicates the excitement and challenge of the field**   An overview of the science of child development should be lively, just as children are. Consequently, I have added more summarizing and transitional statements to clarify the logical connection between one idea and the next. Sentences are shorter and less daunting, although I still choose some challenging vocabulary to deepen comprehension.

■ **Coverage of diversity**   Cross-cultural, international, multi-ethnic, rich and poor—all these words and ideas are vital to appreciating how all our children develop. Studies of various groups make it clear that we all are the same and that each of us is unique. Chapter 1 includes a multifaceted discussion (class-tested with my own students) of where children sleep in various cultures. Similarly, every subsequent chapter refers to differences and similarities, from the many variations of immigrant development to the epigenetic ways in which nature and nurture interact. New research on Romanian adoptees, appreciation of Brazilian street children, cultural variations in childbirth practices, and advantages and disadvantages of various approaches to second-language learning are among the many diversity-related topics discussed throughout the book.

■ **Up-to-date coverage**   My students and my four children help me keep current through their questions and concerns, not only in research but also in practice. My academic mentors nurtured my curiosity as well as a rational suspicion that makes me eager to read and analyze hundreds of journal articles and books on everything from anorexia to zygosity. The recent explosion of research in neuroscience and genetics has challenged me to explain many complex findings and speculative leaps.

■ **Topical organization within a chronological framework**   The book's basic organization remains unchanged. Four chapters begin the book with coverage of definitions, theories, genetics, and prenatal development, used not only as a developmental foundation but also as the structure for explaining the life-span perspective, plasticity, nature and nurture, multicultural understanding, risk analysis, the damage–repair cycle, family bonding, and many other concepts that yield insights for all of human development. The ensuing parts of the book correspond to the major periods of growth. Each part contains three chapters, one for each of the three domains of development: biosocial, cognitive, and psychosocial. The topical organization within the chronological framework is a useful scaffold for student understanding of the interplay between age and domain as children actually experience it. The chapters are color-coded with tabs in the margins: The pages of the biosocial chapters have pale green tabs; the cognitive chapters have lilac tabs; and the psychosocial chapters have peach tabs.

■ **Relevant features**   In some books, boxes are tacked on to make the text seem more current or multicultural than it really is. In this edition, four series of deeper discussions appear as integral parts of the text, and only where they are relevant. These features include two series that readers have particularly liked in earlier editions (called "Changing Policy" and "In Person") and two series that are new to this edition (called "A Case to Study" and "Thinking Like a Scientist"). You will see that these are not spin-offs or add-ons; they are extensions of ideas explored in the text, and thus provide material for critical thinking.

■ **Pedagogical aids**   Each chapter ends with a summary, a list of key terms (with page numbers indicating where the word is introduced and defined), and key questions for reviewing important concepts. Terms are defined in the margins where they are introduced (in boldface) in the text and again in a glossary at the back of the book. The outline on the first page of each chapter and the system of major and minor subheads facilitate the widely used survey–question–review method of study. Observational quizzes inspire readers to look more closely at data and photographs, and the "Especially for . . ." questions in the margins apply concepts to real life (examples of these features are shown in the margin).

Examples of an "Especially for . . . " question, an Observational Quiz for a graph, and an Observational Quiz for a photograph are presented below and on the next page.

?Especially for Educators: An infant day-care center has a new child whose parents speak a language other than the one the teachers speak. Should the teachers learn basic words in the new language, or should they expect the baby to learn the majority language? (See answer, page 190.)

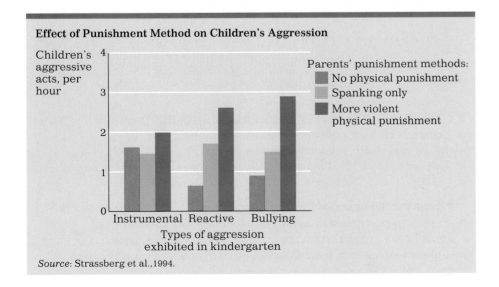

Effect of Punishment Method on Children's Aggression

Source: Strassberg et al., 1994.

FIGURE 10.1 Punishment and Aggression All the children, regardless of how their parents punished them, were about equally likely to exhibit instrumental aggression. The typical child did so once or twice an hour. By contrast, children who were severely punished by their parents were most often the bullies. The most interesting result involves reactive aggression. Children who were spanked interpreted such actions as hostile, and thus as requiring an aggressive response, twice as often as children who had not been physically punished.

?Observational Quiz (see answer, page 316): Could young children become bullies if their parents never spanked them?

■ **Photographs, tables, and graphs that are integral to the text**   Students learn a great deal by studying this book's illustrations, because Worth Publishers encourages authors to choose photos, tables, and graphs, to write captions, and to alter designs to better fit the words—not vice versa. As one result, photos and captions are instructional, supplementing and extending the text. Appendix A furthers this process by presenting at least one chart or table per chapter, containing detailed data for further study.

Learning Is Fun The original purpose of the Head Start program was to boost disadvantaged children's academic skills. The most enduring benefits, however, turned out to be improved self-esteem and social skills, as is evident in these happy Head Start participants, all crowded together.

? *Observational Quiz* (see answer, page 291): How many of these children are in close physical contact without discomfort or disagreement?

Content Changes for the Sixth Edition

Human development, like all sciences, builds on past learning. Many facts and concepts must be restated in every edition of a textbook—stages and ages, norms and variations, dangers and diversities, classic theories and fascinating applications. However, the study of development is continually changed by discoveries and innovations, so no paragraph in this sixth edition is exactly what it was in the fifth edition, much less the first. Extensive updating has been done, particularly in the coverage of multiculturalism and diversity—including such subject areas as gender, disabilities, ethnicity, and poverty. This updating is evident on virtually every page. Entire sections that have considerable emphasis on diversity are indicated here by blue bullets.

Chapter 1: Introduction
● ■ "Butterflies and Warfare" section (various trajectories of change)
● ■ Emphasis on the cultural contexts of development
● ■ "Who Sleeps with Whom?" section (cultural values)
● ■ A Case to Study: "This Sense of Liberation" (growing up on a Georgia farm)
● ■ Thinking Like a Scientist: Race and Biology (archaic and current concepts)

Chapter 2: Theories of Development
■ Increased coverage of behaviorism, including social learning
■ Updated and expanded coverage of epigenetic systems theory
● ■ Greater emphasis on sociocultural theory, including Vygotsky's work

- ●▪ Application of theory: continuity–discontinuity, difference–deficit, nature–nurture
- ▪ Thinking Like a Scientist: What Is a Mother For? (Harlow's surrogate mothers)
- ▪ In Person: My Beautiful, Hairless Babies (why I adore my children)

Chapter 3: Heredity and Environment
- ▪ The practices and controversies surrounding genetic testing (especially in the context of the Human Genome Project)
- ●▪ A Case to Study: What Do People Live to Do? (a young couple's quandary over their Down syndrome fetus)
- ●▪ Changing Policy: Too Many Boys? (sex selection before birth)
- ●▪ In Person: Whose Baby Is It? (alternate reproduction techniques)
- ●▪ Changing Policy: Genetic Counseling: Decisions and Values

Chapter 4: Prenatal Development and Birth
- ●▪ Prenatal testing to prevent transmission of HIV
- ▪ Recent discoveries about fetal learning and sensation (especially hearing)
- ▪ Changing Policy: Preventing Drug Damage (extensively updated)

Chapter 5: The First 2 Years: Biosocial Development
- ▪ New research on sleep at various ages
- ▪ Expanded discussion of brain growth, including expansion, pruning, sculpting
- ●▪ New information on nutrition, malnutrition, and undernutrition
- ▪ A Case to Study: Toni's Well-Child Visit (identifying the signs of early deprivation)
- ●▪ Thinking Like a Scientist: Plasticity and Young Orphans (Romanian adoptees)
- ●▪ Changing Policy: SIDS Among Asian Infants (cohort and cultural insights)

Chapter 6: The First 2 Years: Cognitive Development
- ▪ Research-based challenges to Piaget's theories of early cognition
- ▪ Changing Policy: Policy Implications of Some Modern Research Methods
- ▪ Expanded coverage of information processing
- ●▪ The effects of culture on language acquisition
- ▪ Three views of how infants learn language

Chapter 7: The First 2 Years: Psychosocial Development
- ▪ Expanded coverage of temperament, including exuberance, fearfulness
- ▪ More on emotions and social context (synchrony, social referencing)
- ●▪ Expanded coverage of attachment (not only types A, B, and C but also type D)
- ▪ Expanded discussion of infant day care and father care, including a table on characteristics of high-quality care
- ▪ A Case to Study: Jacob's Parents on Autopilot (a boy's need to develop social connections)

Chapter 8: The Play Years: Biosocial Development
- ▪ Significance of brain development, especially the prefrontal cortex (with implications for education)
- ●▪ Gender, cultural, and age variations in development of motor skills
- ●▪ Updated coverage of injury control and of primary, secondary, and tertiary prevention of injury
- ●▪ Updated discussion of incidence and prevention of child maltreatment, including failure to thrive, shaken-baby syndrome, and post-traumatic stress disorder
- ▪ A Case to Study: The Neglect of Neglect: A 2-Year-Old Boy (early recognition of warning signs)

Chapter 9: The Play Years: Cognitive Development
- Expanded coverage of Vygotsky's theory
- Thinking Like a Scientist: What Did Cinderella Do with the Pumpkin? (comparing theories)
- More explanations and data on theory of mind, including theory-theory
- Expanded coverage of children's information-processing abilities (simple arithmetic, memory, and theory of mind)
- New insights into language development, including the role of cognition
- The pros and cons of early schooling (including the qualities of good pre-K programs)

Chapter 10: The Play Years: Psychosocial Development
- Importance of emotional regulation and emotional intelligence
- Updated, multicultural research on prosocial and antisocial behavior
- Section on the influence of television and video games (reviews harm and benefits)
- Changing Policy: Turning Off the TV (who decides—parents or society?)
- New cross-cultural comparisons of parenting practices

Chapter 11: The School Years: Biosocial Development
- In Person: Two Mexican-American Children in California
- Relationship between brain development and motor control
- Updated coverage of autism, Asperger's, AD/HD, and ADD
- New data and tables on special education in the United States
- A Case to Study: Billy: Dynamo or Dynamite? (parents, teachers, and AD/HD)
- Changing Policy: Changing Tests (multiple intelligences)

Chapter 12: The School Years: Cognitive Development
- International data on children's understanding of logic
- Information processing in the school years (emphasizing brain development)
- Applications of moral education: Kohlberg, Gilligan, Rest
- Various approaches to teaching reading, math, and languages
- New discussion of educational standards and class size

Chapter 13: The School Years: Psychosocial Development
- Updated research on ways to treat and discourage bullying
- New section on prosocial behavior, including gender differences
- Updated coverage of family functions and structures (including adoptive and foster families)
- Rethinking relationship between stress and poverty, particularly family function
- Changing Policy: More Divorce, More Trouble?

Appendix A: Supplemental Charts, Graphs, and Tables
- Quantitative data (in chart, graph, or table form) or further exploration, keyed to each chapter

Appendix B: More About Research Methods
- Discussion of library research, observation, and the case study
- Section on how research validity can be enhanced (through representative sampling, use of a comparison group)
- Listing of key books and journals
- Hints about using the Internet for research

Appendix C: Three Research Assignments

Supplements

As an instructor myself, I know how important good supplements are. I have been known to reject a textbook adoption if the publisher produced inferior and inaccurate ancillaries. Fortunately, Worth Publishers has a well-deserved reputation for the high quality of the supplementary materials it produces for both professors and students, and Worth's sales representatives are the most knowledgeable and helpful in the business. Accompanying this edition you will find the following:

Exploring Child Development: A Media Tool Kit for Understanding Development

This CD series (also available for instructors on VHS and DVD) was prepared by a talented team of instructors, including Lisa Huffman (Ball State University), Tom Ludwig (Hope College), Tanya Renner (Kapiolani Community College), Stavros Valenti (Hofstra University), Catherine Robertson (Grossmont College), and Connie Varnhagen (University of Alberta). Combining video, animations, self-tests, and interactive exercises, the *Media Tool Kit* offers students hands-on, interactive learning. These activities range from investigations of classic experiments (e.g., the visual cliff and the Strange Situation) to observations on children's play. The student tool kit includes more than 40 interactive video-based activities, quizzes, and flashcards tied to every chapter of the book. The instructor tool kit includes more than 200 video clips and animations, along with teaching tips and discussion starters.

Journey Through Childhood Observational Video

Bringing observational learning to the classroom, this new two-video set allows students to watch and listen to real children as a way of amplifying their reading of the text. The video enables students to observe children from birth through adolescence, in settings from day-care centers to schools, homes, and doctors' offices, and from a multitude of cultures and communities across the globe (Africa, Europe, Latin America, and Asia). Noted experts in child development—among them Patricia Greenfield, Charles Nelson, Barbara Rogoff, and Carolyn Rovee-Collier—talk about their work in areas ranging from the biology of early brain development to prosocial behavior in middle childhood. This video set contains more than four hours of footage, including one hour of unnarrated observational clips. An observation workbook for the instructor provides teaching and activity tips. A student workbook helps students sharpen their observational skills and relate text material to real-life settings.

The *Scientific American Frontiers* Videos for Developmental Psychology

This remarkable resource provides instructors with 17 video segments of approximately 15 minutes each, on topics ranging from language development to nature–nurture issues. The videos can be used to launch classroom lectures or to emphasize and clarify course material. The *Faculty Guide* by Richard O. Straub (University of Michigan) describes each segment and relates it to specific topics in the text.

Child Development Telecourse

This new Child Development TeleWeb Course, developed by Coast Learning Systems and Worth Publishers, teaches the fundamentals of child development. The course also explores the variety of individual and developmental contexts that influence development, such as socioeconomic status, culture, genetics, family, school, and society. Each video lesson includes real-life examples interwoven with commentary by experts. In addition, video lessons describe the whole child, while others focus on topics such as fathers, maltreatment, and school. The course includes 26 half-hour video lessons, a *Telecourse Study Guide,* and a *Faculty Manual* with test bank.

Instructor's Resources

This collection of resources, compiled by Richard O. Straub, has been hailed as the richest in developmental psychology. This manual features chapter-by-chapter previews and lecture guides, learning objectives, springboard topics for discussion and debate, handouts for student projects, and supplementary readings from journal articles. Course planning suggestions, ideas for term projects, and a guide to audiovisual and software materials are also included. New to this edition are additional media teaching suggestions.

Study Guide

The *Study Guide,* by Richard O. Straub, helps students evaluate their understanding and retain their learning longer. Each chapter includes key concepts, guided study questions, and reviews that encourage students' active participation in the learning process; two practice tests and a challenge test help them assess their mastery of the material. New to this edition are additional application and observation activities for each chapter of the book.

PowerPoint Slides

A number of presentation slides are available on the Web site or on a CD-ROM. There are two prebuilt PowerPoint slide sets for each text chapter—one featuring chapter outlines, the other featuring all chapter illustrations. These slides can be used as is or customized to fit individual needs. Catherine Robertson has also produced a set of lecture slides featuring tables, graphs, and charts from the book.

The Worth Image and Lecture Gallery

Using Worth's Image and Lecture Gallery, located at www.worthpublishers.com/ilg, instructors can browse, search, and download illustrations from every Worth title and prebuilt PowerPoint presentation files for specific chapters, containing all chapter art or all chapter section headings in text form. Users can also create personal folders on a personalized home page for easy organization of the materials.

Overhead Transparencies

This set of 75 full-color transparencies consists of key diagrams, charts, graphs, and tables from the textbook.

Test Bank and Computerized Test Bank

The test bank, by the author and Clark Alexander, includes at least 80 multiple-choice and 50 fill-in, true-false, and essay questions for each chapter. Each question is keyed to the textbook by topic, page number, and level of difficulty. The Diploma computerized test bank, available for Windows and Macintosh, guides instructors step-by-step through the process of creating a test. It allows instructors to add an unlimited number of questions, edit questions, format a test, scramble questions, and include pictures, equations, and multimedia links. Online testing is also available.

Companion Web Site

The book's companion Web site (www.worthpublishers.com/berger) is an online educational setting for students and instructors. The companion Web site is free and does not require any special codes or passwords. Student resources include: chapter outlines, annotated Web links, online quizzes with immediate feedback and instructor notification, interactive flashcards and frequently asked questions about developmental psychology. For instructors, the Web site includes a full array of teaching tools, such as PowerPoint Slides, syllabus posting, an online gradebook, and links to various resources, including WebCT, Blackboard, and the Worth Image and Lecture Gallery.

Thanks

I'd like to thank those academic reviewers who have read this book in every edition and who have provided suggestions, criticisms, references, and encouragement. They have all made this a better book. I want to mention especially those who have reviewed and commented on this edition:

Mary Beth Ahlum *Nebraska Wesleyan University*
Joseph Allen *University of Virginia*
Leonard Austin *Black Hills State University*
Janette B. Benson *University of Denver*
Chris Boyazis *Bucknell University*
Priscilla Coleman *University of the South*
Tim Croy *Eastern Illinois University*
Peggy DeCooke *State University of New York, Purchase*
Ruth Doyle *Casper College*
Rosanne Dlugosz *Scottsdale Community College*
M. J. Eliason *University of Iowa*
Eugene Geist *Ohio University*
Tracey R. Gleason *Wellesley College*
Michelle de Haan *University College, London*
Robin Harwood *University of Connecticut*
Rebecca Hendrix *Northwest Missouri State University*
Christie Honeycutt *Stanly Community College*
Doug Hughey *Mount San Antonio College*
Andrew Johnson *Park University*
Mary Kay Jordan-Fleming *College of Mount St. Joseph*
Ken Kallio *State University of New York, Geneseo*

Laurie Katz *Middle Tennessee State University*
Kathleen Kleissler *Kutztown University*
Ada Lie *Milwaukee Area Technical College*
Harriett Light *North Dakota State University*
Martha G. Maddox *Houston Baptist University*
Angela Provitera McGlynn *Mercer County Community College*
Julie Ann McIntyre *Russell Sage College*
Joyce Munsch *Texas Tech University*
Barbara J. Myers *Virginia Commonwealth University*
David A. Nelson *Brigham Young University*
Larry J. Nelson *Brigham Young University*
Gail Overby *Southeast Missouri State University*
Susan Rogala *University of Michigan*
Pamela Schulze *University of Akron*
Fred Smiley *Cameron University*
Ken Springer *Southern Methodist University*
Siu-Lan Esther Tan *Kalamazoo College*
Grace van Thillo *Mount San Jacinto College*
Luis G. Valerio *University of Southern Colorado*

Dedication

Whenever I tell my story of how a junior assistant professor became an author writing the sixth edition of a textbook, I am struck by my good fortune. An eager, innocent novice found the best textbook publisher in the industry. Bob Worth himself promised that if I signed with Worth Publishers, I would have to work much harder than with any other company, but the final product would be better. Peter Deane, the book's first developmental editor, proved him right. Throughout the years, many editors, artists, designers, sales representatives, marketing managers, and CEOs have guided my work from its beginning as streams of words and ideas to its current position as a leading textbook sold in twelve nations, four languages, and every state of the United States. The process continues; my latest team of helpers includes Jessica Bayne, Cele Gardner, Tracey Kuehn, Renée Altier, and Catherine Woods—each of whom has taken a personal interest in my work, far beyond professional requirements. I thank them all, and dedicate this edition to them.

Kathleen Stassen Berger

July 2002

The Developing Person
Through Childhood

course before age 13. Two years later, another survey asked the same questions of most of the same boys, now in the eleventh grade; this time, only 8 percent reported having had sex before age 13 (Centers for Disease Control, August 14, 1998; CDC, June 9, 2000). Bravado? Bragging? Embarrassment? See page 25 for more on this.

To summarize, both the passage of time and changes over time sometimes seem obvious, as does continuity; but to know why and how they occur requires looking both forward and backward. Developmentalists examine the present moment, but they also look at what happened before and what happens after, always seeking the links that make a life, remembering that causes and consequences may not be what they seem. Change in one area of life dynamically alters the other areas, but minor changes can have a powerful effect and major events are not always traumatic.

A Life-Span Perspective

To understand all the dynamic systems over time, scientists look beyond childhood, not only because adults help guide the next generation and because every adult is a grown-up child but also because a firm understanding of what the future may hold is needed to help each child now. The scientific study of child development has benefited enormously from the scientific study of the entire life span (Dixon & Lerner, 1999; Smith & Baltes, 1999). In the "reciprocal connection" between the study of childhood and adulthood (Baltes et al., 1998), the **life-span perspective** helps us see sources of *continuity* from the beginning of life to the end (such as with biological sex, family of origin, and perhaps personality) and *discontinuity* (such as with language skills in infancy and with health habits in adulthood).

The life-span perspective actually envisions five distinct characteristics of development, each of which is illustrated throughout this text (Baltes et al., 1998; Smith & Baltes, 1999). Development is all of the following:

- **Multidirectional:** Change is not always linear, as we have just seen. Gains and losses, compensations and deficits, predictable growth and unexpected transformations are all part of the human experience.
- **Multicontextual:** Each human life must be understood as embedded in many contexts, as further described in this chapter.
- **Multicultural:** Many cultural settings—each with a distinct set of values, traditions, and tools for living—must be understood and appreciated, as is also illustrated in this chapter.
- **Multidisciplinary:** Many academic fields—especially psychology, biology, education, and sociology, but also neuroscience, economics, medicine, anthropology, history, and more—contribute data and insight to the science of development, as is apparent throughout this book.
- **Plastic:** Every individual, and every trait within each individual, can be altered at any point in the life span, as we will now explain.

This last characteristic, *plasticity,* or the capability of change, is probably the most encouraging tenet of the life-span perspective. The term *plasticity* denotes two complementary aspects of development: Human characteristics can be molded into different forms and shapes (as plastic can be), yet people maintain a certain durability (again, like plastic). Plasticity provides both hope and motivation—hope because change is possible, and motivation because what occurs at any moment helps lay the foundation for what follows. At the same time, plasticity emphasizes a sobering truth: People cannot become what they are not. We each have unique genes, families, and experiences, and those provide the raw material from which we mold and shape our lives.

life-span perspective A view of human development that takes into account all phases of life, not just childhood or adulthood.

multidirectional A characteristic of development, referring to its nonlinear progression—gains and losses, compensations and deficits, predictable and unexpected changes.

multicontextual A characteristic of development, referring to the fact that each human life takes place within a number of contexts—historical, cultural, and socioeconomic.

multicultural A characteristic of development, which takes place within many cultural settings worldwide and thus reflects a multitude of values, traditions, and tools for living.

multidisciplinary A characteristic of development encompassing the idea that dozens of academic disciplines contribute data and insight to the science of development.

plastic A characteristic of development that indicates that individuals—including their personalities as well as their bodies and minds—change throughout the life span.

<table>
<tr><td colspan="3" align="center">**DOMAINS OF HUMAN DEVELOPMENT**</td></tr>
<tr><td align="center">**Biosocial Development**</td><td align="center">**Cognitive Development**</td><td align="center">**Psychosocial Development**</td></tr>
<tr><td>Includes all the growth and change that occur in a person's body, and the genetic, nutritional, and health factors that affect that growth and change. Motor skills— everything from grasping a rattle to driving a car—are also part of the biosocial domain. In this text, this domain is called biosocial, rather than physical or biological, because social and cultural factors affect biological growth.</td><td>Includes all the mental processes that a person uses to obtain knowledge or to think about the environment. Cognition encompasses perception, imagination, judgment, memory, and language—the processes people use to think, decide, and learn. Education—not only the formal curriculum within schools but also the informal learning— is part of this domain as well.</td><td>Includes development of emotions, temperament, and social skills. Family, friends, the community, the culture, and the larger society are particularly central to the psychosocial domain. For example, cultural differences in "appropriate" sex roles or in family structures are part of this domain.</td></tr>
</table>

FIGURE 1.3 The Three Domains The division of human development into three domains makes it easier to study, but remember that very few factors belong exclusively to one domain or another. Development is not piecemeal but holistic: Each aspect of development is related to all three domains.

Three Domains of Development

To organize this multifaceted study, we can divide development into three major domains (see Figure 1.3): body, mind, and spirit, or the biosocial, cognitive, and psychosocial domains:

biosocial domain The realm of the brain and body, as well as changes in our biological selves and in the social influences that direct our physical growth.

- The **biosocial domain** includes the brain and body, as well as changes in our biological selves and in the social influences that direct our physical growth.

cognitive domain Our thought processes, perceptual abilities, and language mastery, as well as the educational institutions that encourage our intellectual growth.

- The **cognitive domain** includes thought processes, perceptual abilities, and language mastery, as well as the educational institutions that encourage our intellectual growth.

psychosocial domain Our emotions, personality, and interpersonal relationships with family, friends, and the wider community.

- The **psychosocial domain** includes emotions, personality, and interpersonal relationships with our family, friends, and the wider community.

All three domains are important at every age. For instance, understanding an infant involves studying his or her health (biosocial), curiosity (cognitive), and temperament (psychosocial), as well as dozens of other aspects of development from all three domains. Similarly, understanding adolescents requires studying the physical changes that turn a child's body into an adult one, the intellectual development that allows logical thinking about sexual passion and future goals, and the new patterns of friendship and courtship that lead to the intimate relationships of adulthood.

In practical terms, given a particular developmental change, it is not always obvious which domain it belongs to. Where would you place infertility, or learn-

!Answer to Observational Quiz (from page 4): Loose, printed t-shirts, backward baseball caps, and plastic lidded spout cups were rare before 1980.

ing a second language, or being a classroom bully? If you guessed biosocial, cognitive, and psychosocial, respectively, you are in accord with the placement of these topics in this text. But you also probably realized that there is overlap. For instance, a child is a bully for biological and cognitive reasons as well as social ones. Each person grows as an integrated whole.

All Kinds of People

Development is not only about many types of changes, reciprocal systems, and three major domains; it is also about *all kinds of people*. Remarkable similarities as well as dramatic differences are apparent among the 6 billion humans now alive and the billions more who once lived. Some aspects of development are universal for almost everyone: learning to walk and talk, developing relationships with family and friends, seeking love and learning. Many other aspects of life vary, depending on place, time, and circumstance. To highlight both the universal and the unique, this book includes many examples, quotations, anecdotes, and descriptions of many individuals.

A Case to Study

"This Sense of Liberation"

As you read the following passage, notice not only the impact of all three domains but also similarities and differences between this person and the children you know. Which aspect of this boy's life are true for everyone, which ones are true for most people but not all, and which ones seem unique?

My most persistent memory as a farm boy was of the earth. There was a closeness, almost an immersion, in the sand, loam, and red clay that seemed natural, and constant. The soil caressed my bare feet, and the dust was always boiling up from the dirt road that passed fifty feet from our front door, so that inside our clapboard house the red clay particles, ranging in size from face powder to grits, were ever present, particularly in the summertime, when the wood doors were kept open and the screen just stopped the trash and some of the less adventurous flies. . . .

There is little doubt that I now recall those days with more fondness than they deserve. . . . From as early in March until as late in October as weather and my parents permitted, I never wore shoes. The first warm days of the year brought not only a season of freshness and rebirth, but also a time of renewed freedom for me, when running, sliding, walking through mud puddles, and sinking up to my ankles in the plowed fields gave life a new dimension. I enjoyed this sense of liberation. . . .

There were some disadvantages to bare feet. There was always the possibility of stepping on old barbed wire or a rusty nail, with the danger of tetanus. Another problem was

at school. The pine floors were not sanded and polished but rough, the dust kept down by regular applications of used motor oil. We soon learned to pick up our feet with each step, because splinters were prevalent and a threat to bare feet that slid for even an inch across the surface.

Our most common ailments were the endemic ground itch, ringworm, boils and carbuncles, and sties on our eyes, plus the self-inflicted splinters, cuts, abrasions, bruises, wasp or bee stings. . . . On different occasions, I had both arms and three ribs broken, but my most memorable injury was just a small splinter in my wrist. . . . My arm was swollen only slightly, but I couldn't bend my wrist or move my fingers without intense pain, so I stayed at home instead of going to the field. One day, after our noon meal, as Daddy was leaving to go to work, he said, "The rest of us will be working while Jimmy lies here in the house and reads a book." I was stricken by his remark, knowing that he was disgusted with me when he called me "Jimmy" instead of "Hot." . . . My good reputation as a worker was important to me, and my father's approval was even more precious.

Not knowing what to do, I went out into the pasture near our home, ashamed of my laziness while my Daddy had to work even harder than usual. Desperate for a cure, I finally put my hand against a fencepost with my fingers upward, wrapped my belt tightly around it, and then slowly raised my arm to force my wrist to bend. All of a sudden, to my delight, there was a big eruption of pus, in the midst of which was a half-inch piece of blackened wood. I ran back to the house, got on my bicycle, pedaled it as fast as possible to the cotton field, and reported to Daddy for work. When I showed him the splinter, he smiled and said, "It's good to have you back with us, Hot."

[Carter, 2001, pp. 15, 29, 78–82]

It is easy to see the interplay of the three domains in this excerpt. Jimmy's desire for his father's approval (psychosocial) gave him the idea (cognitive) of strapping his hand to a fence to self-treat the infection in his arm (biosocial).

Both the universal and the unique are evident as well. Jimmy's attitudes and emotions are common among all children, including not only his wish for respect from adults but also his acceptance of conditions (dust, heat, bare feet) that those growing up in other places might think intolerable. By contrast, some specific conditions are very unusual: Perhaps you guessed from the red clay, dirt road, and clapboard house that Jimmy lived in rural Georgia, not far from Alabama, at a place and time that most people alive today would find strange.

It is also apparent that development is dynamic, ever-changing: Childhood for this happily barefoot lad is unlike that of any young child today, many of whom "need" several costly pairs of name-brand shoes. These differences highlight the crucial importance of the historical, cultural, and economic contexts of development.

A Clapboard Home Long grass now covers the loam and red clay that eighty years ago felt liberating to the boy named Jimmy. He sometimes slept with the farm family who lived here, although his own home was larger, with more windows, a stone's throw away.

PHYLLIS PICARDI / STOCK SOUTH / PICTUREQUEST

The Contexts of Development

As you might imagine, neither in a single book nor in everyday life can anyone simultaneously consider all the contextual factors that bear on any aspect of development. Throughout this text, we will examine a great many such factors, including families, schools, and nations, exploring how they push development in one direction or another. They are all interactive and reciprocal, with a small change sometimes becoming the butterfly whose wingbeat produces a major shift and a massive disaster sometimes not being strong enough to alter an individual's life course.

At the outset, however, we need to describe and define three contexts that can affect virtually every phase of development: the historical context, the cultural context, and the socioeconomic context. As Figure 1.4 suggests, these three contexts do not act in isolation.

The Historical Context

cohort A group of people whose shared birth year, or decade, means that they travel through life together experiencing the same major historical changes.

All persons born within a few years of one another are said to be a **cohort**, a group of people whose shared age means that they travel through life together (although they don't necessarily know one another). The idea is that all the people in a particular cohort are subject to the same history—the same prevailing assumptions, important public events, technologies, and popular trends. How

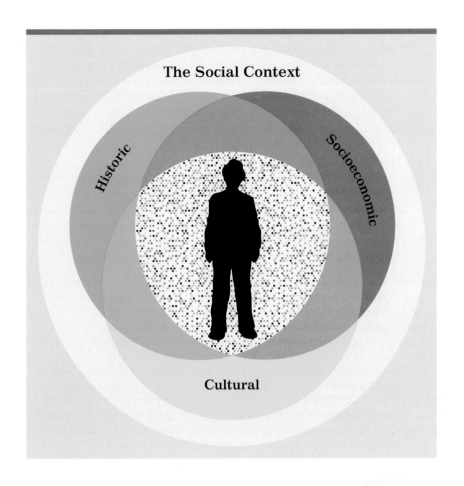

FIGURE 1.4 Contexts Within Contexts Three broad contexts within the social context—history, socioeconomic status, and culture—affect human development in many ways—sometimes distantly, sometimes directly, sometimes individually, sometimes in combination. Because these three contexts overlap, it is often impossible to determine whether a particular effect comes from cohort, social class, or ethnic heritage.

? *Observational Quiz* (see answer, page 10) Can you guess the significance of the multicolored dots?

history affects the lives and thoughts of a specific person depends partly on how old the person was when a given historical experience occurred. People in a specific cohort tend to be affected in the same way; those in different cohorts are generally affected differently. You can confirm this by asking members of other generations of your family about the war in Vietnam, Princess Diana's death, smoking marijuana, or even the appropriate use of a cell phone.

As profound economic, political, and technological changes occur over the years, basic concepts about how things "should be" are influenced by how things *were* before such changes took place. Scholars have discovered that our most cherished assumptions about how things should be are not always generally accepted. Instead, such an assumption is likely to be a **social construction**, an idea built more on shared perceptions of social order than on objective reality. As social shifts occur, social constructions also change.

Right now, for example, perceptions about the role of computers in society are shifting, cohort by cohort. The oldest cohorts tend to fear computers and are quick to see the Internet as a source of problems—pornography, social isolation, obesity, crime. The middle cohorts see computers as powerful tools to be mastered. The youngest cohorts see them as appliances, no more remarkable than toothbrushes or bicycles; they want fast, colorful, and audible ones in their bedrooms. Each cohort is partly correct; each has its own social construction. In fact, new inventions, from the radio to the automobile, and probably even the first campfire or plowed field, have always been judged by the older generations who grew up without them as corrupting the youth, who no longer do things the traditional way (Wartella & Jennings, 2000).

Even the most basic ideas about human development can change. For example, our very concept of childhood, as a precious and extended stage of life, is a

social construction An idea that is built more on shared perceptions of social order than on objective reality.

"You'd better ask your grandparents about that, son—my generation is very uncomfortable talking about abstinence."

Changing Values To some extent, the experiences and values of late adolescence influence each cohort for a lifetime. Maturity does not usually change those values, but at least it can make each generation realize the limitations of its historical context.

culture The specific manifestations of a social group's design for living, developed over the years to provide a social structure for the group members' life together.

! *Answer to Observational Quiz* (from page 9): Note that the dots are the same colors as the contexts and the overlap between the contexts. That means the dots signify that every context is apparent in some way in every immediate circumstance.

social construction. In many historical contexts, children were nurtured only until they could care for themselves (at about age 7). Then they entered the adult world, working in the fields or at home and spending their leisure time engaged in the activities of grown-ups (Ariès, 1962). Further, the social construction that children are born "little angels" would lead to quite different child rearing than would the once-common idea that adults have to "beat the devil out of them" in order to turn children into proper, God-fearing adults (Hwang et al., 1996; Straus, 1994).

The historical context of development is thus continually changing because "differences in year of birth expose people to . . . different priorities, constraints, and options" (Elder et al., 1995). For instance, the barefoot farm boy in A Case to Study lived in a southern community that accepted racial segregation without question. He was White, and A.D., his best friend, was Black. He writes that sometimes

Daddy let A.D. and me go to Americus to see a movie by ourselves. We had to walk up the railroad to Archery, find the little red leather flag left for the purpose, and stick it upright in a hole in the end of a crosstie. The engineer would see the signal and stop so we could board in front of the section foreman's house. It cost fifteen cents each, and we parted company during the ride to sit in the seats marked "white" and "colored." When we arrived in Americus we walked together to the Rylander Theater and separated again, A.D. paying his dime at a back entrance and sitting in the high third level while I went in to sit either downstairs or in the first balcony. Afterward, we would go back home, united in friendship though physically divided on the segregated train. Our only strong feeling was one of gratitude for our wonderful excursion; I don't remember ever questioning the mandatory racial separation, which we accepted like breathing.

[Carter, 2001, pp. 95–96]

When they got older, both Jimmy and A.D. fought against racial segregation, which they came to believe was very wrong. But their childhood historical and cultural context had created a racist social construction that was "accepted like breathing."

The Cultural Context

Culture is the second pervasive context of development. When social scientists use the term **culture**, they include hundreds of specific manifestations of a social group's *design for living*, developed over the years to provide a social structure for the group members' life together (Kluckhohn, 1949). Culture includes values, assumptions, and customs, not only physical objects (clothing, dwellings, cuisine, technologies, works of art, and so on). The term *culture* is sometimes used rather loosely, as in "the culture of poverty," "the culture of children," or "the culture of America." However, whenever culture is considered as part of the social context, the emphasis is more on values, behaviors, and attitudes than on the specific foods, clothes, and objects of daily life.

Survival Within the Cultural Context

Culture guides human development in a multitude of interrelated ways, helping families thrive within their communities. Here is one example: In many marginal agricultural communities, children are an economic asset because they work on the family's farm. Later, they perpetuate the family unit by remaining on the land, raising their own children, and caring for their aged parents. Thus, every newborn benefits the entire family group. If that family is also poor and dependent on subsistence farming, then nutrition and medical care are inadequate. As a

Cherish the Child Cultures vary tremendously in how much they value children. China's "one-child" policy urges every family to limit reproduction, which could be taken as a sign either that children are not as valuable as older people or that each child is destined to be precious.

? *Observational Quiz* (see answer, page 14): What three signs suggest that this community enjoys this boy?

result, infant mortality is high—a serious loss to the family unit, which needs a new generation to work the land. Therefore, infant care is designed to maximize survival and emphasize cooperation. Typical cultural practices for babies in poor rural communities include the following:

- Breast-feeding on demand
- Immediate response to crying
- Close body contact, frequent touching, and caressing
- Keeping the baby beside the mother at night
- Constant care by siblings and other relatives

All these measures protect the fragile infant from an early death while establishing the value of interdependence among family members (LeVine et al., 1994).

In contrast, middle-class parents in postindustrial nations need not fear that their infant will die, but they have other concerns. They buy cribs, strollers, disposable diapers, high chairs, car seats, and educational toys—all quite expensive items that rural families never purchase. Even food, child care, and shelter are far more costly in an urban than a rural community, which is one reason most women in developed nations want only one or two children and most women in developing countries want three to five (Tsui et al., 1997) (see Appendix A, Chapter 1). The payoff for urban parents comes not when the child begins herding the sheep but when the young adult graduates from college and lands a prestigious job.

Therefore, hoping to ensure their children's future success in a technological and urbanized society, middle-class parents focus their child-rearing efforts on intellectual growth and emotional independence. They typically provide intense cognitive stimulation, talking to their babies more than touching them, putting them to sleep by themselves in their own cribs in their own rooms, and ignoring their young children's whining, crying, fussing, and clinging so as not to "spoil" them.

Who Sleeps with Whom?

As noted above, a specific cultural difference appears when parents decide where their children will sleep. Suppose you are asked to arrange the sleeping places for a family of six moving into a new apartment. The family consists of a

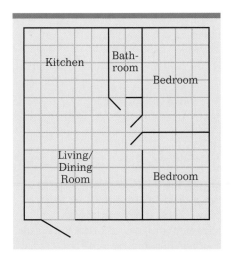

Who Sleeps Where? A six-person family needs to sleep in the apartment shown above. Can you figure out where? We have a mother, father, two daughters ages 2 and 15, and two sons ages 6 and 9.

LIBRARY OF CONGRESS

Why Not Put the Children to Work? The current view of childhood as a special period given over to formal education and play is a fairly recent one. As late as 1900, one out of every five children between the ages of 10 and 16 in the United States worked, often at dirty and dangerous jobs in factories, mills, and mines. These "breaker" boys, who usually started their work at age 10, had the task of picking out slate and rubble from crushed coal as it came down shutes from giant processors. Their hours were long; their environment was choked with coal dust; and their pay was less than a dollar a day.

husband and wife, two daughters aged 15 and 2, and two sons aged 6 and 9; the apartment has a living–dining room, a kitchen, one bathroom, and two bedrooms. Think a moment and see the figure at left before reading on. Have you figured it out? If you are from a non-Western culture, you see two easy solutions: Either the males sleep in one room and the females in another, or everyone sleeps in one room, perhaps on mats on the floor, with the second bedroom as the reading, studying, and computer room. What might seem like crowding may be preferred by people from the many cultures whose members always seek the company of others, awake or asleep (Schweder et al., 1998).

If you are from a Western culture, however, you believe in

> the ritualized isolation of children during the night, the institution of "bedtime," and the protection of the privacy of the "sacred couple" upheld by a cultural norm mandating the exclusive co-sleeping of the husband and wife.
>
> *[Schweder et al., 1998, p. 873]*

Your Western culture has taught you that husband and wife must sleep together, without the children. You have been warned that it is important for even young infants to sleep in separate cribs (Nakamura et al., 1999). You also believe that the 15-year-old is not a child, but a young woman who needs some privacy. This family has a problem without a solution, except the one my students suggested: "They must move."

Sleeping places are only one of hundreds of cultural variations. Each culture endorses certain parental strategies—not just for sleeping but also for talking, feeding, disciplining, encouraging, playing, and so on—that guide children to develop abilities, values, and expectations that are well suited for that place and time. Everyone grows up to "promote, promulgate, and share their understandings and practice with their children" (Schweder et al., 1998, p. 866). How does this relate to sleeping arrangements? Children who sleep with their parents are taught to depend on their parents for warmth and protection; children who sleep alone are taught to be independent of their families, becoming bold and independent as adults. Both practices seem to result in reasonably healthy adults, albeit with contrasting attitudes about their relationships with their parents, with Western young adults eager to get their own place, and non-Westerners often continuing to live with their parents even after marriage.

The Children's House For about 20 years, a third practice was common in hundreds of *kibbutzim* (the plural of *kibbutz*, a kind of farming commune developed in Israel, whose members share work, meals, income, and child care). In every kibbutz, the children once spent several hours each day with their parents, but slept in the same room with other children in a "Children's House," without adults. (The adults took weekly turns monitoring the children by intercom, in case an emergency arose during the night.) This custom changed, first in a few kibbutzim, then in others.

These changing patterns offered an opportunity for scientists to compare sleeping practices, as one researcher did. Three groups of 16- to 18-year-olds who had been raised in more than a dozen kibbutzim were studied; 33 had spent all their nights away from their parents; 34 had begun life sleeping in Children's Houses but switched before age 6 to sleeping near their parents; and 33 had always slept near their parents. This study also included a fourth group of 31 adolescents who had never lived on a kibbutz but had been raised in the city in their parents' homes. When the researcher evaluated these four groups of adolescents, particularly their emotions regarding their parents, the last three groups were quite normal (see Figure 1.5). However, many who had always slept apart from their parents, especially the boys, had difficulty talking about and relating to their family members (Scharf, 2001), a result similar to that of other research on kibbutz-raised children (Aviezer et al., 1994). Virtually all Israeli kibbutzim now

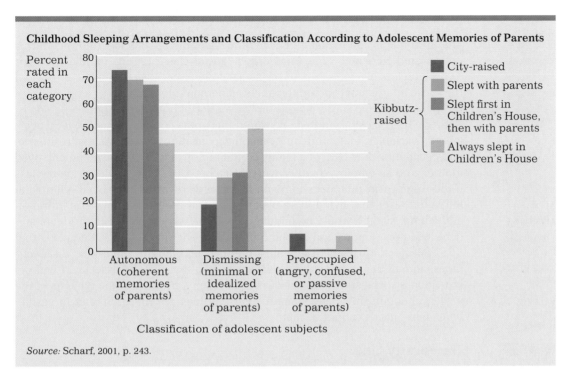

Childhood Sleeping Arrangements and Classification According to Adolescent Memories of Parents

Legend:
- City-raised
- Kibbutz-raised:
  - Slept with parents
  - Slept first in Children's House, then with parents
  - Always slept in Children's House

Source: Scharf, 2001, p. 243.

FIGURE 1.5 **The Cost of Early and Continuing Nighttime Separation from Parents** The adolescent subjects' tape-recorded reminiscences about their parents were rated by trained researchers who did not know which of the four sleeping arrangements the subjects had experienced in childhood. The subjects were rated as autonomous, dismissing, or preoccupied, according to the criteria established for the Adult Attachment Interview. The subjects who, as children living on a kibbutz, had slept in a Children's House rather than near their parents were least likely to be rated as autonomous. Overall, the three groups of kibbutz-raised subjects were more likely to be rated as dismissing, with distorted memories of their parents, than were the city-raised subjects.

encourage parents to have their infants and children sleep near them; the Children's Houses are empty at night (Oppenheim, 1998).

The Need for Parents Extensive research led to the contemporary idea that children develop best if their parents are nearby (Bowlby, 1969, 1973, 1988). Today children who are hospitalized usually have their parents beside them (40 years ago the parents were kept away, to minimize infections). Families in the midst of war (such as the Bosnian mothers) stay together. Before the research, during World War II, thousands of English children were sent away from the cities (which were targets for German bombing) to stay with foster families in the countryside; they survived, but many developed psychological problems as debilitating as physical injury might have been (Burlingham & Freud, 1942).

Looking at cultural contexts makes it apparent that there are numerous wonderful and diverse ways to raise children, and each society and each set of parents make choices that could have been quite different. However, comparing cultures also makes it clear that some human needs are universal. For example, although most cultural variations in child rearing make sense within a given cultural context, raising children without a dedicated caregiver (though not necessarily a biological parent) is never satisfactory. Studies of orphans adopted from Romania as well as abused foster children from the United States suggest that children can recover from early separations if the caregivers are loving and patient, but it is much better to avoid the need for such recovery in the first place (Bowlby, 1988; Chisholm, 1998; Dozier et al., 2001).

Especially for Social Scientists: Can you think of any cultural assumptions that might have led to the now-universal practice in Israel of having kibbutz children sleep near their parents?

Especially for Parents: If you think one-year-olds should not sleep in their parents' room, why do you think that?

The Socioeconomic Context

The third major contextual influence on development is **socioeconomic status**, abbreviated **SES** and sometimes called "social class" (as in "middle class" or "working class"). SES is part of the social context because it influences many of the social interactions and opportunities a person might have.

Socioeconomic status is *not* simply a matter of how rich or poor a person is. Rather, SES is most accurately measured through a combination of several overlapping variables, including family income, educational level, place of residence, and occupation. The SES of a family consisting of, say, an infant, a nonemployed mother, and an employed father who earns $12,000 a year would be lower-class if the wage earner happens to be an illiterate dishwasher employed full time at minimum wage and living in an urban slum. But the same family configuration and annual income would be middle-class if the wage earner is a graduate student living on campus and teaching part time. The point of this example is that SES reflects not just financial status: It entails *all* the advantages and disadvantages, and *all* the opportunities and limitations, that may be associated with an individual's social status. Social class is as much a product of the mind as of the wallet, although obviously some mental attitudes are more difficult to sustain when basic needs cannot be met.

The Poverty Line

In official government statistics, SES is usually measured solely by family income (adjusted for inflation and family size), perhaps because the effects of education and occupation are difficult to quantify. In 2002 in the contiguous United States, a family of four with an annual income below $18,100 was considered to be at the bottom of the SES scale (U.S. Department of Health and Human Services, 2002). Their $18,100 was a dollar amount called the **poverty line**, which is calculated as the minimum amount needed to pay for basic necessities. (In Alaska and Hawaii, the poverty line is set somewhat higher.)

Looking only at family income is simplistic yet sometimes useful, especially when income falls below the poverty line. The reason is that inadequate family income both signals and creates a social context of limited opportunities and heightened pressures. These, in turn, make life much more difficult to manage than it is for families higher up on the socioeconomic ladder. For example, throughout the world infant mortality, child neglect, inadequate schools, and adolescent violence are all much more common among the poor than among the affluent (McLoyd, 1998). Of particular concern in the United States is that the poorest age group is also the youngest, in part because most publicly subsidized benefits (health care, food, housing, Social Security) that are age-related begin after age 65 (see Figure 1.6 and a state-by-state breakdown in Appendix A, Chapter 10).

Families and Neighborhoods

Although low income is a rough but useful indicator of poverty, and although poverty is a rough but useful signal for severe problems, we cannot simply say that lack of money creates overwhelming developmental difficulties. A better and more precise indicator is needed to differentiate between those low-SES individuals, families, and neighborhoods that are overcome by poverty and those that seem relatively protected.

Supportive relationships within the family are one crucial variable. For example, studies of children living in poverty find that some are "resilient: bouncing back from adversity, they become well-adjusted and successful, while others become angry, lonely, law-breaking, and failures" (Werner & Smith, 1992; see also Rutter et al., 1998). One difference is nurturant, involved parents. Even if adults

---

socioeconomic status (SES) An indicator of a person's social and economic standing, measured through a combination of family income, educational level, place of residence, occupation, and other variables.

❗Answer to Observational Quiz (from page 11): At least four adults are smiling at him; he is eating an apple that was brought to the market for sale; he is allowed to sit on the table with the food. If you noticed another sign—his new green sandals—give yourself bonus credit.

poverty line The minimum annual income a family needs to pay for basic necessities, as determined by the federal government. A family whose income falls below that amount is considered poor.

Response for Social Scientists (from page 13): Researchers as well as leaders in Israel assume that children should have strong relationships with their parents. Could this assumption itself be a social construction?

Response for Parents (from page 13): If you think the child should be in a separate room because the parents need privacy, you should know that children always sleep near their parents in India—and yet that country has an overpopulation problem. People obviously can have sex in many places and times other than in their shared bedroom at night. If your reason has to do with teaching the child, at a young age, to be independent, you are correct: The child is likely to learn not to depend on the parents for warmth and comfort while sleeping.

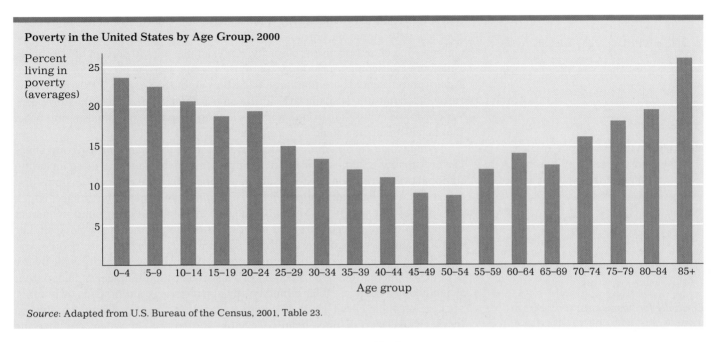

Poverty in the United States by Age Group, 2000

Percent living in poverty (averages)

Source: Adapted from U.S. Bureau of the Census, 2001, Table 23.

FIGURE 1.6 Children Are the Poorest Someone who goes to bed hungry, in a crumbling house or apartment, in a crime-ridden community is more likely to be a child than an adult. To those who study child development, this seems unfair—especially because some older adults who are not actually poor "spend down" their assets in order to qualify for government subsidies. Who should support the poor of other generations—the society as a whole or the family members of those who are poor?

are poor, unmarried, and victims of childhood neglect and abuse, they can become good parents, and the quality of parenting is the single most sensitive predictor of a resilient child (Duncan & Brooks-Gunn, 2000; Wyman et al., 1999).

Neighborhoods are another crucial variable, as you might guess from the emphasis on the mesosystem. If people show concern for each other and for their immediate surroundings—getting rid of trash on the street, repairing broken windows, and so on—the children will be healthier and more successful than children of equally poor families who live in neighborhoods where the adults care only about themselves. The importance of "collective efficacy," which is the ability of the neighbors to create a functioning community, has been shown in detailed, block-by-block analyses in Chicago and New Orleans (Cohen et al., 2000; Sampson et al., 1997) and probably is true overall. Finally, again as our understanding of development would predict, a change in income level is more influential than the absolute level. For example, one study of impoverished families whose income improved over three years—even though it was still below average—found that the children did as well as middle-class children (Dearing et al., 2001).

Don't Go There Not just poverty but neglect and crime are evident in this scene on Chicago's South Side. In communities where incomes are low but the residents care about the neighborhood, abandoned cars are towed away, not stripped, and empty buildings are rebuilt, demolished, or at least boarded up, not left with broken windows for rats and drug addicts to enter.

Economics and Ethnic Groups

To say, as we did earlier, that "social class is as much a product of the mind as of the wallet" is not to say that money does not matter. It *does* matter, but it is only one of several factors that constitute social class, and social class is only one of the factors that affect child development. To complicate matters, socioeconomic status often overlaps with ethnic background, so a particular pattern of development can be connected to either income or ethnicity. For example, only 10 percent of European-American households include six or more people, but 25 percent of Hispanic-American households are that large (U.S. Bureau of the Census, 2000). Is that the result of income (the Hispanic average income is about 60 percent of the European-American) or culture (a strong emphasis among Hispanics on familism, the belief that family members should stay together)?

ethnic group A collection of people who share certain attributes, almost always including ancestral heritage and often including national origin, religion, customs, and language.

What exactly is an ethnic group? Briefly, members of an **ethnic group** share certain attributes, almost always including ancestral heritage and often including national origin, religion, customs, and language. (*Heritage* refers to customs and traditions from past generations; *national origin* merely means birthplace, which may or may not signify customs.) Because of this shared background, members of an ethnic group recognize and identify with one another. They have similar attitudes and daily encounters with the social world, especially with people who realize they are members of that ethnic group. Accordingly, ethnicity is partly the product of perceptions and reactions. This social recognition aspect is apparent when people broadcast their ethnicity—by, for instance, putting flags or bumper stickers on their cars ("Honk if you're Italian") or wearing distinctive apparel (neck chains, jackets, pins, head coverings, and so on)—or when they take the opposite approach, working to rid themselves of an accent or mannerism that reveals their ethnic roots.

Especially for Immigrants: Why might it be unwise for you to abandon the customs of your native culture?

One of the many complications of ethnicity (and one of the reasons people are not always happy when others recognize their ethnic heritage) is that, in every nation of the world, economic opportunities, occupational choices, and residential patterns are linked to ethnic identity. Any research that finds differences between people based on ethnicity or race may actually be uncovering differences in SES, or vice versa (Bradley et al., 2001). Becoming aware of this problem is an essential step for students and researchers, but it is often impossible to disentangle SES, culture, ethnicity, and race (Smith, 2000), as the Thinking Like a Scientist feature explains.

race A social construction by which biological traits (such as hair or skin color, facial features, and body type) are used to differentiate people whose ancestors came from various regions of the world.

Thinking Like a Scientist

Race and Biology

Sometimes *race* is considered an element of ethnicity. Indeed, outsiders mistakenly assume that people of the same racial background are also from the same ethnic background, and statisticians often categorize people by race rather than by ethnicity. However, as social scientists emphatically point out, **race**—defined as the biological traits (such as hair or skin color, facial features, and body type) that people use to distinguish one group from another—is much less influential on development than ethnic background (Goodman, 2000). The Human Genome Project (discussed in Chapter 3) has found that genetic distinctions *between* racial groups are few and insignificant compared with genetic distinctions between members of one family or another *within* any racial group.

For this reason, social scientists prefer to discuss ethnicity, not race, although sometimes data are reported only by race. In that case, race is used as the only available marker for ethnicity.

Ethnic identity, however, is not primarily genetic; it is a product of the social environment and the individual's consciousness. Two people may look like close relatives but may have quite different upbringings, heritages, and community settings and therefore quite different ethnic identities. Or two people may be very different in appearance but still share an ethnic identity. This is readily apparent in many Latin American ethnic groups. These groups include people of African, European, and Indian descent who are united in a single ethnicity by their common language and original homeland. Similarly, people of African descent who lived for many generations in the Caribbean do not generally consider themselves black, at least as people born in the United States define "black" (Waters, 2000). In fact, immigrant children from many nations resent being categorized racially (Suarez-Orozco & Suarez-Orozco, 2001). They recognize that racial designations can be used artificially to set them apart and exclude them; people from the Middle East, for instance, are categorized as white in the United States but as non-white in England.

The realizations that ethnic categories are not genetic and that racial categories are misleading are changing the way scientists report research. For example, the 1970 U.S. census used only three racial categories—white, Negro, and other. Millions of Spanish-speaking citizens insisted that they did not belong in these categories, and millions of Asian-Americans and Native Americans resented being dismissed as "other." Three new categories were added in 1980: "Asian and Pacific Islander," "American Indian, Eskimo, Aleut," and "Hispanic, may be of any race" (although those who checked off "Hispanic" were also asked to designate "white" or "black"). Allowing Hispanics to be tallied separately has

been particularly useful for those who care about the well-being of children; the census has revealed that the proportion of children under age 18 who are of Spanish heritage has doubled since 1980, from 9 to 18 percent; this increase lends urgency to the need to improve bilingual education as well as many other social services for children.

For the 2000 census, some scientists advocated getting rid of all racial categories, but this idea was rejected. Instead, a sixth category was created, separating "Asian" from "Native Hawaiian, and Pacific Islander." Respondents were also allowed to check several new racial categories, including "More than one race."

Social scientists increasingly recognize that all racial categories are imprecise, because each contains at least a dozen quite distinct ethnic groups. More and more studies try to specify the ethnic background of the subjects. At this point in the historical context, ethnic and racial categories remain socially and economically powerful, affecting how children develop, and therefore they are often reported in research. Data collected prior to 2000 are often reported using the old racial categories. By the 2010 census, these classifications may change again.

The Person Within Systems and Contexts

Awareness of the overlaps among culture, SES, and ethnicity leads to another, even more important, realization: Although each context always affects how an

individual develops, a person within a context or system is never like a part in a complex machine, responsive only to the mechanical pushes and pulls of that context. No one is exactly like the statistically "average" person of his or her cohort, socioeconomic status, or culture. Not only is each person guided in divergent directions by many contextual influences, whose power varies from individual to individual, age to age, situation to situation, and family to family, but also each person has unique genes and experiences.

Consequently, each of us differs in unexpected ways from any stereotypes or generalities that might seem pertinent, and our individual differences demand as much scientific respect and scrutiny as any of the commonalities that link us to a particular group. In

Not the Usual Path If we were to consider only this woman's past history or the cultural values that her dyed hair and polished fingernails suggest, we would say that she belongs at home with her grandchildren and old-age pension. However, individual uniqueness can override contextual limitations—which explains why she is about to walk the Appalachian Trail from Maine to Georgia. If we use a life-span perspective, this is not a surprise, because she always enjoyed exercise and the outdoors, and covering the trail's entire 2,160-mile length was her lifelong ambition.

VINCE DE WITT / STOCK, BOSTON

Jimmy Carter in Havana, Cuba, in 2001.

fact, each of us is an active participant in every context that includes us. We contribute to the history of our cohort, we help form our economic circumstances, and we construct our own personal meanings from our cultural background (Rogoff, 1997; Valsiner, 1997). This power of the developing individual is demonstrated by every person who is the focus of the features in this book called "A Case to Study." Remember that barefoot farm boy from southwest Georgia? Given his historical, cultural, and economic contexts, he was destined to become a farmer like his father. But he did not. He went to the U.S. Naval Academy (the first in his family to attend college), became an engineer, and at the age of 52 was elected the 39th president of the United States. Today Jimmy Carter is a renowned humanitarian on the world stage. To reinforce the same point—that domains interact and that contexts are powerful—the In Person feature presents a personal story, that of my brother's son David.

In Person

My Nephew David

In the spring of 1967, in rural Kentucky, an epidemic of rubella (German measles) struck two particular victims— David's mother, who had a rash and a sore throat for a couple of days, and her 4-week-old embryo, who was damaged for life. David was born in November, with a life-threatening heart defect and thick cataracts covering both eyes. Other damage included minor malformations of the thumbs, feet, jaw, and teeth, as well as of the brain.

The historical context was crucial. Had David been conceived a decade later, widespread use of the rubella vaccine would have protected him from damage. Had he been born a few years earlier, he would have died. Indeed, some doctors expected David to live briefly as a severely retarded child requiring custodial care. But in 1967 the new miracle of microsurgery saved his tiny heart and his life.

My brother is a professor and his wife is a nurse; their cultural and socioeconomic contexts encouraged them to seek outside help rather than accept their fate. They asked advice from a teacher at the Kentucky School for the Blind, who told them to stop blaming themselves and stop overprotecting David. If their son was going to learn about his world, he had to explore it. For example, rather than confining David to a crib or playpen, they were to provide him with a large rug for a play area. Whenever he crawled off the rug, they were to say "No" and place him back in the middle of it. He would learn to use his sense of touch to decide where he could explore safely without bumping into walls or furniture. They followed this advice.

Nonetheless, progress was slow. Rubella had damaged much more than David's eyes and heart. At age 3, he could not yet talk, chew solid food, use the toilet, coordinate his fingers, or even walk normally. An IQ test showed him to be severely mentally retarded. Fortunately, although most children with rubella syndrome have hearing defects, David's hearing was normal.

David's fifth birthday occurred in 1972. By then, the social construction that children with severe disabilities are unteachable was being seriously challenged. David's parents found four schools that would accept a child with multiple handicaps. In accordance with the family's emphasis on education, they enrolled him in all four. He attended two schools for children with cerebral palsy: One had morning classes, and the other—40 miles away—afternoon classes. (David ate lunch in the car with his mother on the daily trip.) On Fridays these schools were closed, so he attended a school for the mentally retarded. On Sundays he spent two hours in church school, which was his first experience with "mainstreaming"—the then-new idea that children with special needs should be educated with normal children. Particularly in the church community, the cultural-ethnic context of northern Kentucky benefited David, for accepting the disabled and helping neighbors are basic Appalachian values.

At age 7, David entered a public school, one of the first severely disabled children to be mainstreamed. Rubella continued to hinder his biosocial, cognitive, and psychosocial development. His motor skills were poor (among other things, he had difficulty controlling a pencil); his efforts to read were limited by the fact that he was legally blind; and his social skills were seriously impaired (he pinched people he didn't like, hugged girls too tightly, cried and laughed at inappropriate times).

During the next several years, development in the cognitive domain proceeded rapidly. By age 10, David had skipped a year of school and was a fifth-grader. He could read—with a magnifying glass—at the eleventh-grade level and was labeled "intellectually gifted" according to tests of verbal and math skills. Outside of school he began to learn a second language, play the violin, and sing in the choir.

David now calls his college experience an "adversity," and certainly many of his peers and professors were unprepared for a student like him. He sometimes seemed to learn too well, asking precise questions and remembering numbers and words that most students would forget. He sometimes took offense at inadvertent slights. But he finally graduated, a double major in Russian and German. He studied in Germany to refine his translating skills and now earns his living as a translator (an interesting choice for someone who cannot see social nuances of facial expressions and therefore learned to listen carefully). His latest report is that he is

> generally quite happy, but secretly a little happier lately, especially since November, because I have been consistently getting a pretty good vibrato when I am singing, not only by myself but in congregational hymns in church. [He explained vibrato:] when a note bounces up and down within a quarter tone either way of concert pitch, optimally between 5.5 and 8.2 times per second.
>
> *[David, 2002]*

Amazing. David is both knowledgeable and happy, and he continues to develop his skills. He also has a wry sense of humor. When I told him that I wasn't progressing as fast as I wanted to in revising this text, even though I was working very hard every day, he replied, "That sounds just like a certain father I know." As his aunt, I have watched David defy many pessimistic predictions. The rubella damage will always be with him, limiting his development. But David proves again that no human is entirely or inevitably restricted by any of life's domains, systems, or contexts.

Three Brothers Studying the development of other people is fascinating in many ways, not the least of which is that no human is untouched by understanding the personal story of another. I have learned many things from David, shown in this recent family photo with his two older brothers, Bill (left) and Michael (right). One is the role of siblings: Bill and Michael protected their younger brother, but David also taught them, making them more nurturant than most young men in their community. I know this firsthand—these boys were the closest thing my daughters had to big brothers, and they tolerated teasing that some older cousins would have put a stop to.

KATHLEEN BERGER

Developmental Study as a Science

Because the study of human development is a science, it follows objective rules of evidence. Because it concerns human life and growth, it is also laden with personal implications and applications. This interplay of the objective and the subjective, of the individual and the universal, of young and old, of past, present, and future makes developmental science a dynamic, interactive, and even transformative study. Of all the sciences, the study of human development is the least static, least predictable, and least narrow. It also may have the most noble goal: "explaining, assessing, and promoting change and development" (Renninger & Amsel, 1997, p. xi). In other words, developmental scientists seek not only to understand and measure human change but also to use their knowledge to help all people develop their full human potential.

This lofty goal is of vital importance. Everyone has heartfelt opinions about how children should grow and why they turn out the way they do. By definition, opinions are subjective and tend to be biased, or influenced by our particular

Response for Immigrants (from page 16): Since cultures develop for reasons, a custom that seems superficial and old-fashioned in your new country may be part of an interdependent design for living; changing one custom may affect many other aspects of your life. This does not mean that change is bad; it simply means that aspects of both the old culture and the new culture should be examined before being adopted or discarded.

backgrounds and experiences. To move beyond opinions and controversy, developmentalists use the scientific method to seek evidence—not biased or wishful thinking—to gain the knowledge we need to use (Shonkoff, 2000; Thompson & Nelson, 2001). In fact, one of the goals of all science is to question assumptions, to disprove what "everyone knows," and even to reexamine the results of other scientific research (Feynman, 1985; Popper, 1965).

The Scientific Method

The **scientific method**, as it applies to developmental study, involves four basic steps and sometimes a fifth:

1. *Formulate a research question.* On the basis of previous research or a particular theory or personal observation, pose a question about development.
2. *Develop a hypothesis.* Reformulate the question into a **hypothesis,** which is a specific prediction that can be tested.
3. *Test the hypothesis.* Design and conduct a research project that will provide evidence—in the form of data—about the hypothesis.
4. *Draw conclusions.* Use the evidence to support or refute the hypothesis. Describe any limitations of the research and any alternative explanations for the results.
5. *Make the findings available.* Publishing the research is often the fifth step in the scientific method. It involves describing the procedure and results in sufficient detail that other scientists can evaluate the conclusions or replicate the research. **Replication** is the repetition of a scientific study, using the same procedures on another group of subjects, to verify or refute the original study's conclusions.

Some Complications

In actual practice, scientific investigation is less straightforward than these five steps would suggest. The linkages among question, hypothesis, test, and conclusion are sometimes indirect, and the design and execution of research are influenced by (fallible) human judgment (Bauer, 1992; Howard, 1996). Human biases tend to guide the choice of which topics to examine, which methods to use, and how to interpret the results.

Sometimes major industries that have an economic stake in the results of scientific studies either sponsor or subsidize research and distort the conclusions. It has been proven in court that the tobacco industry has done this regarding the harm done by nicotine and other toxins in cigarettes for years, and they continue to hamper scientific studies of the effects of advertising, international marketing, and secondhand smoke (Ong & Glantz, 2001). Most other social practices have economic implications, such as creating more public day-care centers, reducing the amount of lead in old houses, providing vouchers for private schools, funding contraception or abortion, using drugs to quiet disruptive children—although in all these cases the evidence is less clear-cut than it was for tobacco. Minimizing the effects of cultural values, political pressures, personal wishes, and financial support is a challenge. It is also one goal of the methods and procedures of science—and not an easy goal to reach (Hunt, 1999; Shonkoff, 2000).

Further, there is always a question of whether researchers are aware of all the relevant **variables**—qualities that may differ, or vary, during an investigation. People vary in sex, age, education, ethnicity, economic status, nationality, values, jobs, family background, personality—the list could go on and on. Moreover, developmental researchers must deal with both *intrapersonal variation,* which is variation within one person from day to day, and *interpersonal variation,* which

scientific method An approach to the systematic pursuit of knowledge that, when applied to the study of development, involves five basic steps: Formulate a research question, develop a hypothesis, test the hypothesis, draw conclusions, and make the findings available.

hypothesis A specific prediction that is stated in such a way that it can be tested and either confirmed or refuted.

replication The repetition of a scientific study, using the same procedures on another group of subjects, to verify or refute the original study's conclusions.

variables The qualities that may differ, or vary, during a scientific investigation.

is variation between people or between groups of people. The two kinds of variation are not always easily distinguished.

Partly because of this complexity, certain controversies echo throughout the study of development, each time with different issues and questions—and often with different responses:

- *Nature–nurture.* How much and which aspects of development are affected by genes and how much and which aspects by environment?
- *Continuity–discontinuity.* How much of human growth builds smoothly and gradually on previous development, and how much transformation occurs suddenly?
- *Difference–deficit.* When a person develops differently from most other people, when is that difference considered diversity to be celebrated and when is it considered a problem to be corrected?

Each of these controversies is further explained and explored throughout this text, especially in Chapter 2, on theories of development.

Two other issues seem contentious to those unfamiliar with developmental study, though they are not issues for developmentalists:

- *Religion–science.* Do the tenets of religious faith and the methods of science necessarily conflict?
- *Individual–society:* Can we study the individual person without studying the family, the community, and the culture?

To both of these questions, the answer from scientists who study development is "no." Religion and science are complementary, not conflicting (Gould, 1999), and individuals are inextricably involved with their social group (Cole, 1996). Some of the most emotional questions about human life—who should have sex with whom, who should hurt whom, who should be rich or poor, and when and how all these things might happen—benefit from the scientific method and the perspective of other cultures and cohorts. Prepare for some new ideas.

Research Methods

Between the questions developmental scientists ask and the answers they find lies their methodology—not only the steps of the scientific method but also the specific strategies used to gather and analyze data. These strategies are critical because "the ways that you attempt to clarify phenomena in large measure determine the worth of the solution" (Cairns & Cairns, 1994). In other words, *how* research is designed affects the *validity* (does it measure what it purports to measure?), *accuracy* (are the measurements correct?), *generalizability* (does it apply to other populations and situations?), and *usefulness* (can it solve real-life problems?) of the conclusions.

Some general strategies to make research valid, accurate, and useful are described in Appendix B. Now we turn to specific methods of testing hypotheses: observations, experiments, surveys, and case studies. Remember, the overall goal is to find evidence that answers questions and minimizes human biases.

Observation

An excellent method to test hypotheses regarding human development is **scientific observation**—that is, observing and recording, in a systematic and objective manner, what people do. Observations often occur in a naturalistic setting, such as at home, in a workplace, or on a public street. Typically, the observing scientist tries to be as unobtrusive as possible, so that the people being studied (the research subjects) act as they normally do.

scientific observation A method of testing hypotheses by unobtrusively watching and recording subjects' behavior either in a laboratory or in a natural setting.

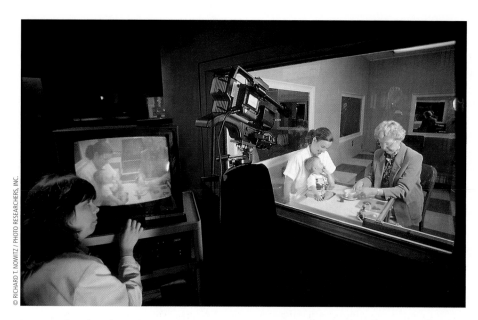

Observation can also occur in a laboratory. In this setting, the scientists sometimes are not visibly present at all; they may sit behind one-way windows that allow them to peer, unnoticed, into the experimental room, or they may record data with a video camera placed on the wall. In the laboratory, scientists study many aspects of behavior, such as the rate and duration of eye contact between infant and caregiver, the patterns of dominance and submission that emerge as an entire family discusses its vacation plans, the heart rate and brain activity of a child watching a frightening movie, and many more.

Already mentioned at the beginning of this chapter is observational research on the moment-by-moment

Do Not Disturb: Science in Progress Does any 6-month-old understand that cups go on saucers, that circles are not squares, and that mothers know the answers when a child does not? In this laboratory observation, one scientist elicits the answers while another videotapes the results for later analysis.

interaction between a parent and an infant. This is sometimes done with great precision, using two video cameras and analyzing the tapes frame by frame on a computer to see whether a new baby really can observe a parent's rapidly changing facial expression or vocalization and respond to it. The answer is "yes," a finding that could not have been made without very careful and objective observations (Rochat, 2001).

Observation has one major limitation. It does not indicate what causes the behavior we observe. If we notice that one mother spanks her children and another does not, or that one 11-year-old sneaks a beer and another abstains, *why* do such differences appear? Naturalistic observation can note many characteristics of these two 11-year-olds, but it cannot explain why one variable occurs with another. For instance, in the United States, young adolescents who abuse alcohol are more likely to be male than female and more likely to be non-Hispanic white (European-American) than black (African-American) (Johnston et al., 2001). But why?

correlation A number indicating the degree of relationship between two variables, expressed in terms of the likelihood that one variable will occur when the other variable does. A correlation is not an indication that one variable *causes* the other.

Naturalistic observation provides no definitive answers about causes. The data can prove that certain variables correlate with other variables, not that one causes another. A **correlation** exists between two variables if one variable is more (or less) likely to occur when the other occurs. For example, a correlation exists between being a male European-American teenager and drinking beer. Are hormones, upbringing, advertising, or peer pressure the reason? Correlation indicates a connection, but it does not specify the reason for that connection. Are African-American adolescents better protected from alcohol abuse by religion, income, or family influences than European-Americans? Correlation cannot provide the answer.

Even when two variables are strongly (or highly) correlated, we should not, even must not, say that one variable causes the other. Table 1.1 illustrates the three types of correlational connections, using the correlation between wealth and education as an example.

TABLE 1.1 There Is a Strong Positive Correlation Between Wealth and Education

Possible explanation:	Income → education (Wealthy families pay for good schools and colleges.)
Possible explanation:	Education → income (Well-educated people earn more.)
Possible explanation:	Family values → income → education (Hard work and no drugs produce higher levels of both income and education.)
Conclusion:	Education and income are somehow connected.

Whenever there is a strong correlation between two variables, either of the variables could be the cause or both could be caused by a third variable. Correlation is not causation.

A correlation is *positive* if the occurrence of one variable makes it *more* likely that the other will occur. A correlation is *negative* if the occurrence of one variable makes it *less* likely that the other will occur. Because of the way correlation is calculated, the highest positive correlation is expressed as +1.0 and the greatest negative correlation as –1.0. Most actual correlations are neither so high nor so low: A correlation of 0.5 is impressive. Two variables that are not related at all have a correlation of zero, or 0 (exactly halfway between +1.0 and –1.0). We mentioned earlier that observation has confirmed that some parents spank their children more often than others. Correlation suggests reasons for this variation. As you can see from Table 1.2, the reason does not seem to be the child's sex, at least for 4- to 5-year-olds. This study found a positive correlation between spanking and behavior problems, and a negative one between spanking and the warmth of the parent's feelings toward the child. This link is intriguing—but once again, other research needs to reveal what causes what. The best way to do this is to conduct an experiment.

The Experiment

An **experiment** is an investigation designed to untangle cause from effect. In the social sciences, experimenters typically expose a group of people to a particular treatment or condition to see if their behavior changes as a result. In technical terms, experimenters manipulate an **independent variable** (the imposed treatment or special condition). They then note how that change affects the specific behavior they are studying, which is called the **dependent variable.** Thus, the independent variable is the new, special treatment; the dependent variable is the response (which may or may not be affected by the independent variable). Finding out which independent variables affect which dependent variables, and how great that effect may be, is the purpose of an experiment.

By comparing changes in a dependent variable that occur after an independent (experimental) variable has been imposed, researchers are often able to uncover the link between cause and effect. This is the reason experiments are performed: No other research method can so accurately pinpoint what leads to what.

In a typical experiment (diagrammed in Figure 1.7), two groups of subjects are studied: an **experimental group,** which is given a particular treatment (the independent variable), and a **comparison group** (also called a *control group*), which does not get the special treatment but is similar to the experimental group in other ways (such as age, ethnicity, SES). In the study of the Bosnian refugees mentioned at the beginning of this chapter, data were collected on a dozen variables for all the mothers and children. Half of the mothers were then given special counseling (the independent variable) to help them cope with their children's reactions to their wartime experiences. These women's children constituted the experimental group. The other mothers received no counseling; their children were the comparison group.

After five months, all the children were examined again. Few significant differences were found between the experimental and comparison groups of children. (*Significant* and *insignificant* are statistical terms that indicate the likelihood that the results did or did not occur by chance. In this study, improvements in the experimental group were so slight, and the total number of children involved was so small, that most changes were insignificant—that is, they could have happened by chance.) The one significant change was biological: The experimental children gained more weight over the five-month period than the other children (Dybdahl, 2001). In trying to understand why the counseling sessions were not more effective, the author speculates that the treated mothers shared what they learned with the comparison-group mothers, so that all benefited from an

TABLE 1.2 Correlations Between Spanking of 4- to 5-year-olds and Other Variables

Child is female	–0.06
Parent is warm toward child	–0.23
Child has behavior problems	+0.46

Source: McLoyd & Smith, 2002.

experiment A research method in which the researcher tries to determine the cause-and-effect relationship between two variables by manipulating one variable (called the *independent variable*) and then observing and recording the resulting changes in the other variable (called the *dependent variable*).

independent variable In an experiment, the variable that is introduced or changed to see what effect it has on the dependent variable.

dependent variable In an experiment, the variable that may change as a result of the introduction of or changes made in the independent variable.

experimental group In an experiment, the subjects who are given a particular treatment.

comparison group In an experiment, the subjects who are not given special treatment but who are similar to the experimental group in other relevant ways. (Also called the *control group.*)

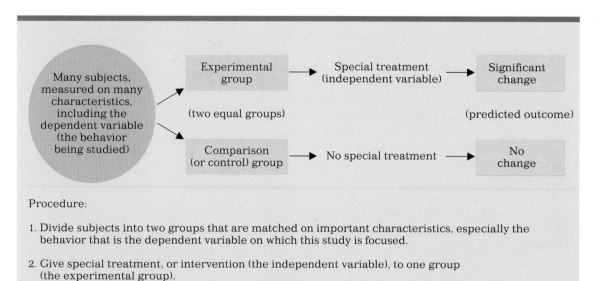

Procedure:

1. Divide subjects into two groups that are matched on important characteristics, especially the behavior that is the dependent variable on which this study is focused.

2. Give special treatment, or intervention (the independent variable), to one group (the experimental group).

3. Compare the groups on the dependent variable. If they now differ, the cause of the difference was probably the independent variable.

4. Publish the results.

FIGURE 1.7 How to Conduct an Experiment

? *Observational Quiz* (see answer, page 26):
Does the experimental group always change?

intervention that was intended for only half of them. It is also possible that counseling did not produce changes that helped the children emotionally (remember, they were all surprisingly unscathed by the civil war) but did help the mothers focus on nutrition—an important factor, since all these children had been underfed.

With all experiments, other questions remain. First, to what degree do the findings from an artificial experimental situation apply in the real world? A major problem with many experiments is that the controlled situation, with the scientist manipulating the independent variable, is different in important ways from normal, everyday life.

In addition, in most experiments (except those with very young children) the participants know they are research subjects. Subjects, especially adults, may attempt to produce the results they believe the experimenter is looking for, or, especially if they are adolescents, they may try to undermine the study. Even if the subjects do not react in either of these ways, almost all experimental subjects are more nervous than they otherwise would be. This reaction leads to the third problem: Is it ethical to make people nervous in such a way? Perhaps, but not always, as is discussed at the end of this chapter. Certainly it is not ethical to harm subjects in any way. It would be highly unethical (as well as artificial) to try to learn more about spanking, for instance, by asking some parents to spank their children more often.

Ideally, an experiment avoids these pitfalls by relying on natural conditions, which become the independent variable. Natural conditions can create an experimental and a comparison group. In the study of the kibbutz children, the independent variable was children's sleeping conditions (either near or apart from their parents), and the dependent variable was the adolescents' emotional relationships to family members. This study was a *natural experiment,* recommended as the most accurate and ethical way to conduct developmental research on children (Bronfenbrenner, 1979).

The Survey

In the research method called the **survey**, information is collected from a large number of people by personal interview, by written questionnaire, or by some other means. This is an easy, quick, and direct way to obtain data. Surveys are especially useful when scientists want to learn about children, since an obvious way of doing so is to ask parents or teachers.

Unfortunately, getting valid data through an interview or questionnaire is more difficult than it seems, because these methods are vulnerable to bias from both the researcher and the respondents. In addition, many people who are interviewed give answers that they think the researchers want, or that express opinion rather than fact, or that they think will make them seem wise or good.

For example, remember the survey that asked 5,000 boys if they had had sex before age 13? In ninth grade, 14 percent said "yes," but in the eleventh grade only 8 percent of the same boys said "yes." This was a paper-and-pencil survey conducted in classrooms, and researchers had no way to question the boys more closely. It could be that boys are likely to boast in ninth grade (is it "cool" to say "yes" to sex at that age?) or that they were more ashamed by eleventh grade (is it "good" to postpone sex at that age?). Or maybe the phrase *sexual intercourse* means something different at ages 14 and 16, or perhaps some of the early-experienced boys had left school or were out sick or refused to answer the questions in eleventh grade—or perhaps they really did forget. Since, for ethical reasons, the survey was confidential and anonymous, the researcher did not know which of the boys gave conflicting answers on the two surveys, much less why they did so. As you can see, surveys are useful for collecting a great deal of data, but accuracy and interpretations are problematic.

The Case Study

A **case study** is an intensive study of one individual. Typically, the case study is based on interviews with the subject regarding his or her background, current thinking, and actions; it may also utilize interviews of people who know the individual. Additional case-study material may be obtained through observation, experiments, and standardized tests, such as personality inventories and intelligence tests. A true case study is much more detailed than the excerpts presented in the feature called "A Case to Study" in this book.

Case studies can provide a wealth of detail, which makes them rich in possible insights. Many developmentalists prefer case studies precisely for that reason: The complexity of a human life is easier to comprehend through the rich *qualitative,* or descriptive, information of a case study than through a *quantitative* study involving sheer numbers.

However, the collection and interpretations of case-study information reflect the biases as well as the wisdom of the researcher. Even when a case study is carefully collected and interpreted, the conclusions apply with certainty to only one person. The case study has two important uses:

▪ To understand a particular individual very well
▪ To provide a provocative starting point for other research

However, no confident conclusions about people in general can be drawn from a sample size of 1, or even 10 or 20, no matter how deep and detailed the study is.

Clearly, there are many ways to gather developmental data, and each method compensates for the weaknesses of the others. Researchers can observe people in naturalistic or laboratory settings, or they can experimentally elicit reactions under controlled conditions or take advantage of unusual natural experiments. They can survey hundreds or even thousands of people, or interview a smaller

survey A research method in which information is collected from a large number of people by personal interview, by written questionnaire, or by some other means.

case study A research method in which one individual is studied intensively.

! Answer to Observational Quiz (from page 24): No. Note the word *predicted*. The hypothesis is that change will occur for the experimental group and not the control group, but the reason for doing the experiment is to discover whether that prediction does indeed come true.

number of people in great depth, or study one life in detail. Because each method has weaknesses, none of them provide data with ample scope and precision to merit broad conclusions. But each brings researchers closer to the issues and answers. Together they can either support or refute theories and hypotheses.

Studying Changes over Time

Remember the definition on page 1: The scientific study of human development seeks to understand how and why people—all kinds of people—change, and how and why they remain the same, as they grow older. Accordingly, for research to be truly developmental, it must be able to deal with things that change and continue *over time*. Developmental scientists need to design their research so that it includes time, or age, as a factor. Usually they accomplish this with one of three basic research designs: cross-sectional, longitudinal, or cross-sequential (as illustrated in Figure 1.8).

Cross-Sectional Research

cross-sectional research A research method in which groups of people who differ in age but share other important characteristics are compared.

The most convenient, and thus more common, way to include age in a developmental study is by designing **cross-sectional research.** In a cross-sectional study, groups of people who differ in age but share other important characteristics (such as level of education, socioeconomic status, and ethnic background) are compared.

Cross-sectional design seems simple enough, but it is very difficult to ensure that the various groups being compared are similar in every important background variable except age. Let's look at a simple, hypothetical example of cross-sectional research.

Suppose a group of 10-year-olds are found to be taller by about 12 inches (30 centimeters) than a comparable group of 6-year-olds. It seems reasonable to conclude that during the four years between ages 6 and 10, children gain a foot in height. However, even such an obvious conclusion might be wrong. In fact, other research shows that most children grow less than that—about 10 inches (25 centimeters)—between those ages. It could be that the particular 10-year-olds in the study were better nourished throughout their lives than the particular 6-year-olds or that they had some other relevant characteristic that was not accounted for. Certainly, if the 10-year-old group included more boys than girls or more Africans than Asians than the 6-year-old group, the height difference would reflect sex or ethnicity as well as age.

Compare These with Those The apparent similarity of these two groups in gender and ethnic composition makes them candidates for cross-sectional research. Before we could be sure that any difference between the two groups is the result of age, we would have to be sure the groups are alike in other ways, such as socioeconomic status and religious affiliation. These two groups are not exactly the same, but we cannot tell whether the cross-sectional differences are significant or not.

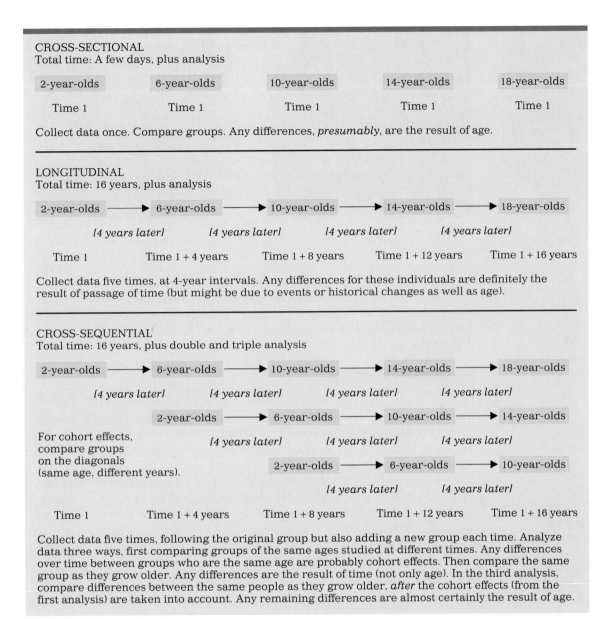

FIGURE 1.8 Which Is Best? Cross-sequential research is the most time-consuming and most complex approach, but it also yields the best information about development. This is one reason why hundreds of scientists conduct research on the same topics, replicating one another's work—to gain some of the advantages of cross-sequential research without having to wait all those years.

Of course, good scientists try to make cross-sectional groups similar in every major background variable. Nevertheless, even if two cross-sectional groups were identical except for age, they would still reflect cohort differences because each age group was born in a different historical period. In this example, even four years could make a difference in the typical diet, as some additives are banned and as new snacks are introduced each year.

More broadly, factors in any domain could change over four years. Biological: A particular childhood disease might have been controlled and then eliminated (as polio was) or nutrition could have dramatically decreased over a four-year period (if, for instance, a nation were torn by civil war). Cognitive: Popular opinion about ideal weight could make children so weight-conscious that many of them undereat. Psychosocial: How children spend their time within

each society changes. For example, between 1950 and 1954, children's television watching increased from zero to an average of almost three hours a day, making children less active and thus fatter, and fatter children begin their adolescent height spurt sooner. Any of these historical patterns could affect average height, and thus cross-sectional results would be deceptive because they ignore cohort differences.

Longitudinal Research

longitudinal research A research method in which the same individuals are studied over a long period of time.

To help discover whether age, rather than some other background or historical variable, is really the reason for an apparent developmental change, scientists undertake **longitudinal research**, studying the *same individuals* over a long period of time. Because longitudinal research compares information about the same people at different ages, it eliminates the effects of background variables, even those that researchers are not aware of. If we know how tall a group of children were at age 6 and how tall the same children are at age 10, it is easy to figure out how much they grew, on average, during the four intervening years.

Longitudinal research is particularly useful in studying development over a long age span (Elder, 1998). It has yielded valuable and sometimes surprise findings on many topics, including the following:

- *Children's adjustment to divorce.* The negative effects linger, but not for every child (Hetherington & Kelly, 2002).
- *The role of fathers in child development.* Even 50 years ago, fathers were far more influential regarding their children's future happiness than the stereotype of the distant dad implies (Snarey, 1993).
- *The consequences of an early delay in motor or language abilities.* Motor delays often disappear; language delays usually persist (Silva, 1996).
- *Prevention of teenage delinquency.* One factor is patient parenting at age 5, using conversation rather than physical punishment to correct the child's behavior (Pettit et al., 2001).

Repeated longitudinal research can uncover not only change but also the process of change. Do children learn to read suddenly, by "breaking the code," or gradually? The answer could not be found by simply comparing preliterate 4-year-olds and fluently reading 8-year-olds. However, following children month by month reveals the answer: Reading is usually a gradual process, although certain aspects can be grasped quite suddenly (Adams et al., 1998).

You will learn the results of many longitudinal studies throughout this book. Nevertheless, this design has some serious drawbacks. Over time, some subjects may withdraw, move far away, or die. These changes can skew the ultimate results if those who disappear differ from those who stay in the study (more rebel-

A Longitudinal Look at Kirsten Longitudinal research is ideal for discovering, as the definition of developmental study on page 2 states, "how and why people change, and how and why they remain the same, as they grow older." These photographs of Kirsten at 5 months, 18 months, 5 years, 8 years, and 12 years illustrate this well. In some ways, change is obvious—from baldness to chest-length hair, for instance. Similar changes can be seen for almost all children, although Kirsten's pattern was somewhat unusual since she didn't really start to grow a full head of hair until she was almost 3 years old. In other ways, continuity is clear: She is emotionally engaging at every age. This is most obvious when, as a toddler, she hid something forbidden from her parents, but it is apparent in the other snapshots as well.

Now, at age 13, it is not surprising that she is distinctive in predictable ways, such as her ballet, writing, social sensitivity, and cheerleading. She is also typical of her cohort in other ways—she likes boys, computers, and television—as cross-sectional research would show as well. Longitudinal research (and, in this case, even longitudinal photos) also helps spot the impact of unusual events, which are not typical of either that child or children in general.

? *Observational Quiz* (see answer, page 31): Kirsten's parents got divorced. Can you spot when?

lious? of lower SES?). In addition, the research itself may affect those who remain (who might "improve" over a series of tests, for example, only because they become increasingly familiar with the questions). This makes the results of longitudinal research less applicable to the average developing person, who is not in such a study.

Perhaps the biggest problem of all is that a longitudinal investigation is very time-consuming and expensive. It involves far more commitment from scientists and funding agencies than does cross-sectional research.

Cross-Sequential Research

As you can see, both cross-sectional research and longitudinal research allow scientists to look at development over time, but each design has flaws. Because these two methods tend to make up for each other's disadvantages, scientists have devised various ways to use the two together (Hartman & George, 1999). The simplest is **cross-sequential research** (also referred to as *cohort-sequential* or *time-sequential* research) (Schaie, 1996). With this design, researchers first study several groups of people of different ages (a cross-sectional approach) and then follow those groups over the years (a longitudinal approach).

Using cross-sequential design, we can compare findings for a group of, say, 50-year-olds with findings for the same individuals at age 30, as well as with findings for groups who were 50 a decade or two earlier and groups who are 30 years old now. Cross-sequential research thus allows scientists to disentangle differences related to chronological age from those related to historical period. Scientists using this method are like prospectors for gold, sifting through other elements to find genuine nuggets of age-related development. In fact, every method is useful, and none are perfect, as Figure 1.8 illustrates. A better metaphor might be trying to assemble a jigsaw puzzle, with each study contributing a piece but none of them making a complete picture in themselves.

cross-sequential research A hybrid research method in which researchers first study several groups of people of different ages (a cross-sectional approach) and then follow those groups over the years (a longitudinal approach). (Also called *cohort-sequential* or *time-sequential research*.)

Ethics and Science

Every scientist must be concerned with the ethics of conducting and reporting research. At the most basic level, researchers who study humans must ensure that their subjects are not harmed and that subjects' participation is voluntary and confidential. Each academic discipline and professional society involved in the study of human development has a **code of ethics**, or set of moral principles. In developmental studies, the need to protect the participants is especially acute when they are children.

code of ethics A set of moral principles that is formally adopted by a group or organization.

Ethics for Child Development Researchers

The Society for Research in Child Development (SRCD, 1996) includes the following precautions in its code of ethics:

- The investigator should use no research operation that may harm the child either physically or psychologically.
- Before seeking consent or assent from the child, the investigator should inform the child of all features of the research that may affect his or her willingness to participate and should answer the child's questions in terms appropriate to the child's comprehension. [The child is free to] discontinue participation at any time.
- Investigators working with infants should take special effort to explain the research procedures to the parents and be especially sensitive to any indicators of discomfort in the infant.
- The investigators should keep in confidence all information obtained about research participants.
- In reporting results, . . . the investigator should be mindful of the social, political, and human implications.

Such ethical guidelines—developed and enforced partly as a result of past abuses—deal with only part of the problem. For contemporary researchers, the thorniest issues arise not during but before and after the research. Every proposed study must be analyzed ahead of time to see if its benefits will outweigh its costs in time, money, and even momentary distress.

In human development, the possibility of distress varies with the subject's age and condition (Thompson, 1992). A young child may become upset by a few minutes of separation from a caregiver; older children are more susceptible to loss of self-esteem and privacy; parents of adolescents may not want anyone to ask their offspring anything about sex, drugs, or discipline. Often, the studies with the greatest potential benefit involve the most vulnerable groups, such as infants who have been maltreated or children who are suspended from school. Ironically, some groups (women, children, drug addicts) were excluded as subjects of research into drug treatments for AIDS because experimental drugs might have done them unexpected harm; as a result, the first AIDS treatments proven effective had never been tested on the people who might need them most (Kahn et al., 1998).

Especially for Future Researchers: What question in child development do you think needs to be further investigated? What do you think the problems with such research might be?

The Implications of Research

Once an investigation has been completed, additional ethical issues arise concerning the reporting of research findings. An obvious breach of scientific ethics is to "cook" the data, arranging the numbers so that a particular conclusion seems the only logical one. Sometimes this can be done unintentionally, which is one reason replication is so important. Deliberate deception regarding the data is cause for ostracism from the scientific community, dismissal from a teaching or research position, and, in some cases, criminal prosecution. Further, *"in reporting results, . . . the investigator should be mindful of the social, political, and human implications of his [or her] research"* (SRCD, 1996).

What does "mindful" of implications mean? An example makes it clear. A storm of controversy was evoked by a study of college students who had become sexually involved with adults before reaching the legal age of consent (Rind et al., 1998). The research correctly reported that the consequences depended on many factors. The actual article was a *meta-analysis,* which is a compilation of data from many other sources, so no research subjects were directly involved.

However, talk-show hosts and political candidates condemned the study—not because of its results, but because of their own misinterpretation of it. Such misinterpretation occurred for many reasons, but one reason was that the authors and editors were not sufficiently mindful of the inferences that other people might draw. The basic problem is that:

> Scientists are committed to verifying their claims in terms of the logic-based system of thinking. . . . Scientists sometimes forget that media personalities, elected politicians, and many others operate under very different rules from psychologists and other scientists. . . . Like it or not, scientists operate not only within a scientific context but also a societal one.
>
> *[Sternberg, 2002, pp. 193, 194]*

In another research project, a group of college students who listened to Mozart before taking a cognitive test scored higher than another group who heard no music (Rauscher et al., 1993; Rausher & Shaw, 1998). This "Mozart effect" was also misinterpreted; the governor of Georgia ordered that all newborns receive a free Mozart CD in order to improve their intelligence, and Florida passed a law requiring every state-funded infant day-care center to play classical music. The actual initial study was irrelevant to infants, and the results for college students could not be replicated (Nantais & Schellenberg, 1999; Steele et al., 1999).

As these examples demonstrate, even when the scientific method is carefully used and proper safeguards for the subjects are in place, ethics requires a concern for the implications of the results. Conclusions must be honestly and carefully reported; hasty generalizations are often false. Scientific methodology and integrity are the bases of our study of human development, and that is all the more reason to make sure the implications are carefully interpreted.

What Should We Study?

Finally, every reader of this book should consider the most important ethical issue of all: Are scientists studying the issues that are crucial to human development?

- Do we know enough about infant growth to ensure that every baby reaches full potential?
- Do we know enough about human sexual urges and actions to prevent sexually transmitted diseases, stop unwanted pregnancy, halt sexual abuse, and cure infertility?
- Do we know enough about stress, poverty, and prejudice to enable humans to be happier and healthier?
- Do we know enough about angry children to prevent a child from becoming a bully, a delinquent, and then a violent criminal?

The answer to all these questions is a loud *NO!* Sometimes the particulars of informed consent and confidentiality distract us from the larger ethical concerns, such as answering the questions just posed.

Ethics means far more than taking care of the subjects and reporting research carefully and honestly. It also means choosing to investigate issues that should be explored and then reporting results conscientiously and accurately. This chapter has noted many social problems that have been relieved by developmental research, including racial segregation, premature death of disabled children, and distorted parent–child interactions. Many more examples in which scientific findings have enhanced child development are cited throughout this book. Other issues still need research. Children still suffer because many questions have not been answered, or even asked. The next cohort of developmental scientists will continue this work, building on what is known. Read on.

!Answer to Observational Quiz (from page 29): Kirsten's parents ended their marriage about when Kirsten was 8 (fourth picture). Signs of this disruption are that she is thoughtful, unsmiling, with arms held close.

Response for Future Researchers (from page 30): Almost any issue that you care about is a valid subject for research, partly because scientists work best if they truly want to learn the answers. Beyond the problems of time, money, and protection of subjects, the crucial question is whether you are prepared to obtain results that contradict your own social constructions. Some of the best and bravest scientists surprise themselves as well as their culture.

SUMMARY

Definitions: Change over Time

1. Human development is a science that seeks to understand how people change over time. Sometimes these changes are linear—gradual, steady, and predictable—and sometimes not.

2. Development is the product of dynamic systems. Any one change affects an interconnected system, and any one person affects all the other people in a family or social group.

3. Change may be small or large, caused by something seemingly insignificant, like the flap of a butterfly's wings, or something large and pervasive, like a civil war. Development can seem to be continuous, or unchanging, for a period of time, and then a massive transformation can suddenly occur.

4. The life-span perspective reminds us that development is multidirectional, multicontextual, multicultural, multidisciplinary, and plastic. *Plasticity* means that change is always possible but never unrestricted: Childhood becomes the foundation for later growth.

5. Development can be divided into three broad aspects, called domains. The biosocial domain includes physical growth, the cognitive domain includes intellectual growth, and the psychosocial domain includes emotions and the social context. All three are important for every person at every point of development.

The Contexts of Development

6. Each individual develops within three contexts: historical, cultural, and socioeconomic. Since each person has unique genes and experiences, contexts do not determine an individual's development, but they always influence it.

7. The historical context is crucial, with all people in each cohort affected by the events and the social beliefs that prevailed when they were young. Such beliefs are often social constructions, or values that shift as the historical context changes.

8. Communities raise children in diverse ways, with each culture encouraging habits and personality traits that will help people function well in that culture.

9. Family income and residence, as well as the education level of the parents, determine a child's socioeconomic status. Particularly if family income falls below the poverty line, children are handicapped by their SES in crucial ways, including health, education, and even survival.

10. It is not easy to disentangle the effects of income and ethnicity. Although it is sometimes used in popular speech, scientists now find "race" a confusing and misleading category. Scientists prefer to group people by ethnicity, SES, age, or culture.

Developmental Study as a Science

11. The scientific method leads researchers to question assumptions and gather data to test conclusions. Although far from infallible, scientific methods help researchers avoid biases and guide them in asking questions that might not otherwise be asked.

12. Among the research methods used by scientists are observation, experiments, surveys, and case studies. Each method has strengths and weaknesses.

13. The most robust (solid) conclusions can be drawn when similar results are found in replications using various methods with many subjects in diverse cultures. Well-designed experiments are useful but difficult to conduct in human development, unless natural circumstances happen to create an experimental group.

14. Many statistical methods further scientific research. One is correlation, the calculation of a number that indicates how two variables are connected, though it does not prove that one variable causes the other. Another statistic is significance, which indicates the degree of possibility that a particular result occurred by chance.

15. To study growth over time, scientists use three strategies: cross-sectional research (comparing people of different ages), longitudinal research (studying the same people over time), and cross-sequential research (combining the first two methods).

Ethics and Science

16. Ethics is crucial in all sciences, perhaps especially in developmental research when children are involved. Not only must subjects be protected, but results must be clearly reported and understood.

17. Appropriate application of insights from scientific research depends partly on the integrity of the scientific methods used but even more on careful explanation and interpretation of the conclusions. The most important ethical issues of all are: Are the critical questions being asked, and is needed research being conducted?

KEY TERMS

scientific study of human
　development (p. 1)
linear change (p. 2)
dynamic systems (p. 2)
butterfly effect (p. 2)
life-span perspective (p. 5)
multidirectional (p. 5)
multicontextual (p. 5)
multicultural (p. 5)
multidisciplinary (p. 5)

plastic (p. 5)
biosocial domain (p. 6)
cognitive domain (p. 6)
psychosocial domain (p. 6)
cohort (p. 8)
social construction (p. 9)
culture (p. 10)
socioeconomic status (SES)
　(p. 14)
poverty line (p. 14)

ethnic group (p. 16)
race (p. 16)
scientific method (p. 20)
hypothesis (p. 20)
replication (p. 20)
variables (p. 20)
scientific observation (p. 21)
correlation (p. 22)
experiment (p. 23)
independent variable (p. 23)

dependent variable (p. 23)
experimental group (p. 23)
comparison group (p. 23)
survey (p. 25)
case study (p. 25)
cross-sectional research (p. 26)
longitudinal research (p. 28)
cross-sequential research
　(p. 29)
code of ethics (p. 29)

KEY QUESTIONS

1. Give an example of each of several kinds of change in human development.

2. What are some of the contexts and systems that would be particularly relevant in shaping your personal development? Explain your choices.

3. What are some of the reasons that a major social change might *not* affect a child's development very much?

4. How do researchers in child development benefit from the life-span perspective?

5. Give an example (not from the book) of development that is affected by all three domains.

6. How might the historical context differ for someone born in 1950 and someone born in 2000?

7. How might a young child's sleeping situation affect his or her adult values and personality?

8. Why is income not identical with socioeconomic status?

9. How does the condition of a child's neighborhood moderate or magnify the effects of poverty?

10. Why do people sometimes confuse SES, ethnicity, and race?

11. Pick two of the four methods of research, and show how the advantages of one compensate for the disadvantages of the other.

12. Why is cross-sectional research the easiest way to study development?

13. What are the advantages of cross-sequential research?

14. In what ways does the scientific method reduce human biases?

15. What are the most difficult ethical issues in the study of human development?

Chapter Two

Theories of Development

As we saw in Chapter 1, the scientific effort to understand human development usually begins with questions. One of the most basic is: How do people develop into the persons they ultimately become?

- Do early experiences—of breast-feeding or bonding or abuse—linger into adulthood, even if they seem to be forgotten?
- How important are specific school experiences in human intelligence?
- Can a person develop moral values without being taught them?
- Do a person's chances of becoming a violent adult depend on whether he or she grows up in, say, Chile or Cambodia or Canada?
- If your parents or grandparents suffer from depression, schizophrenia, or alcoholism, will you develop the same condition?

For every answer, more questions arise: Why or why not? When and how? And, perhaps more important of all, so what?

What Theories Do

Each of the five questions listed above is answered by one of the five major theories described in this chapter. To frame various questions, and to begin to answer them, we need some way to determine which facts about development are relevant. Then we need to organize those facts to lead us to deeper understanding. In short, we need a theory.

A **developmental theory** is a systematic statement of principles and generalizations that provides a coherent framework for studying and explaining development. Developmental theorists "try to make sense out of observations . . . [and] construct a story of the human journey from infancy through childhood or adulthood" (Miller, 2002, p. 2). Such a story, or theory, is more than a set of assumptions and facts; it connects facts and observations, putting the details of life into a meaningful whole. Theories are also quite practical, in three ways:

- Theories offer insight and guidance for everyday concerns by providing a broad and coherent view of human development.
- Theories form the basis for hypotheses that can be tested by research studies. Thus, theories "provide a point of departure," " a conceptual context" for individual scientists who study according to their own particular research interests (Renninger & Amsel, 1997, p. ix).

developmental theory A systematic statement of principles and generalizations that provides a coherent framework for studying and explaining development.

■ Theories generate discoveries: "New facts change the theory, and changes in the theory generate new experiments and thus new facts" (Miller, 2002, p. 4).

Not just five, but hundreds of theories are relevant to the study of development. Some originated with extraordinary intellectual leaders, who fashioned what are called **grand theories**, "because each offered a powerful framework for interpreting and understanding change and development [and was] meant to apply to the change and development of all individuals, in all contexts, across all contents" (Renninger & Amsel, 1997, p. ix). Some are called **minitheories**, because they are intended to explain only a part of development or to relate to only a particular group of people, rather than to explain everything, everywhere, for everyone (Parke et al., 1994). And some are called **emergent theories**, because they arise from several accumulated minitheories and may become the new systematic and comprehensive theories of the future.

In this chapter we will focus on three grand theories—psychoanalytic theory, behaviorism, and cognitive theory—and two emergent theories—sociocultural theory and epigenetic systems theory. These five theories, and several others, will be further described and applied in relevant discussions later in this book.

Grand Theories

In the first half of the twentieth century, two opposing theories—psychoanalytic theory and behaviorism (also called learning theory)—began as theories of psychology and later were applied to human development more broadly. By mid-century, cognitive theory had overtaken these first two, becoming the dominant seedbed of research hypotheses. In regard to some ideas, proponents of each of these grand theories often scorned the other two; yet all of them agreed on many basic principles. Before we examine the points of disagreement and agreement, we will briefly describe each theory.

Psychoanalytic Theory

Psychoanalytic theory interprets human development in terms of intrinsic drives and motives, many of which are irrational and unconscious, hidden from awareness. These basic underlying forces are viewed as influencing every aspect of a person's thinking and behavior, from the smallest details of daily life to the crucial choices of a lifetime. Psychoanalytic theory also sees these drives and motives as providing the foundation for the universal stages of development that every human experiences. For everyone, each stage entails specific developmental tasks, from the formation of human attachments in infancy to the quest for emotional and sexual fulfillment in adulthood.

Freud's Ideas

Psychoanalytic theory originated with Sigmund Freud (1856–1939), an Austrian physician who developed this theory based on his clinical work with patients suffering from mental illness. He listened to their accounts of dreams and fantasies, as well as to their "uncensored" streams of thought, and constructed an elaborate, multifaceted theory. According to this theory, development in the first six years occurs in three stages, each characterized by sexual interest and pleasure centered on a particular part of the body. In

---

grand theories Comprehensive theories that have traditionally inspired and directed thinking about development. Psychoanalytic theory, behaviorism, and cognitive theory are all grand theories.

minitheories Theories that focus on some specific area of development but are less general and comprehensive than the grand theories.

emergent theories Recently formulated theories that bring together information from many minitheories but that have not yet cohered into theories that are comprehensive and systematic.

psychoanalytic theory A grand theory of human development that holds that irrational, unconscious drives and motives, many of which originate in childhood, underlie human behavior.

(Freud's Ideas) Erikson's

Freud at Work In addition to being the world's first psychoanalyst, Sigmund Freud was a prolific writer. His many papers and case histories, primarily descriptions of his patients' bizarre symptoms and unconscious sexual urges, helped make the psychoanalytic perspective a dominant force for much of the twentieth century.

AKG / PHOTO RESEARCHERS, INC.

Childhood Sexuality? The girl's interest in the statue's anatomy may reflect simple curiosity, but Freudian theory would maintain that it is a clear manifestation of the phallic stage of psychosexual development, when girls are said to feel deprived because they lack a penis.

infancy, that body part is the mouth (the *oral stage*); in early childhood, it is the anus (the *anal stage*); in the preschool years, it is the penis (the *phallic stage*). (See Table 2.1 for descriptions of the stages in Freud's theory.)

Freud maintained that at each of these stages, sensual satisfaction from stimulation of the mouth, anus, or penis is linked to the major developmental needs and challenges that are associated with that stage. During the oral stage, for example, the baby not only gains nourishment through sucking but also experiences sensual pleasure and becomes emotionally attached to the mother, who provides this oral gratification. During the anal stage, pleasures related to control and self-control—initially with defecation and toilet training—are paramount.

One of Freud's most influential ideas was that each stage includes its own potential conflicts between child and parent, as, for instance, when an adult tries to wean a baby from the beloved bottle. According to Freud, how the child experiences and resolves these conflicts—especially those related to weaning, toilet training, and childhood sexual curiosity—determines the person's lifelong personality and patterns of behavior. An adult may not know it, but the fact that he or she smokes cigarettes (oral), or keeps careful track of money (anal), or is romantically attracted to a much older partner (phallic) signifies unconscious problems rooted in a childhood stage.

Another developmental aspect of Freud's theory is its conception of the personality as consisting of three distinct systems: id, ego, and superego. The *id* represents the unconscious psychic energy that we devote to satisfying our basic urges toward survival, aggression, and reproduction. The *superego* is a strict moral judge, especially of impulses that the parents or culture would condemn. The *ego* tries to make rational choices and to cope with the reality of daily life, partly by keeping the id's unconscious lust and the superego's guilt under control. Infants are governed primarily by the id: They want their own needs to be met immediately, including their psychosexual need for oral pleasure. As children grow older, their egos develop; they continue to assert themselves but also begin to accommodate the external world's demands. Especially in early childhood, at about the phallic stage, parents and the society teach the child which impulses need to be controlled and thus foster development of the superego. The emotionally healthy person develops a strong ego, able to cope with the urges of both the id and the superego.

CORBIS

Erikson's Ideas

Freud had many followers who became famous psychoanalytic theorists in their own right. Although they all acknowledged the importance of unconscious, irrational forces and of early childhood, each expanded and modified Freud's ideas. The most notable of these neo-Freudians was Erik Erikson (1902–1994), who formulated his own version of psychoanalytic theory.

Erikson spent his childhood in Germany, his adolescence wandering through Italy, and his young adulthood in Austria. Just before World War II, he arrived in the United States, where he studied Harvard students, children at play, and Native American cultures. Erikson proposed eight developmental stages covering the entire life span, each of which is characterized by a particular challenge, or *developmental crisis,* which is central to that stage of life.

As you can see from Table 2.1, Erikson's first five stages are closely related to Freud's stages. Erikson, like Freud, believed that problems of adult life echo unresolved conflicts of childhood. For example, an adult who has difficulty establishing a secure, mutual relationship with a life partner may never have resolved the crisis of early infancy, *trust versus mistrust.* However, Erikson's stages differ significantly from Freud's in their emphasis of the person's relationship to the family and culture, not just to his or her own sexual urges.

In Erikson's theory, the resolution of each developmental crisis depends on the interaction between the individual's characteristics and whatever support is provided by the social environment. In the stage of *initiative versus guilt,* for example, children between ages 3 and 6 often want to undertake activities that exceed their abilities or the limits set by their parents. Their efforts to act independently leave them open to pride or failure, depending partly on how they go about seeking independence, partly on the reactions of their parents, and partly on their culture's expectations. As an example of the last influence, some cultures *encourage* assertive 5-year-olds as being creative spirits who know their own minds; other cultures *discourage* them as being rude or fresh children. The children internalize, or accept, these reactions, and later, as adults, some are much bolder and others are more self-critical than their peers in other cultures.

Developmentalists owe a debt of gratitude to Freud and to the neo-Freudians who extended and refined his concepts. Many psychoanalytic ideas are widely accepted today—for example, that unconscious motives affect our behavior and that the early years are a formative period of personality development.

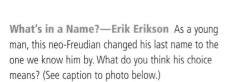

What's in a Name?—Erik Erikson As a young man, this neo-Freudian changed his last name to the one we know him by. What do you think his choice means? (See caption to photo below.)

SYLVAIN GRANDADAM / PHOTO RESEARCHERS, INC.

Who Are We? The most famous of Erikson's eight crises is the identity crisis, during adolescence, when young people find their own answer to the question "Who am I?" Erikson did this for himself by choosing a last name that, with his first name, implies "son of myself" (Erik, Erik's son). Although the identity crisis is universal, particulars vary from place to place and time to time—with each cohort distinguishing itself from the slightly older cohort in some way.

? *Observational Quiz* (see answer, page 40): Where and when do you think this photograph was taken?

TABLE 2.1 Comparison of Freud's Psychosexual and Erikson's Psychosocial Stages

Approximate Age	Freud (Psychosexual)	Erikson* (Psychosocial)
Birth to 1 year	**Oral Stage** — The mouth, tongue, and gums are the focus of pleasurable sensations in the baby's body, and sucking and feeding are the most stimulating activities.	**Trust vs. Mistrust** — Babies learn either to trust that others will care for their basic needs, including nourishment, warmth, cleanliness, and physical contact, or to lack confidence in the care of others.
1–3 years	**Anal Stage** — The anus is the focus of pleasurable sensations in the baby's body, and toilet training is the most important activity.	**Autonomy vs. Shame and Doubt** — Children learn either to be self-sufficient in many activities, including toileting, feeding, walking, exploring, and talking, or to doubt their own abilities.
3–6 years	**Phallic Stage** — The phallus, or penis, is the most important body part, and pleasure is derived from genital stimulation. Boys are proud of their penises, and girls wonder why they don't have one.	**Initiative vs. Guilt** — Children want to undertake many adultlike activities, sometimes overstepping the limits set by parents and feeling guilty.
7–11 years	**Latency** — This is not a stage but an interlude, during which sexual needs are quiet and children put psychic energy into conventional activities like schoolwork and sports.	**Industry vs. Inferiority** — Children busily learn to be competent and productive in mastering new skills or feel inferior and unable to do anything well.
Adolescence	**Genital Stage** — The genitals are the focus of pleasurable sensations, and the young person seeks sexual stimulation and sexual satisfaction in heterosexual relationships.	**Identity vs. Role Diffusion** — Adolescents try to figure out "Who am I?" They establish sexual, political, and career identities or are confused about what roles to play.
Adulthood	Freud believed that the genital stage lasts throughout adulthood. He also said that the goal of a healthy life is "to love and to work."	**Intimacy vs. Isolation** — Young adults seek companionship and love with another person or become isolated from others because they fear rejection and disappointment. **Generativity vs. Stagnation** — Middle-aged adults contribute to the next generation through meaningful work, creative activities, and/or raising a family, or they stagnate. **Integrity vs. Despair** — Older adults try to make sense out of their lives, either seeing life as a meaningful whole or despairing at goals never reached.

*Although Erikson described two extreme resolutions to each crisis, he recognized that there is a wide range of outcomes between these extremes. For most people, the best resolution of a crisis is not either extreme but, rather, a middle course.

Behaviorism

The second grand theory arose in direct opposition to psychoanalytic theory. Early in the twentieth century, John B. Watson (1878–1958) argued that if psychology was to be a true science, psychologists should study only what they could see and measure: human behavior, not human thoughts and hidden urges. In Watson's words:

> Why don't we make what we can *observe* the real field of psychology? Let us limit ourselves to things that can be observed, and formulate laws concerned only with those things. . . . We can observe behavior—what the organism does or says.
>
> [Watson, 1924/1998, p. 6]

According to Watson, anything can be learned. He said:

> Give me a dozen healthy infants, well-formed, and my own specified world to bring them up in and I'll guarantee to take any one at random and train him to become any type of specialist I might select—doctor, lawyer, artist, merchant

! *Answer to Observational Quiz* (from page 38): The signs suggest Asia, and the fact that overt rebellion is difficult in a small Asian town suggests a large city. If you guessed Tokyo, score one correct. A sharp eye on the T-shirt and an accurate memory of when Mohawk hairstyles were in fashion would give you another correct answer—probably 1992.

behaviorism A grand theory of human development that focuses on the sequences and processes by which behavior is learned. (Also called *learning theory.*)

John B. Watson

conditioning According to behaviorism, any process in which a behavior is learned. See *classical conditioning* and *operant conditioning.*

classical conditioning The process by which a neutral stimulus becomes associated with a meaningful stimulus so that the organism responds to the former stimulus as if it were the latter. (Also called *respondent conditioning.*)

chief, and yes, even beggar-man and thief, regardless of his talents, penchants, tendencies, abilities, vocations, and race of his ancestors.

[Watson, 1924/1998, p. 82]

Other psychologists agreed, partly because they found it difficult to study the unconscious motives and drives identified in psychoanalytic theory. Actual behavior, by contrast, could be studied far more objectively and scientifically. Thus was developed the theory called **behaviorism.** It is also called *learning theory* because the focus is on the ways we learn specific behaviors—ways that can be described, analyzed, and predicted with far more scientific accuracy than the unconscious drives proposed by psychoanalysts (Horowitz, 1994; Uttal, 2000).

Laws of Behavior

Laws of behavior are said to apply to every individual at every age, from newborn to octogenarian. These laws provide insights into how mature competencies are fashioned from simple actions and how environmental influences shape individual development. In the view of behaviorists, all development involves a process of learning and, therefore, does not occur in specific stages that depend on age or maturation (Bijou & Baer, 1978).

Learning occurs through **conditioning,** as a particular response comes to be triggered by a particular stimulus (see Figure 2.1). There are two types of conditioning: classical and operant.

Classical Conditioning A century ago, Russian scientist Ivan Pavlov (1849–1936) began to study the link between stimulus and response. While doing research on salivation in dogs, Pavlov noted that his experimental dogs began to drool not only at the sight of food but also, eventually, at the sound of the approaching attendants who brought the food. This observation led him to perform his famous experiment in which he taught a dog to salivate at the sound of a bell. Pavlov began by ringing the bell just before presenting food to the dog. After a number of repetitions of this bell-then-food sequence, the dog began salivating at the bell's sound even when there was no food nearby.

This simple experiment was one of the first scientific demonstrations of **classical conditioning** (also called *respondent conditioning*). In classical conditioning, an organism (any type of living creature) comes to associate a neutral stimulus with a meaningful one and then responds to the former stimulus as if it were the latter. In Pavlov's original experiment, the dog associated the sound of

The Founder of Behaviorism John Watson was an early proponent of learning theory whose ideas are still influential today.

A Contemporary of Freud Ivan Pavlov was a physiologist who received the Nobel Prize in 1904 for his research on digestive processes. It was this line of study that led to his discovery of classical conditioning.

> **Learning occurs through:**
>
> ▪ **Classical conditioning**   Through association, neutral stimulus becomes conditioned stimulus.
> ▪ **Operant conditioning**   Through reinforcement, weak or rare response becomes strong, frequent response.
> ▪ **Social learning**   Through modeling, observed behaviors become copied behaviors.

FIGURE 2.1 Three Types of Learning
Behaviorism is also called learning theory, because it emphasizes the learning process, as shown here.

the bell (the neutral stimulus) with food (the meaningful stimulus) and responded to the sound as though it were the food itself. That response was a conditioned response, which meant learning had occurred.

Operant Conditioning   The most influential North American proponent of behaviorism was B. F. Skinner (1904–1990), who agreed with Watson that psychology should focus on the scientific study of behavior. Skinner also agreed with Pavlov that classical conditioning explains some types of behavior. However, Skinner believed that another type of conditioning—**operant conditioning** (also called *instrumental conditioning*)—plays a much greater role in human behavior, especially in more complex learning. In operant conditioning, the organism learns that a particular behavior produces a particular consequence. If the consequence is useful or pleasurable, the organism will tend to repeat the behavior to achieve that response again. If the response is unpleasant, the organism will tend not to repeat the behavior.

Once a behavior has been conditioned (learned), animals (including humans) continue to perform it even if pleasurable consequences occur only occasionally. Almost all of a person's daily behavior, from socializing with others to earning a paycheck, can be understood as a result of operant conditioning. For instance, when a baby first gives a half smile in response to a full stomach, a mother might smile back. Soon the baby is conditioned by the mother's responsive smile to give a bigger smile, and the mother picks the baby up to reinforce the smile. As time goes on, the baby becomes a smiling toddler, a cheerful child, an outgoing adolescent, and a friendly adult—all because of early operant conditioning and periodic reinforcing.

In operant conditioning, the process of repeating a consequence to make it more likely that the behavior in question will recur is called **reinforcement** (Skinner, 1953). A consequence that increases the likelihood that a behavior will be repeated is therefore called a *reinforcer*. The mother's early reinforcement produces a socially responsive, smiling adult.

The study of human development has benefited from behaviorism. That theory's emphasis on the causes and consequences of observed behavior has led researchers to see that many behavior patterns that seem to be inborn, or to result from deeply rooted emotional problems, are actually learned. If something is learned, it can be unlearned, which is a very hopeful message. Although it is not easy to break old habits and patterns, we are never stuck in our past. This realization has encouraged scientists to find ways to eliminate particular problem behaviors— among them temper tantrums, phobias, and addictions—by analyzing all the reinforcements and past conditioning and then breaking the stimulus–response chains that sustained the unwanted behaviors.

Like any good theory, behaviorism has also been a source of hypotheses for scientific experiments, such as those described in Thinking Like a Scientist.

operant conditioning The process by which a response is gradually learned via reinforcement or punishment. (Also called *instrumental conditioning*.)

reinforcement The process by which a behavior is followed by results that make it more likely that the behavior will be repeated. This occurs in operant conditioning.

Rats, Pigeons, and People   B. F. Skinner is best known for his experiments with rats and pigeons, but he also applied his knowledge to human problems. For his daughter, he designed a glass-enclosed crib in which temperature, humidity, and perceptual stimulation could be controlled to make her time in the crib enjoyable and educational. He wrote about an ideal society based on principles of operant conditioning, where, for example, workers in less desirable jobs would earn greater rewards.

© SAM FALK

Thinking Like a Scientist

What Is a Mother For?

Because theories help organize perceptions, they make it easier for scientists to interpret their observations. True scientists welcome not only findings that confirm a theory but also data that don't fit their expectations. For example, Harry Harlow's experiments confirmed some conventional wisdom about mother–infant attachment and disproved other aspects.

Both behaviorism and psychoanalytic theory originally assumed that the reason children love their mothers is that the mothers satisfy basic hunger and sucking needs. In other words, they held that "the infant's attachment to the mother stemmed from internal drives which triggered activities connected with the libations of the mother's breast. This belief was the only one these two theoretical groups ever had in common" (Harlow, 1986).

Harlow, a psychologist who studied learning in infant monkeys, observed something that made him question the centrality of food:

> We had separated more than 60 of these animals from their mothers 6 to 12 hours after birth and suckled them on tiny bottles. The infant mortality rate was a fraction of what would have obtained had we let the monkey mothers raise their infants. Our bottle-fed babies were healthier and heavier than monkey-mother-reared infants. . . . During the course of our studies we noticed that the laboratory-raised babies showed strong attachment to the folded gauze diapers which were used to cover the . . . floors of their cages.
>
> [Harlow, 1986, p. 103]

In fact, the infant monkeys seemed more emotionally attached to the cloth diapers than to their bottles. This was contrary to the two prevailing theories. Psychoanalytic theory would say that the infant would love whatever satisfied its oral needs (the nipple), and behaviorism would predict that the infant would become attached to whatever provided reinforcing food (the bottle). Accordingly, Harlow set out to make a "direct experimental analysis" of human attachment via his monkeys.

Using monkeys to study emotional processes in humans may seem a stretch to some people, but not to Harlow, who had been trained as an experimental psychologist. He knew that it would be unethical to separate human infants from their mothers, but he believed that "the basic processes relating to affection, including nursing, contact, clinging, and

HARLOW PRIMATE LABORATORY, UNIVERSITY OF WISCONSIN

Clinging to "Mother" Even though it gave no milk, this "mother" was soft and warm enough that infant monkeys spent almost all their time holding on to it. Many infants, some children, and even some adults cling to a familiar stuffed animal when life becomes frightening. According to Harlow, the reasons are the same: All primates are comforted by something soft, warm, and familiar to touch.

even visual and auditory exploration, exhibit no fundamental differences in the two species" (Harlow, 1958).

Harlow provided infant monkeys with two "surrogate" (artificial) mothers, both the right size, with a face that included obvious eyes. One surrogate was made of bare wire, and the other was made of wire covered by soft terrycloth. He divided his monkeys into two groups. One was fed by a bottle periodically put through the chest of the cloth "mother"; the other was fed by a bottle put through the chest of the wire "mother." The hypothesis to be tested was that the cloth surrogate might be reinforcing, even for the monkeys that were fed by the wire mother.

To collect his data, Harlow measured how much time each baby spent holding on to one or the other of the two surrogates. The monkeys who had a cloth mother that provided milk clung to it and ignored the bare-wire, nonfeeding mother. However, beyond the few minutes needed to suck the milk, even the babies that fed from the wire mother had no interest in holding on to it, going to it only when hunger drove them to do so. No attachment to, or love for, the nourishing wire mother could be observed, but the cloth mothers seemed to win the infants' affection (see Figure 2.2).

This reaction was so strong that Harlow then wondered whether the cloth surrogate mothers might also reassure infant monkeys when frightening events occurred, just as a real mother does when a scared youngster runs to her. He set up another experiment, putting an unfamiliar mechanical toy into a cloth-reared infant monkey's cage. The monkeys immediately sought comfort from its cloth mother, scrambling to cling to it with one hand and then timidly exploring the new object with the other.

Wire mothers provided no such reassurance. Monkeys who were exposed to the same stress without the cloth mother's presence showed obvious signs of fright—freezing, screaming, shivering, hiding, urinating. It seems, then, that mothering is not primarily about feeding, but about touching, comforting, and holding, which Harlow called "contact comfort" or "love" (Harlow, 1958).

Harlow's research is a classic example of the use of theories. Although his study disproved an aspect of both behaviorism and psychoanalytic theory, that is not the most significant point. Remember, theories are meant to be useful, not necessarily true. (If they were known to be true in every aspect, they would be scientific laws, not theories.)

In this example, because he knew what the psychoanalytic and behavioral theories said about love and comfort, the baby monkeys' interactions with the gauze diapers caught Harlow's attention. That led to closer observation, a hypothesis, a clever series of experiments, and some amazing results. For decades, perhaps centuries, no one had questioned the idea that feeding creates loyalty—until actual observations conflicted with both grand theories. This conflict prompted an alert scientist to ask new questions.

Both psychoanalytic theory and behaviorism were revised and expanded in response to Harlow's experiments and to other evidence. Advice to caregivers changed as well: Crying infants should be picked up and cuddled, even if they are not hungry. The result has been much more cradling and less crying—all because a scientist compared a theoretical prediction with his own observations and performed ingenious experiments to test his hypothesis.

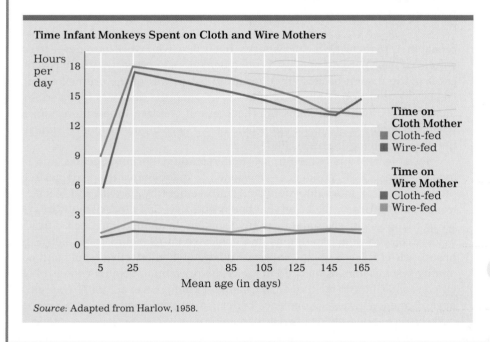

Time Infant Monkeys Spent on Cloth and Wire Mothers

Hours per day

Time on Cloth Mother
■ Cloth-fed
■ Wire-fed

Time on Wire Mother
■ Cloth-fed
■ Wire-fed

Mean age (in days)

Source: Adapted from Harlow, 1958.

FIGURE 2.2 Softer Is Better During the first three weeks of Harlow's experiment, the infant monkeys developed a strong preference for the cloth-covered "mothers." That preference lasted throughout the experiment, even among the monkeys who were fed by a wire-covered mother.

? *Observational Quiz* (see answer, page 46): At five days, how much time did the wire-fed monkeys spend on the cloth mothers compared with the cloth-fed monkeys?

Social Learning

Originally, behaviorists sought to explain all behavior as arising directly from a chain of learned responses, the result of classical and operant conditioning. However, one characteristic of every grand theory is that it is sufficiently comprehensive and thought-provoking that later scientists revise and extend it. One revision of behaviorism, based on thousands of studies, began with the realization that all creatures appreciate the touch, warmth, reassurance, and example of other similar beings. This extension is called **social learning theory.** Humans, even more than other animals, learn many behaviors by observing the behavior of others, without personally experiencing any reinforcement. Humans also strive for the feelings of pride and acceptance that other people can give.

An integral part of social learning is **modeling,** when people observe behavior and then copy it. For children, parents are the first models. Modeling is not simply imitation, because people model only some actions, of some individuals, in some contexts. For example, you undoubtedly know some adults who

Especially for Older Brothers and Sisters: Psychologists believe that the best role models for children are older siblings and other people they know well and see daily, rather than sports stars or political heroes. Why?

social learning theory An application of behaviorism that emphasizes that many human behaviors are learned through observation and imitation of other people.

modeling In social learning theory, the process in which people observe and then copy the behavior of others.

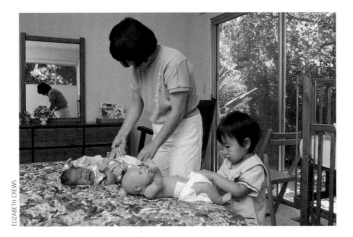

Social Learning in Action Social learning validates the old maxim "Actions speak louder than words." If the moments here are typical for each child, the girl in the left photo is likely to grow up with a ready sense of the importance of this particular chore of infant care. Unfortunately, the boy on the right may become a cigarette smoker like his father—even if his father warns him of the dangers of this habit.

?Observational Quiz (see answer, page 46): Beyond what they are doing, what else shows that these children imitate their parents?

self-efficacy In social learning theory, the belief that one is effective; self-efficacy motivates people to change themselves and their contexts.

cognitive theory A grand theory of human development that focuses on the structure and development of thinking, which shapes people's attitudes, beliefs, and behaviors.

Jean piaget

Would You Talk to This Man? Children loved talking to Jean Piaget, and he learned by listening carefully—especially to their incorrect explanations, which no one had paid much attention to before. All his life, Piaget was absorbed with studying the way children think. He called himself a "genetic epistemologist"—one who studies how children gain knowledge about the world as they grow up.

repeat their parents' behavior patterns, but others who work hard never to copy certain of their parents' actions. From a behaviorist perspective, both reactions confirm the theory, because they testify to the power of the original example. Generally, modeling is most likely to occur when the observer is uncertain or inexperienced (which explains the readiness of children to use modeling) and when the model is someone admirable and powerful, nurturing, or similar to the observer (Bandura, 1986, 1997).

Social learning is related to self-understanding, social reflection, and feelings of efficacy. Self-confidence—developed from looking at the examples set by others as well as more directly from reinforcement by parents and teachers—leads to **self-efficacy,** the belief that one is effective. Self-efficacy motivates people to change themselves and their environment. In an individual, self-efficacy is associated with high aspirations and achievement (Bandura et al., 2001). In a group, self-efficacy becomes *collective efficacy* when effective family and community systems join, as they did in the crime-preventing neighborhoods of New Orleans and Chicago mentioned in Chapter 1 (Sampson et al., 1997). Overall, behaviorism encourages action, since better conditioning with precise reinforcers is likely to change a child, a family, or a culture.

Cognitive Theory

The third grand theory is **cognitive theory,** which focuses on the structure and development of thought processes and understanding. Cognitive researchers try to determine how a person's thinking, and the expectations that result from a particular understanding, affect the development of attitudes, beliefs, and behaviors. In other words, to understand people, don't delve into what they have forgotten from childhood (as in psychoanalytic theory) or what has happened to them (as in behaviorism), but instead find out what they think.

Jean Piaget (1896–1980) was the major pioneer of cognitive theory. Although originally trained in the natural sciences, Piaget became interested in human thought processes when he was hired to field-test questions for a standard intelligence test for children. Piaget

TABLE 2.2 Piaget's Periods of Cognitive Development

Approximate Age Range	Name of Period	Characteristics of the Period	Major Gains During the Period
Birth to 2 years	Sensorimotor	Infant uses senses and motor abilities to understand the world. There is no conceptual or reflective thought; an object is "known" in terms of what an infant can *do* to it.	The infant learns that an object still exists when it is out of sight (*object permanence*) and begins to think through mental actions as well as physical actions.
2–6 years	Preoperational	The child uses *symbolic thinking,* including language, to understand the world. Sometimes the child's thinking is *egocentric,* causing the child to understand the world from only one perspective, his or her own.	The imagination flourishes, and language becomes a significant means of self-expression and of influence from others. Children gradually begin to *decenter,* that is, become less egocentric, and to understand and coordinate multiple points of view.
7–11 years	Concrete operational	The child understands and applies logical operations, or principles, to help interpret experiences objectively and rationally rather than intuitively.	By applying logical abilities, children learn to understand the basic concepts of conservation, number, classification, and many other scientific ideas.
12 years through adulthood	Formal operational	The adolescent or adult is able to think about abstractions and hypothetical concepts and to reason analytically, not just emotionally.	Ethics, politics, and social and moral issues become more interesting and involving as the adolescent becomes able to take a broader and more theoretical approach to experience.

was supposed to find the age at which most children could answer each question correctly, but he found the children's wrong answers much more intriguing.

How children think is much more important and more revealing of mental ability, Piaget concluded, than *what* they know. Moreover, understanding how people think reveals how they interpret their experiences and thus explains how they construct their values and assumptions.

Piaget maintained that there are four major periods, or stages, of cognitive development: the *sensorimotor* period, the *preoperational* period, the *concrete operational* period, and the *formal operational* period (see Table 2.2). These are age-related, and, as you will see in later chapters, each has features that permit certain types of knowing and understanding (Piaget, 1952b, 1970a,b).

Movement from one period to another is propelled by the human need for **cognitive equilibrium**—that is, a state of mental balance. What Piaget meant is that each person attempts to make sense of new experiences by reconciling them with his or her existing understanding. Cognitive equilibrium occurs when one's present understanding "fits" new experiences, whether this fitting involves a baby's discovery that new objects can be grasped in the same way as familiar objects or an adult's explanation of shifting world events as consonant with his or her political philosophy.

Figure 2.3 diagrams how the need for cognitive equilibrium is fulfilled. When a new experience does not seem to fit existing understanding, the individual falls into a state of *cognitive disequilibrium,* an imbalance that initially produces confusion. Disequilibrium then leads to cognitive growth when the person modifies old concepts and constructs better ones to fit the new experience if

cognitive equilibrium In cognitive theory, the state of mental balance that enables a person to reconcile new experiences with existing understanding. People strive to attain cognitive equilibrium.

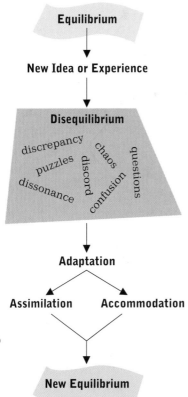

FIGURE 2.3 Challenge Me Most of us, most of the time, prefer the comfort of our conventional conclusions. According to Piaget, however, when new ideas disturb our thinking, we have an opportunity to expand our cognition with a broader and deeper understanding.

necessary, thus moving to a higher stage. In Piaget's terminology, cognitive adaptation occurs in two ways:

■ Reinterpreting new experiences so that they fit into, or *assimilate* with, the old ideas
■ Revamping old ideas so that they can *accommodate* the new

Assimilation is easier, since it does not require much adjustment. But accommodation is sometimes necessary, and it produces significant intellectual growth—a new form of thinking that is more inclusive than before.

You may experience cognitive disequilibrium, for example, when a friend's argument reveals logical inconsistencies in your views, when your favorite chess strategy fails against a skilled opponent, or when your mother does or says something you never expected her to. In the last example, you might assimilate your mother's unusual statement by deciding that it was just something she heard and didn't really mean. Growth occurs if, instead, you adjust your previous conception of your mother to accommodate a new, expanded, and more comprehensive view of who she is.

How to Think About Flowers A person's stage of cognitive growth influences how he or she thinks about everything, including flowers. (a) To a baby, in the sensorimotor stage, flowers are "known" through pulling, smelling, and perhaps tasting. (b) A slightly older child might be egocentric, wanting to pick and eat the vegetables now. (c,d) At the adult's formal operational stage, flowers can be part of a larger, logical scheme—either to earn money or to cultivate beauty. Note, however, that thinking is an active process throughout the life span.

According to cognitive theory, babies poke, pull, and taste everything they get their hands on; preschool children ask thousands of questions; school-age children become avid readers and information collectors; adolescents try out a wide variety of roles and experiences; and adults continually increase their knowledge and expertise in areas that interest them—all because people at every age seek cognitive challenges.

Recognition of this active searching is the very essence of Piaget's theory of human cognitive development. Unlike psychoanalytic and learning theories, which depict children as buffeted and shaped by influences beyond their control, cognitive theory portrays a much more active person, one who seeks ways to comprehend the world.

Not What He Expected Water spraying out of a pipe that he can hold in his hand—a surprising event that is likely to trigger first cognitive disequilibrium and then cognitive growth.

? *Observational Quiz* (see answer, page 48): This boy is 14 months old, in the sensorimotor period, and at an age when he loves to experiment. What is he likely to do next?

Limitations of the Grand Theories

All three of the theories we have just described deserve to be called "grand." They are insightful and provocative, stimulating not only for researchers in human development but also for historians, educators, novelists, and, particularly, psychotherapists. Thousands of clinical professionals still use techniques originated by Freud, Skinner, or Piaget. Further, each of these three theories has made significant contributions to developmental science, as already shown.

However, the grand theories, as they attempted to explain the development of all humans everywhere, were probably too wide-ranging. The central idea that every person, in every culture, in every nation, passes through certain fixed stages (Freud, Erikson, Piaget) or can be conditioned according to the same laws of reinforcement (Watson, Pavlov, Skinner) does not seem applicable to the actual diversity of human beings worldwide. Careful observation of any living, breathing, growing person evokes surprise and puzzlement, no matter what grand theory or basic assumption the observer might hold. This is already evident from the surprising examples in Chapter 1: the butterfly effect, the Bosnian 5-year-olds unscathed by war, and the eleventh-graders who seemed to forget that they had had sex before age 13.

In other words, all three grand theories seem much less comprehensive and inclusive now than they once did. This is apparent in the central controversies of development (continuity/discontinuity, difference/deficit, nature/nurture), discussed at the end of this chapter. It also becomes apparent when the theories of physics and biology are compared with the theories about human development in terms of their scientific rigor. As one critic writes:

> No field of biology can match the precision and power of physics, because unlike electrons or neutrons, all organisms are unique. But the differences between, say, two *Escherichia coli* bacteria or two leafcutter ants are trivial compared to the differences between any two humans, even those who are genetically identical. Each individual mind may also change dramatically when its owner is spanked, learns the alphabet, reads *Thus Spoke Zarathustra*, takes LSD, falls in love, gets divorced,

No Theories Allowed These three elderly women are in a nursing home where research in human development has not yet been applied. Being confined to wheelchairs, unable to see or hear each other, means that they are cut off from the comforts of human contact (psychoanalytic), of homemade food (behaviorism), and of intellectual stimulation (cognitive theory). Although none of the grand theories are considered comprehensive in the twenty-first century, any one of them could suggest improvements in the situation depicted here.

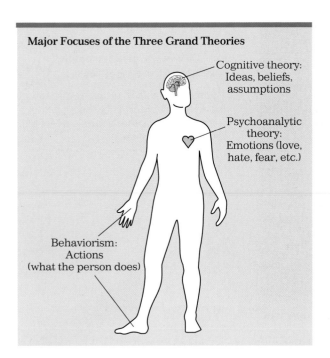

Major Focuses of the Three Grand Theories

Cognitive theory:
Ideas, beliefs,
assumptions

Psychoanalytic
theory:
Emotions (love,
hate, fear, etc.)

Behaviorism:
Actions
(what the person does)

FIGURE 2.4 **Major Focuses of the Three Grand Theories**

undergoes Jungian dream therapy, suffers a stroke. The variability and malleability of minds enormously complicate the search for general principles of human nature.

[Horgan, 1999, p. 6]

Each grand theory begins with a different focus: human emotions (psychoanalytic theory), actions (behaviorism), and thoughts (cognitive theory) (see Figure 2.4). The main conflict among the three theories involves what should be studied and how. As you might imagine, psychoanalytic theorists typically rely on case studies, behaviorists do experiments, and cognitive theorists observe and ask questions. However, all three grand theories seem to ignore major cultural differences and to underestimate the power of genes. New theories are needed to fill the gap, and at least two are emerging (Greene, 1997; Overton, 1998).

Emergent Theories

The three grand theories originated almost a century ago as theories of psychology. By contrast, the two emergent theories are recent and multidisciplinary. They include observations, mini-theories, and hypotheses from all the many sciences—in addition to psychology—that currently study human development. *Sociocultural theory* draws on research in education, sociology, and history; *epigenetic systems theory* is based on research from biology, genetics, ethology, and neuroscience. In part because of their scope and in part because of their recency, neither theory has become a comprehensive, coherent whole. However, as you will now see, both provide significant frameworks for the study of human development.

Sociocultural Theory

Although "sociocultural theory is still emerging and is not a single consolidated view," it stresses a new appreciation of the social context that developmentalists now recognize (Rogoff, 1998, p. 687). **Sociocultural theory** seeks to explain the growth of individual knowledge, development, and competencies in terms of the guidance, support, and structure provided by the society. Social change over time results from individual choices. Note the bidirectional influence of culture and person: People are affected by society, but people also change society.

The central thesis of sociocultural theory is that human development is the result of dynamic interaction between developing persons and their surrounding culture. According to this theory, culture is not simply an external variable that impinges on the developing person; it is integral to development (Cole, 1996).

The power of culture cannot be understood simply by comparing one particular practice in one place or ethnic group with another, as "cross-cultural" research did in the past. Instead, each culture is seen as a unique "design for living," and children learn that design from objects and people—from their parents, teachers, and peers, in their homes, schools, and neighborhoods. Consider a very simple example: What do you do if a 6-month-old baby starts to fuss? You could find a pacifier, turn on a musical mobile, change the diaper, give a bottle, pick up the baby and walk around, sing a lullaby, offer a breast, shake a rattle, or close the door so the noise won't bother anyone. Each of these is "the right thing to do" according to parents in some cultures but not in others. Few of these parents are aware that their culture has so shaped their attitudes that they respond to a baby's cry in a particular way, yet this is precisely what happens, according to sociocultural theory.

sociocultural theory An emergent theory that holds that human development results from the dynamic interaction between each person and the surrounding culture, including all the social forces, near and distant, that affect that person.

!*Answer to Observational Quiz* (from page 47): He will want to use all his senses and motor skills, so he might put the pipe to his mouth to taste it, rub it on his belly to feel the cold, shake it up and down to see and hear what happens, and—watch out—aim it at you to see your reaction.

Guided Participation

A major pioneer of the sociocultural perspective was Lev Vygotsky (1896–1934), a psychologist from the former Soviet Union. Vygotsky was particularly interested in the cognitive competencies that developed among the culturally diverse people of his huge country, including such skills as the proper use of tools in an agricultural community and the appropriate use of abstract words among people who had never been to school. In the sociocultural view, these competencies develop from interactions between novices and more skilled members of the society, who act as tutors or mentors in a process called an **apprenticeship in thinking** (Rogoff, 1990, 1998).

COURTESY OF DR. MICHAEL COLE, LABORATORY OF COMPARATIVE HUMAN COGNITION, UC, SAN DIEGO

The Founder of Sociocultural Theory Lev Vygotsky, now recognized as a seminal thinker whose ideas on the role of culture and history are revolutionizing education and the study of development, was a contemporary of Freud, Skinner, Pavlov, and Piaget. Vygotsky did not attain their eminence in his lifetime, partly because his work, conducted in Stalinist Russia, was largely inaccessible to the Western world and partly because he died young, at age 38.

The implicit goal of this apprenticeship is to provide the instruction and support that novices need in order to acquire the knowledge and capabilities that are valued by their culture. The best way to accomplish this goal is through **guided participation:** The tutor engages the learner in joint activities, offering not only instruction but also direct involvement in the learning process.

Note that this apprenticeship depends on social interaction, not on a student's own discovery or on a teacher's lecture. Neither student nor teacher is ever passive; one person learns from another, through the words and activities that they engage in *together* (Karpov & Haywood, 1998). This is one crucial difference between sociocultural theory and the grand theories of the past: "Cognitive development occurs in and emerges from social situations" (Gauvain, 1998, p. 191). Adults learn from children as well as vice versa, and both adults and children learn as much from their peers as from older or younger individuals.

The concept that a culture's patterns and beliefs are social constructions (as explained in Chapter 1) is easy for sociocultural theorists to understand. However, the fact that something is socially constructed does not reduce its power or importance; quite the opposite. Values are among the most potent forces, shaping the development of every member of the culture. This point was stressed by Vygotsky, who himself was a teacher and argued that mentally and physically disabled children can learn (Vygotsky, 1925/1994). If people believe that "every child can learn," they are likely to find a way to teach every child.

The Zone of Proximal Development

According to sociocultural theory, *what* people need to learn depends on their cultures, but *how* they learn is always the same, whether they are learning a manual skill, a social custom, or a language. Cultural context, social customs, and guided participation are always part of the process.

apprenticeship in thinking In sociocultural theory, the process by which novices develop cognitive competencies through interaction with more skilled members of the society, often parents or teachers, who act as tutors or mentors.

guided participation In sociocultural theory, the process by which a skilled person helps a novice learn by providing not only instruction but also a direct, shared involvement in the learning process.

Especially for Teachers: Following Vygotsky's precepts, how might you teach reading to an entire class of first-graders at various skill levels?

R. ROWAN / PHOTO RESEARCHERS, INC.

A Temporary Support Structure Scaffolds support workers as they construct a new building or repair an existing one, such as the California state capitol in Sacramento, shown here. Similarly, expert teachers erect educational scaffolds, using hints, ideas, examples, and questions to support the novice learner until a solid cognitive structure is formed.

zone of proximal development In sociocultural theory, the range of skills that a learner can exercise and master with assistance but cannot yet perform independently. According to Vygotsky, learning can occur within this zone.

Response for Teachers (from page 49): First of all, you wouldn't teach them "to read"; you would find out where each child was and what he or she was capable of learning next, so that instruction would be tailored to each child's zone of proximal development. For some this might be letter recognition; for others, comprehension of paragraphs they read to themselves. Second, you wouldn't teach the whole class. You would figure out a way to individualize instruction, maybe by forming pairs, with one child teaching the other, by setting up appropriate computer instruction, or by having parents or ancillary teachers work with small groups of three or four children.

For learning to occur, a teacher (who can be a parent or peer as well as a professional) draws the learner into his or her **zone of proximal development**, which is the range of skills that the learner can exercise and master with assistance but cannot yet perform independently. Through sensitive assessment of the learner's ability and capacity for growth, the teacher engages his or her participation, guiding the transition from assisted performance to independent achievement. The teacher must avoid two ever-present dangers, boredom and failure, both of which are outside that ideal zone. Some frustration is permitted, but the learner must be actively engaged, never passive or overwhelmed (see Figure 2.5).

To make this rather abstract-seeming process more concrete, let's take a simple example—a father teaching his 5-year-old daughter to ride a bicycle. He probably begins by slowly rolling her along, supporting her weight while telling her to keep her hands on the bars and her feet on the pedals, to push the right and left pedals in rhythm, and to look straight ahead. As she becomes more comfortable and confident, he begins to roll her along more quickly, noting out loud that she is now able to keep her legs pumping in a steady rhythm. Within another lesson or two he is jogging beside her, holding on to just the handlebar. When he senses that, with a little more momentum, she could maintain her balance by herself, he urges her to pedal faster and slowly loosens his grip until, perhaps without her even realizing it, she is riding on her own.

Note that this is not instruction by rote. First, some children need more assurance than others; from the start the instruction process is modified for the particular learner. Second, even knowing the child, a parent needs to listen and

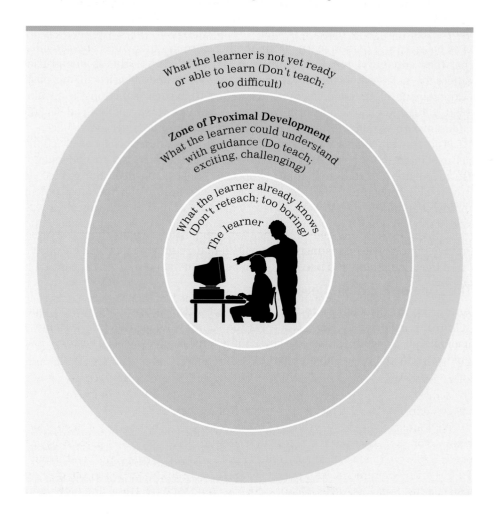

FIGURE 2.5 The Magic Middle Somewhere between the boring and the impossible is the zone of proximal development, where interaction between teacher and learner results in knowledge never before grasped or skills not already mastered. The intellectual excitement of that zone is the origin of the joy that both instruction and study can bring.

9. Piaget believed that cognitive development is an active and universal process. Curiosity is guided by the search for cognitive equilibrium, which is a person's ability to explain a new situation with existing understanding. When disequilibrium occurs, people develop cognitively by modifying their understanding to cover the new situation.

Emergent Theories

10. Sociocultural theory explains human development in terms of the guidance, support, and structure provided by culture. For Vygotsky, learning occurs through the social interactions learners share with more knowledgeable members of the society. They guide learners through the zone of proximal development.

11. Epigenetic systems theory begins by noting that genes are powerful and omnipresent, potentially affecting every aspect of development. This theory also stresses an ongoing interaction between the genes and environmental forces, which can range from prenatal toxins to lifelong stresses. This interaction can halt, modify, or strengthen the effects of the genes, both within the person and, over time, within the species.

12. Epigenetic systems theory also focuses on the systems, within the individual as well as the species, that support development. In one such system, infants are born with various drives and reflexes that help ensure their survival, while adults are normally also equipped with innate predispositions to nurture babies, no matter what sacrifices might be required.

Comparisons and Controversies

13. Psychoanalytic, learning, cognitive, sociocultural, and epigenetic systems theories have each contributed to the understanding of human development, yet no one theory is broad enough to describe the full complexity and diversity of human experience.

14. Each of the five major theories reviewed here has a somewhat different position on the issues of development. The continuity–discontinuity controversy concerns the question of whether development occurs smoothly or in stages. The difference–deficit controversy asks when something that is unusual (a difference) becomes harmful (a deficit).

15. The nature–nurture controversy centers on how much influence heredity has on development, as compared to how much influence the environment has. Every researcher agrees, however, that both factors influence human development.

16. Each theory provides a useful perspective; none is complete in itself. Most developmentalists are eclectic, adopting aspects of various theories rather than following any single theory.

KEY TERMS

developmental theory (p. 35)
grand theories (p. 36)
minitheories (p. 36)
emergent theories (p. 36)
psychoanalytic theory (p. 36)
behaviorism (p. 40)
conditioning (p. 40)

classical conditioning (p. 40)
operant conditioning (p. 41)
reinforcement (p. 41)
social learning theory (p. 43)
modeling (p. 43)
self-efficacy (p. 44)
cognitive theory (p. 44)

cognitive equilibrium (p. 45)
sociocultural theory (p. 48)
apprenticeship in thinking (p. 49)
guided participation (p. 49)
zone of proximal development (p. 50)

epigenetic systems theory (p. 51)
selective adaptation (p. 52)
ethology (p. 54)
nature (p. 60)
nurture (p. 60)
eclectic perspective (p. 62)

KEY QUESTIONS

1. What functions does a good theory perform?
2. What is the major assumption of psychoanalytic theory?
3. What are the key differences between Freud's and Erikson's ideas concerning development?
4. What is the major focus of behaviorism?
5. What are the differences between classical conditioning and operant conditioning?
6. According to Piaget, how do periods of disequilibrium lead to mental growth?
7. What are the main differences among the grand theories?
8. According to sociocultural theory, how does development occur?
9. Give an example of guided participation that is not in the text.
10. According to epigenetic systems theorists, how can genetic instructions change?
11. What are the main differences between the two emergent theories?
12. What are the three main ongoing controversies in development?
13. Pick one controversy, and explain the different perspectives taken by the five theories.

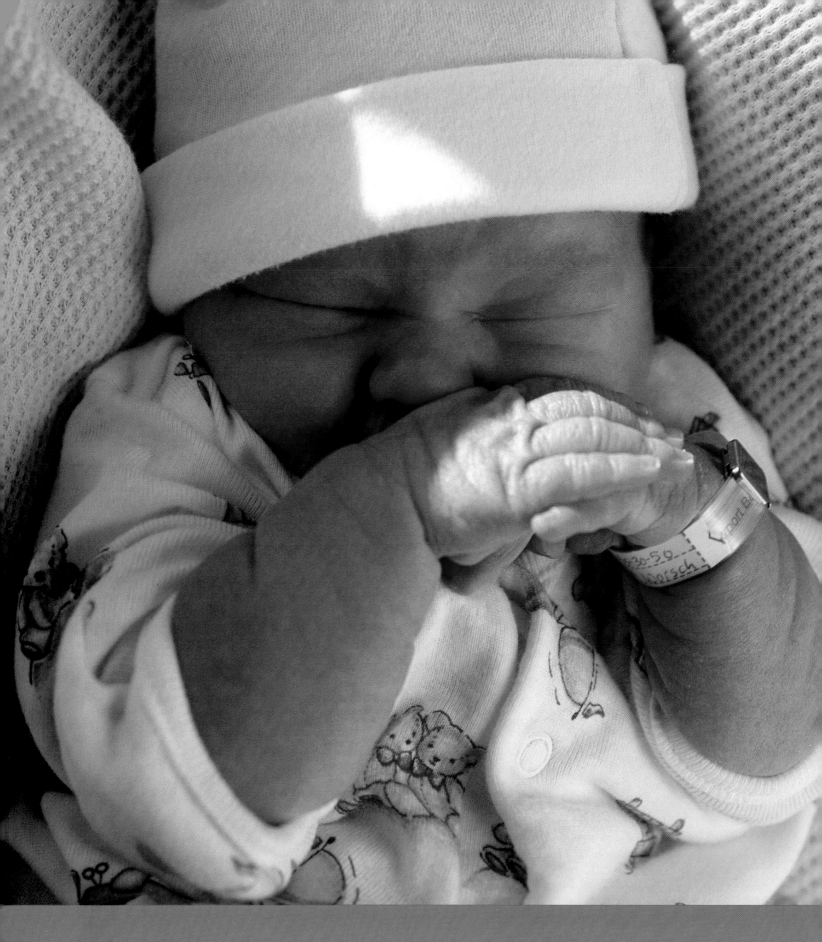

Part I

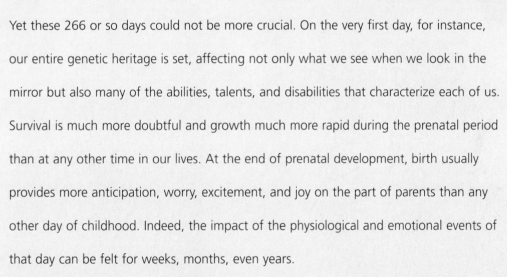

When considering the human life span, most people ignore or take for granted the time from conception through birth. Indeed, among all the nations of the world, China seems to have been the only one to include the prenatal period when reckoning age. Yet these 266 or so days could not be more crucial. On the very first day, for instance, our entire genetic heritage is set, affecting not only what we see when we look in the mirror but also many of the abilities, talents, and disabilities that characterize each of us. Survival is much more doubtful and growth much more rapid during the prenatal period than at any other time in our lives. At the end of prenatal development, birth usually provides more anticipation, worry, excitement, and joy on the part of parents than any other day of childhood. Indeed, the impact of the physiological and emotional events of that day can be felt for weeks, months, even years.

These early days, usually uncounted and underemphasized, are the focus of the next two chapters.

The Beginnings

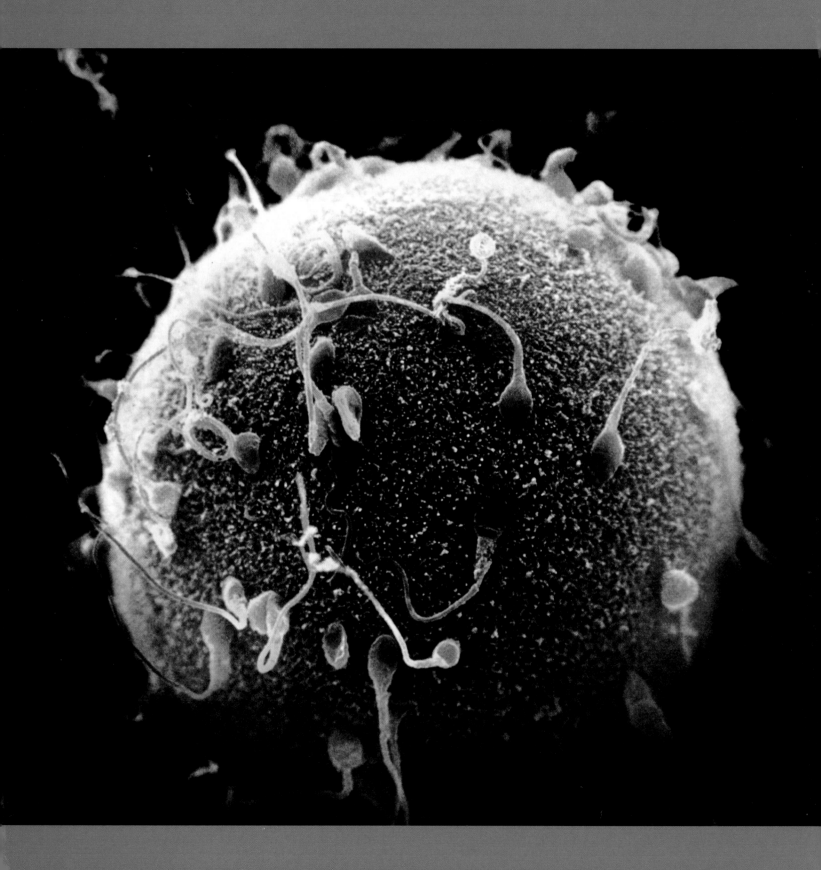

Heredity and Environment

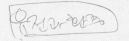

Genetics has taken a lead role in the drama of human development. Prospective parents seek to predict which physical and psychological traits their children will inherit; the Human Genome Project promises to decipher the invisible genetic code that directs human growth; everyone consulting a doctor about any pain or peculiarity is questioned about ancestral and familial conditions; and anyone who studies child development realizes that genes are the foundation of all the growth we seek to understand.

Yet in many ways genetics remains a mystery, a plot difficult to follow, with strange twists and turns. This chapter goes behind the scenes to explain not only what genes are but how they work. Genes are pervasive and powerful, and you will learn more about the many ways in which their influence becomes apparent in each developing person.

Remember from Chapter 2, however, that genetic influence is actually *epigenetic.* Genes are influenced by their ongoing interaction with the *environment,* which includes everything nongenetic, from the nourishment of the fetus to the macrosystem of the growing child. The interaction between heredity and the environment, or between nature and nurture, is dynamic, complex, and varied. Indeed, "it may well be that outcome variability is built into individual development as a fact of nature" (Wachs, 2000). Rather than determining the course of our lives, genes are a major cause of the variability, diversity, and surprises that make human development the fascinating subject that it is. Understanding the basic facts about genes—what they are, where they are located, how they work together, and when they interact with the environment—is the topic of this chapter, one that you are likely to find surprising and fascinating.

Genetics: Foundations in Biology and Ethics

As you know from Chapter 1, a central tenet of human growth is *plasticity:* People are molded by their life experiences. Yet plasticity requires some raw material to be shaped, some basic substance to start the developmental process. Genes provide that raw material. Understanding them aids in understanding all past, present, and future generations and individuals, including me and you. How do your genes distinguish you from everyone else? How do they restrict, guide, and motivate you—in ways that your parents never wished or you yourself never imagined?

The general facts about child development and the specific questions about each of us lead directly to practical applications and ethical quandaries surrounding genetics—human cloning, selective abortion, surrogate parenthood, eugenics, disability accommodation, genetic testing, sex selection, donor gametes, infertility treatment, international adoption, to name just a few. We cannot duck these topics, because "once we take development seriously, we must also take genetics seriously" (Pennington, 2001). The question "What can humans become?" raises another question: "What *should* people become?"

Accepting people as they are, yet using genetic knowledge for the good of all humanity, has both ethical and logical pitfalls. To introduce this urgent topic, we look in on a couple who are arguing about the baby they are expecting.

A Case to Study

What Do People Live to Do?

John and Martha are in their 20s, both graduate students at Harvard, expecting their second child in five months. Martha's initial prenatal screening revealed abnormally low levels of alpha-fetoprotein (AFP). A low AFP level could indicate that her fetus has Down syndrome, in which each cell of the body has 47 chromosomes (instead of the usual 46) and which produces distinctive facial characteristics, serious health problems, and mental retardation. To recheck the AFP results (Down syndrome is rare when the parents are under 35) and to allow time for a more definitive test called amniocentesis, another blood test was immediately scheduled.

John met Martha at a café after a nurse drew the second blood sample, before the laboratory reported the new levels. Later, Martha wrote about their conversation.

"Did they tell you anything about the test?" John said. "What exactly is the problem?" . . .

"We've got a one in eight hundred and ninety-five shot at a retarded baby."

John smiled, "I can live with those odds."

I tried to smile back, but I couldn't. . . . I wanted to tell John about the worry in my gut. I wanted to tell him that it was more than worry—that it was a certainty. Then I realized all over again how preposterous that was. "I'm still a little scared."

He reached across the table for my hand. "Sure," he said, "That's understandable. But even if there is a problem, we've caught it in time. . . . The worst case scenario is that you might have to have an abortion, and that's a long shot. Everything's going to be fine."

. . . "I might *have to have* an abortion?" The chill inside me was gone. Instead I could feel my face flushing hot with anger. "Since when do you decide what I *have to* do with my body?"

John looked surprised. "I never said I was going to decide anything," he protested. "It's just that if the tests show something wrong with the baby, of course we'll abort. We've talked about this."

"What we've talked about," I told John in a low, dangerous voice, "is that I am pro-choice. That means I decide whether or not I'd abort a baby with a birth defect. . . . I'm not so sure of this."

"You used to be," said John.

"I know I used to be." I rubbed my eyes. I felt terribly confused. "But now . . . look, John, it's not as though we're deciding whether or not to have a baby. We're deciding what *kind* of baby we're willing to accept. If it's perfect in every way, we keep it. If it doesn't fit the right specifications, whoosh! Out it goes.". . .

John was looking more and more confused. "Martha, why are you on this soapbox? What's your point?"

"My point is," I said, "that I'm trying to get you to tell me what you think constitutes a 'defective' baby. What about . . . oh, I don't know, a hyperactive baby? Or an ugly one?"

"They can't test for those things and—"

"Well, what if they could?" I said. "Medicine can do all kinds of magical tricks these days. Pretty soon we're going to be aborting babies because they have the gene for alcoholism, or homosexuality, or manic depression. . . . Did you know that in China they abort a lot of fetuses just because they're female?" I growled. "Is being a girl 'defective' enough for you?"

"Look," he said, "I know I can't always see things from your perspective. And I'm sorry about that. But the way I see it, if a baby is going to be deformed or something, abortion is a way to keep everyone from suffering—*especially* the baby. It's like shooting a horse that's broken its leg. . . . A lame horse dies slowly, you know? . . . It dies in terrible pain. And it can't run anymore. So it can't enjoy life even if it doesn't die. Horses live to run; that's what they do. If a baby is born not being able to do what other people do, I think it's better not to prolong its suffering."

". . . And what is it," I said softly, more to myself than to John, "what is it that people do? What do we live to do, the way a horse lives to run?"

[Beck, 1999, pp. 132–133, 135]

The second AFP test came back low but in the normal range, "meaning there was no reason to fear that Adam had Down syndrome" (p. 137).

This episode reminds us of the subjective values and opinions that surround the objective facts about genetic differences. We will return to John and Martha, and to other values and opinions, later. First, however, let us outline those "objective facts about genetic differences."

From One Cell to Trillions

Human development begins very simply, when a male reproductive cell, or *sperm* (plural: *sperm*), penetrates the membrane of a female reproductive cell, or *ovum* (plural: *ova*). Each human **gamete** (the name for any reproductive cell, whether it comes from a male or female) contains more than a billion genetic instructions in the form of chemical codes.

At conception, when the sperm and ovum combine, the two gametes form a complete set of instructions for creating a person. Those instructions are not always followed to the letter. They must be read and interpreted, and the necessary components must be found. Genetic instructions begin by directing growth and become more complex as life unfolds (Johnston & Edwards, 2002).

Growth Begins

For the first hour or so after a sperm enters an ovum, the two cells maintain their separate identities, side by side, enclosed within the ovum's membrane. Suddenly they fuse, and a living cell called a **zygote** is formed: Two reproductive cells have literally become one, and the genetic material from one parent matches up with the genetic material from the other.

Within hours, the zygote begins the first stages of growth through a process of *duplication* and *division*. First, the combined genetic material from both gametes duplicates itself, forming two complete sets of the genetic code for that person. Then these two sets move toward opposite sides of the zygote, and the zygote divides neatly down the middle. Thus, the one-celled zygote has become two cells, each containing a complete set of the original genetic code. These two cells duplicate and divide to become four; these four, in turn, duplicate and divide to become eight; and so on.

At about the eight-cell stage, a third process, *differentiation,* is added to duplication and division. Cells begin to specialize, taking different forms and reproducing at various rates, depending on where in the growing mass they are. Before differentiation, any one of the cells could become a whole person; after differentiation, this is no longer true. The next nine months of development from a mass of cells to a newborn baby are described in Chapter 4. But now you need to know about genes and cells.

When you (or I, or any other person) were newborn, your body had about 10 trillion cells, almost half of them in your immature brain. By adulthood, your cells have increased to more than 100 trillion. But no matter how many cells you have, and no matter how much division, duplication, differentiation, and specialization has occurred, each body cell carries a copy of the complete genetic instructions inherited by the one-celled zygote. This explains why DNA testing of any body cell can identify "the real father" or "the guilty criminal" or "the long-lost twin" when the traditional methods of identification fail.

The Genetic Code

The basic unit of genetic instruction is the **gene.** A gene is a discrete segment of a **chromosome,** which is a molecule of *DNA* (*deoxyribonucleic acid*). Except for sperm and ova, every normal human cell has 23 pairs of chromosomes (46 chromosomes in all), which collectively carry between 30,000 and 40,000 distinct

gamete A reproductive cell; that is, a cell that can reproduce a new individual if it combines with a gamete from the other sex.

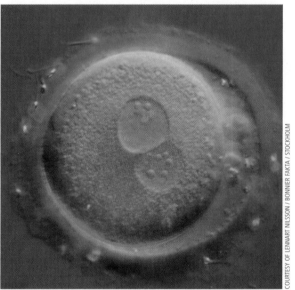

COURTESY OF LENNART NILSSON / BONNIER FAKTA / STOCKHOLM

The Moment of Conception The ovum shown here is about to become a zygote. It has been penetrated by a single sperm, whose nucleus now lies next to the nucleus of the ovum. Shortly, the two nuclei will fuse, bringing together about 40,000 genes that will guide future development.

zygote The single cell formed from the fusing of a sperm and an ovum.

gene The basic unit for the transmission of heredity instructions.

chromosome A carrier of genes; one of the 46 molecules of DNA (in 23 pairs) that each cell of the body contains and that, together, contain all human genes.

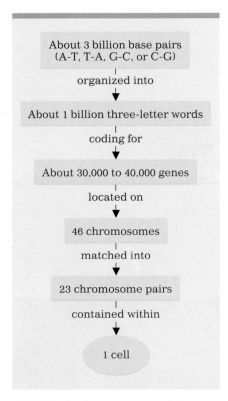

About 3 billion base pairs
(A-T, T-A, G-C, or C-G)

organized into

↓

About 1 billion three-letter words

coding for

↓

About 30,000 to 40,000 genes

located on

↓

46 chromosomes

matched into

↓

23 chromosome pairs

contained within

↓

1 cell

FIGURE 3.1 What Every Human Cell Contains

genetic code The sequence in which pairs of chemical bases appear along each segment of the DNA molecule.

Human Genome Project An international effort to map the complete human genetic code.

genes (see Figure 3.1). Each cell has the same DNA message. In fact, with rare exceptions, even when a human has an abnormal number of chromosomes (as in the 47 chromosomes of Down syndrome), every body cell still has those same chromosomes with those same genes.

The instructions from each gene are "written" in a chemical code made up of pairs of only four chemical *bases*—adenine, guanine, cytosine, and thymine, abbreviated A, G, C, and T, respectively. These chemical bases normally combine in only four pairings, A-T, T-A, G-C, and C-G, a fact that might seem to provide a very limited genetic vocabulary. In fact, there are approximately 3 billion base pairs in the DNA of every human and thousands of base pairs in every gene, which means that many, many sequences are possible.

On each gene the code letters are written in a particular sequence of three-letter words that direct the formation and combination of twenty amino acids. These amino acids, in turn, direct the synthesis of hundreds of different kinds of proteins, including enzymes that serve as the body's building blocks and regulators. Following genetic instructions, certain cells become neurons (brain cells), others become the lens of the eye, others become the valves of the heart, and so on throughout the body.

The influence of genes doesn't stop there. Through some sort of on–off switching mechanism, genes control life itself, instructing cells to grow, to repair damage, to take in nourishment, to multiply, to atrophy, to die. Even certain kinds of cognitive development involve genes that switch on at particular ages, propelling maturation in specific areas of the brain (Plomin et al., 2001).

The Human Genome Project

The precise nature of a gene's instructions is determined by the **genetic code**—that is, the sequence in which the pairs of chemical bases appear along each segment of the DNA molecule. The **Human Genome Project** is an international effort to map the complete genetic code. (A *genome* is all the genetic information, or hereditary material, that an organism possesses.) Originally scheduled to be completed by 2005, the Human Genome Project progressed so rapidly that two rough drafts were ready in 2000. The two drafts are similar overall, but different in details; both are still missing several segments, and both have already been enormously useful in locating genetic disabilities and developing treatments.

We now know that about 99 percent of all the genes are basically the same for all humans worldwide. Moreover, we share this genetic base with many other species of animals. This makes it easy to learn more about people by studying mice, monkeys, and even flies and worms.

For example, every mammal embryo is genetically commanded to make seven neck bones. Because of the influence of other genes, those seven bones in a whale's neck become flat, thin disks; those in a giraffe's neck become elongated; and those in a human's neck are in between—probably more than we would need if our bodies were perfectly designed to avoid neck injuries, but adequate as a template to accommodate mammalian diversity (Barnett, 1998). Thus, to learn about human neck injuries, we can study the neck of any mammal.

Reading the Code A small segment of a DNA molecule is sequenced into bands, with one color for each of the base pairs. These pairs direct the synthesis of enzymes and proteins that, in turn, direct the formation of a living creature. One small change in a gene might result in a physical anomaly or a mental quirk. A few hundred different genes might result in a giraffe instead of a whale.

Similarly, the gene that produces the legs of a butterfly is exactly the same gene that shapes the four legs of a cat, the many legs of a centipede, and the two legs of a person. The differences between your legs and those of other creatures are governed by a regulator gene that advises the leg gene as to the particular shape and number of legs to make (Pennisi & Roush, 1997).

The regulator genes, which guide growth and development throughout the body, make up much of the 1 percent of genetic differentiation between humans and other animals, and between one human and another. One percent may not seem like a lot, but it means that "about 3 million of our 3 billion base pairs differ among people" (Plomin et al., 2001, p. 51). A minor difference can have a major impact, as seen with genes that vary by just a letter or two.

"Reading" the Genome

Matt Ridley, who has written extensively on genetics, has provided a useful analogy between the human genome and a book.

> Imagine that the genome is a book.
>
> There are twenty-three chapters, called CHROMOSOMES.
> Each chapter contains several thousand stories, called GENES.
> Each story is made up of paragraphs, called EXONS, which are interrupted by advertisements called INTRONS.
>
> Each paragraph is made up words, called CODONS.
> Each word is written in letters called BASES.
>
> There are one billion words in the book, which makes it . . . as long as 800 Bibles. If I read the genome out to you at the rate of one word per second for eight hours a day, it would take me a century. If I wrote out the human genome, one letter per millimetre, my text would be as long as the River Danube. This is a gigantic document, an immense book, a recipe of extravagant length, and it all fits inside the microscopic nucleus of a tiny cell that fits easily upon the head of a pin.
>
> [Ridley, 1999, p. 7]

A normal alteration is called an **allele,** one of several possible letter sequences that some genes have. Note that everyone has one allele or another of those variable genes; it is not that there is a standard, normal version and a mutant form. An allele makes it less likely that you will be a flaming redhead, a fluent reader, or senile when you are very old. Other alleles make it more likely that those things will happen. An allele even makes you more or less fearful (Hariri et al., 2002)

allele One of the normal versions of a gene that has several possible sequences of base pairs.

Continuity and Diversity

Paradoxically, the common and universal characteristics of human development are contrasted with unique and distinctive ones. Both are always apparent and both are crucial. Interpretation of developmental events is continually switching from universal to unique, from half-full to half-empty, depending on whether one prefers to emphasize that humans are all one species or that each human is an individual.

Now we consider some aspects of this paradox, as manifested in chromosomes, in sex determination, in species-specific characteristics, and in genetic diversity (as it relates to twins and as it is achieved through alternate means of conception).

Chromosomes: Same Cells, Different People

As we have noted, each human usually has 46 chromosomes, which are duplicated in every body cell except gametes. The chromosomes are arranged in 23 distinct pairs. One member of each pair is inherited from the mother, and the

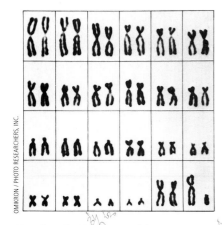

Mapping the Karyotype A *karyotype* portrays a person's chromosomes. To create a karyotype, a cell is grown in a laboratory, magnified, and then usually photographed. The photo is cut into pieces and rearranged, matching the pairs of chromosomes, from pair 1, the largest pair (*top left*) to pair 23, here the XY of a normal male (*bottom right*).

? *Observational Quiz* (see answer, page 74): Is this the karyotype of a normal human?

twenty-third pair The chromosome pair that, in humans, determines the zygote's (and hence the person's) sex, among other things.

XX A twenty-third pair that consists of two X-shaped chromosomes, one from the mother and one from the father.

XY A twenty-third pair that consists of one X-shaped chromosome from the mother and one Y-shaped chromosome from the father.

other one is inherited from the father. When the chromosomes pair off, the genes pair off, too, again with one from each parent (although, since many genes can have several alleles, a specific gene from one parent may not exactly match its mate from the other parent).

This very specific genetic and chromosomal pairing is encoded for life in every cell—with one important exception. When the human body makes sperm or ova, cell division occurs in such a way that each gamete receives only one member of each chromosome pair. This is why sperm and ova each have only 23 chromosomes: to ensure that when they combine, the new organism will have a total of 46 chromosomes. In other words, genetically, we are whatever we are: Every cell of your body, from the soles of your feet to the lining of your gut to the dancing neurons of your brain, contains the distinct code that makes you you, and every cell of my body contains the unique code that makes me me. And half of every cell's code is from your mother and half from your father.

The one exception becomes relevant if you and I reproduce. My gametes each contain only half of my genes; your gametes each contain only half of your genes. This means that our children would be neither yours nor mine but ours—half you, half me. It also guarantees genetic diversity in each child, male or female.

Sex Determination

Of the 23 pairs of human chromosomes, 22 are closely matched pairs called autosomes, with the two chromosomes of each pair containing similar genes in almost identical positions and sequence. The **twenty-third pair**, which is the pair that determines the individual's sex (among other things), is a different case. In the female, the twenty-third pair is composed of two large X-shaped chromosomes. Accordingly, it is designated **XX**. In the male, the twenty-third pair is composed of one large X-shaped chromosome and one much smaller Y-shaped chromosome. It is designated **XY**.

Obviously, because a female's twenty-third chromosome pair is XX, every ovum that her body creates will contain either one X or the other—but always an X. And because a male's twenty-third pair is XY, half of his sperm will contain an X chromosome and half will contain a Y. That Y chromosome (but not the X) contains a gene (called SRY) that directs a developing fetus to make male organs.

FIGURE 3.2 Determining a Zygote's Sex Any given couple can produce four possible combinations of sex chromosomes; two lead to female children, and two to male. In terms of the future person's sex, it does not matter which of the mother's Xs the zygote inherited. All that matters is whether the father's Y sperm or X sperm fertilized the ovum. However, for X-linked conditions it matters a great deal, since typically one, but not both, of the mother's Xs carries the trait.

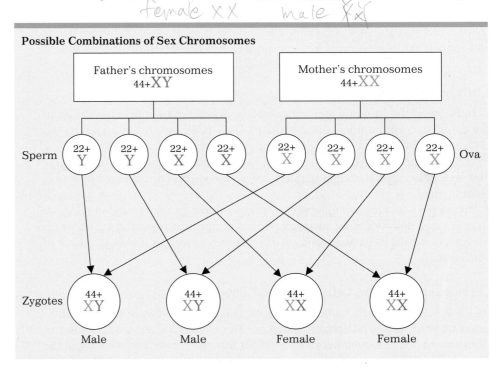

Possible Combinations of Sex Chromosomes

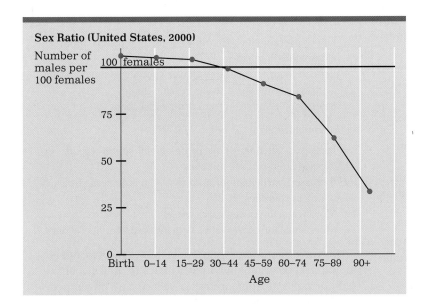

Sex Ratio (United States, 2000)

FIGURE 3.3 Too Many Baby Boys? Worldwide, slightly more males than females are born each year. Given the slightly higher rate of death among males in childhood (and assuming no unequal, major killer, such as war), the result is a roughly equal number of men and women of reproductive age. In the past, many women died in childbirth, whereas today heart attacks kill many more men than women—which is the main reason why the sex ratio now favors women after age 45. (Men are also somewhat more likely than women to die from other causes.) What would be the effect on marriage and divorce rates, on health costs, on crime statistics, and on population growth if couples had far more boys than girls, or vice versa?

Thus, the critical factor in the determination of a zygote's sex is which sperm reaches the ovum first—a Y sperm, creating a male (XY), or an X sperm, creating a female (XX) (see Figure 3.2).

Every now and then, a gene carried by a man renders either his X sperm or his Y sperm immobile, so that he can father only sons or only daughters. Other factors can also affect the survival of male or female embryos. However, the overall sex ratio (the proportion of males to females in a given population) at birth has always been roughly equal, and females increasingly outlive males with advancing age (see Figure 3.3). Now our expanding knowledge of genetics allows humans to alter the sex ratio dramatically. Whether or not to use that knowledge is an ethical issue, as the following Changing Policy feature explains.

Changing Policy

Too Many Boys?

Unless wars, epidemics, or other catastrophes occur, about an equal number of men and women reach young adulthood, the prime reproductive age. Should nations, or individuals, be allowed to change the natural sex ratio?

Some have tried. Numerous societies have allowed female infanticide (a practice so common that it had to be explicitly forbidden in the Koran) or have allowed husbands to divorce or even kill wives who produced only daughters (as did England's Henry VIII). For centuries, pregnant women were advised to eat certain foods, sleep on one side, or pray to the moon to make sure their baby was a boy or girl.

Today we know better:

■ Sperm, not ova, determine a baby's sex.
■ Each zygote is already XX or XY; no prenatal action can change that.

Moreover, we now have the potentially dangerous ability to discover, via prenatal testing, whether an embryo is destined to be male or female. This knowledge has been put to use in China, where, each year between 1990 and 1993, more than a million couples aborted female fetuses because sons are favored and couples are forbidden to have more than one child. In reaction, the Chinese government has outlawed abortion for the purpose of sex selection; as a result, virtually all the Chinese infants available for international adoption are girls. The same problem emerged in India, where laws against sex selection exist but are not enforced. In the state of Punjab, only 79 females are born for every 100 males (Duggar, 2001).

Couples in the United States who do not wish to abort have another alternative. For decades, cattle breeders have successfully used sperm sorting and artificial insemination to produce only male or only female calves, depending on whether beef or milk is the desired product. A similar sperm-sorting technique is available experimentally for humans and is said to have a 95 percent success rate (Grifo et al., 1994).

Do we need a social policy to regulate this new technology? Before answering, consider the social consequences if only half as many girls were born as are born today:

In family life

■ Fewer single mothers, fewer widows, more never-married men

■ Weaker family ties between siblings, parents and children, grandparents and grandchildren (because women maintain the family network)

■ More children per woman, fewer children per man

■ More children with learning disabilities, hyperactivity, conduct disorders; fewer adolescents with depression, eating disorders

In economic life

■ More engineers, architects, billionaires; fewer nurses, teachers, secretaries

■ Greater demand for fast food, fast cars, guns, prostitutes

■ Less demand for fashionable clothes, household furnishings, kitchen equipment

■ More violent crimes of all kinds, and thus a greater need for police, judges, prisons

In health care

■ Lower average life span, more accidental deaths, more suicides, more homicides

■ Less ongoing medical care; fewer specialists in gynecology, arthritis, gerontology; fewer nursing homes

■ More people suffering from drug and alcohol abuse

In community life

■ Increased attendance at professional sports events; decreased attendance at libraries

■ Increased participation in sports teams; decreased participation in churches

■ More wars; fewer day-care centers

■ More votes for conservative policies; fewer for liberal ones

Do you disagree, insisting that cultural practices, not biological sex, determine who participates in athletics or religion or politics? Your protest is valid for all fifteen items. Neither genes nor chromosomes determine behavior, although sex-linked hormones do make one sex more likely to act in certain ways than the other (Ridley, 1999).

If you had only one child, would you prefer a son or a daughter? The Ethics Committee of the American Society for Reproductive Health (2001) reported that sperm sorting is still experimental and should not have "widespread use" but may be permitted in some cases. What do you think?

The Human Species

The vast majority of each person's genes are identical to those of every other human being, male or female, related or not (Plomin et al., 2001). As a result of the instructions carried by genes, each new member of the human race shares certain characteristics with everyone else, alive or dead or not yet born:

■ Common physical structures (such as the pelvic alignment that allows humans to walk upright)

■ Common behavioral tendencies (such as the urge to communicate through language)

■ Common reproductive potential (allowing any male and female human to produce a new member of the species)

These species-specific characteristics, and thousands of others, have been fashioned throughout a long evolutionary history, promoting survival by enabling humans to live successfully on Earth (Ridley, 1999).

The remainder of each person's genes differ in various ways from those of other individuals. Such a difference usually takes the form of an allele that has only one or two changes in the thousands of letter combinations. The diversity that these small variations in the genetic code provide, over generations, is essential for human adaptation to new environments and needs. Thus, the fact that each human differs genetically from others means that our species is able to survive as conditions and circumstances change. For example, some genetic variants confer special resistance to malaria, cholera, tuberculosis, or alcoholism (Ridley, 1999).

! Answer to Observational Quiz (from page 72): No, there are 24 pairs here. This photo shows the two different possibilities for the twenty-third pair. (The normal female XX is just to the left of the normal male XY.)

Additive Genes

One common pattern of interaction among genes begins with an **additive gene**. When genes interact additively, the phenotype reflects the contributions of all the genes that are involved. The many genes that affect height, hair curliness, and skin color, for instance, usually interact in an additive fashion.

Consider an unlikely scenario: A tall man whose parents and grandparents were all very tall marries a short woman whose parents and grandparents were all very short. Assume that every one of his height genes is for tallness and that hers are all for shortness. The couple's children will inherit tall genes via the father's sperm and short genes via the mother's ova. Because the genes affecting height interact additively, the children will be of middling height (assuming that their nutrition and physical health are adequate). None of them will be as tall as their father or as short as their mother, because each will have at least one gene for tallness and one gene for shortness, somehow "averaged" together.

In actuality, most people have both kinds of ancestors—relatively tall ones and relatively short ones—so children are often taller or shorter than both their parents. My daughter Rachel is of average height, which is shorter than my husband or me, but taller than either grandmother. Rachel must have inherited a grandmother's shortness genes from our genotypes, even though it is not apparent in our phenotypes. How any additive trait turns out depends on all the contributions of whichever genes (half from each parent's varied genotype) a child happens to inherit. Every additive gene that is on a person's genotype has some impact on the phenotype. I myself am tall because my father was very tall; I would have been even taller if my mother had not been so short.

Dominant and Recessive Genes

Less common are *nonadditive patterns,* in which the phenotype shows the influence of one gene much more than that of others. One kind of nonadditive pattern is the *dominant–recessive pattern.* When a gene pair interacts according to this pattern, the phenotype reveals the influence of the more powerful gene, called the **dominant gene.** The other, weaker gene, the **recessive gene,** is not expressed in any obvious way.

Sometimes the dominant gene completely controls the characteristic and the recessive gene is merely carried, with its influence not evident at all in the phenotype. In other instances, the outcome reflects *incomplete dominance,* with the phenotype influenced primarily, but not exclusively, by the dominant gene.

Hundreds of physical characteristics are determined according to the dominant–recessive pattern (with some epigenetic modification due to environmental factors and the influence of other genes). Blood types A and B are both dominant and O is recessive, leading to a complex relationship of genotype and phenotype in blood inheritance. (See Appendix A.) Brown eyes are also said to be dominant over blue eyes, and many genetic diseases are recessive. However, with eye color and many diseases, additive interactions are also apparent.

X-Linked Genes

Some genes are called **X-linked** because they are located only on the X chromosome. If an X-linked gene is recessive—as are the genes for most forms of color blindness, many allergies, several diseases, and some learning disabilities—the fact that it is on the X chromosome is critical. Recall that males have only one X chromosome. Thus, whatever recessive genes a male happens to inherit on his X chromosome cannot be counterbalanced or dominated by genes on his second X chromosome—he has no second X. Any recessive genes on his X chromosome will be expressed in his phenotype. This explains why traits

additive gene A gene that, through interaction with other genes, affects a specific trait (such as skin color or height).

THOMAS DIGORY / STOCKPHOTOS / THE IMAGE BANK

Skin Color Is Inherited But . . . Using "black," "white," "red," and "yellow" to denote human skin color is misleading, because humans actually have thousands of skin tones, each resulting from the combination of many genes, and none of them is one of these four colors. Depending on which half of each parent's skin-color genes children happen to inherit, each child can be paler, ruddier, lighter, darker, more sallow, more olive, or more freckled than either parent. This is particularly apparent in many African-American families, like this one, whose ancestors came from at least three continents.

dominant gene The stronger of an interacting pair of genes.

recessive gene The weaker of an interacting pair of genes.

X-linked Referring to a gene that is on the X chromosome.

Especially for History Students: Some genetic diseases may have changed the course of history. For instance, the last czar of Russia had four healthy daughters and one son with hemophilia. Once called the royal disease, hemophilia is X-linked. How could this rare condition affect the monarchies of Russia, England, Austria, Germany, and Spain?

Inheritance of an X-Linked Recessive Trait
The phenotypes on lines 1 and 2 are normal because their genes are normal. Those on lines 3 and 4 are normal because the abnormal X-linked gene is recessive and the normal gene is dominant. Those on lines 5 and 6 are color-blind because they have no dominant, normal X.

TABLE 3.1 The 23rd Pair and X-Linked Color Blindness

X indicates an X chromosome with the X-linked gene for color blindness

23rd Pair	Phenotype	Genotype	Next Generation
1. XX	Normal woman	Not a carrier	No color blindness from mother.
2. XY	Normal man	Normal X from mother	No color blindness from father.
3. XX	Normal woman	Carrier from father	Half her children will inherit her X. The girls with her X will be carriers, the boys with her X will be color-blind.
4. XX	Normal woman	Carrier from mother	Half her children will inherit her X. The girls with her X will be carriers, the boys with her X will be color-blind.
5. XY	Color-blind man	Inherited from mother	All his daughters will have his X. None of his sons will have his X. All his children will have normal vision, unless their mother also had an X for color blindness.
6. XX	Color-blind woman (rare)	Inherited from both parents	Every child will have one X from her. Therefore, every son will be color-blind. Daughters will be only carriers, unless they also inherit an X from the father, as their mother did.

carried on the X chromosome can be passed from mother to son but not from father to son (since the Y does not carry the trait). (See Table 3.1.)

More Complications

As complex as the preceding descriptions of gene interaction patterns may seem, they make gene–gene interaction appear much simpler than it actually is. That is because, to be able to discuss interaction at all, we are forced to treat genes as though they were separately functioning "control devices." But, as we have noted, genes merely direct the creation of 20 amino acids, the combination of which directs the synthesis of thousands of kinds of proteins and enzymes, which then form the body's structures and direct its biochemical functions. The proteins of each body cell are continually affected by other proteins, enzymes, nutrients, and toxins that direct the cell's functioning (Masoro, 1999).

The genes themselves do not always function as the textbooks say they do. For example, a dominant gene might not actually "penetrate" the phenotype completely. Such incomplete penetrance may be caused by temperature, stress, or many other factors. Sometimes the split of a chromosome pair at or before conception is not precise, resulting in a person who is a *mosaic,* that is, who has a mixture of cells, some with a dominant gene, some without. A person could have one blue eye and one brown, or many other mosaicisms. And in the additive pattern, some genes contribute substantially more than others, either because they are naturally partially dominant or because their influence is amplified by the presence of certain other genes.

Moreover, certain genes behave differently depending on whether they are inherited from the mother or from the father. The full scope of, and the reason for, this parental **genetic imprinting,** or tagging, of certain genes has yet to be determined. We know that imprinting involves hundreds of genes but does not

genetic imprinting The tendency of certain genes to be expressed differently when they are inherited from one parent rather than the other.

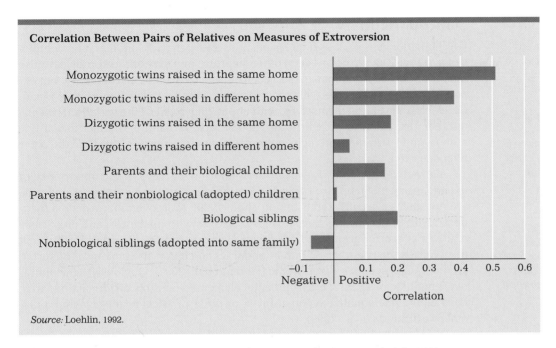

Correlation Between Pairs of Relatives on Measures of Extroversion

Source: Loehlin, 1992.

FIGURE 3.4 Both Nature and Nurture These correlations suggest that genes are quite influential in how shy or outgoing people feel. Note especially the much higher correlations between monozygotic than dizygotic twins.

? *Observational Quiz* (see answer, page 86): Can you see three indications from these correlations that the environment also affects this trait?

The study also showed that emotional expression and brain patterns in some infants changed between the ages of 4 months and 4 years. Inhibition was particularly likely to decrease if the child was placed in a good day-care center before age 2 (Fox et al., 2001). Apparently, the day-care experience, which includes regular interaction with other infants, encouraged the shy children to be more outgoing, and that was enough to shift the genetic pattern.

Alternatively, if a shy child's parents are themselves very shy and avoid contact with strangers, but nonetheless blame their child for being fearful, the child might grow up much more socially timid than if the parents were outgoing—and might be dramatically more inhibited than most other children.

The point here is not that genetically based tendencies disappear as life experiences accumulate. Shy people probably always feel a twinge of inhibition when entering a new school, for instance, or arriving at a party full of strangers—and these tendencies affect their life course. But life experiences and cultural context do make a difference. A longitudinal study in the United States found that shyness slowed down young men's career advancement, but this was not found to be the case in similar longitudinal research in Sweden. The researchers speculated on one reason for the difference:

> Swedish culture values shy, reserved behavior . . . and support systems of various sorts made it possible for Swedish boys to enter universities and careers without being assertive.
>
> *[Kerr et al., 1996]*

The same conclusion applies to other psychological traits that have strong genetic influences, including intelligence, activity level, aggression, and even religiosity. In each case, various dimensions of environment can enhance, inhibit, or alter the phenotypic expression of a person's heredity (Wachs, 2000).

Schizophrenia

Psychopathologies such as depression, antisocial behavior, phobias, and compulsions, as well as virtually every other neurotic or psychotic disorder, are also genetically based traits that are subject to strong environmental influence. For example, relatives of people with schizophrenia have a higher-than-normal risk of developing the illness themselves, with about 75 percent of the variation in schizophrenia traceable to genes (Rutter, 2002). Most striking is the fact that if one monozygotic twin develops schizophrenia, about two-thirds of the time the other twin does, too.

Viewed another way, however, the same statistic reveals the importance of the environment: One-third of monozygotic twins whose twin has schizophrenia are not themselves afflicted (Cannon et al., 1999). Moreover, many people diagnosed with schizophrenia have no close relatives with the illness, and most close relatives of schizophrenics do not themselves develop the disorder. Even if that relative was their mother or father, about 88 percent of the biological offspring are *not* diagnosed as schizophrenic (Plomin et al., 2001). Obviously, schizophrenia is multifactorial, with environmental elements—possibly a slow-acting virus, head injury, inadequate oxygen at birth, or other physical insult—playing a pivotal role (Cannon et al., 1999).

Using genetic and epidemiological techniques, scientists are advancing in the treatment and prevention of schizophrenia. It is now known that one gene that predisposes for schizophrenia is on chromosome 6 (Sherman & Waldman, 1999). This gene does not act alone: Some people with the gene do not develop schizophrenia; some people without it, do. One predisposing factor is birth during late winter, probably because some virus more prevalent in late fall or early winter can affect a vulnerable fetus (Mortensen et al., 1999).

A similar scenario is apparent for Alzheimer's disease. Early-onset Alzheimer's is genetically dominant; if a person inherits the gene, he or she develops the disease before age 50. But late-onset Alzheimer's is multifactorial. A gene on chromosome 19 comes in several alleles. People with ApoE4 are more likely to develop the disease, and those with another allele (ApoE2) almost never do. A double dose of the ApoE4 allele (one from each parent) almost always leads to Alzheimer's if the person lives long enough. Nevertheless, a few people with two copies of this destructive allele never develop the disease, because they benefit from other, protective genes and a favorable environment (Vickers et al., 2000).

Alcoholism

At various times, drug addiction, including alcoholism, has been considered a moral weakness, a personality flaw, and a sign of psychopathology (Leonard & Blane, 2000). Alcoholics were once locked up in jails or in mental institutions. When that didn't stop the problem, entire nations banned alcohol, as the United States did during Prohibition, from 1919 to 1933. People who are not alcoholics have long wondered why some people just can't stop drinking to excess, and alcoholics have kept trying and failing to stop after one or two drinks.

Now we know that some people's inherited biochemistry makes them highly susceptible to alcohol addiction. Anyone can abuse alcohol, but each person's genetic makeup creates an addictive pull that can be overpowering, extremely weak, or something in between.

Evidence for "alcoholism genes" is found in the fact that some ethnic groups (such as those from the British Isles and from northern Russia) have a much higher proportion of alcoholics than others. Biochemistry allows some people to "hold their liquor," drinking so much that they become alcoholics, and causes others, notably many East Asians, to sweat and become red-faced after just a few sips of alcohol. This embarrassing response, particularly for women, is an incentive to avoid alcohol (McGue, 1995). Some people become sleepy, others nauseated, others aggressive, and others euphoric when alcohol hits their brains, and each person's reaction increases or decreases the eagerness to have another drink.

Alcoholism is not simply a biochemical reaction; it is psychological as well as physical. Not surprisingly, genes predispose a person to have certain personality traits that correlate with abusive addictions: a quick temper, a readiness to take risks, and a high level of anxiety. Thus, alcoholism is polygenic, with almost every alcoholic inheriting a particular combination of biochemistry-affecting and temperament-affecting genes that push him or her toward abusive drinking. Originally this was more true for men than women, because women were typically discouraged by their cultures from drinking to excess. Now that women in many cultures are free to follow their genetic impulses, the heritability of alcoholism in females is more than 50 percent (Heath et al., 1997).

Alcoholism Genes and Cultural Pressures

Although no ethnic group or gender is immune to alcoholism, the disease is much more prevalent in some ethnic groups (such as the British) than others (such as the Japanese) and, until recently, was much more common in men than women. There are three reasons behind these trends: selective adaptation, religious prohibition, and public policy.

For centuries in the British Isles, beer and wine were actually healthier for people than water, because the fermentation process killed many of the harmful bacteria that thrived in drinking water. Thus, being able to drink alcohol in quantity was adaptive in most of Europe. East Asians had a different solution to the problem of bacteria: They boiled their water and drank it as tea. This explains why about half of all Asians lack the gene for an enzyme necessary to fully metabolize alcohol: Their ancestors didn't need it.

Culture counts. If a person with a strong genetic tendency toward alcoholism spends a lifetime in an environment where alcohol is unavailable (in a devout Islamic family in Saudi Arabia, for example), the genotype will never be expressed in the phenotype. Similarly, if the person lives in a nation where alcohol is readily available (such as the United States or Japan) but belongs to a religion that forbids it (Mormon or Adventist, for instance) or a gender that never gets drunk (Japanese women), they are likely to escape their genetic destiny.

In contrast, if the same person is allowed to drink frequently at an early age, the potential of the genes will be released, as is true in Russia and Australia, among other places. Further, if a culture promotes alcohol consumption, with peer pressures that lead to alcohol abuse, genetically susceptible people become active alcoholics. Even for them, personal choices dramatically alter the outcome. Some alcoholics die of the disease before they are 30; others spend decades alternating among abuse, controlled drinking, and abstinence; still others recognize the problem, get help, and are sober and productive throughout a long life.

Developmental issues also have an impact. A person is most likely to become an active alcoholic between ages 15 and 25, even though the genotype has been present since conception. Another vulnerable period is old age: When the metabolism shifts, older people are more likely to become abusive drinkers. Among some ethnic groups, alcohol is taboo for women, which is one reason Mexican-American babies almost never have fetal alcohol syndrome unless the mother was raised in the United States and became acculturated. Among some American Indian tribes on reservations, alcohol is forbidden; among other tribes, it is readily available, with disastrous results for all who are affected—especially newborns, teenagers, and the elderly.

All Alcoholics? Probably not. These farm workers in Provence, France, pause for a meal—complete with bread, wine, glasses, and a tablecloth. Drinking alcohol with friends and food is not a sign of alcoholism; habitually drinking alone is. Of course, cultural pressure to drink creates problems, which is one reason France has a high rate of cirrhosis, but this might not be a pressure group: One of the two bottles is water.

Can public policy have any effect here? Apparently yes. In the United States between 1980 and 1990, alcohol consumption per capita was reduced by 10 percent. Moreover, between 1980 and 1999, stricter enforcement of drunk-driving laws reduced the number of fatal accidents involving drunk drivers—from 26 percent to 17 percent overall and from 24 percent to 14 percent among 16- to 20-year-olds (U.S. Bureau of the Census, 2001). Workplace employee-assistance programs and insurance policies that consider alcoholism as a treatable disease have also had an effect, but this seems to have diminished recently. Drinking and alcohol-related problems were at the same level or worse at the end of the 1990s as at the beginning (Greenfield et al., 2000; Midanik & Greenfield, 2000).

These examples—painful shyness, schizophrenia, and alcoholism—make it quite clear that genes, the prenatal and postnatal biochemical environment, and the more distant social environment are all powerful influences on human development. Their complex interaction is involved in every aspect of development at every age and in every era. And in each person's life, the results of earlier genetic–environmental interactions guide further development. That said, we must also stress that the outcome is never predetermined, even at age 70 or 80. As one biologist explains:

> At every stage of development, from moment to moment, the growing organism is interacting with a varying environment; and the form of each interaction depends on the outcome of earlier interactions. This process is indescribably complicated—which is why it is never described and rarely even acknowledged. The extreme of intricacy is reached in human development, for the conditions which we and our children experience are often the products of deliberate, sometimes intelligent, choice.
>
> *[Barnett, 1998]*

Response for College Students Who Enjoy a Party (from page 86): Your friend's ability to "hold his liquor" is an ominous sign; his body probably metabolizes alcohol differently from the way most other people's do. Alcoholics are often deceptive about their own drinking habits, so you might ask him about the drinking habits of his relatives. If he has either alcoholics or abstainers in the family, you should be concerned, since both are signs of a genetic problem with alcohol. Ask him whether he can have only one drink a day for a month. Alcoholics find such restricted drinking virtually impossible.

On a practical level, this means we must not ignore the genetic component in any given trait—whether it be something wonderful, such as a wacky sense of humor; something fearful, such as a violent temper; or something quite ordinary, such as the tendency to get bored with our routine. However, we must not forget that the environment affects every trait, in ways that change as maturational, cultural, and historical processes unfold, with an impact that can be chosen or changed, depending on the people and society. Genes are always part of the tale, influential on every page, but they never determine the plot or the final paragraph.

Inherited Abnormalities

We now give particular attention to genetic and chromosomal abnormalities, for three reasons:

- Disruptions of normal development provide insight into the complexities of genetic interactions.
- Knowledge of the origins of genetic and chromosomal abnormalities suggests how to reduce or limit their harmful consequences.
- Misinformation and prejudice compound the problems of those who are affected by chromosomal and genetic abnormalities.

Chromosomal Miscounts

Sometimes when gametes are formed, the 46 chromosomes divide unevenly, producing a sperm or an ovum that does not have the normal complement of exactly 23 chromosomes. If such a gamete fuses with a normal gamete, the result is a zygote with more or fewer than 46 chromosomes. This is not unusual. An estimated half of all zygotes have an odd number of chromosomes. One count found 9,080 different chromosomal abnormalities in which part of or a whole chromosome was missing or misplaced (Borgaonkar, 1997). Most such zygotes do not even begin to develop, and most of the rest never come to term—usually because a **spontaneous abortion**, or *miscarriage,* occurs. About 5 percent of stillborn (dead-at-birth) babies also have more than 46 chromosomes (Miller & Therman, 2001).

Once in about every 200 births, a baby survives with 45, 47, or, rarely, 48 or 49 chromosomes. In every case, the chromosomal abnormality leads to a recognizable *syndrome,* a cluster of distinct characteristics that tend to occur together. In many cases—for instance, trisomy-18 (Edwards') and trisomy-13 (Patau) syndromes—the newborn lives for only a short time.

Prenatal Detection

Over the past 30 years, researchers have refined prenatal tests that are used selectively to detect whether chromosomal abnormalities are indeed present (Goetzel & D'Alton, 2001).

Alpha-Fetoprotein Assay A sample of the mother's blood can be tested for the level of alpha-fetoprotein (AFP), an indicator of neural-tube defects, multiple embryos, or, as Martha and John feared in this chapter's Case to Study, Down syndrome. About 10 percent of all pregnant women exhibit high or low AFP, but most of these are false alarms, caused by miscalculation of the age of the fetus or some other normal variation. The test itself is not risky, but unexpected AFP levels indicate that additional testing is needed, as Martha and John learned.

Ultrasound A sonogram, or ultrasound image, uses high-frequency sound waves to produce a "picture" of the fetus. If done early in pregnancy, sonograms can reveal problems such as an abnormally small head or other body malformations, excess spinal fluid accumulating on the brain, and several diseases (for instance, of the kidney). In addition, sonograms are used to diagnose twins, to estimate fetal age, to determine the position of the placenta, and to reveal the rate of fetal growth. No known risks to mother or fetus result from sonograms, unlike the X-ray that it replaced. Sonograms are routine in England and Canada, but in the United States they are used only about half the time. The reasons for the differences are cultural and political, in that England and Canada, but not the United States, provide free prenatal care to everyone (Heyman & Henriksen, 2001).

spontaneous abortion The naturally occurring termination of a pregnancy before the fetus is fully developed. (Also called *miscarriage.*)

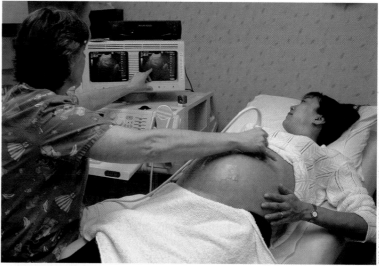

CHAD EHLERS / INDEX STOCK IMAGERY

There's Your Baby For many parents, their first glimpse of their future child is an ultrasound image. The outline of the fetus's head and body are visible once an expert points them out. Measuring the width of the head is the best way to estimate fetal age, and the presence of more than one heartbeat is the first signal that a multiple birth is expected.

Amniocentesis In amniocentesis, about half an ounce of the fluid inside the placenta is withdrawn through the mother's abdominal wall. The fluid contains sloughed-off fetal cells that can be cultured and analyzed to detect chromosomal abnormalities as well as many other genetic and prenatal problems. The amniotic fluid also reveals the sex of the fetus (useful knowledge if an X-linked disorder is likely). Amniocentesis cannot be safely performed until midpregnancy (at least 14 weeks), and many detected abnormalities have uncertain consequences. Both these facts make the woman's decision about continuing the pregnancy very difficult. About once in 200 pregnancies, amniocentesis causes a spontaneous abortion.

Chorionic Villi Sampling In chorionic villi sampling (CVS), a sample of the placental tissue that surrounds the fetus is obtained and analyzed. This test provides the same information as amniocentesis, but CVS is usually performed earlier, at about the 10th week of pregnancy (Goetzel & D'Alton, 2001). This benefit comes at a price, however: Compared to amniocentesis, CVS is slightly less accurate and three times as likely to cause a spontaneous abortion.

Pre-Implantation Testing New techniques allow genetic testing to occur even earlier than CVS. If conception occurs in vitro ("in glass," or in a laboratory dish, with sperm being added to ova that have been surgically removed from the mother), one cell can be removed from each zygote at the four- or eight-cell stage and analyzed genetically. If a possible genetic defect is *not* found, the remaining developing cells can be inserted into the uterus. About 25 percent of the time, the cell mass implants, grows, and becomes a newborn without the chromosomal or genetic abnormality that the couple sought to avoid.

Pre-implantation testing is controversial and unusual, available only in specialized centers that screen for about 20 of the most commonly inherited conditions (Simpson et al., 1999). But some couples would not risk reproduction without the assurance of pre-implantation analysis. Experimenting on lower animals, researchers have added a gene or chromosome at the pre-implantation stage to replace a defective one—a measure not yet performed on human embryos.

Risks and Benefits of Testing The ideal (not always attained) is to reserve testing for suspected cases of serious, well-understood conditions, for which diagnosis is quite accurate and treatment or prevention is available (Wingerson, 1998). Unfortunately, uncertain diagnosis, especially of unusual chromosomal abnormalities, means that many pregnant couples are faced with puzzling results (either positive or negative) or ambiguous findings. Doctors usually decide which tests should be done and when, and prospective parents are often unprepared to interpret the data. As a consequence, nations differ in when and to whom prenatal tests are offered, and couples with identical results sometimes make opposite decisions.

In fact, doctors vary widely in the way they present prenatal tests to prospective parents. For instance, in one British hospital that required doctors to offer genetic tests to all pregnant patients, one doctor spoke to a patient of the "tremendous amount of heartache if we get a false positive" (quoted in Heyman & Henriksen, 2001, p. 100). Another told a patient to ask herself, "How do I feel about having a Down syndrome baby?" (p. 145) and then work back from there to decide about getting tested. Not surprisingly, the patient of the first doctor decided to have no genetic tests, and the second doctor's patient had amniocentesis. In this hospital, women over age 35 were warned about their increased risk of having a baby with Down syndrome but were not told about other relatively common syndromes or serious complications. Concern focuses on the problem that is lifelong and more readily dealt with by abortion, not on those whose victims die in early infancy or those that are apparent after birth.

As for Martha and John, even though their second AFP test indicated that their fetus was unlikely to have Down syndrome, Martha still had a gut feeling that something was wrong. She volunteered for amniocentesis and got bad news: Her fetus had the extra chromosome of Down syndrome after all. She decided not to abort and gave birth to Adam. Years later, when Martha was talking to a group about her decision to continue her pregnancy, a woman in the audience said that she had been in the same situation but had made the "wrong" decision. Martha replied that there was no right or wrong decision; every decision about prenatal testing is difficult, and each choice has costs (Beck, 1999). (We return to John and Martha in Chapter 4.) Let's look at Down syndrome in more detail.

Down Syndrome

Down syndrome is the most common extra-chromosome condition: There is a third chromosome at the twenty-first pair, which is why the syndrome is also called trisomy-21. Most embryos and newborns with trisomy-21 die. A few decades ago, almost all such children died in early childhood, but advances in treatment mean that now most survive well into adulthood (though seldom into old age).

Some 300 distinct characteristics can result from the presence of that extra chromosome, but no individual with Down syndrome is quite like another, either in symptoms or in their severity. Despite this variability, almost all people with trisomy-21 have certain specific facial characteristics—a thick tongue, round face, slanted eyes—as well as distinctive hands, feet, and fingerprints. Many also have hearing problems, heart abnormalities, muscle weakness, and short stature.

In terms of neurological development, almost all individuals with Down syndrome experience mental slowness. Their eventual intellectual attainment

MACPHERSON

Earning His Daily Bread This man with Down syndrome works in a cafeteria, and, by all reports, is a steady, conscientious employee.

? *Observational Quiz* (see answer, page 93): Visible are four signs of Down syndrome; not visible (and perhaps not present) are at least four other signs. Name all eight.

varies: Some are severely retarded; others are average or even above average. Usually—but not always—those who are raised at home and given appropriate cognitive stimulation progress to the point of being able to read and write and care for themselves (and often much more), while those who are institutionalized tend to be, and to remain, much more retarded (Carr, 1995).

Many young children with trisomy-21 are unusually sweet-tempered; they are less likely to cry or complain than most other children. Temperament may be a liability, however. If a Down syndrome child is more passive and less motivated to learn than others, that characteristic produces a slower learning rate and a lower IQ as time goes on (Wishart, 1999).

People with Down syndrome age faster than other adults. For them, the ailments of old age begin in middle adulthood (Hassold & Patterson, 1999). By that time, they "almost invariably" develop Alzheimer's disease, which severely impairs their limited communication skills and makes them much less compliant (Czech et al., 2000). They are also prone to a host of other problems more commonly found in older persons, including cataracts and certain forms of cancer. Consequently, their mortality rate begins to rise at about age 35, and their life expectancy is lower than that of other mentally retarded adults and much lower than that of average people (Strauss & Eyman, 1996).

This generally pessimistic description, however, does not reflect the actual experience of many individuals with Down syndrome. It is true that all have language difficulties, and many have other serious medical problems. But they may still become happy, proud, and successful young adults. One gave the following advice to others:

> You may have to work hard, but don't ever give up. Always remember that you are important. You are special in your own unique way. And one of the best ways to feel good about yourself is to share yourself with someone else.
>
> [Christi Todd, quoted in Hassold & Patterson, 1999]

Abnormalities of the Twenty-Third Pair

Every newborn infant has at least one X chromosome in the twenty-third pair; an embryo cannot develop without an X. However, about 1 in every 500 infants either is missing a sex chromosome (thus the X stands alone) or has two or more other sex chromosomes in addition to the first X. These abnormalities usually impair cognitive and psychosocial development as well as sexual maturation. In many cases, treatment with hormone supplements can alleviate some of the physical problems, and special education may remedy some of the deficits related to psychological functioning.

The specific features of any syndrome vary considerably from one individual to another. In fact, in many cases, the presence of abnormal sex chromosomes goes undetected until a seemingly normal childhood is followed by an abnormally delayed puberty. This is particularly likely for a boy who has *Klinefelter syndrome, XXY*. Such a boy will be a little slow in elementary school, but it is usually not until puberty—when his penis does not grow and fat begins to accumulate around his breasts—that his parents wonder if something is seriously wrong.

The Fragile X One of the most common syndromes associated with the sex chromosomes is **fragile-X syndrome**, which is genetic in origin. In some individuals, part of the X chromosome is attached to the rest of it by such a thin string of molecules that it seems about to break off (hence the name of the syndrome). This abnormality in the chromosome is caused by the mutation of a single gene, which has more than 200 repetitions of the "word" CGG (Plomin et al., 2001). The mutation involved in the fragile X intensifies as it is passed from one generation to the next, with more repetitions.

fragile-X syndrome A genetic disorder in which part of the X chromosome is attached to the rest of it by a very thin string of molecules; often produces mental deficiency in males who inherit it.

Of the females who carry it, most are normal (perhaps because they also carry one normal X chromosome), but one-third show some mental deficiency. Among the males who inherit a fragile-X chromosome, about 20 percent are apparently completely normal, about 33 percent are somewhat retarded, and the rest are severely retarded. The last group is relatively large: The cognitive deficits caused by fragile-X syndrome represent the most common form of inherited mental retardation. In addition to cognitive problems, the fragile X is often associated with inadequate social skills and extreme shyness (Dykens et al., 1994; Hagerman, 1996).

The wide range of effects produced by this disorder is somewhat unusual. However, the more we learn about other abnormal genes, chromosomes, and syndromes, the more diversity we find in their effects. For example, schizophrenia, as you already learned, is genetic, but the specific form (e.g., hebephrenic, paranoid) is not (Plomin et al., 2001).

Causes of Chromosomal Abnormalities

Chromosomal abnormalities are caused by many factors, some genetic and some environmental (such as the parents' exposure to excessive radiation). However, the variable that most often correlates with chromosomal abnormalities is maternal age. According to one detailed estimate, a 20-year-old woman has about 1 chance in 800 of carrying a fetus with Down syndrome; a 39-year-old woman has 1 chance in 67; and a 44-year-old woman has 1 chance in 16 (see Appendix A for the month-by-month, age-specific incidence).

Other chromosomal abnormalities are less common, but virtually all follow an age-related pattern (Snijders & Nicolaides, 1996). Because about half of all fetuses with these abnormalities are aborted spontaneously and some others are aborted by choice, the actual birth rate of infants with chromosomal abnormalities is lower than these statistics would suggest. Many doctors recommend prenatal testing for chromosomal abnormalities whenever a pregnant woman is 35 or older, although this step is controversial.

Harmful Genes

While relatively few people are born with abnormal chromosomes, everyone has at least 20 genes (usually additive or recessive) that could produce serious diseases or handicaps in the next generation (see Table 3.3.). Most of the 7,000 *known* genetic disorders are dominant, since whenever a dominant gene is inherited, it is apparent in the person's phenotype. With a few exceptions, dominant disorders are not seriously disabling because people with disabling dominant disorders are unlikely to have children and thus are unlikely to pass their genes on. One exception is *Huntington's chorea,* a central nervous system disease caused by a genetic mutation (again, too many triplets, this time more than 35 CAGs) that remains inactive until adulthood, by which time a person could have had many children (as the original Mr. Huntington did).

Another dominant disorder that can be severe is *Tourette syndrome,* which is quite common but variable. About 30 percent of those who inherit the gene exhibit recurrent uncontrollable tics and explosive outbursts of verbal obscenities. The remaining 70 percent experience milder symptoms, such as an occasional twitch that is barely noticeable and a postponable impulse to speak inappropriately.

Recessive and multifactorial disorders are less likely to be recognized but actually claim many more victims, largely because such disorders can pass unchecked (and unnoticed) from carrier to carrier for generations. As a result, carrier status can easily become widespread in a population. Among the more commonly known recessive disorders are cystic fibrosis, thalassemia, and sickle-cell anemia, with as

!Answer to Observational Quiz (from page 91): Four visible signs: round head, short stature, large hands, slanted eye sockets. Not visible: mental retardation, heart abnormalities, muscle weakness, thick tongue.

TABLE 3.3 Common Genetic Diseases and Conditions

Name	Description	Prognosis	Probable Inheritance	Incidence*	Carrier Detection†	Prenatal Detection?
Albinism	No melanin; person is very blond and pale.	Normal, but must avoid sun damage.	Recessive.	Rare overall; 1 in 8 Hopi Indians is a carrier.	No	No
Alzheimer's disease	Loss of memory and increasing mental impairment.	Eventual death, often after years of dependency.	Early onset— dominant; after age 60— multifactorial.	Fewer than 1 in 100 middle-aged adults; 20 percent of all adults over age 80.	Yes, for some genes; ApoE4 allele increases incidence	No
Breast cancer	Tumors in breast that can spread.	With early treatment, most are cured; without it, death within 3 years.	BRCA1 and BRCA2 genes seem dominant; other cases, multifactorial.	1 woman in 8 (only 20 percent of breast cancer patients have BRCA1 or 2).	Yes, for BRCA1 and BRCA2	No
Cleft palate, cleft lip	The two sides of the upper lip or palate are not joined.	Correctable by surgery.	Multifactorial.	1 in every 700 births; more common in Asian-Americans and American Indians.	No	Yes
Club foot	The foot and ankle are twisted.	Correctable by surgery.	Multifactorial.	1 in every 200 births; more common in boys.	No	Yes
Cystic fibrosis	Mucous obstructions, especially in lungs and digestive organs.	Most live to middle adulthood.	Recessive gene; also spontaneous mutations.	1 in 2,500; 1 in 20 European-Americans is a carrier.	Sometimes	Yes, in most cases
Diabetes	Abnormal sugar metabolism because of insufficient insulin.	Early onset (Type I) fatal without insulin; for adult onset (Type II), variable risks.	Multifactorial; for adult onset, environment is crucial.	Type I: 1 in 500 births; more common in American Indians and African-Americans. Type II: 1 adult in 10.	No	No
Deafness (congenital)	Inability to hear from birth on.	Deaf children can learn sign language and live normally.	Multifactorial; some forms are recessive.	1 in 1,000 births; more common in people from Middle East.	No	No
Hemophilia	Absence of clotting factor in blood.	Death from internal bleeding; blood transfusions prevent damage.	X-linked recessive; also spontaneous mutations.	1 in 10,000 males; royal families of England, Russia, and Germany had it.	Yes	Yes
Hydro-cephalus	Obstruction causes excess water in the brain.	Brain damage and death; surgery can make normal life possible.	Multifactorial.	1 in every 100 births.	No	Yes

*Incidence statistics vary from country to country; those given here are for the United States. All these diseases can occur in any ethnic group. When certain groups have a high or low incidence, it is noted here.
†Studying the family tree can help geneticists spot a possible carrier of many genetic diseases or, in some cases, a definite carrier. However, here "Yes" means that a carrier can be detected even without knowledge of family history.

Name	Description	Prognosis	Probable Inheritance	Incidence*	Carrier Detection†	Prenatal Detection?
Muscular dystrophy (13 diseases)	Weakening of muscles.	Inability to walk, move; wasting away and sometimes death.	Duchenne's is X-linked; other forms are recessive or multifactorial.	1 in every 3,500 males develops Duchenne's.	Yes, for some forms	Yes, for some forms
Neural-tube defects (open spine)	Anencephaly (parts of the brain missing) or spina bifida (lower spine not closed).	Anencephalic— severe retardation; spina bifida— poor lower body control.	Multifactorial; defect occurs in first weeks of pregnancy.	Anencephaly—1 in 1,000 births; spina bifida—3 in 1,000. More common in Welsh and Scots.	No	Yes
Phenylketo–nuria (PKU)	Abnormal digestion of protein.	Mental retardation, hyperactivity; preventable by diet.	Recessive.	1 in 10,000 births; 1 in 100 European-Americans is a carrier; especially Norwegians and Irish.	Yes	Yes
Pyloric stenosis	Overgrowth of muscle in intestine.	Vomiting, loss of weight, eventual death; correctable by surgery.	Multifactorial.	1 male in 200, 1 female in 1,000; less common in African-Americans.	No	No
Schizo-phrenia	Severely distorted thought processes.	No cure; drugs hospitalization, psychotherapy, relieve symptoms.	Multifactorial.	1 in 100 people develop it by early adulthood.	No	No
Sickle-cell anemia	Abnormal blood cells.	Possible painful "crisis"; heart and kidney failure; treatable with drugs.	Recessive.	1 in 500 African-Americans; 1 in 10 African-Americans and 1 in 20 Latinos is a carrier.	Yes	Yes
Tay-Sachs disease	Enzyme disease.	Apparently healthy infant becomes weaker, usually dying by age 5.	Recessive.	1 in 4,000 births; 1 in 30 American Jews and 1 in 20 French-Canadians are carriers.	Yes	Yes
Thalassemia	Abnormal blood cells.	Paleness and listlessness, low resistance to infections.	Recessive.	1 in 10 Greek-, Italian-, Thai-, and Indian-Americans is a carrier.	Yes	Yes
Tourette syndrome	Uncontrollable tics, body jerking, verbal obscenities.	Often imperceptible in children; worsens with age.	Dominant, but variable penetrance.	1 in 250 births.	Sometimes	No

Sources: Briley & Sulser, 2001; Klug & Cummings, 2000; Mange & Mange, 1999; McKusick, 1994; National Academy of Sciences, 1994; Shahin et al., 2002.

genetic counseling A process of consultation and testing that enables individuals to learn about their genetic heritage, including conditions that might harm any children they may have.

many as 1 in 12 North Americans being a carrier for one or another of the three. Most genetic research has been done in Europe and North America; undoubtedly, many other dominant and recessive conditions are prevalent in Asia, Africa, and South America that have not yet been named and described (Wright, 1998).

Genetic counseling, which is the process of testing a person to discover what genetic conditions are present on the genotype and then advising that person how likely the condition is to occur in his or her offspring's phenotype, is widely available in developed nations. Often, but not always, a couple can learn what their chances are of bearing a child with a specific genetic disease and can seek advice about how to prevent such an outcome. In the United States, genetic counselors try to follow two ethical guidelines.

■ The results are kept confidential, beyond the reach of insurance companies and out of public records.
■ The final decision is made by the clients, not by the counselor, whose job is to provide facts and options, not to impose values and conclusions.

A problem arises in interpreting these guidelines, however. Should test results be kept confidential, even from other family members who are directly affected? And should a client be allowed to make a decision that the counselor believes is unethical? Most counselors answer "yes" to both questions, but many members of the public answer "no." The disagreement is explained in the following Changing Policy feature.

Changing Policy

Genetic Counseling: Decisions and Values

Until recently, after the birth of a child with a serious or even fatal genetic or chromosomal disorder, couples thought fate rather than genetics was to blame. They often went on to have more children, who were likely to have the same problem or be carriers of it.

Today, many couples worry about their genes even before they marry. Almost every adult has a relative with a serious disease that may well be genetic. Genetic counseling can help relieve such worries, although it also requires careful decision making by the prospective parents.

In general, prenatal, preconceptual, or even prenuptial genetic counseling and testing are recommended for:

■ Individuals who have a parent, sibling, or child with a serious genetic condition
■ Couples who have a history of early spontaneous abortions, stillbirths, or infertility
■ Couples who are from the same ethnic group or subgroup—especially if the group is a small one and most particularly if the couple are close relatives
■ Women age 35 or older

When a couple begins genetic counseling, the counselor constructs a family history, charting patterns of health and

sickness over the generations, particularly with regard to early deaths and unexplained symptoms. The counselor then explains specific conditions based on age, ethnicity, and genetic history and discusses what the options will be if testing reveals high risk of serious conditions. This last step is crucial; as options increase, so do choices. The couple then decides whether to proceed with genetic testing.

There is an interesting paradox here. Genetic counselors, scientists, and the general public usually believe it best to proceed with testing because some information is better than none. However, high-risk individuals (who are most likely to hear bad news) do not necessarily agree, especially if the truth might jeopardize the marriage, health insurance coverage, or the chances of parenthood (Duster, 1999). If the genetic tests would reveal only the risk to the adult, not to a prospective child, most high-risk adults say they would rather not know about their own fate.

As a result of testing, couples can know the approximate odds that their prospective child will have a serious genetic problem. Of course, odds are risk assessments, not guarantees. If both partners have the recessive gene for sickle-cell anemia, for instance, and the couple plans to have several children, then all of them, some of them, or none of them

KEY TERMS

gamete (p. 69)
zygote (p. 69)
gene (p. 69)
chromosome (p. 69)
genetic code (p. 70)
Human Genome Project (p. 70)
allele (p. 71)
twenty-third pair (p. 72)
XX (p. 72)

XY (p. 72)
monozygotic twins (p. 75)
dizygotic twins (p. 76)
infertile (p. 76)
assisted reproductive
  technology (ART) (p. 76)
in vitro fertilization (IVF)
  (p. 76)

polygenic (p. 78)
multifactorial (p. 78)
genotype (p. 78)
phenotype (p. 78)
carrier (p. 78)
additive gene (p. 79)
dominant gene (p. 79)
recessive gene (p. 79)

X-linked (p. 79)
genetic imprinting (p. 80)
behavioral genetics (p. 81)
molecular genetics (p. 83)
spontaneous abortion (p. 89)
fragile-X syndrome (p. 92)
genetic counseling (p. 96)

KEY QUESTIONS

1. How many zygotes, genes, and chromosomes make one person?

2. How can detectives use genetic information to prove a person guilty or innocent of a crime?

3. How is genetic diversity among people ensured, and why is diversity important for the human species?

4. How do alleles affect human development?

5. What is the difference between genotype and phenotype?

6. What are the differences and similarities between the two types of twins?

7. Why does a person's sex affect the expression of a recessive X-linked gene?

8. What research strategies are used to distinguish genetic from environmental influences?

9. How can environment influence physical traits, such as height and weight, that are strongly genetic?

10. Why is alcoholism more common in some nations than in others?

11. Compare the severity and frequency of human dominant and recessive disorders.

12. What factors affect a child's odds of being born with genetic abnormalities?

13. Why might one couple with a Down Syndrome fetus get an abortion and another continue with the pregnancy?

14. Why are privacy and confidentiality important values for genetic counselors?

Prenatal Development and Birth

태아정신

germinal period The first two weeks of development after conception; characterized by rapid cell division and the beginning of cell differentiation.

embryonic period Approximately the third through the eighth week after conception, the period during which the rudimentary forms of all anatomical structures develop.

fetal period The ninth week after conception until birth, the period during which the organs grow in size and complexity.

O ur primary focus in this chapter is on the astounding biological transformation from a single-cell zygote to a fully formed baby. As you will see, this is a social, not just biological, event. The mother-to-be's health habits and activities, the community's laws and practices, and the culture's customs regarding birth are just some of the myriad contextual factors that make some newborns—those fortunate enough to be born to certain mothers in certain communities and cultures—much better prepared for a long and happy life than others. Fathers also can make a difference, and so can the fetus itself—especially if the mother is particularly concerned about its well-being.

From Zygote to Newborn

The most dramatic and extensive transformation of life occurs from the beginning to the end of the prenatal period. The entire process is awesome, but to make it easier to study, human growth before birth is often divided into three main periods. The first 2 weeks of development are called the **germinal period**; the third through the eighth week is the **embryonic period**; and the ninth week until birth is the **fetal period**. (Alternative terms for these and other milestones of pregnancy are discussed in Table 4.1 on page 104.)

Germinal: The First 14 Days

You learned in Chapter 3 that, within hours after conception, the one-cell zygote, traveling slowly down the fallopian tube toward the uterus, begins the process of cell division and growth (see Figure 4.1 on page 104). At about the eight-cell stage the process of differentiation begins. The cells take on distinct characteristics and gravitate toward particular locations that foreshadow the types of cells they will become. One unmistakable sign of differentiation occurs about a week after conception, when the multiplying cells (now numbering more than 100) separate into two distinct masses. The outer cells form a protective circle that will become the *placenta* (the organ that surrounds and protects the developing creature), and the inner cells form a nucleus that will become the embryo.

germinal
2+
embryo 3+
fetal 9+

266 days
38 weeks
9 month

trimester

TABLE 4.1 Timing and Terminology

Popular and professional books use various confusing phrases to segment pregnancy. This may help.

- *Beginning of pregnancy*: In this text, pregnancy begins at conception, which is also the starting point of *gestational age*. However, the organism does not become an *embryo* until about two weeks later, and pregnancy does not affect the woman (and cannot be confirmed by blood or urine testing) until implantation. Paradoxically, many obstetricians date the onset of pregnancy from the date on which the woman's last menstrual period (LMP) began, about 14 days *before* conception.

- *Length of pregnancy*: Full-term pregnancies last 266 days, or 38 weeks, or 9 months. If the LMP is used as the start, pregnancy lasts 40 weeks, sometimes expressed as 10 lunar months.

- *Trimesters*: Instead of *germinal period, embryonic period,* and *fetal period,* some writers divide pregnancy into three-month periods called *trimesters*. Months 1, 2, and 3 are called the *first trimester;* months 4, 5, and 6, the *second trimester;* and months 7, 8, and 9 the *third trimester.*

- *Due date*: Although doctors assign a specific due date (based on the woman's LMP), only 5 percent of babies are born on their exact date. Babies born between three weeks before and up to two weeks after are considered "on time." Babies born earlier are called *preterm;* babies born later are called *post-term.*

implantation Beginning about a week after conception, the burrowing of the organism into the lining of the uterus, where it can be nourished and protected during growth.

The first task of the outer cells is to achieve **implantation,** that is, to embed themselves in the nurturant environment of the uterus. The cells nestle into the uterine lining, rupturing tiny blood vessels in order to obtain nourishment and to build a connective web of membranes and blood vessels linking the mother and the developing organism. This connective web allows the organism to grow over the next nine months or so.

Implantation is far from automatic, however. At least 60 percent of all natural conceptions and 70 percent of all in vitro conceptions that are inserted into the uterus fail to properly implant (see Table 4.2; Bentley & Mascie-Taylor, 2000). Most new life ends even before the embryo begins to form or the woman suspects she is pregnant.

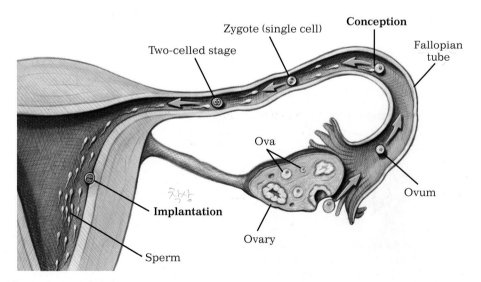

FIGURE 4.1 The Most Dangerous Journey In the first 10 days after conception, the organism does not increase in size because it is not yet nourished by the mother. However, the number of cells increases rapidly as the organism prepares for implantation.

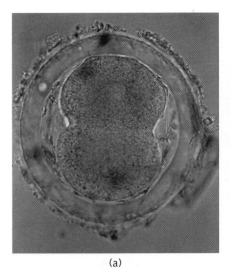
(a)

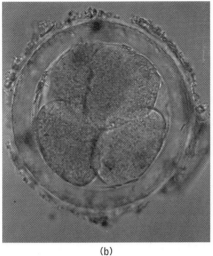
(b)

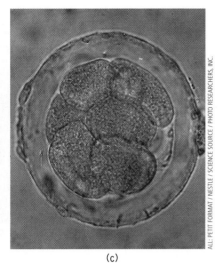
(c)

ALL: PETIT FORMAT / NESTLE / SCIENCE SOURCE / PHOTO RESEARCHERS, INC.

First Stages of the Germinal Period
The original zygote as it divides into (a) two cells, (b) four cells, and (c) eight cells. Occasionally at this early stage, the cells separate completely, forming the beginning of monozygotic twins, quadruplets, or octuplets.

TABLE 4.2 **Vulnerability During Prenatal Development**

The Germinal Period
At least 60 percent of all developing organisms fail to grow or implant properly, and thus do not survive the germinal period. Most of these organisms are grossly abnormal.

The Embryonic Period
About 20 percent of all embryos are aborted spontaneously, most often because of chromosomal abnormalities.

The Fetal Period
About 5 percent of all fetuses are aborted spontaneously before viability at 22 weeks or are stillborn, defined as born dead after 22 weeks.

Birth
About 31 percent of all zygotes grow and survive to become living newborn babies.

Sources: Bentley & Mascie-Taylor, 2000; Moore & Persaud, 1998.

Embryo: From the Third Through the Eighth Week

The start of the third week after conception initiates the *embryonic period,* during which the formless mass of cells becomes a distinct being—not yet recognizably human but worthy of a new name, *embryo.* First the developing organism begins differentiating into three layers, which eventually form key body systems. Then a perceptible sign of body formation appears, a fold in the outer layer of cells. At 22 days after conception this fold becomes the **neural tube,** which will later develop into the central nervous system, including the brain and spinal column (Larsen, 1998).

The head starts to take shape in the fourth week after conception. It begins as a featureless protrusion. Eyes, ears, nose, and mouth start to form within days. Also in the fourth week, a blood vessel that will become the heart begins to pulsate, making the cardiovascular system the first to show any activity. By the fifth week, buds that will become arms and legs appear, and a tail-like appendage extends from the spine. The upper arms and then forearms, palms, and webbed

neural tube A fold of outer embryonic cells that appears about three weeks after conception and later develops into the central nervous system.

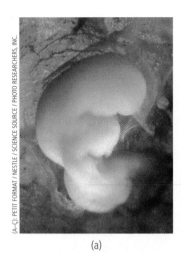
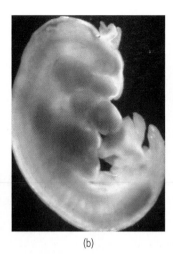
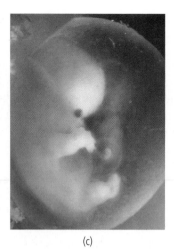
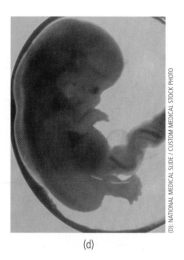

(a)   (b)   (c)   (d)

(A–C): PETIT FORMAT / NESTLE / SCIENCE SOURCE / PHOTO RESEARCHERS, INC.

(D): NATIONAL MEDICAL SLIDE / CUSTOM MEDICAL STOCK PHOTO

The Embryonic Period (a) At 4 weeks past conception, the embryo is only about ⅛ inch (3 millimeters) long, but already the head (top right) has taken shape. (b) At 5 weeks past conception, the embryo has grown to twice the size it was at 4 weeks. Its primitive heart, which has been pulsing for a week now, is visible, as is what appears to be a primitive tail, which will soon be enclosed by skin and protective tissue at the tip of the backbone (the coccyx). (c) By 7 weeks, the organism is somewhat less than an inch (2½ centimeters) long. Eyes, nose, the digestive system, and even the first stage of toe formation can be seen. (d) At 8 weeks, the 1-inch-long organism is clearly recognizable as a human fetus.

fingers appear about 5 weeks after conception. Legs, feet, and webbed toes, in that order, emerge a few days later, each having the beginning of a skeletal structure (Larsen, 1998).

At 8 weeks after conception, the embryo weighs about 1/30 ounce (1 gram) and is about 1 inch (2½ centimeters) long. The head has become more rounded, and the features of the face have formed. The embryo has all the basic organs and body parts (except sex organs) of a human being, including elbows and knees. The fingers and toes separate (at 52 and 54 days after conception, respectively), and the "tail" is no longer visible, having been incorporated into the lower spine at about 55 days.

Fetus: From the Ninth Week Until Birth

The organism is called a *fetus* from the ninth week after conception until it is born. That one name covers tremendous change, from a tiny, sexless creature smaller than the final joint of your thumb to a boy or girl who could nestle comfortably in your arms. We will now describe some of the details of this transformation.

The Third Month

Although the zygote already has a pair of chromosomes that determines sex, it seems as if sex organs are an afterthought in biological development. Not until the third month do the sex organs take discernible shape. Earlier, at the sixth week, the *indifferent gonad* appears, a cluster of cells that can develop into male or female sex organs. Through the seventh week, males and females are virtually identical (Larsen, 1998). Then, if the embryo is male (XY), the SRY gene on the Y chromosome sends a biochemical signal that initiates the development of male sexual organs. If the embryo is female (XX), no such signal is sent and the indifferent gonad develops female sex organs—first the vagina and uterus and then the external structures (Koopman et al., 1991).

Sex organs take several more weeks to develop, but by the twelfth week after conception the external genital organs are fully formed. Another sex-related development is that the newly formed organs begin to send hormones to the developing brain, directing small variations, depending on the sex of the developing person. Most functions of the brain are gender-neutral, and all sex-related functions are epigenetic, depending on internal and external factors that continue throughout life. However, the sex differences in brain organization occur, for the most part, in mid-gestation (Cameron, 2001).

are two critical periods. The first is at the very beginning of pregnancy, when stress during the germinal period can impede implantation. The second critical period is toward the end of pregnancy, when the fetus most needs to gain weight and when the cortex of the brain is developing. At this time the fetus is particularly vulnerable to damage that can cause learning disabilities. Further, near the end of pregnancy, instability of the mother's body systems (for instance, if she has chills or the shakes) can loosen the placenta or cause hormonal changes, both of which can precipitate birth.

Note that for behavioral teratogens there is no safe period. The brain and nervous system can be harmed throughout prenatal development and infancy.

Amount of Exposure

A second important factor is the dose and/or frequency of exposure. Some teratogens have a **threshold effect;** that is, they are virtually harmless until exposure reaches a certain level, at which point they "cross the threshold" from being innocuous to being damaging. Indeed, a few substances, such as vitamin A, are actually beneficial in small amounts but fiercely teratogenic in large quantities (Kraft & Willhite, 1997). Vitamin A is an essential part of a good prenatal diet, so vitamin A is a component of most multivitamins for pregnant women; but more than 10,000 units per day may be too much.

For most teratogens, experts are reluctant to specify a threshold below which the substance is safe. One reason is that many teratogens have an **interaction effect;** that is, one poison intensifies the effects of another. Alcohol, tobacco, and marijuana are among the substances that interact, together doing more harm than any one of them would do alone.

Genetic Vulnerability

A third factor that determines whether a specific teratogen will be harmful, and to what extent, is the developing organism's genes. When a woman carrying dizygotic twins drinks alcohol, for example, the twins' blood alcohol levels are exactly equal; yet one may be more severely affected than the other (Maier et al., 1996). This difference probably involves a gene affecting a specific enzyme (alcohol dehydrogenase) that is crucial to the breakdown of alcohol. Similar genetic susceptibilities are suspected in other birth disorders, including cleft palate and club foot (Hartl & Jones, 1999). Because of epigenetic variability, even monozygotic twins may be affected differently. For example, all four of the monozygotic Genain quadruplets (born in 1930) developed schizophrenia, but the severity and type of each woman's condition varied (Plomin et al., 2001).

Genes are also implicated in the teratogenic effect of a deficiency of folic acid (a B-complex vitamin) in the mother-to-be's diet. Researchers have known for several years that folic-acid deficiency can produce *neural-tube defects*—either *spina bifida,* in which the spine does not close properly, or *anencephaly,* in which part of the brain does not form. Neural-tube defects occur more commonly in certain families and ethnic groups (specifically, Irish, English, and Egyptian) and not often in others (most Asian and African groups). That fact led to research that found the source: A defective gene produces an enzyme that prevents the normal utilization of folic acid (Mills et al., 1995).

In some cases, genetic vulnerability is related to the sex of the developing organism. Generally, male (XY) embryos and fetuses are at greater risk than female (XX). This is one explanation for a known fact: Male fetuses are more often aborted spontaneously. In addition, newborn boys have more birth defects, and older boys have more learning disabilities and other problems caused by behavioral teratogens. Autism, for instance, is largely genetic, but about four times as many boys as girls are autistic.

Especially for the Friend of a Pregnant Woman: Suppose that your friend is frightened of having an abnormal child. She refuses to read about prenatal development because she is afraid to learn about what could go wrong. What could you tell her?

threshold effect The phenomenon in which a particular teratogen is relatively harmless in small doses but becomes harmful once exposure reaches a certain level (the threshold).

interaction effect The phenomenon in which a teratogen's potential for causing harm increases when it is combined with another teratogen or another risk factor.

Response for the Friend of a Pregnant Woman (from page 113): Reassure her that almost all pregnancies turn out fine, partly because most defective fetuses are spontaneously aborted and partly because protective factors are active throughout pregnancy. Equally important, the more she learns about teratogens, the more she will learn about protecting her fetus. Many birth defects and complications can be prevented with good prenatal care.

human immunodeficiency virus (HIV) A virus that gradually overwhelms the body's immune responses, leaving the individual defenseless against a host of pathologies that eventually manifest themselves as AIDS.

Hope for the Future Marilis and Anol, of the Dominican Republic, are especially delighted with their 18-month-old daughter, Yolanda, because their first child died of AIDS at age 2. Both parents are HIV-positive, but Yolanda is not. To avoid transmitting the virus to her baby, Marilis took the anti-AIDS drug AZT during her pregnancy, delivered Yolanda by cesarean section, and gives the baby formula rather than breast-feeding her. Yolanda, too, received AZT for the first 6 weeks of her life. Marilis and Anol hope that their story will inspire other people to do all they can to reduce the transmission of HIV.

Specific Teratogens

Because of the many variables involved, risk analysis cannot precisely predict the results of teratogenic exposure in individual cases (Jacobson & Jacobson, 1996). However, decades of research have revealed the possible effects of some of the most common and damaging teratogens. More important, much has been learned about how individuals and society can reduce the risks.

Diseases

Many diseases, including most viruses and virtually all sexually transmitted diseases, can harm a fetus. Here we will focus on only two conditions, rubella and HIV, that also illustrate the potential for public health measures to prevent birth defects.

Rubella One of the first teratogens to be recognized was *rubella* (sometimes called *German measles*). Rubella was long considered a harmless childhood disease. But 50 years ago doctors discovered that if a woman contracts rubella early in pregnancy, her embryo might suffer blindness, deafness, heart abnormalities, and brain damage. (Some of these problems and their effects were apparent in my nephew David's story in Chapter 1.)

The seriousness of this teratogen became all too evident in a worldwide rubella epidemic in the mid-1960s. In the United States alone, 20,000 infants had obvious rubella-caused impairments, including hundreds who were born both deaf and blind (Franklin, 1984). Thousands more showed no immediate effects because damage was done only to the brain, but behavioral or learning problems appeared later in childhood (Enkin et al., 1989).

Since that epidemic, widespread immunization—either of preschool children (as in the United States) or of all adolescent girls who are not already immune (as in England)—has reduced the rubella threat. Consequently, only two rubella-syndrome infants were born in the United States in 2001 (CDC, January 4, 2002). Other teratogenic diseases (for example, chicken pox) likewise have been controlled by immunization and now rarely damage fetuses.

Pediatric AIDS No immunization is yet available for the most devastating viral teratogen of all: the **human immunodeficiency virus (HIV).** HIV gradually overwhelms the body's natural immune response, becoming *AIDS (acquired immune deficiency syndrome)* when the person's immune system can no longer fight off any of dozens of debilitating and deadly infectious diseases.

Pregnant women with HIV transmit the virus, prenatally or during birth, to about 25 percent of their infants. HIV overwhelms a very young body faster than a fully grown one. Consequently, worldwide, most of the 570 million HIV-positive infants born in 2000 will die before age 5 (Parker, 2002). In medically advanced nations, hundreds of HIV-positive children survive to adolescence, attending school, making friends, and understanding their illnesses (Brown et al., 2000). Like other children with innate vulnerability (to conditions such as juvenile diabetes, sickle-cell anemia, and asthma), HIV-positive children enjoy their lives; but their survival makes the need for prevention more obvious, because parents, doctors, and the children themselves suffer year after year.

Prevention of pediatric AIDS may now be possible. If a pregnant HIV-positive woman takes antiretroviral drugs (such as ZDV and AZT) starting 14 weeks after conception and gives birth by cesarean section and if the newborn is given antiretroviral drugs and is not breast-fed, then mother-to-child transmission of HIV is reduced from about 25 percent to 8 percent. Indeed, comprehensive counseling and free treatment for all pregnant women in the state of Michigan reduced the known rate of transmission from 19 percent to 3 percent in just seven years (1993–2000) (CDC, February 8, 2002). Most of the mothers who actually transmitted the virus during these seven years did not start taking antiretroviral drugs by mid-pregnancy. Michigan's success makes it clear why half a million children still develop AIDS each year. For successful prevention, the medical infrastructure must provide early counseling, adequate prenatal care, and free antiretroviral drugs. None of these steps are taken in the nations of sub-Saharan Africa, where 20 million adults carry the virus, or in many other countries (Jha et al., 2001).

In addition, women must go to a doctor early in pregnancy, learn their HIV status, and take the drugs. Each step of this process demands some courage. One woman from central Africa said, "I am going to die anyway. My baby might live but what is the point, as there will be no mother to raise my baby" (quoted in Bassett, 2002). (She has a point; even HIV-negative African babies are likely to die if their mother dies of AIDS.) Even in most of the United States, some pregnant women choose not to know their HIV status, and some obstetricians do not routinely test for HIV. In contrast, Michigan law requires confidential counseling and testing to be offered to all pregnant women, "regardless of their race, age, or marital or socioeconomic status" (CDC, February 8, 2002).

In short, early and diligent prenatal care can reduce the dangers posed to the fetus by infectious diseases, but such care is often lacking. Even in the United States, the wealthiest nation of the world, 240 newborns had congenital syphilis in 2001 (CDC, January 4, 2002); the severe damage that this disease causes to the fetal brain and body can easily be prevented if the mother is diagnosed, treated, and cured early in pregnancy. Overall, about 25 percent of pregnant women in the United States who choose to give birth also choose not to obtain prenatal care until after the critical first trimester (CDC, April 26, 2002).

Medicines and Drugs

The vital importance of prenatal counseling and care is underscored by the evidence on the many medicines that can damage a fetus. The list of proven teratogenic medicines includes tetracycline, anticoagulants, bromides, anticonvulsants, phenobarbital, retinoic acid (a common treatment for acne, as in Accutane), and most hormones. Other prescription drugs and nonprescription drugs (such as aspirin, antacids, and diet pills) may be teratogenic. Obviously, then, women who might become pregnant, or who are pregnant, should avoid taking any medication unless it is recommended by a doctor who is both well versed in teratology *and* aware of the possible pregnancy.

Prenatal damage is also caused by *psychoactive drugs*—that is, drugs that affect the psyche (see Table 4.4). Beer and wine, liquor, cigarettes and smokeless tobacco, heroin and methadone, LSD, marijuana, cocaine in any form, inhalants, and antidepressant pills are the most common preventable teratogens. All psychoactive drugs slow down fetal growth and increase the risk of premature labor. All can affect the developing brain, producing both short-term and long-term deficits. For days or weeks after birth, infants who were prenatally addicted to any of these drugs sleep fitfully, startle easily, cry unhappily, suck voraciously, eat erratically, and show other signs of drug withdrawal.

As they develop, such children may exhibit learning difficulties, impaired self-control, poor concentration, and overall irritability. Beyond these general effects, each drug varies in its specific effects. Thus, tobacco causes low birthweight, while alcohol causes **fetal alcohol syndrome (FAS)**, the leading teratogenic cause of mental retardation. Definitive longitudinal data on both FAS and the less severe

Especially for Social Workers: When is it most important to convince women to be tested for HIV—a month before pregnancy, a month after conception, or immediately after birth?

BOB DAEMMRICH / THE IMAGE WORKS

Drug Abuse Smoking and drinking are an essential part of daily life for millions of young women, many of whom find these habits impossible to give up when they become pregnant. If you met this woman at a party and you thought complete abstinence was too much to ask, temperance might be a reasonable suggestion. Taking a few puffs and a few sips, or using just one drug and not the other, might prevent damage to the fetus's developing body and brain.

fetal alcohol syndrome (FAS) A cluster of birth defects, including abnormal facial characteristics, slow physical growth, and retarded mental development, that is caused by the mother's drinking excessive quantities of alcohol when pregnant.

TABLE 4.4 Effects of Psychoactive Drugs on Prenatal Development

Drug	Usage	Effects
Alcohol	3 or more drinks daily, or binge drinking of 5 or more drinks on one occasion early in pregnancy	Causes *fetal alcohol syndrome (FAS)*. Symptoms include a small head, abnormal facial characteristics (wide spacing between the eyes, a flattened nose and a narrow upper lip, unusual eyelids, and missing skin indentation between nose and upper lip), overall growth retardation, learning disabilities, and behavior problems (including poor concentration and impaired social skills).
	More than ½ oz. of absolute alcohol a day	Causes *fetal alcohol effects (FAE)*. FAE does not observably affect facial appearance or physical growth, but it affects brain functioning. The first sign is noisy, higher-frequency cries at birth. Later signs, on cognitive tests, include lower IQ (by about 5 points).
	Moderate drinking: less than 1 or 2 servings of beer or wine or 1 mixed drink a few days per week	Probably has no negative effects on prenatal development, although this is controversial.
Tobacco	Maternal smoking early in pregnancy	Increases risk of certain rare abnormalities, including malformation of the limbs and the urinary tract.
	Maternal smoking late in pregnancy	Reduces birthweight and size. Babies born to habitual smokers weigh, on average, about 9 oz. (250 g) less, and they are shorter, both at birth and in the years to come. They may have asthma.
	Paternal smoking	Reduces birthweight by about 2 oz. (45 g) on average.
Marijuana	Heavy use	Affects the central nervous system, as evidenced by the tendency of affected newborns to emit a high-pitched cry that denotes brain damage.
	Light use	Has no proven long-term effects.
Heroin	Any use	Because of the physiological "highs" and "crashes" of the addiction (such as the reduction of oxygen, irregular heartbeat, and sweating and chills that occur during withdrawal), heroin causes slower fetal growth and premature labor. (See also *methadone,* below.)
Methadone	Later in pregnancy	Moderates the effects of heroin withdrawal during pregnancy but is as addictive as heroin. Heavily addicted newborns require regulated drug doses in the first days of life to prevent the pain and convulsions of sudden opiate withdrawal.
Cocaine	Any use	Causes overall growth retardation, problems with the placenta, and specific learning problems in the first months of life. Research on long-lasting effects is confounded by the effects of poverty and the ongoing addiction of the mother. The major concern is in language development.
Solvents	Especially early in pregnancy	Causes smaller heads, crossed eyes, and other abnormalities.

Overall sources: Larsen, 1998; Lyons & Rittner, 1998.

condition called FAE (fetal alcohol effects) are now available. The data leave no doubt that alcohol is a behavioral teratogen. It increases hyperactivity, reduces concentration, and causes specific learning deficits, particularly in spatial reasoning and arithmetic (Streissguth & Connor, 2001).

Such definitive longitudinal research on the effects of specific illegal drugs is not available, because it is virtually impossible to locate a sizable representative sample of newly pregnant women who use one, and only one, illicit drug at a steady and measurable dose. Illicit drug users almost always use several legal as well as illegal drugs—not just their drug of choice—so interactive effects are common.

Furthermore, when a mother-to-be is *addicted* to an illicit drug, the fetal hazards are compounded by her erratic sleeping and eating habits; her bouts of anxiety, stress, and depression; and her increased risk of accidents, violence, and sexual abuse. One study of more than 3,000 women found that most of those who used psychoactive drugs quit during pregnancy. The unfortunate exceptions were the 100 or so who were physically abused by their partners; they were more likely to continue drug abuse (Martin et al., 1996). Finally, severely addicted women are

Response for Social Workers (from page 115): Voluntary testing and then treatment can be useful at any time, since women who learn that they are HIV-positive are more likely to get treatment, in order to reduce the likelihood of transmission, and to avoid pregnancy. If pregnancy does occur, diagnosis early in pregnancy is best, since abortion is one option and taking antiretroviral drugs such as AZT is another—one that prevents many cases of pediatric AIDS.

BOTH: GEORGE STEINMETZ

Differences and Similarities The differences between these two children are obvious at a glance: One is an African American teenager, the other a Swedish toddler. One similarity is obvious, too: Both are girls. However, the most important similarity—fetal alcohol syndrome—is apparent only on closer observation.

? *Observational Quiz* (see answer, page 119): How many of the five visible facial characteristics of fetal alcohol syndrome can you see in both girls?

often malnourished and sick, unsupported by concerned family members, and without medical care. After a baby is born, all these problems typically surround the child for years, along with possible additional stresses from an absent or abusive father and a poor and dangerous neighborhood. So targeting prenatal use of a particular illegal drug as *the* cause of the child's learning problems is obviously unscientific. Targeting it as a signal that a woman is in serious trouble, and that she and her fetus need ongoing, intensive help, makes sense.

Changing Policy

Preventing Drug Damage

Despite the ambiguity of much of the longitudinal research on drug use, the evidence leads to a strong recommendation: Pregnant women should avoid drugs entirely, because nothing is risk-free, even an occasional indulgence.

Nevertheless, many women in their prime reproductive years drink alcohol, smoke cigarettes, or use illicit drugs. Most continue their drug use in the first weeks before they realize that they are pregnant. It is already late, after the early formation of the embryo. To make matters worse, those who are addicts, alcoholics, or heavy users of multiple drugs are least likely to stop on their own, least likely to recognize their condition in the first few weeks and obtain early medical care, and often excluded from residential drug treatment programs.

General education is not enough. For example, the danger of tobacco and alcohol use during pregnancy is well known, and warning signs are displayed on cigarette packs and in liquor stores and bars. Yet about one in six pregnant women in the United States smoked during the final three months of pregnancy, with those under age 25 twice as likely to smoke as those over age 35 (CDC, September 24, 1999). Similarly, in a 1999 U.S. survey, 13 percent of pregnant women admitted drinking, at least a little, and 3.3 percent said that they had drunk a lot within the previous month—at least one

drink per day or five or more drinks on one occasion, a level that is definitely risky (see Figure 4.4 on page 118). This rate has not declined substantially in the past decade (CDC, April 5, 2002). Worse, the actual amount and prevalence of drinking are undoubtedly higher, because many alcoholics hide the extent of their drinking. A careful assessment in Seattle, Washington, of babies born in 1981 found that 3 in 1,000 had fetal alcohol syndrome and another 6 in 1,000 had less obvious brain damage (Sampson et al., 1997). The overall rate, about 1 in 100, shows that while not every pregnant drinker harms her fetus, far too many do. In fact, alcohol remains the leading teratogenic cause of mental retardation (Jacobs et al., 2000).

What can be done, beyond general education? The research suggests five protective steps:

1. *Abstinence from all drugs even before pregnancy.* The best course is to avoid drugs altogether. This can make a dramatic difference, as is shown by data on babies born to women who have recently emigrated to North America. For many reasons, including poverty and lack of medical care, immigrants are at high risk for prenatal and birth complications of every kind. However, their newborns weigh more, are born with fewer defects, and show less evidence of behavioral teratogens than do native-born children of the same

ethnicity (Beiser et al., 2002; Hernandez & Charney, 1998). One reason is that immigrants are more often drug-free, not only because of cultural patterns but also because their husbands and parents discourage any substance use in pregnancy.

2. *Abstinence from all drugs after the first month.* The teratogenic effects of psychoactive drugs accumulate throughout pregnancy. Thus, early prenatal care, with routine testing for drug use and effective treatment toward abstinence, would reduce fetal brain damage substantially. In fact, because the last three months of pregnancy are critical for brain development, a drug-free second half of pregnancy *may* be enough to prevent brain damage if drug use during the first half was moderate (Maier et al., 1996). Since alcohol and tobacco are at least as teratogenic as illegal drugs, they need to be tested for and targeted just as much as cocaine, heroin, marijuana, and the like.

3. *Moderation throughout pregnancy* (if abstinence from all drugs is impossible). The prenatal effects of psychoactive drugs are dose-related, interactive, and cumulative. Therefore, each dose that is reduced, each drug that is eliminated, and each day that is drug-free represents less damage that can be caused.

4. *Social support.* Maternal stress, psychological problems, loneliness, and poor housing correlate with prenatal complications as well as with drug use (Kramer et al., 2001). In fact, the correlation between psychoactive drugs and prenatal problems may be due, in part, to a hidden factor—psychological difficulties (Robert, 1996). If this is true, then befriending, encouraging, and assisting pregnant drug users may not only reduce their use of teratogens but also aid fetal development, even without directly affecting drug use. (Of course, the assistance should not include any help in obtaining or using drugs.)

5. *Postnatal care.* Babies born with alcohol, cocaine, or even heroin in their systems sometimes become quite normal, intelligent children if they receive optimal care (Koren et al.,

1998; Richardson, 1998). Thus, another way to protect children is to ensure sensitive nurturance after birth (through parenting education, preventive medicine, home visits, early day care, and, if necessary, adoption). Social prejudices work against these children. For instance, the assumption that "crack babies" are destined to have serious learning problems might reduce educational outreach. Social intervention to repair the damage from maternal alcohol abuse is minimal: 80 percent of such children are cared for by someone other than their mothers but very few receive any special services (Streissguth & Connor, 2001). One study found that cocaine-exposed infants whose mothers received help were significantly better off, physically and cognitively, by age 3 than a comparison group from similar low-SES families who neither were exposed to cocaine before birth nor received special services afterward (Kilbride et al., 2000).

One preventive measure that does *not* seem to help is prosecuting pregnant women who use drugs. Jailing such women enforces drug abstinence, and, ironically, imprisoned pregnant women have healthier babies than their peers outside the walls (Martin et al., 1997). However, the threat of prosecution and imprisonment keeps thousands of pregnant women away from prenatal care. This increases fetal damage that might have been prevented (Lyons & Rittner, 1998). When it comes to imprisoning drug addicts, the math is simple. If preventing drug abuse in one pregnant woman by keeping her in jail results in ongoing drug abuse in 99 other women who avoid all prenatal care, the harm far exceeds the benefit. If there were some way to get all 99 to reduce their drug use, however, the benefits might be substantial.

How much harm is prevented by any measure short of total abstinence before pregnancy starts? No one knows for certain. We cannot know until all newborns who were exposed to drugs before birth are assured of excellent care after birth—a distant goal (Byrd et al., 1999).

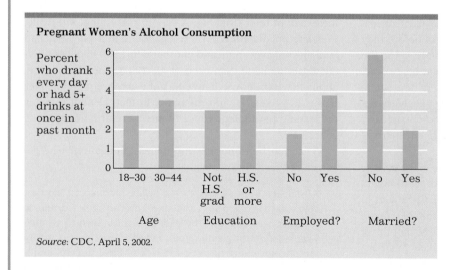

FIGURE 4.4 Wisdom Doesn't Cut It Logically, one might think that older women and women with job experience and education would never drink to the point of endangering their fetus, but this isn't so. The only factor that seemed to make a powerful difference was marriage.

Adults usually don't change much in a year or two. Sometimes their hair gets longer or grows thinner, or they gain or lose a few pounds, or they become a little wiser. But if you were to be reunited with friends you haven't seen for several years, you would recognize them immediately.

If, in contrast, you were to care for a newborn twenty-four hours a day for the first month, and then did not see the baby until a year later, you probably would not recognize him or her. After all, would you recognize a best friend who had quadrupled in weight, grown 14 inches, and sprouted a new head of hair? Nor would you find the toddler's behavior familiar. A hungry newborn just cries; a hungry toddler says "more food" or climbs up on the kitchen counter to reach the bananas.

A year or two is not much time compared to the almost eighty years of the average life span. However, children in their first two years reach half their adult height, develop cognitive abilities that have often surprised researchers, and learn to express almost every emotion—not just joy and fear but also many others, including jealousy and shame. And two of the most important human abilities, talking and loving, are already apparent.

The next three chapters describe these radical and wonderful changes.

The First 2 Years: Infants and Toddlers

Chapter Five

The First 2 Years: Cognitive Development

This chapter is about infant *cognition,* a word that means "thinking" in a very broad sense. Cognition involves intelligence and learning, memory and language, facts and concepts, beliefs and assumptions, teaching and education. You might wonder, "Intelligence in babies?" Yes, indeed.

Imagine, for a moment, that you are a newborn, just beginning to have thoughts. New and constantly changing images, sounds, smells, and body sensations bombard your limited consciousness. You try to make sense of them, connecting smells with visual images, tastes with feelings. You develop perceptions of objects, of people, even of parts of your own body; you figure out which relate to you, and how, and when. Then you put it all together: sensations, sequences, objects, people, events, permanent and transient features, causes and effects. And this is just the beginning of your cognition.

By the end of the first year—and often much sooner—you will have categories for organizing and thinking about the objects you experience, you will understand how your own actions can make things happen, you will have goals and know how to reach them, and you will begin to talk. By the end of the second year, you will speak in sentences, think before acting, and pretend to be someone or something (a mother, an airplane) that you know you are not.

No wonder, then, that infant intelligence is a major topic: There is much to describe.

We begin with the framework provided by Jean Piaget for observing the amazing intellectual progress from newborns who know nothing, on to toddlers who are able to make a wish and blow out their birthday candles. Then we consider more recent research on affordances, categories and concepts, and memory, that suggests that infant brain and perceptual development is faster and deeper than even Piaget realized. This all comes to fruition in child language—an intellectual accomplishment that actually begins before birth, even though the first words are not spoken until about age 1, followed by gradual acquisition of grammar. How all this happens is a topic of great interest and controversy, as you will learn.

Sensorimotor Intelligence

It is impossible to understand the first two years of cognitive development without referring to Piaget, a Swiss scientist born in 1896. By carefully observing his own three children, Piaget discovered that infants are active learners. From those detailed observations and from hundreds of studies of other children, Piaget concluded that humans of every age and circumstance actively seek to comprehend their world and that their understanding occurs in four specific, age-related periods. Each of these periods is characterized by a particular kind of thinking, a way to understand the world.

The first of those periods begins at birth, then accelerates so rapidly that six distinct substages occur before age 2. Because infants learn through their senses and motor skills, Piaget called this first period **sensorimotor intelligence.** Piaget's works (including 26 major books) "continue to be an important source of inspiration for contemporary infant research" (Rochat, 2001, p. 7).

All developmentalists owe Piaget a great deal, especially regarding infancy. The following passage is one of thousands that exemplify his contributions. Piaget is observing his 3-month-old son, Laurent:

> I place the string which is attached to the rattle in his right hand, merely unrolling it a little so that he may grasp it better. For a moment nothing happens, but at the first shake due to chance movement of his hand, the reaction is immediate: Laurent starts when looking at the rattle and then violently strikes his right hand alone, as if he felt the resistance and the effect. The operation lasts a full quarter of an hour during which Laurent emits peals of laughter. The phenomenon is all the more clear because, the string being slack, the child must stretch his arm sufficiently and put the right amount of effort into it.

> *[Piaget, 1952b, p. 162]*

This passage illustrates three of Piaget's attributes: his keen powers of observation; his close attention to sequence, the essence of development; and his fascination with the details of infant discovery. In all these, Piaget has been a role model for generations of developmentalists, who not only use careful observation, paying particular attention to sequence, but also share Piaget's fascination with the details and the delights of infant behavior. You remember from Chapter 2 that some specific conclusions reached by Piaget are no longer considered valid. We will discuss these deficiencies further in this chapter. But to benefit from Piaget's insights, we present the six stages of sensorimotor intelligence (see Table 6.1).

Stages One and Two: Primary Circular Reactions

The first two stages of sensorimotor intelligence are examples of **primary circular reactions,** which are reactions that involve the infant's own body. Stage one, called the *stage of reflexes*, lasts only for a month. It includes reflexes (described on page 150), such as sucking and grasping, and also senses, which are so responsive at birth that they seem like reflexes. Simple inborn actions and reactions are all that newborns can use for sensorimotor intelligence, but these simple reflexes soon begin to help infants think as well as react. Sensation becomes perception, which becomes cognition; reflexes become deliberate.

At this point, the baby enters stage two, *first acquired adaptations* (also called the stage of first habits). This change from reflexes to deliberate action occurs because repeated use of reflexive responses provides information about what the body does and how that action feels. Infants adjust their body reactions in accord with this information from their body. This adjustment still involves their own body (making it a primary circular reaction), but it also ushers in **adaptation** of reflexes and senses to the specifics of the context. *Adaptation* is a key word in Piaget's understanding of cognition, meaning that taking in new information and responding to it become part of the thinking process.

Assimilation and Accommodation

Adaptation occurs in two complementary ways: by assimilation and by accommodation (as you learned in Chapter 2). **Assimilation** means taking new information into the mind by incorporating it into previously developed mental categories, or

---

sensorimotor intelligence Piaget's term for the intelligence of infants during the first (sensorimotor) period of cognitive development, when babies think by using their senses and motor skills.

primary circular reactions The first of three types of feedback loops, this one involving the infant's own body, in which the infant takes in experiences and tries to make sense of them.

adaptation The cognitive process by which new information is taken in and responded to.

assimilation The process of taking new information into the mind by incorporating it into previously developed mental categories, or schemas.

TABLE 6.1 The Six Stages of Sensorimotor Intelligence

For an overview of the stages of sensorimotor thought, it helps to group the six stages into pairs. The first two stages involve the infant's responses to its own body (sometimes called *primary circular reactions*):

Stage One
(birth to 1 month)

Reflexes—sucking, grasping, staring, listening.

Stage Two
(1–4 months)

The first acquired adaptation (assimilation and coordination of reflexes)—sucking a pacifier differently from a nipple; grabbing a bottle to suck it.

The next two stages involve the infant's responses to objects and people (sometimes called *secondary circular reactions*):

Stage Three
(4–8 months)

An awareness of things—responding to people and objects.

Stage Four
(8–12 months)

New adaptation and anticipation—becoming more deliberate and purposeful in responding to people and objects.

The last two stages are the most creative, first with action and then with ideas (sometimes called *tertiary circular reactions*):

Stage Five
(12–18 months)

New means through active experimentation—experimentation and creativity in the actions of the "little scientist."

Stage Six
(18–24 months)

New means through mental combinations—considering before doing provides the child with new ways of achieving a goal without resorting to trial-and-error experiments.

action patterns—in Piaget's terminology, "schemas." **Accommodation** means taking new information into the mind in such a way as to readjust, refine, or expand previous schemas.

Adaptive processes occur throughout life. Indeed, for Piaget, adaptation is the essence of intelligence. There are numerous definitions of *intelligence* (according to my Webster's dictionary, it includes the abilities to learn, to understand, to respond quickly, to remember), but for Piaget, an unintelligent person is rigid, stuck, unable or unwilling to adapt his or her cognitive processes to include new ideas, to find a new equilibrium.

In the first two stages of infancy, adaptation via both assimilation and accommodation is obvious: Babies eagerly and actively adapt their reflexes and senses to whatever experiences they have. The reflexive grasp, for instance, is automatic and tight whenever something is put in the newborn's hand; within a few months, however, the baby grasps only certain things, because accommodation has occurred. Similarly, the senses assimilate everything at first but then begin to accommodate the particular sights and sounds of the infant's immediate surroundings—focusing on faces, for instance, and ignoring the bright lights that first captured the attention. Sucking is another example of this assimilation/accommodation process, one that we will explain in detail.

accommodation The process of taking new information into the mind in such a way as to readjust, refine, or expand previous mental categories, or schemas.

Sucking as a Stage-Two Adaptation

Newborns suck anything that touches their lips; sucking is one of the strongest and most apparent reflexes. In fact, newborns turn their heads to try to suck anything that touches their cheeks. These reflexes of rooting and sucking confirm that for the newborn, everything is assimilated into the general schema "the world is for sucking"; no accommodation is needed.

Stage Two Sucking everything is a mere reflex in the first month of life, but by 3 months Katie has already learned that some objects afford better sucking than others. Many infants her age have learned not to suck on people's faces, but with this mother, that adaptation is not necessary.

ROBERT ULLMAN

However, at about the age of 1 month, infants start to adapt sucking. Some items, such as the nipple of a bottle (for a breast-fed infant), merely require assimilation: The same old sucking reflex brings nourishment. Others require more accommodation: Pacifiers need to be sucked without the tongue-pushing and swallowing reflexes, since they do not provide food. This adaptation is a sign that infants have begun to organize their perceptions; they are "thinking."

In other words, adaptation in the early weeks relies primarily on reflexive assimilation—everything suckable is assimilated as worthy of being sucked until accommodation occurs. After several months, new responses are established because adaptation has occurred, organizing the sucking reflex into nonreflexive actions: Suck some things to soothe hunger, suck others to bring comfort, and suck still others (fuzzy blankets, large balls) not at all. If the baby is hungry, only familiar nourishing nipples will do—all other objects are rejected. Similarly, when babies are not hungry but want the reassurance of rhythmic sucking, they will suck a pacifier. If no pacifier has been offered in the stage of reflexes, infants begin sucking their thumbs, fingers, or knuckles (a choice that depends on whatever the baby first assimilates). If infants a few months old are full and their stomachs hurt, sucking is probably not what they want: They push away a bottle stuck into their crying mouth and may resist a pacifier as well. They want pain relief, perhaps available only if someone carries them, putting pressure on their bellies.

Especially for Parents: When should parents decide whether to feed their baby only by breast, only by bottle, or using some combination, and when should they decide whether or not to offer a pacifier?

Stages Three and Four: Secondary Circular Reactions

In stages three and four, development switches from primary circular reactions, involving the baby's own body (stages one and two), to **secondary circular reactions,** involving the baby with an object or with another person.

secondary circular reactions The second of three types of feedback loops, this one involving people and objects, in which the infant takes in experiences and tries to make sense of them.

Stage Three: Making Interesting Sights Last

During stage three (age 4 to 8 months), infants interact diligently with people and objects to produce exciting experiences. Realizing that rattles make noise, for example, they shake their arms and laugh whenever someone puts a rattle in their hand. Even the sight of something that normally delights an infant— a favorite toy, a favorite food, a smiling parent—can trigger an active attempt at interaction.

Vocalization of all sorts increases a great deal at this time, and not just in a chorus (as with younger infants—when one newborn in the nursery cries, they all tend to cry). Now that babies realize that other people can and will respond, they love to make a noise, listen for a response, and answer back. Interestingly, by the age of 3 or 4 months, babies are already unlikely to make sounds at the same moment that someone is talking to them, causing a deceptive downward shift in the frequency of vocalization at about 4 months (Hsu et al., 2000). This is an example of a secondary circular reaction, because infants incorporate other people into their cognitive schema. The "interesting sights" are outside their own bodies.

Overall in this third stage, infants become more aware of objects and of other people; they recognize some of the specific characteristics of the things in their environment, and they develop ways to continue whatever sensation they seek. Sometimes they repeat a specific action that has just elicited a pleasing response from some person or thing.

Stage Four: New Adaptation and Anticipation

Stage four, which occurs from about 8 months to 1 year, is sometimes called "the means to the end," because babies now think about a goal and begin to understand how to reach it. This is a much more sophisticated kind of thinking than occurs in stage 3, when babies merely understand how to continue an experience once it is underway.

In stage four, babies adapt in new, more deliberate ways. They anticipate events that will fulfill their needs and wishes, and they try to make such events occur. A 10-month-old girl who enjoys playing in the tub might see a bar of soap, crawl over to her mother with it as a signal to start her bath, and then remove all her clothes to make her wishes crystal clear—finally squealing with delight when she hears the bath water being turned on. Similarly, if a 10-month-old boy sees his mother putting on her coat to leave without him, he might begin tugging at it to stop her or he might drag over his jacket to signal that he is coming along.

Senses and motor skills (and probably brain maturation as well) advance to make such anticipation possible. Careful experimental studies have found that at 8½ months, but not before, infants search for a concealed object using "landmarks" (visible spatial clues) (Lew et al., 2000). At about the same age, but not before, they anticipate where an interesting sight will appear and they look in that direction (Reznick et al., 2000). Organizing spatial perceptions in the brain and remembering the location of past sights require some neurological associations between memory and place, which is probably impossible before certain dendrite networks form.

All our examples of anticipation also reveal **goal-directed behavior**—that is, purposeful action. The baby's obvious goal-directedness at this age stems from the development of an enhanced awareness of cause and effect as well as better memory for actions already completed (Willatts, 1999). That cognitive awareness coincides with the emergence of the motor skills infants need to achieve their goals.

Thus, a stage-four baby might see something from across the room, be attracted to it, and crawl toward it, ignoring many interesting distractions along the way. Or the baby might grab a forbidden object—a box of matches, a thumbtack, a cigarette—and cry with rage when it is taken away. Because the baby is now goal-directed, the wailing continues even if the infant is offered a substitute that he or she normally finds fascinating.

Piaget thought that the concept of **object permanence** begins to emerge during stage four. Object permanence refers to the awareness that objects or people continue to exist when they are no longer in sight. At this point—and usually not before—infants actively search for objects that are no longer in view. Researchers have since shown that the concept of object permanence actually begins to emerge much earlier. However, the *goal-directed* search for toys that have fallen from the baby's crib, rolled under a couch, or disappeared under a blanket does not begin to emerge until about 8 months, just as Piaget indicated.

LAURA DWIGHT

Stage Three This 7½-month-old knows that a squeal of delight is one way to make the interesting experience of a tickle from Daddy last.

Response for Parents (from page 170): Within the first month, the stage of reflexes. If parents wait until the infant is 4 months or older, they may discover that they are too late. It is difficult to introduce a bottle to a 4-month-old who has been exclusively breast-fed or a pacifier to a baby who has already adapted the sucking reflex to a thumb.

goal-directed behavior Purposeful action initiated by infants in anticipation of events that will fulfill their needs and wishes.

object permanence The realization that objects (including people) still exist even when they cannot be seen, touched, or heard.

Thinking Like a Scientist

Object Permanence Revisited

Peek-a-Boo The best hidden object is Mom under an easily moved blanket, as 7-month-old Elias has discovered. Peek-a-boo is the most fun from about 7 to 12 months. In another month, Elias will search for more conventionally hidden objects. In a year or two, his surprise and delight at finding Mom will disappear.

Although it no doubt seems obvious to you that an object, an animal, and your mother continue to exist when you cannot see them, Piaget discovered that it is not at all obvious to very young infants. If a 5-month-old sees a ring of keys, for instance, and reaches for it, simply moving it out of reach is likely to create a fuss and frustration, but "disappearing" it behind your back or even in your closed hand produces only a fleeting expression of disappointment. No further crying or reaching transpires.

Quite literally, out of sight is out of mind. When an infant does demonstrate object permanence (in this case by trying to pry open your hand to get the keys), that is considered a marker of intelligence. Consequently, object permanence has been the subject of intense developmental research. The design and implications of that research continue to be controversial (Baillargeon, 1999).

To understand that controversy, we begin with an appreciation of Piaget's discovery. Before Piaget, it was assumed that infants understood objects in the same way that adults do. Piaget developed a simple experiment that proved that assumption wrong. An adult shows an infant an interesting toy and then covers it up with an easy-to-remove blanket or cloth. If the infant then removes the cover to get the toy, that means that he or she realizes that the toy still exists, even though it was momentarily out of sight.

Various forms of this experiment have been replicated with thousands of infants in virtually every university, every city, and every nation of the world. The findings:

- Infants younger than 8 months do not search for hidden objects.
- At about 8 months, infants search if they can do so immediately but lose interest or forget if they have to wait a few seconds.
- By 2 years, the concept of object permanence is quite well understood. However, even 3-year-olds playing hide-and-seek may become fearful that someone has really disappeared, or they may hide themselves in obvious places (such as behind a coat rack with their feet still visible or as a big lump under a sheet on a bed).

Does failure to search mean the infant has no concept of object permanence? Could other weaknesses of the young brain or body—lack of motivation, imperfect motor skills, or fragile memory—mask an understanding that objects still exist when they are not seen? For almost 50 years, the scientific community accepted Piaget's conclusions. Then, beginning in the 1980s, some researchers raised questions and set about answering them (Spelke, 1993).

One clever experiment startled developmental researchers when it was first published (Baillargeon, 1987). Infants age 3 to 5 months sat directly in front of a screen attached on one side to a table. The screen was made to pivot upward, front to back, from flat to full height and then down to flat again (see Figure 6.1). This action took place immediately in front of the baby, and the screen was tall, so that at its full height everything behind it was hidden from view. The experimenter made the screen pivot many times, until the infants were no longer interested in watching it rise and fall. When babies seemed bored with the routine rise and fall, a large, solid box was placed on the far side of the table, positioned so that the screen would hit it as it pivoted backward.

Two experimental conditions followed. In one, called the *possible event,* the screen pivoted again, up and then back, until it hit the box and stopped, as one would expect. In the other, called the *impossible event,* the screen pivoted up and down as before, through the entire 180-degree arc, as if no box were in the way. (In fact, although the babies couldn't see it happen, the box dropped through a trap door before the screen reached it.)

(a) Habituation

(b) Placing the box

(c) Possible event

(d) Impossible event

FIGURE 6.1 The Old Screen-and-Box Game The basic steps of Renée Baillargeon's test of object permanence—a test that does not depend on the infant's searching abilities or motivation to search. (a) The infant is habituated to the movement of a hinged screen that rotates through a 180-degree arc toward and (as shown) away from the infant. (b) With the infant observing, a box is placed in the backward path of the screen. Then the infant witnesses two events: (c) the "possible" event in which the screen's movement through the arc is stopped by the box, and (d) the "impossible" event, in which the screen completes its movement through the arc as though the box did not exist. Infants as young as 4½ months stare longer at the "impossible" event, indicating their awareness that the box does exist even though they cannot see it behind the screen.

By 4½ months, infants stared longer at the "impossible" event than at the "possible" one, as recorded on videotape and counted in milliseconds. Their longer stares signified their expectations that the box continued to exist when it was hidden from view. This means that the 4½-month-old infants had some concept of object permanence and were surprised when an object seemed to disappear. Apparently Piaget was mistaken in concluding that infants younger than 8 months have no notion of object permanence. As one leading researcher summarizes:

> Until fairly recently, the study of children's cognitive development was dominated by the theory of Jean Piaget. Piaget's theory was detailed, elaborate, comprehensive, and, in many important respects, wrong.

> *[Tomasello, 2000, p. 37]*

Most developmentalists still respect Piaget's work and commend him for his two most basic ideas: (1) Infants do not understand everything that adults assume they understand and (2) young infants are smarter than many people realize. Piaget's error was in not realizing that infants are more intelligent, at younger ages, than even he knew.

Where's Rosa? At 18 months, Rosa knows all about object permanence and hiding. Her only problem here is distinguishing between "self" and "other."

Tertiary
2nd year

Especially for Parents: One parent wants to put all the breakable or dangerous objects away because their toddler is now able to move around independently. The other parent says that the baby should learn not to touch certain things. Who is right?

BOB DAEMMRICH PHOTO, INC.

A boy with a purpose At ten months, this little boy is goal-oriented, stuffing the bread into his mouth with his left hand. In a few months, he will also experiment, probably by dropping crumbs on the floor, dipping the bread in gravy, or conducting many other creative experiments.

tertiary circular reactions The third of three types of feedback loops, this one involving active exploration and experimentation, in which the infant takes in experiences and tries to make sense of them.

"little scientist" Piaget's term for the stage-five toddler (age 12 to 18 months), who actively experiments with objects to learn about their properties.

mental combinations Sequences of actions that the toddler in Piaget's stage six of sensorimotor intelligence (age 18 to 24 months) develops intellectually before actually performing them.

deferred imitation A mental combination in which an infant perceives something that someone else does and then performs the same action a few hours or even days later.

Stages Five and Six: Tertiary Circular Reactions

In their second year, infants begin experimenting in thought and deed. Actually, they experiment first in deed and then in thought, because toddlers typically act first and think later. **Tertiary circular reactions** mean that, rather than simply responding to their own bodies (primary reactions) or to other people or objects (secondary reactions), 1-year-olds take independent and varied actions to actively discover the properties of people and objects. They not only take such action, they delight in their discoveries. Remember that Toni, in our case study in Chapter 5, was "always busy"? That is just as it should be. Indeed, discovery is so rewarding that a toddler might do something that is uncomfortable (taste detergent, squeeze under a bed) to learn more about the world.

Stage Five: New Means Through Active Experimentation

Stage five (age 12 to 18 months) builds directly on the accomplishments of stage four, as infants' goal-directed and purposeful activities become more expansive and creative after the first birthday. Toddlerhood is a time of active exploration and experimentation, a time when babies "get into everything," as though trying to discover all the possibilities their world has to offer.

Because of the experimentation that characterizes this stage, Piaget referred to the stage-five toddler as a **"little scientist"** who "experiments in order to see." Having discovered some action or set of actions that is possible with a given object, stage-five infants seem to ask, "What else can I do with this? What happens if I pour water on the cat?" Their scientific method is one of trial and error, but their devotion to discovery sounds familiar to every adult researcher—and to every parent.

Stage Six: New Means Through Mental Combinations

In the final stage of sensorimotor intelligence (age 18 to 24 months), toddlers begin to anticipate and solve simple problems by using **mental combinations,** a kind of intellectual experimentation that supersedes the active experimentation of stage five. They try out various actions mentally, before actually performing them, to think about the consequences their actions might bring. Thus stage-six children can invent new ways to achieve a goal without resorting to trial-and-error experiments. Consider how Piaget's daughter Jacqueline solved a problem she encountered at the age of 20 months:

> Jacqueline arrives at a closed door with a blade of grass in each hand. She stretches out her right hand toward the knob but sees that she cannot turn it without letting go of the grass. She puts the grass on the floor, opens the door, picks up the grass again and enters. But when she wants to leave the room, things become complicated. She puts the grass on the floor and grasps the doorknob. But then she perceives that in pulling the door toward her she will simultaneously chase away the grass which she placed between the door and the threshold. She therefore picks it up in order to put it outside the door's zone of movement.
>
> [Piaget, 1952b, p. 162]

Being able to use mental combinations also makes it possible for the child to pretend. A toddler might lie down on the floor, pretend to go to sleep, and then jump up laughing. Or a child might sing to a doll before tucking it into bed. This is in marked contrast to the behavior of the younger infant, who might treat a doll like any other toy, throwing it, biting it, or banging it on the floor.

As you can see, mental combinations include thinking about consequences before acting and pretending—both quite sophisticated intellectual accomplishments. One other significant intellectual accomplishment involving both thought and memory begins at stage six, according to Piaget. **Deferred imitation,** when an infant sees (or hears, or otherwise perceives) something that someone else does and then imitates that behavior, is another example of a mental combination (Piaget, 1962). He describes an incident involving Jacqueline, who at 16 months observed another child

> who got into a terrible temper. He screamed as he tried to get out of a playpen and pushed it backward, stamping his feet. Jacqueline stood watching him in amazement, never having witnessed such a scene before. The next day, she herself screamed in her playpen and tried to move it, stamping her foot lightly several times in succession.
>
> *[Piaget, 1962, p. 63]*

You may have noticed that Jacqueline was not yet 18 months old, the age at which stage 6 begins. Actually, Piaget was not rigidly age-bound. He cites several instances when his own children were slightly ahead of the norms. He was quite adamant about sequences, though: The behaviors of stage six follow, never precede, those of stage five. However, as with object permanence, later research has shown that he was mistaken: Deferred imitation can begin as early as 9 months. To understand how Piaget again underestimated children, it is useful to realize how scientific methods, and consequently public policies regarding infant development, changed in the course of the twentieth century.

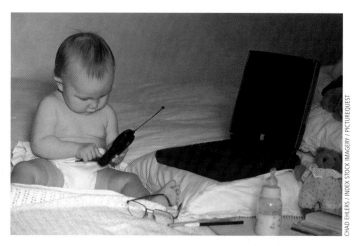

Can You Hear Me Now? How does this baby know about using a cellular phone? Months of watching adults have led to this moment of deferred imitation.

Changing Policy

Policy Implications of Some Modern Research Methods

Scientific investigation has advanced since Piaget's day. A major innovation is the development of complex statistical methods, which can detect small differences (such as milliseconds of visual attention) and can compile data from hundreds of subjects to prevent overgeneralization from a small sample (as Piaget did with his own three children). A related insight is that background factors—not only age but also sex, family structure, socioeconomic status, culture, cohort, and so on—can make a major difference in how a child develops.

Two important research tools not available to Piaget are habituation studies and fMRI. **Habituation** (from the word *habit*) refers to the process of getting used to an object or event through repeated exposure to it, as when an infant hears the same sound or sees the same picture again and again until he or she seems to lose interest in it. One of the wonderful characteristics of very young infants is that they enjoy novel stimuli and soon become habituated to (or bored by) the same old experience. Habituation is thus a boon for researchers studying infant development.

If a baby becomes habituated to one stimulus and then is presented a new one, any of several indicators—a longer or more focused gaze; a faster or slower heart rate; more or less muscle tension around the lips; a change in the rate, rhythm, or pressure of suction on a nipple—reveal that the baby detects a difference between the two stimuli. If no change occurs, that means the baby cannot yet perceive the difference. By watching for signs of habituation, scientists have learned, for instance, that even 1-month-olds can detect the difference between a *pah* sound and a *bah* sound, between a circle with two dots inside it and a circle without any dots, between a smooth pacifier and a bumpy one.

fMRI (functional magnetic resonance imaging, a brain-imaging technique) reveals brain activity by showing increases in oxygen supply to various parts of the brain as a person tries to remember a word or watches an exciting movie (Casey et al., 2001). The fMRI depicts the brain areas where, for instance, the recognition of faces and the recognition of places occur. Probably the most important insight to date from fMRI and other brain scans is that various parts of the brain are specialized for various activities but that no one part functions alone (Casey et al., 2001). Connections between parts are thus crucial, and experience helps form those connections (as explained in Chapter 5). (The major new brain-scanning techniques are listed in Table 6.2.)

The main conclusion relevant to public policy is that the early years of life, once thought to be intellectually empty, are now known to be prime time for cognitive development. Indeed, developmentalists now worry about the opposite danger: Since we know that substantial cognitive development occurs in the first three years, some politicians and members of the media act as if those years are the only ones that provide a foundation for learning. Not so. As a report from 20 leading developmentalists summarizes:

> Early experiences clearly affect the development of the brain. Yet the recent focus on "zero to three" as a critical or particularly sensitive period is highly problematic, not because this isn't an important period for the developing brain, but simply because the disproportional attention to the period from birth to 3 years begins too late and ends too soon. (National Research Council and Institute of Medicine, 2000)

Experts concerned about the interface between developmental research and public policy worry that the colorful pictures of brain activity may inspire journalists and politicians to make unrealistic conjectures about the pace of cognitive development (Thompson & Nelson, 2001). Piaget himself was concerned about "the American question," which was always asked by audiences in the United States but not elsewhere: "How can we speed up cognitive development?" Piaget pointed out that maturation fosters cognition at the appropriate time, and he developed his theory to show that the intellect evolves over time in a series of stages.

It is possible that all the recent research, especially the sophisticated technology and analyses that are now available, has actually distracted scientists from the essential developmental perspective. As always, the interpretation of the data from scientific research is the crucial contribution from scientists who know the various questions and issues regarding that perspective. Perhaps the makers of public policy need to be reminded that the entire context of development is more important than any specific activity that might stimulate one part of the brain at one stage of development.

habituation The process of getting used to an object or event through repeated exposure to it.

fMRI Functional magnetic resonance imaging, a technique in which the brain's magnetic properties are measured to detect changes in activity levels anywhere in the brain.

TABLE 6.2 Some Techniques Used by Neuroscientists to Understand Brain Function

Technique	Use
EEG (electroencephalogram)	Measures electrical activity in the top layers of the brain, where the cortex is.
ERP (event-related potential)	Notes the amplitude and frequency of electrical activity (as shown by brain waves) in specific parts of the cortex in reaction to various stimuli.
fMRI (functional magnetic resonance imaging)	Measures changes in activity anywhere in the brain (not just the outer layers).
PET (positron emission tomography)	Also (like fMRI) reveals activity in various parts of the brain. Locations can be pinpointed with precision, but PET requires injection of radioactive dye to light up the active parts of the brain.

Because of practical and ethical concerns, none of these techniques have been used with large, representative samples of normal infants.

Information Processing

Piaget was a "grand" theorist of cognition throughout the life span, with an appreciation of shifts in the nature of cognition that occur at about ages 2, 6, and 12. His sweeping stage overview contrasts with another view of infant cognition, one that arises from **information-processing theory**, a perspective on human thinking processes modeled on computer analysis of data. No computer can match the mind's capacity for reflection, creativity, and intuition. However, information-processing theorists suggest that a step-by-step description of the mechanisms of human thought, by analogy to the steps by which computers process data, aids our understanding of the development of cognition at every age.

information-processing theory A perspective that compares human thinking processes, by analogy, to computer analysis of data, from sensory input through brain reactions, connections, and stored memories to output.

Information-processing researchers look not only at such specific fields of study as neuroscience and linguistics, but also at the comprehensive processing of information, from input through output. Information processing begins with input in the form of sensory messages picked up by the five senses; proceeds to brain reactions, connections, and stored memories; and concludes with some form of output. For infants, the output might consist of moving a hand to uncover a hidden object, or saying a word to signify recognition of a person, or focusing the eyes to demonstrate that a stimulus is noticed.

Although many researchers in infant cognition do not explicitly use the information-processing perspective in their work, this perspective helps tie together the various aspects of infant cognition that are the topic of extensive study and exciting discoveries. We will review three of these aspects now: affordances, categories, and memory. Each of these refers to a step in information processing: Affordances concern perception (or, by analogy, input); categories refer to the organization of concepts by the brain (or programming); and memory involves retrieval of ideas already learned or of past experiences (or output).

A Hole Is to Dig As for any scientist, discovery and application are the motivating forces for infant activity. Clamshells have many uses, one for clams, one for hungry people, and another—shown here—for toddlers on the beach.

Affordances

Perception, remember, is the mental processing of information that arrives at the brain from the sensory organs. It is the first step of information processing—the input to the brain. One of the puzzles of adult development is why two people can have radically different perceptions of the same situation. The same question applies to infants.

A lifetime of thought and research led Eleanor and James Gibson to conclude that perception is far from an automatic phenomenon that every baby, everywhere, experiences in the same way (E. Gibson, 1969; J. Gibson, 1979). For infants, as for the rest of us, perception is a cognitive accomplishment that requires selection from a vast array of possibilities: "Perceiving is active, a process of obtaining information about the world. . . . We don't simply see, we look" (E. Gibson, 1988, p. 5).

The Gibsons contend that the environment (people, places, and objects) *affords*, or offers, many opportunities to be perceived and to be used in a wide variety of ways (E. Gibson, 1997). Each of these opportunities for perception and interaction is called an **affordance.** Which particular affordances are perceived and acted on depends on four factors: sensory awareness, immediate motivation, current development, and past experience.

As a simple example, a lemon may be perceived as something that affords smelling, tasting, touching, viewing, throwing, squeezing, and biting (among other things). Which affordance a particular person perceives and acts on depends on the four factors just mentioned. Consequently, a lemon might elicit quite different perceptions from an artist about to paint a still life, a thirsty adult in need of a refreshing drink, and a teething baby wanting something to gnaw on. This example implies (correctly) that affordances require an ecological fit between the individual and his or her environment. Hence, affordances arise both from specific qualities of an object and from the way the individual subjectively perceives the object.

Affordances are not limited to objects; they are also perceived in the physical characteristics of a setting and the living creatures in it (Reed, 1993). A toddler's idea of what affords running might be any unobstructed surface—a meadow, a

affordance An opportunity for perception and interaction that is offered by people, places, and objects in the environment.

Response for Parents (from page 174): It is easier and safer to babyproof the house, because toddlers, being little scientists, want to explore. However, it is also important for both parents to encourage and guide the baby, so it might be better to leave out a few untouchable items for teaching purposes than to get a divorce.

JOE EPSTEIN / DESIGN CONCEPTIONS

It's OK to Grasp Daddy's Nose Infants quickly learn what objects are of the right size and proximity for grasping. If the adults in their life allow it, graspability also affords sociability, an impulse that requires one to distinguish appropriate objects from inappropriate ones.

graspability The perception of whether or not an object is of the proper shape, size, texture, and distance to afford grasping.

long hallway in an apartment building, or an empty road. To an adult eye, the degree to which these places afford running may be restricted by such factors as a bull grazing in the meadow, neighbors in the hallway, or traffic on the road.

Graspable?

All the senses are active processors from the moment of birth. Infants learn what parts of the visual array best afford focusing, what sounds merit listening, and so on. In terms of actions controlled by the infant, the grasping and sucking reflexes are among the first to afford information.

Graspability—whether an object is the right size, shape, and texture for grasping and whether it is within reach—is an early affordance. This is vital information, since infants learn about their world by handling objects. Extensive research has shown that infants perceive graspability long before their manual dexterity enables them to actually grasp successfully. They look intently at objects that seem graspable and ignore ones that do not, even before they are able to aim and adjust their arms and hands to grab the possibly graspable thing (Wentworth et al., 2000). By 5 months, infants are able to grab objects successfully, usually taking longer to coordinate their hand movements than do older babies and adults. This shows that deliberate and thoughtful perception precedes an action that will soon become automatic (McCarty & Ashmead, 1999).

The fact that babies perceive graspability so early helps explain how they explore a face. Once they have some control over their arm and hand movements, they will grab at any face that comes within their reach. But their grabbing is far from haphazard: They do not grab at the eyes or mouth (although they might poke at them), because they already perceive that these objects are embedded and thus do not afford grasping. A tug at the nose or ears is more likely, because these features do afford grasping. Even better are eyeglasses, earrings, and long mustaches—all of which are quickly yanked by most babies, who perceive at a glance the graspability these objects afford.

Sudden Drops

The affordances that an infant perceives in common objects evolve as the infant gains experience with those objects. An example is provided by the **visual cliff**, an apparatus designed to provide the illusion of a sudden dropoff between one horizontal surface and another.

visual cliff An experimental apparatus designed to provide the illusion of a sudden dropoff between one horizontal surface and another.

Depth Perception Like thousands of crawling babies before him, this infant refuses to crawl to his mother because the visual-cliff apparatus makes him think there is a dropoff between himself and her.

? *Observational Quiz* (see answer, page 180): What does he see when he looks down?

INNERVISIONS

The First 2 Years: Psychosocial Development

Psychosocial development, by definition, involves the combination of two elements: the *psyche* (from the Greek word meaning "soul, spirit, feelings") and the *social context* (family, community, culture). This chapter is about that combination: the interaction between an infant's emotions, temperament, and personality, on the one hand, and the entire social world, including mother, father, other caregivers, and society as a whole, on the other. There are many ways in which such an interaction can go well—a "goodness of fit" that allows the baby's temperament and the surrounding social world to come together to support ongoing development. With some adjustments by both partners, this fit usually occurs. We focus first on the infant's contribution to this partnership and then on the caregiving context. Throughout, we note the varieties of interaction, from the infant's secure attachment (whether to mother, father, day-care provider) to development that is detached, disorganized, disturbed, destructive. As we will see, theories lead to practice: What can be done to ensure that every infant achieves that goodness of fit.

Emotional Development in Infancy

In many ways, expressions of emotion become the vital code that enables one person to connect with another, the window that allows outsiders to look into a person's thoughts and allows the person inside to look outward. As the infant becomes older, both processes are at work: The infant's emotions become easier for others to read, just as the infant becomes better able to read the emotional expressions of others.

The diversity of family circumstances and of inborn traits means that some infants develop much more smoothly than others. Of necessity, this chapter describes the typical course of development, but we must not forget the many other psychosocial paths that infants and caregivers take. To help us keep this point in mind, we begin and end the chapter with two cases—Toni (whom we first met in Chapter 5) and Jacob.

A Case to Study

Jacob's Parents on Autopilot

Here is a father's description of his third child, Jacob:

> We were convinced that we were set. We had surpassed our quota of 2.6 children and were ready to engage parental auto-pilot. I had just begun a prestigious job and was working 10–11 hours a day. The children would be fine. We hired a nanny to watch Jacob during the day.
>
> As each of Jacob's early milestones passed we felt that we had taken another step toward our goal of having three normal children. We were on our way to the perfect American family. Yet, somewhere back in our minds we had some doubts. Jacob seemed different than the girls. He had some unusual attributes. There were times when we would be holding him and he would arch his back and scream so loud that it was painful for us.

> *[Jacob's father, 1997]*

Jacob was unable to relate to his parents (or to anyone else) for the first two years of his life, although his parents paid little attention to the problem. They already had two daughters; if they noticed that something was odd, they told themselves "boys are different" and blamed Jacob's inability to talk on a nanny who did not speak English well. His father continues:

> Jacob had become increasingly isolated [by age 2]. I'm not a psychologist, but I believe that he just stopped trying. It was too hard, perhaps too scary. He couldn't figure out what was expected of him. The world had become too confusing, and so he withdrew from it. He would seek out the comfort of quiet, dark places and sit by himself. He would lose himself in the bright, colorful images of cartoons and animated movies.

Jacob was finally diagnosed with a "pervasive development disorder" at age 3. This is a catchall diagnosis that can include autistic reactions (discussed in detail in Chapter 11). At the moment you need to know only that the psychosocial possibilities for Jacob and his parents were unappreciated at this point. First, his despairing parents were advised to consider residential placement, because he would never be normal and they, at least, would no longer be constantly reminded of their "failure." (This recommendation ignored the commitment that most parents feel toward their children.) Second, Jacob's father reports satisfaction that his son successfully passed the "milestones" described in earlier chapters—he gained weight, sat up, walked, played with objects, all on schedule. (Again, a crucial point is ignored: These milestones are connected to biosocial growth, not psychosocial development.) Thus, Jacob's early social problems were overlooked, even though some evidence—such as his reaction to being held and his failure to talk—should have raised the alarm. Other telltale data—smiling, social play, imitation—are not even reported, but should have been.

Toni's situation is another example of the inappropriate focus on biosocial rather than psychosocial difficulties. The case manager's report on Toni does mention some worrisome social factors—the mother went back to work when Toni was about 1 year old, Toni's father is "not in the household," many relatives provide "patchwork care," the mother does not trust strangers to care for Toni—but these are not properly evaluated. For example, if proper evaluation reports that the father is financially supportive and actively involved in her care, it does not matter where he lives; but all we are told is that he does not live in the household. In this chapter we focus on that missing piece: the elements that an infant's emotional and social world should contain for optimal development.

Age Norms

To some extent, early emotional development follows age-graded norms, which are related to physical and cognitive development. For instance, in the first year, before infants walk and talk, they have a smaller range of emotions than in the second year, when more mobility coincides with more emotion. Let us look at the usual sequence of emotional development (which is summarized in Table 7.1).

The First Year

Newborns seem to have only two identifiable emotions: distress and contentment. They cry when they are hungry or in pain, when they are tired or fright-

finely tuned machine (Snow, 1984), an emotional "attunement" of an improvised musical duet (Stern, 1985), and a smoothly flowing "waltz" that is mutually adaptive (Barnard & Martell, 1995). The critical factor is the timing of the interaction, such that each partner responds to the other almost instantly, in a chain of mutual communication. Synchrony helps infants learn to read other people's emotions and to develop some of the basic skills of social interaction, such as taking turns and paying attention, that they will use throughout life.

Synchrony also helps infants learn to express their own feelings. A sensitive parent responds to every hint ("Ooh, are you hungry?" "Aahaaa, you're tired," "Uuumm, you see the rattle?") by mirroring (copying) each expression with exaggerated facial movements and a solicitous tone of voice as well as with actions, such as getting food, putting the head to the shoulder, handing over the rattle (Gergely & Watson, 1999).

Imitation is pivotal. Infants sometimes imitate caregivers: Even newborns can imitate mouth movements, and as their imitation improves over the first year, they begin to feel the emotions that go with the expressions their faces make (just as adults who laugh begin to feel better). But parents' imitation of infants, not infants' imitation of parents, is the force that drives the synchronous activity. If an emotion is visible from an infant's expression (and infants all over the world make the same facial expressions in response to the same stimuli) and the infant sees a familiar face mirroring that emotion, then the infant begins to connect his or her internal state with the external expression (Rochat, 2001).

Learning Through Play

Even though emotional communication is a serious and important job in the first months, synchrony is most evident not in serious dialogue, but in play. Playful interactions may occur in almost any context—during a feeding, a diaper change, or a bath, for example. After a while, they can be initiated by either the adult or the infant: The caregiver might notice the baby's expression or vocalization and echo it (by cooing when the baby coos), or the baby might notice the adult's wide-eyed beaming and break into a grin.

What really distinguishes episodes of synchrony from routine caregiving are the playful, moment-by-moment actions and reactions of both partners. To complement the infant's animated but quite limited repertoire, as well as to elicit new or increased reactions, caregivers perform dozens of actions that seem to be reserved exclusively for babies. Typically, they may open their eyes and mouths wide in exaggerated expressions of mock delight or surprise; make rapid clucking noises or repeat one-syllable sounds ("ba-ba-ba-ba," "di-di-di-di," "bo-bo-bo-bo"); raise and lower the pitch of their voices; change the pace of their movements (gradually speeding up or slowing down); bring their faces close to the baby's and then pull back; tickle, pat, poke, lift, rock, stroke, and do many other simple things. (You may well recognize some of these behaviors as your own spontaneous reaction to a baby—sometimes surprising yourself and amusing those around you!)

Infants' responses complement the actions of adults: They may stare at their partners or look away, vocalize, widen their eyes, move their heads forward or back, or turn aside. A skilled caregiver notices a signal, such as a glance away, that the infant does not want to play. However, some infants need to give very obvious signals—falling asleep, freezing expressionless, or, like Jacob, arching their backs and screaming. Such signals mean that something is wrong in the

Especially for College Men Who Are Not Yet Fathers Imagine you have a male friend who has an infant niece. He says he is afraid he might look silly if he tried to play with her. What do you tell him?

!Answer to Observational Quiz (from page 207): The quiet babies changed the most, perhaps because they were neither distinctly fearful nor distinctly outgoing at 4 months.

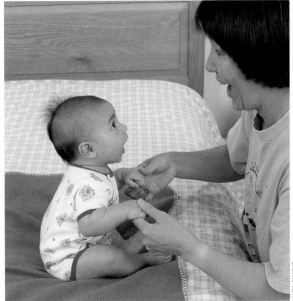

Emotion Shared Three-month-old Mathias and his mother experience synchrony, with eyes wide and staring, mouths open, and hands touching. What would you call the emotion they are sharing—excitement, pride, exhilaration? The experience may be too powerful for any ordinary word to describe.

social interaction: Either the caregiver is too intrusive, not letting the baby rest, or the baby is overwhelmed.

Crucial in all this is that the caregiver be responsive, realizing that babies sometimes just want to look around, to eat, or to sleep. At other times the infant wants interaction but signals that the caregiver's timing or intensity is out of sync. How to repair a failed interaction is as important for both parties to learn as how to sustain interest. Again, the main burden of synchrony falls on the adult: In frame-by-frame studies of videotaped interaction, the caregiver picks up on the baby's signals and elaborates on them more than vice versa (Feldman et al, 1999). Successful breast feeding requires such synchrony, which is one reason it is recommended even when nutrition is not an issue (see Appendix A, Chapter 7).

Reactions to a Still Face

still face technique A method of studying synchrony by assessing the infant's reaction when the caregiver stops engaging in synchronous behavior and merely stares at the baby for a minute or two.

Babies learn to expect certain reactions, as evidenced in a creative experiment using the **still face technique** (Tronick, 1989; Tronick et al., 1978). In the classic condition, a 3- to 4-month-old infant is placed facing the mother, who is first told to play with the baby. Typically, the mother begins the behavior of synchrony, with exaggerated tone, expressions, and so on, and the baby reciprocates with smiles and joy. Then the mother is told to erase all expression and to stare at the baby with a "still face" for a minute or two. Not usually at 2 months, but clearly by 6 months, babies get very upset at the still face: They frown, fuss, drool, look away, kick, or vocalize. Two video cameras record both partners, and then frame-by-frame comparisons reveal the sequence of reactions. The mutuality of the synchrony is apparent, as are the baby's surprise and distress when the mother does not respond. The same conditions and reactions apply with fathers or other significant people, but less so with strangers.

Interestingly, babies are much more upset by their still-faced parents than by their parents' departure for a minute or two (Field, 1994). From a developmentalist's perspective, this is very healthy, because it shows that the baby is used to interactive play. Even more impressive, by 5 months infants have adjusted their style to their social experiences. If a stranger, when placed in front of the infant, responds quickly, with lots of smiling, infants reciprocate *if* their mother acts the same way. However, if their mother is more low-key, infants may be quiet or even cry at an exuberant stranger; they respond better to a stranger whose behavior is similar to their mother's (Bigelow, 1999).

Although synchrony is evident early in life, it becomes more frequent and more elaborate as time goes on; thus, a 6-month-old is a much more active and responsive social partner than a 3-month-old. Parents and infants spend about an hour a day in face-to-face play, although wide variations are apparent from baby to baby, time to time, culture to culture (Baildam et al., 2000; Lee, 2000). Toward the end of the first year, face-to-face play almost disappears; once infants can move around and explore on their own, they are no longer content to stay in one spot and mirror an adult's facial expressions. Even when infants are on the move, however, they look to caregivers for emotional cues, as we will now see.

Social Referencing

social referencing Seeking information about an unfamiliar or ambiguous object or event by observing someone else's expressions and reactions. That other person becomes a reference, consulted when the infant wants to know how to react.

The search for information about another person's feelings is called **social referencing.** A mother's glance of calm reassurance or words of caution, a father's expression of alarm, pleasure, or dismay—each can become a guide to action, telling an infant how to react to an unfamiliar or ambiguous event. (We saw this with the father who allowed his very young daughter's foot to touch the water in the swimming pool.) Social referencing becomes increasingly distinct and important after crawling (at about 9 months) and walking (at about 12 months) make infants independently mobile, when active exploration by Piaget's "little scientist" begins (Derochers et al., 1994). Toddlers search for emotional cues in gaze and facial expressions, pay close attention to outbursts of pleasure or disgust, and watch carefully to detect the intentions behind the actions of others (Baldwin, 2000).

Social referencing is particularly noticeable at mealtime, when infants look to caregivers for cues about new foods. This explains why caregivers the world over smack their lips, pretend to taste, and say "yum-yum" (or the equivalent) as they feed toddlers their first beets, liver, spinach, or whatever. They are trying to lead the infants to like whatever is offered. For their part, toddlers become quite astute at reading expressions, insisting on the foods that the adults *really* like.

Referencing Mom

An everyday example of social referencing is toddlers' willingness to respond to their mother's requests. As every parent knows, toddlers often refuse to do as they are told. In an experiment, only about one toddler in four obeyed their mother's request to pick up dozens of toys that they had not spilled (Kochanska et al., 2001). However, the same toddlers were much more likely to comply when their mothers told them not to touch some very attractive toys within easy reach. Social referencing entered the picture because mothers used tone and expression as well as words to make this prohibition clear and to point out the specifically forbidden toys.

To be specific, when the mothers made it clear to their 1-year-olds that they should not play with certain available toys, about half of the 14-month-olds and virtually all of the 22-month-olds obeyed their mother, even when she was out of sight. Indeed, 80 percent of the older toddlers not only acquiesced but seemed to accept the mother's judgment (which the researchers called *committed compliance*), one even saying "no-no touch" as a reminder (Kochanska et al., 2001). It is interesting to contrast these toddlers' wholesale acceptance of the message they received via social referencing with typical reactions at older ages: Preschoolers more often touch the forbidden toys when the mother is not present, and adolescents ask for reasons and argue back. Unlike these older children, toddlers rely on their parents as reliable social references and accept their judgments, typically looking repeatedly at the adult's facial expression.

Referencing Dad

Early research on the psychosocial context of development usually studied mother–infant relationships, partly for practical reasons and partly because in those days it was assumed that mothers were the main caregivers. Now it has become apparent that people other than mothers can and do provide important care for infants. Research has not caught up to the specific effects of siblings, grandparents, and others (although their influence can be substantial), but much is now known about fathers. Infants use Dad as a social reference as much as Mom, if both are present. In fact, fathers tend to be more encouraging than mothers, who are more protective. As a result, when toddlers are about to begin exploring, they often seek a man's approval as a spur for their curiosity (Parke, 1995).

As researchers looked closely at mothers, fathers, and infants, they discovered a curious difference: Although fathers provide less basic care, they play

MICHAEL S. YAMASHITA / CORBIS

Social Referencing Is it dangerous or joyous to ride in a bicycle basket through the streets of Osaka, Japan? Check with Mom to find out.

Response for College Men (from page 209): Go ahead and play. Infants need adults who are willing to look silly, because making odd noises and facial expressions is part of synchrony and play—both important for infant development. This is not only how infants learn; it is also what fathers throughout the world do, bringing great joy to their babies.

Especially for Grandmothers A grandmother of an infant boy is troubled that the baby's father stays with him whenever the mother is away. She says that men don't know how to care for infants, and she notes that he sometimes plays a game in which he tosses his son in the air and then catches him.

CHROMOSOHM / SOHM / PHOTO RESEARCHERS, INC.

Up, Up, and Away! The vigorous play typical of fathers is likely to help in the infant's mastery of motor skills and the development of muscle control.

Goodness of Fit Attachment to the father can be very strong, especially for boys. If the mother is unavailable for any reason, a secure attachment to the father or another caregiver can make the difference in the child's emotional health.

MICHAEL NEWMAN / PHOTOEDIT

more. In general, infants look to fathers for fun and to mothers for comfort (Lamb, 2000; Parke, 1996). Compared to mothers' play, fathers' play is more noisy, emotional, boisterous, physical, and idiosyncratic (as fathers tend to make up active and exciting games on the spur of the moment).

In the first year of a baby's life, fathers are more likely to move the baby's legs and arms in imitation of walking, kicking, or climbing; to zoom the baby through the air (playing "airplane"); or to tap and tickle the baby's stomach. Mothers tend to caress, murmur, or sing soothingly; to combine play with caretaking routines such as diapering and bathing; or to use standard sequences that involve only one part of the body, such as peek-a-boo and patty-cake. Not surprisingly, young infants typically laugh more, and cry more, when playing with Daddy.

In all probability, physically active play helps the children master motor skills and develop muscle control (Pellegrini & Smith, 1998). In addition, play with Daddy may contribute to the growth of social skills and emotional expression. In one study, one or the other parent sat passively nearby while their 18-month-olds met a stranger. The toddlers were more likely to smile and play with the new person when the father was present than when the mother was; the difference was especially apparent among the boys. The authors of the study speculated that previous boisterous, idiosyncratic interactions with Dad made his presence a signal to be bold and playful (Kromelow et al., 1990).

Similar speculations have been raised about fathers' teasing, which requires the baby's social response to an unpredictable game—and thereby may increase not only excitement but also emotional regulation and social understanding (Pecheux & Labrell, 1994). Another study, this one of very-low-birthweight infants in Japan, found that these high-risk infants were much more likely to develop normal social skills if their fathers were actively involved with them (Itoigawa et al., 1996). And in Israel, father–infant involvement led to an increase in exploratory play (Feldman et al., 1997).

The fact that fathers are good playmates in many cultures does not mean they are limited to that role. If they are called on and their culture allows it, fathers are quite capable of providing all necessary emotional and cognitive nurturing, speaking baby talk, and forming secure relationships as both secondary and primary caregivers (Geiger, 1996; Lamb, 1997).

Diversity is obvious, as each couple cooperates to raise their children. Every set of parents develop their own roles, which may or may not conform to cultural generalities but which work well for their family. In fact, diversity is more evident for fathers' involvement than mothers' (Marsiglio et al., 2000). Nevertheless, fathers' involvement generally benefits children's development, even if fathers forge their own way of caring for their offspring. Cultures or individual mothers who discourage fathers' participation may thus be impairing children's growth. One study found that adolescent boys who did not know their fathers were more likely to abuse drugs and be arrested, as well as to become fathers themselves before age 20 (Fagot et al., 1998). In general, the father's involvement in infant care benefits the mother's self-confidence, the child's later development, and the emotional strength of the father himself (Aldous et al., 1998; Eggebeen & Knoester, 2001; Vandell et al., 1997). Apparently, throughout today's changing world, mothers and fathers together are better able to meet all their infant's needs—biological, cognitive, and psychosocial—than is either parent alone (Cabrera et al., 2000).

Self-Awareness

Another foundation for emotional growth becomes evident in later infancy with the onset of **self-awareness,** which is a person's realization that he or she is a distinct individual whose body, mind, and actions are separate from those of other people. This emerging sense of "me" and "mine" fosters the growth of many self-conscious emotions, from pride and confidence to guilt, shame, and embarrassment. Notice, however, that we discuss self-awareness within our discussion of "emotions in the social context." That's because awareness of self arises from awareness of others, and, simultaneously, self-awareness leads to new consciousness of others. That consciousness fosters other-directed emotions, including defiance and jealousy as well as empathy and affection. As one developmentalist explains:

> With the emergence of consciousness in the second year of life, we see vast changes in both children's emotional life and the nature of their social relationships. . . . With consciousness the child can feel what I have called self-conscious emotions, like pride at a job well done or shame over a failure.
>
> *[Lewis, 1997, p. 132]*

The onset of self-awareness is strikingly evident when infants of various ages are compared. Very young infants have no sense of self. In fact, a prominent psychoanalyst, Margaret Mahler, theorized that for the first 4 months of life infants see themselves as part of their mothers. They "hatch" at about 5 months, and spend the next several months developing a sense of themselves as separate from their mothers (Mahler et al., 1975). Psychoanalytic theories have not been proved to be universally applicable, but there is no doubt that the infant emerges as a self-aware individual occurs gradually over the first year.

During the second year, the period from 15 to 18 months "is noteworthy for the emergence of the Me-self, the sense of self as the object of one's knowledge" (Harter, 1998). This can be seen in the following two examples, one about a series of experiments and the other about one normal toddler.

Rouge on the Forehead

The emerging sense of self was demonstrated in a classic experiment (Lewis & Brooks, 1978). Babies looked in a mirror after a dot of rouge had been surreptitiously put on their noses. If the babies reacted to the mirror image by touching their own noses, that meant they knew they were seeing their own faces. By trying this experiment with 96 babies between the ages of 9 and 24 months, the experimenters found a distinct, age-related developmental shift. None of the babies under 12 months reacted to the mark as if it were on their own faces (they sometimes smiled at and touched the dot on the baby in the mirror). However, most of those between ages 15 and 24 months did react with self-awareness, perhaps by touching their own faces with an expression of curiosity and puzzlement.

The link between self-awareness and self-conscious emotions was shown in a later extension of the rouge-and-mirror experiment (Lewis et al., 1989). In this study, 15- to 24-month-olds who showed self-recognition in the mirror also looked *embarrassed* when they were effusively praised by an adult; that is, they smiled and looked away, covered their faces with their hands, and so on. Infants without self-recognition—that is, those who had not recognized that the rouge was on their own noses—were not embarrassed.

self-awareness A person's realization that he or she is a distinct individual whose body, mind, and actions are separate from those of other people.

Response for Grandmothers (from page 211): Fathers can be great caregivers, and most mothers prefer that the father provide care. It's good for the baby and the marriage. Being tossed in the air is great fun (and no harm, as long as the father is a good catcher!). A generation ago, mothers didn't let fathers care for infants, so today's grandfathers may feel unable to do it. Fortunately, today's mothers less often act as gatekeepers, shutting the fathers out.

A Beautiful Bonnet At 18 months, Austin recognizes himself, obviously delighted by his colander hat. Once self-recognition begins at about this age, many children spend hours admiring themselves with various hats, makeup, and other accessories. Almost every view of themselves is a joy; children are not yet worried about looking stupid or ugly.

Self-awareness soon becomes linked with self-concept, as toddlers figure out the extent of their abilities. One of the interesting aspects is the importance of toddlers' self-evaluations. Toddlers who are told "You're very smart" probably appreciate the compliment, but usually they can already feel quite smart, pleased, and proud about what they have done. In fact, one study found that boys who receive *less* parental praise become *more* proud of themselves, perhaps because they are better able to form their own positive self-evaluations (Belsky et al., 1997). Another longitudinal study found that positive comments from a mother to a 2-year-old did not lead to more pride or less shame by age 3 (Kelley et al., 2000). However, certain negative comments ("You're doing it all wrong") diminished effort and increased shame. Neutral suggestions, in addition to guiding toddlers to complete activities on their own, fostered the willingness to try new challenges later on (Kelley et al., 2000). It seems that building self-esteem is more complicated than simply praising a toddler; it also entails enabling children to accomplish things that make them feel proud.

Juice on the Floor

How can a toddler's own pride be more compelling than parental approval? Look, for example, at Ricky, the grandson of a noted psychologist. Shortly before his second birthday, Ricky teased his mother by deliberately pouring a cup of juice onto a rug. Evidence that Ricky knew he was being naughty was his reaction to his mother's scolding: He was unsurprised and unfazed by her angry words and was quite willing to help her clean up the mess. Only when his mother sent him to his room did he protest angrily, apparently not having anticipated such punishment. Later that day he told his grandmother, "Juice on a floor." Her response was "Juice doesn't go on the floor," delivered somewhat sternly. "Yes, juice on a floor, juice on a floor," Ricky laughingly repeated several times, pretending to turn an imaginary cup upside down. As Ricky's grandmother comments:

> The boy's pleasure at watching the juice spill and anger at being sent to his room are emotions that are typical at all periods of infancy, but his obvious pride at his ability to act counter to convention or his mother's wishes is possible only when self-awareness is firmly established.

[Shatz, 1994]

"I get along fine with people my age and I get along fine with people your age—it's the ones in the middle who give me all kinds of problems."

Parents Are the Problem According to psychoanalytic theory, the inevitable conflicts between parents and young children create the need for personality quirks and defensive measures.

Theories About Caregiving

Thus far we have focused on the infant half of the psychosocial partnership, including both the epigenetic, maturational aspects of emotion and the interface with the social context of development. Here we turn to the other half, the caregiver. We begin by reviewing what our five major theories (introduced in Chapter 2) have had to say about the importance of caregivers, particularly of mothers. As you will see, the theories that developed before the middle of the twentieth century placed mothers at the center of infant growth and development, while more recent theories do not.

Psychoanalytic Theory

By far the strongest emphasis on the early relationship between parent and child arises from psychoanalytic theory, which holds that the first two or three years of life are pivotal for later personality and psychological health. The mother–child relationship is considered particularly crucial. To be specific, there are lifelong consequences if a parent–child relationship goes wrong, these theorists assert, and usually the mother is to blame. Sigmund Freud, who established the framework for this view, believed that the experiences of the first four years "play a decisive part in determining whether and at what point the individual shall fail to master the real problems of life" (Freud, 1918/1963). He thought that the mother was "unique, without parallel, established unalterably for a whole lifetime as the first and strongest love-object and as the prototype of all later love relations" (Freud, 1940/1964).

Freud: Oral and Anal Stages

As we noted in Chapter 2, Freud viewed human development in terms of psychosexual stages that occur at specific ages. According to Freud (1935), psychological development begins in the first year of life with the **oral stage,** so named because the mouth is the young infant's prime source of gratification. In the second year, the infant's prime focus of gratification shifts to the anus—particularly the sensual pleasure of bowel movements and, eventually, the psychological pleasure of controlling them. Accordingly, Freud referred to this period as the **anal stage.**

According to Freud, both the oral and anal stages are fraught with potential conflicts that can have long-term consequences. If a mother frustrates her infant's urge to suck—by, say, weaning the infant from the nipple too early or preventing the child from sucking on fingers or toes—the child may become distressed and anxious and eventually become an adult with an *oral fixation.* Such a person is stuck (fixated) at the oral stage and therefore eats, drinks, chews, bites, or talks excessively, in quest of mouthy pleasures that were denied in infancy.

Similarly, if toilet training is overly strict or if it begins before the child is mature enough to participate (before 18 months), interaction between parents and child may become locked into a conflict over the toddler's refusal or inability to comply. This conflict, too, may have important consequences for the child's future personality. The child becomes fixated and develops an *anal personality;* as an adult, he or she may seek control of self and others and demonstrate an unusual need for regularity in all aspects of life.

Freud's ideas have been extremely influential. The importance of unconscious memories from early childhood and of the mother–infant relationship are still emphasized by many psychoanalytic theorists (Fonagy & Target, 2000). However, research has failed to link specific oral- and anal-stage conflicts with later personality traits. The overall pattern of parental warmth and sensitivity, or coldness and domination, affects the child's emotional development much more than the particulars of either feeding or toilet training. This broader perspective is reflected in the theory of Erik Erikson.

Erikson: Trust and Autonomy

As you remember from Chapter 2, Erikson believed that development proceeds through a series of developmental crises, or challenges, that occur over the life span. In the first crisis of infancy, which Erikson labeled **trust versus mistrust,** the infant learns whether the world is essentially a secure place where basic needs will be readily satisfied or an unpredictable arena where needs are met only after much crying—and sometimes not even then. Erikson (1963) contended that babies begin to develop a sense of security when their mothers provide food and comfort with "consistency, continuity, and sameness of experience." When interaction with the mother inspires trust and security, the child (and later the adult) experiences confidence in engaging with and exploring the world.

oral stage Freud's term for the first stage of psychosexual development, in which the infant obtains pleasure through sucking and biting.

anal stage Freud's term for the second stage of psychosexual development, in which the anus becomes the main source of gratification, particularly the sensual pleasure of bowel movements and, eventually, the psychological pleasure of controlling them.

KEN CAVANAUGH / PHOTO RESEARCHERS, INC

A Moment of Bliss Freud thought that oral gratification through breast feeding was an erotic experience as well as, in his day, a nutritional necessity. Modern psychologists question the power and even the existence of Freud's stages, but his emphasis on the universality of unconscious, primitive urges may not be as far-fetched as some believe.

trust versus mistrust Erikson's term for the first crisis of psychosocial development, in which the infant learns whether the world is essentially a secure place where basic needs are always met or an unpredictable arena where needs (for food, comfort, etc.) are sometimes unmet.

autonomy versus shame and doubt Erikson's term for the second crisis of psychosocial development, in which toddlers either succeed or fail in gaining a sense of self-rule over their own actions and bodies.

The next crisis, which occurs in toddlerhood, is **autonomy versus shame and doubt.** Toddlers want autonomy, or self-rule, over their own actions and bodies. If they fail in their effort to gain it, either because they are incapable or because their caregivers are too restrictive, they feel ashamed of their actions and doubtful of their abilities. According to Erikson, the key to meeting this crisis and gaining a sense of autonomy is parental guidance and protection:

> Firmness must protect him [the toddler] against the potential anarchy of his as yet untrained sense of discrimination, his inability to hold on and let go with discretion. As his environment encourages him to "stand on his own feet," it must protect him against meaningless and arbitrary experiences of shame and of early doubt.
>
> *[Erikson, 1963]*

If parents accomplish this, the child will become increasingly self-confident when new challenges arise.

Like Freud, Erikson believed that problems that begin in early infancy can last a lifetime. He maintained that the adult who is suspicious and pessimistic or who always seems burdened by shame may have been an infant who did not develop sufficient trust or a toddler who did not achieve sufficient autonomy.

Curiosity or Naughtiness? According to Erikson, how parents react to their children's efforts at autonomy can shape how young children resolve the psychosocial crisis of autonomy versus shame and doubt. If you were 21-month-old Shaquille's parent, how would you react to his destructive exploration of a cassette tape?

Behaviorism

From the perspective of behaviorism, or traditional learning theory (discussed in Chapter 2), an infant's emotions and personality are molded as parents reinforce or punish the child's spontaneous behaviors. If parents smile and pick up their baby at every glimmer of an infant grin, the baby will become a child—and later an adult—with a sunny disposition. Responses in early synchrony teach a child some very important lessons about communicating: Take turns, and repair a broken line of communication when necessary. Similarly, if parents continually tease their infant by, say, removing the nipple as the baby is contentedly sucking or by playfully pulling at a favorite toy that a toddler is clutching, that child will develop a suspicious, possessive nature and will not be securely attached to anyone.

The strongest statement of this early view came from John Watson, the leading behaviorist of the time, who cautioned:

> Failure to bring up a happy child, a well-adjusted child—assuming bodily health— falls squarely upon the parents' shoulders. [By the time the child is 3] parents have already determined . . . whether . . . [the child] is to grow into a happy person, wholesome and good-natured, whether he is to be a whining, complaining neurotic, an anger-driven, vindictive, over-bearing slave driver, or one whose every move in life is definitely controlled by fear.
>
> *[Watson, 1928]*

Later theorists in the behaviorist tradition incorporated social learning into their view of personality formation. They found that infants observe and then imitate personality traits of their parents, even if they are not directly reinforced for doing so. A child might develop a quick temper, for instance, if a parent regularly displays anger and in return gets respect—or at least obedience—from other family members.

Social referencing strengthens this learning by observation. Generally, if toddlers receive more signals of interest and encouragement than of fear and prohibition as they explore, they are likely to be more outgoing and less aggressive than they would have been if the opposite messages had been received (Calkins, 1994). If an infant or toddler sees few signals of any kind (as might happen if the primary caregiver is depressed, neglectful, or overtired), the child may become relatively emotionless and passive (Field, 1994).

Like psychoanalytic theorists, behaviorists usually emphasize the importance of the mother in a child's early years. For example, having a social initiative ignored by the mother is a powerful punishment for infants, who naturally strive to make social contact. A depressed mother does not respond to her infant's bids for synchrony, and once the infant is able to move around, her behavior becomes even less encouraging: "Depressed mothers are more likely to withdraw from their children and respond with little emotion or energy, or to become intrusive and hostile toward them" (National Research Council and Institute of Medicine, 2000).

Other Theories

The psychoanalytic and behaviorist theories developed in the early twentieth century and had become popular by mid-century. At that time, it was widely believed that good mothers did not work outside the home, at least until their youngest child entered kindergarten. Other, more recent theories are somewhat less focused on early maternal care.

Cognitive Theory

Cognitive theory holds that a person's thoughts and values determine his or her perspective on the world. Cognitive theorists believe that our early family experiences are important primarily because our thoughts, perceptions, and memories make them so, not because they are buried in our unconscious (as psychoanalytic theory maintains) or burned into our brain patterns (according to behaviorism). Regarding synchrony, cognitive theory suggests that newborns know nothing about whether relationships are supposed to be trusting, encouraging, liberating, or restrictive. What infants do is try to develop a general concept of what to expect from people, in much the same way that, as we saw in Chapter 6, they develop affordances of objects or events.

To be specific, infants use their early relationships to develop a **working model,** a useful set of assumptions that become a frame of reference that can be called upon later in life (Bretherton & Munholland, 1999). It is called a "model" because these early relationships are seen as a prototype or blueprint; it is called "working" because it is useful in practice but is just a guide, not a fixed and final creation.

For example, if a 1-year-old girl develops a working model, based on how her mother responds to her, that people are not to be trusted, then she will use that assumption whenever she meets a new person. All her childhood relationships will be insecure, and as an adult she will be suspicious of humanity, always on guard against further disappointment. To use Piaget's terminology, people develop a cognitive schema to organize their perceptions of all humans, just as babies develop a schema to organize their perception of objects—deciding, for instance, that small objects are graspable. It is the interpretation of early experiences that is crucial, not necessarily the experiences themselves (Schaffer, 2000). This is true for many infant cognitions, such as the concept of self and the role of

working model In cognitive theory, a set of assumptions that are used to organize perceptions and experiences.

temperament traits such as fear and curiosity. We all develop many working models, which are subject to change as the need for adaptation arises.

Sociocultural Theory

The sociocultural perspective emphasizes the many ways in which the entire social context can have a major impact on infant–caregiver relationships. For example, if the culture encourages mothers to nurse at the baby's first whimper and to soothe every distress, the infant will be likely to develop into a trusting, contented adult.

The sociocultural perspective also says that children can change after infancy if their social context changes. A dramatic recent example is the thousands of children in Romania who had been surrendered to orphanages and were adopted by couples from other countries in the early 1990s. None of these children had experienced synchrony or responsive caregiving of any kind in infancy; in fact, "without exception, children adopted from Romania experienced very gross global deprivation" (O'Connor et al., 2000, p. 379). However, some of them developed warm and supportive relationships with their new parents—evidence of sociocultural power.

In truth, many later adoptees who had had a severely deprived infancy did not adapt perfectly: By age 6 they still had not attained normal cognitive or social development. But the fact that some had done so suggests that change after the first year is possible, and that even the worst social context in the early years can be replaced by a better social-cultural situation, to which the children will respond. Other research, with children whose infancy was less disturbed, also finds that personality and emotional traits are affected by current cultural conditions as much as or more than by early ones (O'Connor et al., 2000).

Epigenetic Systems Theory

Epigenetic systems theory holds that each infant is born with a genetic predisposition to develop certain traits that affect emotional development. Temperament is real. As we have seen in our discussion of temperament, the emotions of the infant are universal in their emergence but vary from child to child in the frequency and intensity of their expression. Change is possible, because genes permit selective adaptation to the environment. The central idea of epigenetic systems theory—that all human behavior is imbedded in a social and biological context that changes in mutually adaptive ways over time—seems as true in the first years of life as in the final days.

Each of our five major theories provides useful, and sometimes contrasting, perspectives on two of the most extensively studied aspects of infant psychosocial development: attachment and day care.

Attachment

The relationship between child and parent is lifelong. Even adult children and their aging parents have episodes of quick-response interaction, with mutual glances and laughter, that are similar to the exchanges they had when the child was a few months old and synchrony between parent and child first appeared. Love, affection, and closeness between parents and children are possible at any age. At each stage, however, the expression of that relationship changes, and the usual terminology changes as well.

The term *synchrony* is usually reserved for the first year, when preverbal play predominates. Another term, **attachment**, describes the relationship be-

attachment According to Ainsworth (1973), "an affectional tie that one person or animal forms between himself and another specific one—a tie that binds them together in space and endures over time."

Part II

The Developing Person So Far: The First 2 Years

BIOSOCIAL

Body, Brain, and Nervous System Over the first 2 years, the body quadruples in weight and the brain triples in weight. Connections between brain cells grow into increasingly dense and complex neural networks of dendrites and axons. As neurons become coated with an insulating layer of myelin, they send messages faster and more efficiently. The infant's experiences are essential in "fine-tuning" the brain's ability to respond to stimulation.

Motor Abilities Brain maturation allows the development of motor skills from reflexes to coordinated voluntary actions, including grasping and walking. At birth, the infant's senses of smell and hearing are quite acute; although vision at first is sharp only for objects that are about 10 inches away, visual acuity approaches 20/20 by age 1 year.

Health The health of the infant depends on nutrition (ideally, breast milk), immunization, and parental practices. Survival rates are much higher today than they were even a few decades ago.

COGNITIVE

Perceptual Skills The infant's senses are linked by both inter-modal and cross-modal perception, allowing information to be transferred among senses. The infant is most interested in affordances, that is, what various experiences and events offer to the infant. Movement and personal sensory experiences contribute to the perception of affordances.

Cognitive Skills The infant's active curiosity and inborn abilities interact with various experiences to develop early categories, such as object size, shape, texture, and even number, as well as an understanding of object permanence. Memory capacity, while fragile, grows during the first years. The infant progresses from knowing his or her world through immediate sensorimotor experiences to being able to "experiment" on that world through the use of mental images.

Language Babies' cries are their first communication; they then progress through cooing and babbling. Interaction with adults through "baby talk" teaches them the surface structure of language. By age 1, an infant can usually speak a word or two, and by age 2 is talking in short sentences.

PSYCHOSOCIAL

Emotions and Personality Development Emotions change from quite basic reactions to complex, self-conscious responses. Infants become increasingly independent, a transition explained by Freud in terms of the oral and anal stages, by Erikson in terms of the crises of trust versus mistrust and autonomy versus shame and doubt. While these theories emphasize the parents' role, research finds that much of basic temperament—and therefore personality—is inborn and apparent throughout life.

Parent–Infant Interaction Early on, parents and infants respond to each other by synchronizing their behavior in social play. Toward the end of the first year, secure attachment between child and parent sets the stage for the child's increasingly independent exploration of the world. The infant becomes an active participant in this social interaction, first in directly reacting to others and then in seeking out opinions through social referencing. By age 2, toddlers have definite personalities, the product of the interaction of nature and nurture.

Part III

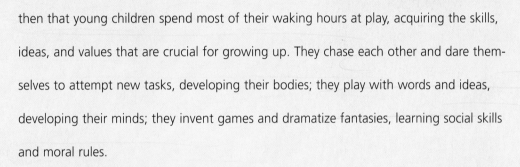

T he period from ages 2 to 6 is usually called early childhood, or the preschool period. Here we shall call it the "play years" as well, to underscore the importance of play during that time. Play occurs at every age, of course, but the years of early childhood are the most playful of all. It is then that young children spend most of their waking hours at play, acquiring the skills, ideas, and values that are crucial for growing up. They chase each other and dare themselves to attempt new tasks, developing their bodies; they play with words and ideas, developing their minds; they invent games and dramatize fantasies, learning social skills and moral rules.

The playfulness of young children can cause them to be delightful or exasperating. To them growing up is a game, and their enthusiasm for it seems unlimited—whether they are quietly tracking a beetle through the grass or riotously turning their play area into a shambles. Their minds seem playful, too, for the immaturity of their thinking enables them to explain that "a bald man has a barefoot head" or that "the sun shines so children can go outside to play."

If you expect them to sit quietly, think logically, or act realistically, you are bound to be disappointed. But if you enjoy playfulness, you will enjoy caring for, listening to, and even reading about children between 2 and 6 years old.

Chapter Eight

The Play Years

The Play Years: Cognitive Development

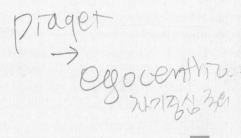

Piaget → egocentric

One of the delights of observing young children is listening to their fanciful and subjective understanding. They beguile us with imaginative, even magical, thinking when they chatter away with an invisible playmate, or wonder where the sun sleeps, or confidently claim that they themselves sleep with their eyes open. At the same time, they startle us when they are confused by metaphors (as in "Mommy is tied up at the office" or "The car's engine just died") and when they are illogical about common occurrences, such as believing that the moon follows them when they walk at night or that buttons are alive because they hold up pants (Carey, 1999). At 3 years of age, they believe that wishes usually come true and that adults, children, and probably cats and dogs (but not babies) can make such wishes (Woolley et al., 1999). Clearly, their thinking is often dictated by their own subjective views, but it also reflects guidance and explicit instruction. This chapter describes both—the magic of what is, and the education that can be.

Research on intellectual development before age 7 has inspired a completely new understanding of early schooling, which was once thought of as merely "day care" but is now considered an important learning experience. One developmental psychologist explains:

> People often call this the "preschool period," but that's not only a mundane name for a magic time, it's also a misnomer. These three-ish and five-ish years are not a waiting time before school or even a time of preparation for school, but an age stage properly called "early childhood" that has a developmental agenda of its own.
>
> [Leach, 1997, p. 431]

The goal of this chapter is to understand that "developmental agenda," from the theories to the facts about cognitive development, from the language explosion to early education.

How Children Think: Piaget and Vygotsky

For many years, the magical and self-absorbed nature of young children's thinking dominated developmentalists' descriptions. In this we were guided by Jean Piaget, the Swiss developmentalist whose theories were discussed in Chapter 2 and who called such thinking *egocentric* (literally, "self-centered"). Piaget thought young children were severely and inevitably limited by their own perspective. The label "egocentric" stuck, not only to the children but also to our thoughts about them.

However, more recent research has highlighted another side of early childhood cognition. This side was suggested first by scientists who skillfully used naturalistic observation to chronicle exactly what children said and did. Analyze the following interaction between a 2-year-old child and his mother, who had been trying to hold his sweet tooth in check:

> *(Child sees chocolate cake on table.)*
> **Child:** Bibby on.
> **Mother:** You don't want your bibby on. You're not eating.
> **Child:** Chocolate cake. Chocolate cake.
> **Mother:** You're not having any more chocolate cake, either.
> **Child:** Why?
> **Mother:** *(No answer)*
> **Child:** *(Whines)* Tired.
> **Mother:** You tired? Ooh! *(Sympathetically)*
> **Child:** Chocolate cake.
> **Mother:** No chance.
>
> *[adapted from Dunn et al., 1987, p. 136]*

Is this 2-year-old illogical, unaware of his social context? Not at all. He is showing strategic skill in pursuing his goal—from asking for his bib (which, unlike cake, is a noncontroversial request) to eliciting his mother's sympathy by feigning fatigue. He is, as Lev Vygotsky would recognize, thinking beyond the bounds of egocentrism. To develop an understanding of both the egocentrism and the social awareness of early cognition, we consider both Piaget and Vygotsky.

Piaget: Preoperational Thought

Piaget's term for cognitive development between the ages of about 2 and 6 is **preoperational thought.** Because he assumed that the ultimate goal of cognition is the ability to reason logically, Piaget emphasized what children cannot do rather than what they can do. Until about age 6 or 7, according to Piaget, children cannot yet think *operationally;* that is, they cannot develop a thought or an idea according to a set of logical principles and then change their conclusions about a given problem when the logical rules change. For instance, they know that Mother is Mother, but they cannot grasp that Mother was once Grandma's baby girl.

Obstacles to Logical Operations

Young children may not yet be capable of logical thought, but that does not mean that they are stupid. Rather, it means that their thinking reflects four prelogical characteristics. The first is **centration,** a tendency to focus thought on one aspect of a situation to the exclusion of all others. We already saw centration in Chapter 6, with the underextension of first words. This continues with later words and concepts. Young children may, for example, insist that lions and tigers are not cats because they center on the house-pet aspect of the cats they know. Or they may insist that Father is a *daddy,* not a brother, because they center on the role each family member fills for them.

A particular type of centration is ego-centration, better known as **egocentrism.** The egocentric child contemplates the world exclusively from his or her personal perspective. In the daddy example above, the fact that the child centers on the man's relationship to the child is an example of egocentrism. As Piaget described it, young children are not necessarily selfish; they would, for example, rush to comfort a tearful parent. But the comfort would come in a decidedly egocentric form, such as a teddy bear or a lollipop.

A second characteristic of preoperational thought is its **focus on appearance** to the exclusion of other attributes. A girl given a short haircut might worry that she has turned into a boy; a boy might refuse to wear a pink shirt because he is

---

Four Aspects of Preoperational Thought

1. Centration
2. Focus on appearance
3. Static reasoning
4. Irreversibility

---

preoperational thought Piaget's term for cognitive development between the ages of about 2 and 6; characterized by centration (including egocentrism), focus on appearance, static reasoning, and irreversibility.

centration A characteristic of preoperational thought in which the young child focuses on one aspect of a situation to the exclusion of all others.

egocentrism A type of centration in which the young child contemplates the world exclusively from his or her personal perspective.

focus on appearance A characteristic of preoperational thought in which the young child ignores all attributes except appearance.

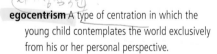

not a girl. Or upon meeting, say, a tall 4-year-old and a shorter 5-year-old, a child might mistakenly insist that "bigger is older."

Third, preoperational children use **static reasoning**, assuming that the world is unchanging, always in the state in which they currently encounter it. If anything does change, it changes totally and suddenly. When she awakened on her fifth birthday, my daughter Rachel asked, "Am I 5 yet?" Told "yes," she grinned, stretched out her arms, and said, "Look at my 5-year-old hands."

Finally, **irreversibility** means that preoperational thinkers fail to recognize that reversing a process can restore whatever existed before the transformation occurred. A 3-year-old who cries because his mother put lettuce on his hamburger might not think to suggest removing the lettuce. Indeed, he might refuse to eat the hamburger even after the lettuce is removed, because he believes that what is done cannot be undone. If his mother takes the contaminated hamburger away, secretly removes the lettuce, and then brings the "new" hamburger, the child might happily eat.

Conservation and Logic

Piaget devised many experiments to test and illustrate the ways in which these four preoperational characteristics—centration, focus on appearance, static reasoning, and irreversibility—limit young children's ability to reason logically. In several experiments, he studied children's understanding of **conservation**, the principle that the amount of a substance is unaffected by changes in its appearance. Piaget found that conservation, which is taken for granted by older children and adults, is not at all obvious to young children. Rather, young children tend to focus exclusively on one facet of shape or placement.

As an example, suppose two identical glasses contain the same amount of liquid. Then the liquid from one of the glasses is poured into a taller, narrower glass. If young children are asked whether one glass contains more liquid than the other, they will insist that the narrower glass, with the higher liquid level, contains more. They make that mistake because they center on the liquid's height, noticing only the static appearance and ignoring the fact that they could reverse the process and re-create the liquid level they had seen a moment earlier.

Similarly, if an experimenter lines up seven pairs of checkers in two rows of equal length and asks a 4-year-old whether both rows have the same number of checkers, the child will usually say "yes." But suppose that, as the child watches, the experimenter elongates one of the rows by spacing its checkers farther apart. If the experimenter asks again whether the rows have the same number

static reasoning A characteristic of preoperational thought in which the young child assumes that the world is unchanging.

irreversibility A characteristic of preoperational thought in which the young child fails to recognize that reversing a process can restore whatever existed before the transformation occurred.

conservation The principle that the amount of a substance is unaffected by changes in its appearance.

Demonstration of Conservation Professor Berger's daughter Sarah, here at 5 ¾, demonstrates Piaget's conservation-of-liquids experiment. First, she examines both short glasses to be sure they contain the same amount of milk. Then, after the contents of one are poured into the tall glass and she is asked "Which has more?" she points to the tall glass, just as Piaget would have expected. Later she added, "It looks like it has more because it's taller," indicating that some direct instruction might change her mind.

HAZEL HANKIN

Tests of Various Types of Conservation

Type of Conservation	Initial Presentation	Transformation	Question	Preoperational Child's Answer
Liquid	Two equal glasses of liquid.	Pour one into a taller, narrower glass.	Which glass contains more?	The taller one.
Number	Two equal lines of checkers.	Increase spacing of checkers in one line.	Which line has more checkers?	The longer one.
Matter	Two equal balls of clay.	Squeeze one ball into a long, thin shape.	Which piece has more clay?	The long one.
Length	Two sticks of equal length.	Move one stick.	Which stick is longer?	The one that is farther to the right.

FIGURE 9.1 Conservation, Please According to Piaget, until children grasp the concept of conservation at (he believed) about age 6 or 7, they cannot understand that the transformations shown here do not change the total amount of liquid, checkers, clay, and wood.

of checkers, most children will reply "no." Other conservation tasks, shown in Figure 9.1, produce similar results. Children are not logical, at least about conservation, until about age 7.

Piaget believed that preoperational children focus on appearances, ignoring or discounting transformations, because they are not yet logical. However, notice that Piaget's operational tests of cognition depend on the child's words, not actions. Other research finds that even 3-year-olds can distinguish appearance from reality if the test is nonverbal (Sapp et al., 2000). Also, children can remember and report transformations in a gamelike setting, such as when a toy puppet, rather than the adult experimenter, does the rearranging. Contemporary researchers now believe that Piaget underestimated conceptual ability during early childhood, just as he did during infancy. He designed his experiments to reveal what young children seemed *not* to understand, rather than to identify what they *could* understand. According to Vygotsky (1978), such underestimation is an error that many adults make: They notice what children cannot do rather than helping them learn what they can.

Vygotsky: Children as Apprentices

Like Vygotsky and Piaget, every developmentalist, every preschool teacher, and every parent knows that young children strive to understand the world that fascinates and sometimes confuses them. One researcher even coined the term **theory-theory** to highlight the idea that children attempt to construct a theory to explain everything they see and hear:

> More than any animal, we search for causal regularities in the world around us. We are perpetually driven to look for deeper explanations of our experience, and broader and more reliable predictions about it. . . . Children seem, quite literally, to be born with . . . the desire to understand the world and the desire to discover how to behave in it.
>
> [Gopnik, 2001, p. 66]

theory-theory Gopnik's term for the idea that children attempt to construct a theory to explain everything they see and hear.

Thus, according to theory-theory, the best conceptualization of, and explanation for, mental processes is that humans always seek reasons, causes, and underlying principles. Although theory-theory is not universally accepted, no one doubts that children are active thinkers, not passive ones; agents, not recipients (Bloom & Tinker, 2001; Brandtstädter, 1998).

Vygotsky also emphasized another point: Children do not strive alone; their efforts are embedded in a social context. They ask questions—how machines work, why weather changes, where the sky ends—assuming that others know the answers.

Meanwhile, parents, as well as older children, early-childhood educators, and many others, do more than just answer. They try to guide a young child's cognitive growth in numerous ways:

- Presenting challenges for new learning
- Offering assistance with tasks that may be too difficult
- Providing instruction
- Encouraging the child's interest and motivation

In many ways, then, a young child is an **apprentice in thinking** whose intellectual growth is stimulated and directed by older and more skilled members of society. With the help of these mentors, children learn to think by means of their **guided participation** in social experiences and in explorations of their universe.

Vygotsky made yet a third important point: The fact that children want to learn, and then do so, is evidence of their cognitive ability. In fact, "What children can do with the assistance of others might be in some sense even more indicative of their mental development than what they can do alone" (Vygotsky, 1978, p. 85).

If this social-apprenticeship aspect of cognitive development seems familiar, that's because it is given particular emphasis in the sociocultural perspective discussed in Chapter 2. Vygotsky's ideas are one basis for extensive research that emphasizes the cultural foundations of growth and development. In contrast to many developmentalists (including Piaget) who regard cognitive growth as a product of individual discovery propelled by personal experience and biological maturation, Vygotsky believed that cognitive growth is driven by culture. More specifically, Vygotsky saw cognition not as a process of private discovery but as a social activity, with parents and other teachers motivating, channeling, and constructing children's learning.

How to Solve a Puzzle

To see how Vygotsky's approach works in practical terms, let's look at an example. Suppose a child tries to assemble a jigsaw puzzle, fails, and stops trying. Does that mean the task is beyond the child's ability? Not necessarily. The child may do better if given guidance that:

- Structures the task to make its solution more attainable
- Focuses attention on the important steps
- Provides motivation

An adult or older child might begin by praising the child for choosing a hard puzzle and then by encouraging the child to look for a missing puzzle piece for a particular section ("Does it need to be a big piece or a little piece?" "Do you see any blue pieces with a line of red?"). Suppose the child finds some pieces of the right size, and then some blue pieces with a red line, but again seems stymied. The tutor might become more directive, selecting a piece to be tried next, or rotating a piece so that its proper location is more obvious, or actually putting a

Guided Participation Through shared social activity, adults in every culture guide the development of their children's cognition, values, and skills. Typically, the child's curiosity and interests, rather than the adult's planning for some sort of future need, motivate the process. That seems to be the case as this Guatemalan girl eagerly tries to learn her mother's sewing skills.

apprentice in thinking Vygotsky's term for the young child whose intellectual growth is stimulated and directed by older and more skilled members of society.

guided participation The process by which young children, with the help of mentors, learn to think by having social experiences and by exploring their universe.

piece in place with a smile of satisfaction. Throughout, the tutor would praise momentary successes, maintain enthusiasm, and help the child recognize that together they are progressing toward the goal of finishing the puzzle.

The critical element in guided participation is that the partners interact to accomplish the task, with the tutor sensitive and responsive to the precise needs of the child. Eventually, as a result of such mutuality, the child will be able to succeed independently—the ultimate goal of Vygotsky's "apprenticeship in thinking."

Such interactive apprenticeships are commonplace and continual. Everywhere in the world, adults provide guidance and assistance to teach various skills that are valued in the culture—perhaps putting together a puzzle, skinning a small snake, or forming a tortilla. Soon, children who are given such guided practice learn to perform the tasks on their own. Eventually, *they* become the tutors, guiding younger children to master skills that other children, who are the same age but live in a distant country, might never dream of trying.

Scaffolding

Key to the success of apprenticeship is the tutor's sensitivity to the child's abilities and readiness to learn new skills. According to Vygotsky (1934/1986),

> The only good kind of instruction is that which marches ahead of development and leads it. It must be aimed not so much at the ripe as at the ripening functions. It remains necessary to determine the lowest threshold at which instructions may begin, since a certain ripeness of functions is required. But we must consider the upper threshold as well: instruction must be oriented toward the future, not the past.

As you saw in Chapter 2, Vygotsky believed that for each developing individual at each skill level, there is a **zone of proximal development (ZPD)**, that is, a range of skills that the person can exercise with assistance but is not quite able to perform independently. How and when children master potential skills depends, in part, on the willingness of others to **scaffold**, or sensitively structure, participation in learning encounters. Most caregivers do this, at least to some extent (Conner et al., 1997; Rogoff, 1998). For example, a study of adults reading to 3-year-olds found very sensitive scaffolding—explaining, pointing, listening—toward the zone of proximal development in response to the child's needs at the moment (Danis et al., 2000).

Vygotsky believed that words can be part of a scaffold and that verbal interaction is a cognitive tool, essential to intellectual growth in two ways. First, internal dialogue, or **private speech**, occurs when people talk to themselves, and this helps them develop new ideas (Vygotsky, 1987).

zone of proximal development (ZPD) Vygotsky's term for a range of skills that a person can exercise with assistance but is not quite able to perform independently.

scaffold A sensitive structuring of the young child's participation in learning encounters.

private speech Vygotsky's term for the internal dialogue which occurs when people talk to themselves and through which new ideas are developed and reinforced.

Language as Mediation One of the problems with cultural transmission of knowledge is that children are ready to learn whatever they are told—as myths about storks or cabbage patches, bogeymen or witches attest.

Calvin and Hobbes

Researchers have found that preschoolers use private speech to review what they know, decide what to do, and explain events to themselves and, incidentally, to anyone else within earshot. Older preschoolers use private speech more selectively and effectively than younger ones (Winsler et al., 2000).

The second way in which language advances thinking, according to Vygotsky, is as the *mediator of the social interaction* that is vital to learning. Whether this **social mediation** function of speech occurs during explicit instruction or only during casual conversation, whether it is intellectual interpretation or simply enthusiastic comment, language as a tool of verbal interaction refines and extends a person's skills. Language allows a person to enter and traverse the zone of proximal development, because words provide a bridge from the child's current understanding to what is almost understood.

social mediation A function of speech by which a person's cognitive skills are refined and extended.

Comparing Piaget and Vygotsky

The theories of Piaget and Vygotsky are "compatible in many ways" (Rogoff, 1998, p. 681). However, each perspective suggests limitations of the other, as a comparison of the two theorists reveals (see Table 9.1).

Thinking Like a Scientist

What Did Cinderella Do with the Pumpkin?

How would scientists figure out whether Piaget or Vygotsky was correct—that is, how egocentric or socially oriented young children actually are? Can you imagine an experiment that would elicit the child's ability to take the perspective of someone other than themselves? In one experiment designed to measure perspective, or egocentrism, in children aged 3 to 5, young children heard two familiar fairy tales, one with the verb *came* or *went,* the other with the verb *take* or *bring.* The first fairy tale included either this passage:

> Little Red Riding Hood was sitting in her bedroom when her mother went (or *came*) and asked her to go to her grandmother's house.

or this one:

> Cinderella was looking and looking in the kitchen for a pumpkin so that she could bring (or *take*) it to her fairy godmother.
>
> *[Rall & Harris, 2000, p. 208]*

The children were then asked questions, such as "Little Red Riding Hood was in her bedroom and what happened next?" The researchers wanted to know whether the children would repeat the verb they had heard or change it. When the verb was consistent with the main character's location (as are *came* and *take* above), most children repeated it exactly, but when it was inconsistent (as are *went* and *bring*), they changed it three times more often than they

repeated it verbatim. For example, although they were told that the mother *went* in, they said the mother *came* in; although they heard that Cinderella wanted to *bring* the pumpkin to her fairy godmother, they said she wanted to *take* it to her.

The authors of this study assert that it shows that Piaget was in error. Specifically:

> The findings of the present study indicate that such perspective-taking is not just an occasional capacity that is sometimes deployed to override a predominantly egocentric stance. The systematic tendency to misrecall inconsistent verbs indicates, rather, that children spontaneously and tenaciously maintain an alternative perspective.
>
> *[Rall & Harris, 2000, p. 206]*

Yet this experiment seems to indicate that neither Piaget nor Vygotsky was completely right. Do children strive on their own to reflect the appropriate perspective? Many contemporary theorists believe that they do—that children are less egocentric than Piaget believed and less dependent on parental guidance than Vygotsky believed. A third perspective is that motivation, self-organization, and social orientation are among the innate characteristics of children. If all three explanations are partly correct, then adults, ideally, should provide: time and opportunity (according to Piaget); guidance and scaffolding (according to Vygotsky); respect and freedom (for the children themselves).

Comparing Two Theories Both theories emphasize that learning is not passive but is affected by the learners. The two theories share concepts and sometimes terminology; the differences are in emphasis.

TABLE 9.1 Concepts from the Theories of Piaget and Vygotsky

Piaget	Vygotsky
Active Learning The child's own search for understanding, motivated by the child's inborn curiosity.	**Guided Participation** The adult or other mentor's aid in guiding the next step of learning, motivated by the learner's need for social interaction.
Egocentrism The preschooler's tendency to perceive everything from his or her own perspective and to be limited by that viewpoint.	**Apprenticeship in Thinking** The preschooler's tendency to look to others for insight and guidance, particularly in the cognitive realm.
Structure The mental assumptions and modalities (schema) the child creates to help him or her organize an understanding of the world. Structures are torn down and rebuilt when disequilibrium makes new structures necessary.	**Scaffold** The building blocks for learning put in place by a "teacher" (a more knowledgeable child or adult) or a culture. Learners use scaffolds and then discard them when they are no longer needed.

Information Processing

As you have just read, developmentalists debate the origins of the cognitive accomplishments that occur during early childhood. However, no one doubts that young children demonstrate amazing competence in many areas. Social competencies are further discussed in Chapter 10; grammar and vocabulary are described at the end of this chapter; the curiosity and creativity of the young child are evident throughout the three chapters on the play years. Now we look closely at mathematics, memory, and theory of mind—all of which are aspects of the particular way that young children process information.

After Ten Comes Eleven The day, the date, the season, and the weather are all concepts that are part of the curriculum of a good preschool. Young children's ability to grasp these concepts—as well as to develop an understanding of number—is a good deal stronger than researchers or educators once imagined.

JOHN LEI / STOCK, BOSTON

Simple Arithmetic

Even infants have some perceptual awareness of quantity, noticing, for example, the difference between two and three objects (although you may remember that researchers do not all agree about the meaning of this perception) (Chiang & Wynn, 2000). The connection between numbers and objects continues to be quite shaky in early childhood. When asked to count a group of objects, younger preschoolers are likely to delete numbers from the number sequence (counting "one, two, four, seven, . . ."), to count the same item more than once, or to omit some items. It takes time to master basic counting principles, which include the following:

■ *Stable order.* In counting, numbers must be said in a fixed order: 1, 2, 3 is not the same as 3, 2, 1.
■ *One-to-one correspondence.* Each item being counted gets one number, and only one.

KEY QUESTIONS

1. How did Piaget and Vygotsky differ in their understanding of the causes of development?

2. Describe how a parent might scaffold a learning skill, such as reading a book.

3. Which counting principles do 3-year-olds understand, and which ones do they not understand?

4. How do contextual and cultural differences affect how easy it is for children to learn to count?

5. What would be easy and what would be difficult for a 3-year-old to remember?

6. How do scientists find out if a child has a theory of mind?

7. How does an imaginary companion help and hinder a child's thought processes?

8. Why is the question whether children should learn a second language so controversial?

9. What is the difference between a child-centered and an academic preprimary school?

10. What are the reasons for and against sending a 3-year-old to early education?

Chapter Ten

The Play Years: Psychosocial Development

Picture a typical 2-year-old and a typical 6-year-old, and consider how emotionally and socially different they are. Chances are the 2-year-old still has many moments of clinging, of tantrums, and of stubbornness, vacillating between dependence and self-assertion. Further, the 2-year-old cannot be left alone, even for a few moments, wherever curiosity might lead to danger or destruction. If a parent takes a 2-year-old and a 6-year-old to the playground, and then gets absorbed in reading the newspaper, after five minutes the 6-year-old will be playing safely nearby with friends, but the 2-year-old may be at the top of a very high slide or tasting a pretend cake in the sandbox or completely out of sight.

In general, by age 6, children have both the confidence and the competence to be quite independent and yet know their limits. A typical 6-year-old does many things alone and is proud of that—perhaps fixing breakfast before school and even helping to feed and dress a younger sibling. This child shows affection toward family members without obvious clinging, exasperating demands, or exaggerated self-will. The 6-year-old might say good-bye to Mom or Dad at the door of the first-grade classroom and then take care of business: following classroom routines, befriending certain classmates and ignoring others, respecting and learning from teachers.

This chapter details how that 2-to-6 transformation occurs and why some 6-year-olds have not yet achieved the emotional control just described. As you will see, parents and peers are pivotal socializing agents in this process, but the child's own maturation and motivation are important, too. This is apparent in all of psychosocial development, but is especially clear in the area of sex and gender.

Emotional Development

As you remember from the chapters on infancy, 2-year-old children have a sense of themselves and their goals, and they are beginning to develop a range of emotions. During the play years all three of these—self, goals, and emotions—come together.

Emotional Regulation

The pivotal accomplishment between ages 2 and 6 is the "ability to inhibit, enhance, maintain, and modulate emotional arousal to accomplish one's goals" (Eisenberg et al., 1997). Pride is tempered by guilt (and vice versa); joy, by sadness; anger, by fear; fear, by rituals. All are regulated and controlled by the 3- or 4-year-old in ways unknown to the exuberant, expressive, and often overwhelmed toddler.

SEAN CAYTON / THE IMAGE WORKS

Close Connection Unfamiliar events often bring temperamental patterns to the surface, as with the curious boy and his worried brother, who are attending Colorado's Pikes Peak or Bust Rodeo breakfast. Their attentive mother keeps the livelier boy calm and reassures the shy one.

?Observational Quiz (see answer, page 298): Mother is obviously a secure base for both boys, who share the same family and half the same genes, but are different ages: One is two and the other is four. Can you tell which boy is younger?

emotional regulation The ability, beginning in early childhood, to direct or modify one's feelings, particularly feelings of fear, frustration, and anger.

externalizing problems Difficulties that arise from a child's tendency to externalize emotions, or experience emotions outside the self, lashing out in impulsive anger and attacking other people or things.

internalizing problems Difficulties that arise from a child's tendency to internalize emotions, or inhibit their expression, being fearful and withdrawn.

This ability, called **emotional regulation**, is developed in response to society's expectations that children "manage frustration" and "modulate emotional expression" (Sroufe, 1996). Most children accomplish this difficult task quite successfully: They are friendly to new acquaintances but not too friendly; angry but not explosive; frightened by a clown but not terrified.

Emotional regulation begins with impulse control. Some children have **externalizing problems:** Their emotions are external or outside them, as they lash out in impulsive anger and attack other people or things. They are "undercontrolled" and need to learn to regulate their anger. Other children have **internalizing problems:** They are fearful and withdrawn. Their inhibition may be an automatic reaction or a fearful strategy, but in any case, "internalizing children appear to lack the spontaneity and flexibility of control that may be needed for positive adjustment" (Eisenberg et al., 2001). Both externalizing and internalizing children must master the art of emotional regulation, first recognizing and accepting their emotions and then regulating expression, exercising some control but not too much.

Maturation and Learning

Part of emotional regulation is neurological, a matter of brain functioning, and part of it is learned, a matter of social awareness. As we saw in Chapter 8, the ability to regulate one's emotions, to think before acting, to decide whether and in what way to display joy or anger or fear, is directly related to the maturation of the prefrontal cortex. Normally, advances occur at about age 4 or 5, as the child becomes less likely to throw a temper tantrum, provoke a physical attack, or burst into uncontrollable giggles. Normally, social experiences reinforce this maturation, as families and communities encourage children to control their emotions.

Not every child develops the ability to regulate emotions at the same age, for four sets of reasons: genes, early stresses on the brain, early care, and current social influences.

Genetic Variations First, genetic influences come into play. Some people are naturally emotionally expressive and others more inhibited, a range found in infants as well as adults. In the study of brain patterns and behavior in 153 children aged 4 months to 4 years described in Chapter 7, considerable stability was found not only in emotional reactions (laughing or crying when a strange clown appeared, for instance) but also in electrical activity in the prefrontal cortex. Just as with adults, young children who were more fearful had greater activity in their right prefrontal cortex, while those who were more exuberant showed more activity in their left prefrontal cortex (Fox et al., 2001). This indicates that some of the variation in emotional expression is genetic. Consequently, some children need to work to regulate their exuberance, others must try to overcome their anxiety, and still others have neither problem, controlling their emotions more easily.

Early Stress The second set of brain-related differences in emotional regulation is the result of damage during brain development, either prenatally (if the pregnant woman was stressed, ill, or a heavy drug user) or postnatally (if the infant was chronically malnourished, injured, or frightened). Repeated exposure to extreme stress kills some of the neurons of the brain and stops others from developing properly (Sanchez et al., 2001), possibly making some young children physiologically unable to regulate their emotions by thinking and remembering. Instead, even an ordinary stressor—such as an unexpected loud noise or a critical remark—could release a flood of stress hormones, particularly a hormone called cortisol. A 4- or 5-year-old might overreact, experiencing terror or fury at something that another child would consider only mildly upsetting (De Bellis, 2001).

To complicate our understanding of the impact of early stress on later brain maturation, some research finds lower, not higher, levels of cortisol in children who had experienced abuse (Gunnar & Vasquez, 2001). Their blunted stress response may be an early sign of depression if it indicates that their emotions are already dampened and distorted instead of regulated. In either case, early stresses can change the electrical activity, dendrite growth, and production of various hormones in the brain.

Care History We already know, from previous chapters, a third set of influences on emotional regulation: the child's early care experiences. These may either soothe or aggravate the child's reaction to the stresses of infancy. We cannot experiment directly on human infants, but one study of rat pups exposed to stresses that usually cause brain abnormalities found that the effects of that stress disappeared if the rats were raised by nurturing, stress-combating mothers. Such mothers licked, nuzzled, groomed, and fed the rat pups even more than an average rat mother would (Kaufman & Charney, 2001). In humans, one particular influence, as you might imagine after reading Chapter 7, is the quality of the child's attachment to the caregiver. Secure children are best able to control their emotional outbursts (Kochanska, 2001; Laible & Thompson, 1998).

The effects of a child's past care are revealed in many ways, including reactions to another child's cry of pain. Children who have been well nurtured and have formed secure attachments regulate their own emotions and express empathy, comforting the hurting child, reassuring the frightened child, or getting help if need be. By contrast, children with insecure attachments respond abnormally to other children's distress. Some do whatever

> . . . would precisely further distress the child (e.g., scaring a child with the very mask that had been frightening, taunting a crying child and calling him or her a "cry baby," or punching a child with a stomach ache in the stomach). . . . [Others] would often become upset themselves when another was distressed (e.g., holding their own lip and seeking a teacher's lap when another child had fallen).
>
> *[Sroufe, 1996]*

Current Experiences Finally, one key difference between humans and most other animals is that human children depend on their parents for years, not merely for

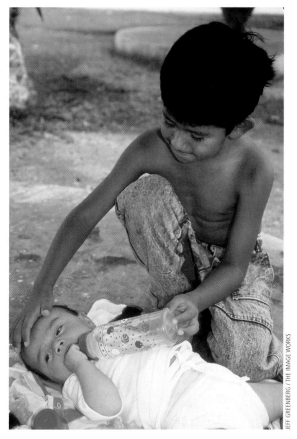

Emotional Regulation Older brothers are not famous for being loving caregivers. However, within the Mayan culture, older children learn to regulate their jealousy and provide major care for younger siblings while their parents work.

? *Observational Quiz* (see answer, page 299): What do you see that suggests that this boy is paying careful attention to his brother?

! *Answer to Observational Quiz* (from page 296): Size is not much help, since children grow slowly during these years and the heads of these two boys appear about the same size. However, emotional development is apparent. Most two-year-olds, like the one at right, still cling to their mothers; most four-year-olds are sufficiently mature, secure, and curious to watch the excitement as they drink their juice.

a few months. Accordingly, it is theoretically possible that parenting practices *after* infancy could be significant in a child's development. Parenting in childhood might have a major impact on emotional regulation, no matter what the child's earliest experiences in infancy had been. Some evidence points in that direction: a mother's current state of depression, current levels of stress hormones, and current patterns of protection seem quite influential in the child's ability to cope with stress and to regulate emotions, sometimes for the better (if a mother who was depressed has recovered) and sometimes for the worse (if a mother becomes depressed) (Susman et al., 2001).

The best research on the relative impact of caregiving in infancy and in early childhood focuses on children who were seriously deprived early in life but then were well nurtured. Such was the experience of the adopted Romanian children mentioned in Chapter 7. Most children adopted before 8 months of age, and some adopted after 8 months, showed normal levels of stress hormones by age 4 or so (Chisholm, 1998; Gunnar et al., 2001). Thus, good caretaking seems able to compensate for high stress and poor caretaking experienced in the early months of life, even repairing the brain damage that may have occurred.

For other adopted children, especially those adopted in toddlerhood, good later caregiving did not prevent emotional difficulties (externalizing or internalizing) or marked delays in emotional regulation. Many were overly friendly, too irritable, or overly distractable. For unknown reasons, some, but not all, children seem to bounce back after early deprivation; resilience probably depends on a combination of genes and experiences (Luthar et al., 2000).

A leading team of developmental researchers summarized:

> In sum, then, there are multiple converging pathways—including not only the neural circuits that are activated by physical, psychological, and immunological stressors, but also the influence of genetics, early experience, and ongoing life events that determine the neural response to different stressors.
>
> *[Cicchetti & Walker, 2001]*

Fear: An Example

Given that some, but not all, caregiving protects against brain abnormalities and that multiple pathways converge, we need to know exactly what parents can do to encourage emotional regulation. One emotion that often seems mishandled by parents in early childhood is fear.

Every normal young child is somewhat fearful. Refusal to go to sleep alone, vivid nightmares, and sudden terror at seeing a masked person are common. However, some parents teach their infants to keep fear at bay by repeatedly responding to the infant's anxiety with reassurance, modulating early fear even at age 1. Comforting touch and tone soothe anxiety at every stage of life. Then, in the "terrible twos," parents teach their children to moderate all the negative emotions, including anger and fear (Kochanska et al., 1997).

The best teacher is example, so ideally parents never express fear when a dog approaches, thunder roars, or a mouse scampers across the floor. The circuits of the child's developing brain respond to such experiences. Gradually, innate emotional triggers are connected to intellectual responses via the corpus callosum, the band of tissue between the brain's hemispheres described in Chapter 8. This connection allows the 4-year-old girl to stand her ground when a circus clown approaches or the 4-year-old boy to restrain himself when another child bumps into him, with neither bursting into tears or launching a self-protective attack.

phobia An irrational fear that is strong enough to make a person avoid the feared object or experience.

Learning can also work in the opposite direction. Some young children develop a **phobia**: an irrational and exaggerated fear that terrifies the person. Phobias probably have their roots in genetic protection of the entire human race:

Our ancestors had good reason to fear spiders, snakes, and heights, which is why many twenty-first-century humans instinctively fear such things more than modern killers such as cigarettes and cars.

Phobias are particularly likely if a child's parents are also somewhat phobic, not only for genetic reasons but also because children become quite astute at sensing their parents' feelings. When a worried parent says "Let's pet the nice doggie," children will notice the hesitant hand, the fast breathing, or the sudden startle if the dog moves. In this case, learning is added to a genetic tendency, and the child becomes afraid.

Thus, emotional regulation is a normal, expected outcome of early childhood, but all four factors—a child's genetics, early physiological stress, early care, and current social context—can delay or distort emotional regulation.

Self-Expression

As you remember, in toddlerhood children gradually realize that they exist as independent people, distinct from others. This awareness becomes, during early childhood, the **self-concept,** which is people's understanding of who they are. By age 2 or 3, a child's self-concept includes such notions as that he or she is a boy or a girl; a brother, sister, or only child; and, of a certain age, religion, and ability. From the self-concept flow many other emotions. In fact, self-concept has been called "the cornerstone of both social and emotional development" (Kagan et al., 1995). Typically, self-concept turns from factual to evaluative, becoming **self-esteem,** or pride in oneself (Davis-Kean & Sandler, 2001). Children with relatively high self-esteem at age 5 tend to be more accepted over the years by other children (Verschueren et al., 2001). Self-esteem that is too high, however, tends to create other problems. A positive, but balanced, self-concept is probably best.

A noteworthy aspect of self-concept and self-esteem is that children in the play years feel older, stronger, and more skilled than younger children or than they themselves once were. One of the worst insults to call a 3-year-old is "baby," and one of the most positive comments is "big boy" or "big girl." The significance of this feeling, as well as young children's skill in negotiation, is shown in this episode involving three 4-year-old girls:

> **Beth:** How about this. Pretend he married two of us and you were the sister. OK? You were the sister of us—OK? Of both of us, cause you were the littler one.
> **Celia:** No, I don't want to be a little one.
> **Beth:** No, you're both, you're big. Um, let's pretend.
> **Annie:** But we were a little bigger.
> **Beth:** You're 20.
> **Celia:** Yeah.
> **Beth:** And both of us are 21.
> **Celia:** OK, so that means . . .
> **Annie:** So, we're one month older than you.
>
> [Furth, 1996]

The young ladies' chronological understanding clearly is immature, but their social skills are not. All three want to maintain their self-esteem as big girls without giving up their social interaction, and they combine assertion and compromise to achieve that end.

For children of all ages, psychologists emphasize the importance of developing a positive self-concept. (In fact, too much self-criticism is one sign of psychosocial problems in a young child.) Normally, young children have no such

Who's Chicken? Genes and good parenting have made this boy neither too fearful nor too bold. Appropriate caution is probably the best approach to meeting a chicken.

self-concept People's understanding of who they are.

self-esteem People's pride in themselves.

! Answer to Observational Quiz (from page 297): Look at his hands, legs, and face. He is holding the bottle and touching the baby's forehead with delicacy and care; he is positioning his legs in a way that is uncomfortable but suited to the task; and his eyes and mouth suggest he is giving the baby his full concentration.

Know-It-Alls Have Something to Learn
Like many preschoolers, Ruthie thinks her art is worth money and she would love to be the rescuer of another child, an animal, or even a bird. In the real world, however, that self-concept will need some modification.

problem; typical 2- to 6-year-olds form quite favorable impressions of themselves. They regularly overestimate their own abilities, believing that they can win any race, skip perfectly, count accurately, and compose beautiful songs. They enjoy undertaking various tasks, and they expect all others—grandparents, playmates, stuffed animals—to be a patient, admiring audience for their showing off. The next day, they might gather the identical audience for a repeat performance. Self-confidence is tied to competence, and competence demands repeated demonstrations of mastery.

Such typically high self-esteem was demonstrated in a laboratory test in which 4- to 6-year-olds were given two minutes to solve an impossible puzzle. When they failed, they were asked to guess how many of two additional puzzles they could solve if they tried. Almost all the children, despite having just failed, answered "both." When the same children were asked to indicate how smart they were by awarding themselves one, two, three, four, or five stars (representing the range from "not smart at all" to "very smart"), more than 90 percent confidently chose five stars (Stipek et al., 1995).

Theories of Emotions

Normal emotional regulation during early childhood has been described by every theorist who has studied this stage. Freud observed a burst of self-importance, anger, and fear during these years; these emotions are submerged by parental actions, so that the next stage, called *latency* (which means quietness and inactivity), can begin. More specifics about many theories, including Freud's, are discussed later in this chapter. Here, however, we need to mention two theorists who have specifically considered the emotions of young children: Erik Erikson and Daniel Goleman.

Initiative Versus Guilt

One crucial aspect of emotional development during early childhood was described by Erik Erikson almost half a century ago. Positive enthusiasm, effort, and self-evaluation characterize ages 3 to 6, according to Erikson's psychosocial theory (first discussed in Chapter 2). During the developmental stage that Erikson calls **initiative versus guilt,** self-esteem is largely defined by the skills and competencies that demonstrate independence and initiative. Most young children leap at almost any opportunity to show that "I can do it!" Spontaneous play becomes goal-directed.

Children do *not* want to do just *anything,* as infants do in Piaget's sensorimotor period and as toddlers do in Erikson's autonomy stage. Now, in the initiative stage, they want to *begin and complete something* and take pride in their accomplishment. Accordingly, attention span becomes much longer. Many 3- or 4-year-olds can spend up to an hour in one episode of pretend play or in practicing a new motor skill or in creating a work of art—something no normal toddler does.

Erikson also believed that, as the larger society motivates them to take on new activities, children develop their sense of themselves and others, feeling guilt when their efforts result in failure or criticism. Guilt is a more mature emotion than is shame. Guilt comes from within the child who is unhappy at having done a bad thing; shame comes from knowing that someone else might see what the child has done and be critical (Tangney, 2001). Both shame and guilt originate from social standards, but guilt indicates that the child has taken on these standards as his or her own.

Erikson's historic overview still applies. Over the last decade of the twentieth century, developmentalists intensely studied the psychosocial development of young children (Eisenberg, 2000). As you remember, all the basic human emotions are already evident by the end of infancy: from early joy and fear to more complex anger and sadness, and, by age 2, self-aware emotions such as jealousy and embarrassment. These emotions continue to be evident during the years from 2 to 6, but now children have an additional developmental task: to express and modulate emotions in ways sanctioned by their social context. As Erikson recognized, when autonomy has become initiative and shame has become guilt, then children have internalized the social standards of their culture and emotions are properly regulated.

Emotional Intelligence

Daniel Goleman (1998) is another theorist who stresses the importance of emotional regulation. He contends that the ability to modulate and direct emotions is crucial to **emotional intelligence,** an understanding of how to interpret and express emotions. Emotional intelligence develops throughout life, but particularly during early childhood. It is during these formative years that the reflective and intellectual areas of the cortex, especially the prefrontal cortex, gradually come to govern the rush of fear, anger, and other passion from the *amygdala,* an emotional hotspot deep within the brain. According to Goleman, when caregivers use children's natural attachment to teach them how and when to express feelings, the children will become balanced and empathetic human beings, neither overwhelmed by nor unresponsive to their own emotions. This is so crucial for any adequate functioning that it is more important than conventional intelligence, according to Goleman.

In Chapter 11 we will discuss various concepts of intelligence, including the conventional definitions that stress verbal and logical abilities. You will also see that a leading alternative view, proposed by Howard Gardner, again stresses emotions—specifically, the ability to understand one's own and other people's

initiative versus guilt The third of Erikson's eight stages of psychosocial development, in which the young child eagerly begins new projects and activities and feels guilt when his or her efforts result in failure or criticism.

emotional intelligence Goleman's term for the understanding of how to interpret and express emotions.

emotions. Similar ideas are expressed in a report from 22 leading researchers on early childhood, who emphasize again and again the importance of learning to regulate emotions (National Research Council and Institute of Medicine, 2000). They write:

> The developmental tasks of this period range from the mastery of essential building blocks for learning and the motivation to succeed in school, to the ability to get along with other children, to make friends, and become engaged in a social group, as well as the capacity to manage powerful emotions.
>
> *[p. 386]*

As you see, in listing six tasks of early childhood, they begin with one cognitive task, then cite four emotional tasks, and conclude with emotional regulation.

Although we have detailed the impact that brain maturation and stress have on emotional growth (including theory of mind in Chapter 9), it is also apparent that human relationships provide essential guidance in emotional expression and regulation. These experts explain:

> Regulation in early development is deeply embedded in the child's relations with others. Providing the experiences, supports, and encouragement that enable children to take over and self-regulate in one area of function after another is one of the most critical elements of good caregiving.
>
> *[National Research Council and Institute of Medicine, 2000, p. 122]*

The rest of this chapter is about those social "experiences, supports, and encouragement" that young children receive from their parents, their peers, and their culture.

Prosocial and Antisocial Behavior

peers People who are about the same age and status as oneself.

Ultimately, emotions are expressed in relation to the social world, particularly behavior related to **peers,** who are other people of about the same age and status as the child. For young children, peers are other children in the neighborhood, play group, and preschool who become friends, acquaintances, or enemies. Many psychologists believe that children learn about their own and other people's emotions through playing with peers. Even the best parent is less desirable than a peer when it comes to the give-and-take of play.

prosocial Behaving in ways that help other people without obvious benefit to oneself.

antisocial Behaving in ways that are deliberately hurtful or destructive.

Few children are neutral in their relationships with peers. Typically they are either **prosocial,** behaving in ways that help another person without obvious benefit to themselves, or **antisocial,** behaving in ways that are deliberately hurtful or destructive (Caprara et al., 2001). In both types of behavior, intent is crucial: Actions that are intended to be hurtful are antisocial, even if they do not actually affect the target. Accordingly, children must be old enough to be able to regulate their emotions before they can justifiably be called either prosocial or antisocial, because they must be able to form the intention to help or harm.

How old is old enough? That is an open question: Some cultures and researchers credit or blame children for their behavior at much younger ages than others. However, most agree that newborns who reflexively cry when another one cries are not yet prosocial and that 1-year-olds who refuse to share are not yet antisocial. By age 4 or 5, though, children should have developed a theory of mind and thus should be able to act in a deliberately prosocial or antisocial manner (Eisenberg, 2000).

Empathy and Sharing

Expressing sympathy, offering to share, and including a shy child in a game or conversation are all examples of prosocial behavior. Such behavior, which is indicative of social competence, appears during the later play years, continues to develop during the school years, and is correlated with emotional regulation (Eisenberg et al., 1997).

Prosocial attitudes also correlate with the making of new friends. Throughout the period from age 2 to 5, violent temper tantrums, uncontrollable crying, and terrifying phobias diminish, and the capacity for self-control—such as not opening a wrapped present immediately if asked to wait—becomes more evident (Kochanska et al., 2001). By school age, children tend to like other children best if they are neither overcontrolled nor undercontrolled in their emotions.

Empathy involves much more than simply following a parent's or teacher's moral prescription to share a toy or comfort another child; it is a prosocial emotion from the heart. **Empathy** is a person's true understanding of the emotions of another, including the ability to figure out what would make that person feel better. It is not egocentric. It is also more complex than mere sympathy, which means feeling sorry *for* someone, not *with* someone.

Because empathy indicates a certain level of understanding of the self and theory of mind, it is not usually evident until about age 4. It is not surprising that prosocial behaviors of all kinds correlate with popularity and friendship during childhood (Ladd, 1999)—and it is empathy that is the source of these helpful impulses. A young child who is lonely and unliked by peers may need special help in developing social skills. Such help can be, and often is, provided by trained teachers in a high-quality preschool—an addition to the list of reasons, given in Chapter 9, that a child's participation in Head Start sometimes affects his or her self-esteem and social relationships in adulthood. Young adults who were well educated in their early years were found, as adults, to be more likely to be married and less likely to be in prison. This amazing longitudinal connection may link empathy, social skills, and one's life situation as an adult.

Aggression

Both prosocial and antisocial behavior take many forms. However, **aggression** is a form of antisocial behavior that is of particular concern; it begins with inadequate emotional regulation during early childhood, and it can become a serious social problem as time goes by (Coie & Dodge, 1998). As one group of researchers reports:

> Children with [emotional] control problems observed by home visitors at ages 3 and 4 years were seen by teachers as more hostile and hyperactive in the classroom at age 5 years. . . . Early onset aggression, in particular, is likely to become entrenched and linked to multiple problems late in development.
>
> [Zahn-Waxler et al., 1996]

In other words, although almost all 2-year-olds are aggressive, a child who is more angry and hurtful at age 3 and 4 than other children is headed for trouble at age 5, 10, or even 15 or 25 (Loeber & Farrington, 2000). Here we will look at the forms, causes, and consequences of aggression that are specific to children aged 2 to 6.

Remember that emotions need to be regulated, not repressed, and that some assertion and self-protection are universal, and probably beneficial, aspects of early development. Accordingly, the consequences of aggressive actions taken by a young child are not always dire: Every normal child sometimes hurts another

What Will She Do? By age three or four, children can respond with empathy to another child's distress, as the girl on the left is doing. Such emotions usually lead to prosocial actions: She is likely to ask the distressed boy at right to play with her at the sand table.

empathy A person's true understanding of the emotions of another, including the ability to figure out what would make that person feel better.

aggression Hostile attitudes and hurtful or destructive actions that stem from anger or frustration.

child or adult by deliberately hitting, kicking, biting, pinching, hair-pulling, name-calling, arm-twisting, or the like. Parents are often shocked when this first happens, especially since they are likely to be the first victims when the angelic infant in their arms suddenly looks at them and then inflicts pain. Typically, parents teach emotional restraint—for instance, by saying "No" and then putting the baby down so that the hurtful action is not repeated. (The parent should never laugh or retaliate; both responses teach the wrong lessons.)

Although parents are no longer likely to be victims by the time the child is 3, other children sometimes are. Aggressive behavior normally increases between ages 1 and 4 because, as children become aware of themselves and their needs and begin to play more with peers, they become more likely to defend their interests. In fact, a 4-year-old who never lashes out is likely to become overwhelmed by anxiety or depression later on, perhaps victimized by bullies or by his or her own fears. But even though 4-year-olds are more aggressive than 2-year-olds, they are usually much more controlled: They do not hurt everyone in their path, but instead choose their issues and targets.

Researchers recognize four forms of aggression:

instrumental aggression Aggressive behavior that is aimed at getting or keeping an object desired by another.

reactive aggression Aggressive behavior that is an angry retaliation for some intentional or accidental act by another person.

relational aggression Aggressive behavior that takes the form of insults or social rejection.

bullying aggression Aggressive behavior that takes the form of an unprovoked physical or verbal attack on another person.

- **Instrumental aggression** is used to obtain or retain something, such as a toy or other object.
- **Reactive aggression** involves angry retaliation for an intentional or accidental act.
- **Relational aggression** is designed to inflict psychic, not physical, pain.
- **Bullying aggression** consists of an unprovoked attack.

Instrumental aggression is common in the play years and is the form of aggression that is most likely to increase from age 2 to 6. Although it should be discouraged as a strategy, instrumental aggression involves objects more than people, is quite normal, and therefore is not of serious concern.

Reactive aggression is more worrisome, because it can indicate a lack of emotional regulation. A 2-year-old might be expected to react to any hurt with aggression, but a 5-year-old should be able to stop and think, figuring out not only whether the hurt was intentional but also whether reciprocal aggression is likely to make the situation better or worse.

Relational aggression, as when a child teases or taunts another, can be even more hurtful than physical aggression (Miller & Olson, 2000). Victims and perpetrators of relational aggression are more likely to be lonely and unwilling to share with others than are victims and perpetrators of instrumental aggression. A 3-year-old who has a toy snatched by another child is likely to cry and try to get it back; but if another child calls him or her dirty, dumb, or bad, the remedy is less obvious. Friendships are severed by relational aggression but not usually by instrumental aggression (Crick et al., 1999).

Bullying aggression is the most troublesome of all. It is not only the most hurtful form of aggression toward other children but also indicates that the bully has a troubled family situation and will probably be involved in worse aggression later. Bullies and victims are discussed in detail in Chapter 13, because the most serious harm occurs during the school years. One aspect, however, is directly relevant to early childhood: Both bullies and victims are characterized by inadequate and immature emotional regulation. This is another reason adults should guide children to understand and control their emotions before the first grade (Mahady et al., 2000).

LAURA DWIGHT

Me First! An increase in aggression by about age 4 is typically accompanied by an increase in self-control. This struggle will not escalate to instrumental aggression if both children have learned some emotional regulation and if neither has been misguided by racism or by a false image of maleness.

Adult guidance is only one of many influences on prosocial and antisocial behavior. To some extent, developmental processes are also at work. It is typical for children to become more prosocial and less aggressive between ages 3 and 6. However, with some children, antisocial behavior does not decrease (Campbell, 1995). The reasons range from genetic and prenatal influences to the impact of school and society. Now we look at an influence that is particularly powerful during early childhood: playing with peers.

Learning Social Skills Through Play

During childhood, play is the most productive and adaptive activity that children can undertake. Indeed, the fact that play is both universal and variable, related to the culture and the gender as well as the age of the playmates, makes it an ideal forum for learning specific social skills (Sutton-Smith, 1997). Although children play when they are alone or with adults, they are much more likely to play with other children.

Compare the peer interactions of a 2-year-old and a 5-year-old. The younger child's social play consists mainly of simple games (such as bouncing and trying to catch a ball and becoming angry or upset if the other child does not cooperate). By contrast, the more sophisticated 5-year-old has learned how to gain entry to a play group, to manage conflict through the use of humor, and to select and keep friends and playmates.

More than 70 years ago, a researcher named Mildred Parten (1932) outlined five types of childhood play, from the least social to the most social:

- *Solitary play.* A child plays alone, seemingly unaware of any other children playing nearby.
- *Onlooker play.* A child watches other children play.
- *Parallel play.* Children play with similar toys in similar ways, but they do not interact.
- *Associative play.* Children interact, sharing materials and emotions, but they don't seem to be playing the same game or to be concerned that the other is not cooperating.
- *Cooperative play.* Children play together, either jointly creating an elaborate game or structure or taking turns.

As you can see, one indicator of social skill development is how children play with peers, because only with age-mates do children themselves assume responsibility for initiating and maintaining harmonious social interaction. Whether learning how to share crayons or sand toys, or how to include everybody in the construction of a spaceship, or how to respond to a friend's accusatory "That's not fair," children must deal with playmates who are not always understanding and self-sacrificing (as a mother might be). Specifically, how does this social play occur? It takes many forms, but two are especially prominent in early childhood; rough-and-tumble play and sociodramatic play.

Rough-and-Tumble Play

One beneficial form of social play is called **rough-and-tumble play**, because it looks quite rough and the children seem to tumble over each other as they play. In fact, the term first came from scientists who studied baby monkeys in East Africa (Jones, 1976). They noticed that the monkeys seemed to chase, attack, roll over in the dirt, and wrestle, quite roughly, but without really hurting each other. If another monkey wanted to play, all it had to do was to come close, catch the eye of a peer, and then run away as if being chased. This was an invitation, which the other monkey almost always accepted. Since the monkeys did not hurt each

rough-and-tumble play Play that mimics aggression through wrestling, chasing, or hitting but that actually occurs purely in fun, with no intent to harm.

LAURA DWIGHT

Male Bonding Sometimes the only way to distinguish aggression from rough-and-tumble play is to look at the faces. The hitter is not scowling, the hittee is laughing, and the hugger is just joining in the fun. Another clue that this is rough-and-tumble play comes from gender and context. These boys are in a Head Start program, where they are learning social skills, such as how to avoid fighting.

other, ethologists called this play, to distinguish it from rough fighting. They noted that the young monkeys who were most likely to fight were least likely to engage in rough-and-tumble play, which led them to conclude that rough-and-tumble play helped monkeys learn to avoid aggression.

When the scientists left the jungle and returned to their families, they were surprised to realize that their own children did the same things as the baby monkeys—that human youngsters also engage in rough-and-tumble-play! It became very obvious that, although a distinguishing characteristic of such play is its mimicry of aggression, rough-and-tumble play is clearly prosocial, not antisocial. Unlike aggression, rough-and-tumble play is both fun and constructive; it teaches children how to enter a relationship, assert themselves, and respond to the actions of someone else while exercising gross motor skills, all without hurting the other person (Pellegrini & Smith, 1998). Adults who are unsure whether they are observing a fight that should be broken up or a social activity that should continue should look for a "play face." Children almost always smile, and often laugh, in rough-and-tumble play, whereas they frown and scowl in real fighting.

Rough-and-tumble play is universal. It has been observed in Japan, Kenya, and Mexico as well as in every income and ethnic group in North America, Europe, and Australia (Boulton & Smith, 1989). There are some cultural and situational differences, however. One of the most important is space and supervision: Children are much more likely to instigate rough-and-tumble play when they have room to run and chase and when adults are not directly nearby. This is one reason the ideal physical environment for children includes ample safe space for gross motor activities, with adults within earshot but not underfoot (Bradley, 1995).

In addition, rough-and-tumble play usually occurs among children who have had considerable social experience, often with each other. Not surprisingly, then, older children are more likely to engage in rough-and-tumble play than younger ones. In fact, the incidence of rough-and-tumble play increases with age, peaking at about age 8 to 10 and then decreasing (Pellegrini & Smith, 1998). Finally, boys are much more likely to engage in rough-and-tumble play than are girls. Indeed, girls typically withdraw from boys' rough-and-tumble play (Fabes, 1994). The reason may be hormonal or cultural or both. (Sex differences are discussed at the end of this chapter.)

Sociodramatic Play

sociodramatic play Pretend play in which children act out various roles and themes in stories that they create themselves.

In the type of social play called **sociodramatic play,** children act out various roles and themes in stories they themselves have created, taking on "any identity, role, or activity that they choose. They can be mothers, babies, Cinderella, or Captain Hook. They can make tea or fly to the moon. Or they can fight, hurt others, or kill or imprison someone" (Dunn & Hughes, 2001). From simple plots at age 2 (a mother–baby script that consists mainly of eating, sleeping, and waking) to elaborate ones by age 5 (such as a trip through the jungle confronting various challenging animals, people, and geological barriers), sociodramatic play provides a way for children to do the following:

- Explore and rehearse the social roles they see being enacted around them
- Test their own ability to explain and convince others of their ideas
- Regulate their emotions through imagination
- Examine personal concerns in a nonthreatening manner

The beginnings of sociodramatic play can be seen in solitary or parallel play, when a toddler "feeds" or "cuddles" or "punishes" a doll or stuffed animal. Sociodramatic play greatly increases in frequency and complexity between the ages of 2 and 6. As young children develop their theory of mind and their emotional regulation, they seek other children to practice what they have learned.

The social experiences that young children have as they negotiate, cooperate, and persuade in let's-pretend play are crucial opportunities (as we saw earlier with the three girls negotiating to be "sisters") (Hobson, 2000). Children can, for instance, use sociodramatic play to try out various means of managing their emotions, as in dealing with a scary situation in the dark (in a tent made of blankets, quickly opened if the darkness becomes overwhelming) or providing nurturance to an injured playmate (who falls down dead and needs to be miraculously revived) or exhibiting courage when the bad guys attack (with machine guns, bombs, or swords). In this sense, then, sociodramatic play is a testing ground for early psychological knowledge, always protecting the self-esteem of the players and teaching them cooperation.

Sociodramatic play can also reveal anger and aggression. In one study comparing hard-to-manage 4-year-olds and their friends, the former were likely to turn sociodramatic play episodes toward violence and death, which are not the usual themes of such play (Dunn & Hughes, 2001). For these children, doctor play became pain and surgery; fantasy play involved killing ("You must go and find your fortune" "Why?" "Because your mother is going to be killed in a minute"); and play fighting became frightening (a hard-to-manage child brandishes a sword saying, "Kill. Kill. Kill me"—to which his friend responds "No" and drops his weapon). This study found that the children whose pretend play was most violent at age 4 became 6-year-olds who were least likely to understand prosocial behavior.

Although both sexes engage in sociodramatic play, girls are more likely to do so, and they are less likely than boys to use violent themes. For their part, boys are more likely to engage in rough-and-tumble play, which seems designed to teach the participants to express their power and strength without actually hurting their playmates. Both sexes apparently learn important prosocial skills as they play. The best setting for children to practice these social skills with peers is a high-quality educational program where children have many friends and where teachers help them master fear and anger and learn to modify their emotional expressions in response to the reaction of their playmates.

In a good early-childhood program, children can develop a wide range of social skills as they interact with peers (National Research Council and Institute of Medicine, 2000). They can also make many friends. Indeed, friendships are remarkably consistent during the play years. Young children choose regular playmates, usually of the same age and sex, and then their ongoing rough-and-tumble play or sociodramatic play together becomes complex, involving more self-disclosure, intimacy, and reciprocity than does their play with casual acquaintances. In fact, two close friends sometimes develop ongoing plots, roles, routines, and scripts, quickly returning to another episode of the same story each time they play together.

Sociodramatic Play Just like the boys in the previous photograph, these girls are developing their social skills—in this case, as store owner and grocery shopper.

? *Observational Quiz* (see answer, page 308): Which specifics of the girls' fantasy play are similar to the real thing, and which are not?

The Influence of Television and Video Games

Young children spend almost 20 hours per week watching television (Nielsen Media Research, 2000), and North American households have more television sets and personal computers than bathrooms—which used to be counted as the indicator of modernity. Other research confirms that 2- to 4-year-olds spend about 3 hours per day watching television and that 5- to 6-year-olds spend about 2 hours, only about 15 minutes of which is educational (Huston et al., 1999).

!*Answer to Observational Quiz* (from page 307): The particular hats, necklaces, and shoes are all quite different from those their mothers would likely wear to the store, and the stock, the money holder, and the grocery bag are quite different. However, the essence of shopping is here: Money is exchanged for goods, and both participants politely play their roles.

It is easy to understand why this is so. Parents quickly learn that the "idiot box" is a good babysitter: It keeps children relatively quiet and in one room for hours at a time. Advertisers know that young children are gullible and demanding, so that a program that keeps their uncritical attention creates a strong market and large profits for junk foods and expensive toys.

Some critics suggest that any time spent watching television is destructive, becausee it keeps children from physical activity, imaginative play, reading, and family interaction. Although this point may be valid, there is no proof that merely viewing TV, hour after hour, is destructive. There is evidence, however, that the messages conveyed on the screen are influential, as confirmed by a longitudinal study that surveyed children at about age 5 and again at about age 16. Those who had watched educational television as young children (mostly *Sesame Street* and *Mr. Rogers' Neighborhood*) became teenagers who earned higher grades and did more reading than other high-school students, especially if they were boys. By contrast, those who watched violent TV programs had lower grades, especially if they were girls (Anderson et al., 2001). Using a variety of statistical safeguards, the researchers found causation, not merely correlation. In other words, those parents who encouraged their children to watch *Mr. Rogers* might also be parents who encouraged their children to get good grades, but this research found that educational television in and of itself had a positive impact.

The fact that content is crucial is one reason video games are of great concern to many developmental researchers. Remember that good science is accumulated slowly and deliberately, with various methods and diverse populations and samples, over a period of years. Developmentalists are reluctant to state flatly that violent video games are worse than violent TV programs, that they lead directly to death and injury. However, it is certain that both are destructive, pushing children to be more violent than they would otherwise be (Bushman & Anderson, 2001). One developmentalist explains, "It seems likely that the impact of watching characters being killed on television will be exceeded for a child playing a computer game who is doing the virtual killing" (Larson, 2001).

Changing Policy

Turning Off the TV

Most policy makers seem resigned to the impact of TV and video games on young children. Instead, they save their criticism for the parents who let infants watch television (an increasing number of programs, such as *Barney* and *Teletubbies,* target youngsters under age 2), or who let their teenagers play violent video games.

Film and TV executives say the media are merely reflecting reality, but critic Michael Medved (1995) asks, if TV violence is part of everyday life,

> . . . then why do so few people witness murders in real life but everybody sees them on TV and in the movies? The most violent ghetto isn't in South Central L.A. or Southeast Washington, D.C.; it's on television. About 350 characters appear each night on prime-time TV, but studies show an average of seven of these people are murdered every night. If this rate applied in reality, then in just 50 days everyone in the United States would be killed and the last one left could turn off the TV.

[pp. 156–157]

Watching television may be particularly harmful in early childhood, not only because of all the hours that are spent in front of the screen but also because young children are just beginning to learn about society, culture, and emotions. Television teaches many potentially destructive lessons. Developmentalists focus on several aspects:

- Advertisements with faulty messages about nutrition, promoting foods high in fat, sugar, and salt
- Perpetuation of sexist, ageist, and racist stereotypes
- Depiction of violent solutions for every problem with no expression of empathy

At 10 A.M. on Saturday mornings, more than half of all North American children are watching TV (Comstock & Scharrer, 1999). What do they see and learn? The "good guys," whether in cartoons or police dramas, do as much hitting, shooting, and kicking as the bad guys, yet the consequences of their violence are sanitized, justified, or made comic. They are never portrayed as bloodthirsty or evil. In cartoons, a person or object blown to smithereens is funny and a person who stops to think about consequences dies. All the good guys are male, even on educational television (Big Bird, Barney, even Bugs Bunny). Virtually no hero, in cartoon or human form, is nonwhite, although villains often are. Women are portrayed as victims or adoring girlfriends of the heroes, almost never as leaders—except in a very few sex-stereotyped programs that few boys watch.

Video games are worse in every respect—more violent, more sexist, more racist. Almost all the characters in 33 popular Nintendo and Sega Genesis video games are male and Anglo, and 80 percent of the games include violence or aggression as an essential strategy the child must use to score points (Dietz, 1998).

Children who watch violent television are likely to be more aggressive than children who do not, and children who are already inclined to be aggressive are likely to watch the most violent programs. In fact, "well over 1,000 studies . . . point overwhelmingly to a causal connection between media violence and aggressive behavior in some children" (U.S. Congress, 2000). Six major organizations concerned with the psychological and physical well-being of children (the American Psychological Association, the American Academy of Pediatrics, the American Medical Association, the American Academy of Child and Adolescent Psychiatry, the American Academy of Family Physicians, and the American Psychiatry Association) suggest that parents turn off the TV.

Obviously, not every child who watches televised violence or plays violent video games becomes a bully or a victim, a racist or a sexist. The impact of video violence has been compared to that of cigarette smoking: Not every smoker is guaranteed to die of lung cancer, but many will (Bushman & Anderson, 2001). To take this comparison a step further: No responsible parent would give a child a cigarette, or even deliberately blow smoke in a child's direction. Why, then, do parents turn on the TV for their children to watch?

The current public policy debate revolves around the question of whether an emphasis on parental responsibility is adequate or whether the judgment and power of parents are overwhelmed by the commercialization of children's television, which requires programs to be as eye-catching as possible in order to draw a wide audience for the unhealthy snacks and the expensive toys of the sponsors. The division of responsibility for such decisions between individual parents and governmental policy is a matter of societal debate. This is an ongoing public policy issue that the next generation may decide.

Wrong Lessons Learned Preschoolers are eager for knowledge, and these boys are learning to shoot the bad guys whenever they appear. The most frightening aspect of television watching at this age is that children absorb it totally, without a firm understanding of the difference between real and pretend.

Parenting Patterns

We have seen that many things—including genes, peers, gender, and culture—affect children's behavior. Parenting patterns are also very influential (Maccoby, 2000; Patterson, 1998). However, it is important to neither exaggerate nor understate the role of parents—mistakes often made in the media or by social scientists of earlier periods.

> Contemporary students of socialization largely agree that early researchers often overstated conclusions from correlational findings; relied excessively on singular, deterministic views of parental influence; and failed to attend to the potentially

confounding effects of heredity. Contemporary researchers have taken steps to remedy many of these shortcomings. Unfortunately, the weaknesses of old studies still permeate presentations of socialization research in introductory textbooks and the mass media, partly because they appeal to preferences for simple generalizations.

[Collins et al., 2000]

In other words, the general public would like to believe that parents alone determine a child's personality, an error made by theorists as dissimilar as Sigmund Freud and John B. Watson 80 years ago (see Chapter 7). Current research places much less emphasis on parents, but the way mothers and fathers relate to their children is still important (Maccoby, 2000).

Baumrind's Three Styles of Parenting

The contemporary study of parenting patterns has been greatly influenced by the early work of Diana Baumrind (1967, 1971), who began with 100 preschool children, all from California and almost all European-American and middle-class. As a careful researcher, Baumrind used many measures of behavior, several of them involving naturalistic observation. First, she observed the children's activities in preschool and, on the basis of their actions, rated their self-control, independence, self-confidence, and other attributes. She then interviewed both parents of each child and observed parent–child interaction in two settings, at home and in the laboratory, in search of possible relationships between the parents' behavior at home and the child's behavior at preschool.

Baumrind found that parents differed on four important dimensions:

- Expressions of *warmth*, or nurturance, which ranged from very affectionate to quite cold
- Strategies for *discipline*, which might involve explanation, criticism, persuasion, and/or physical punishment
- The quality of *communication*, which ranged from extensive listening to demands for silence
- Expectations for *maturity*, evident in how much responsibility and self-control was demanded

On the basis of these four dimensions, Baumrind identified three basic styles of parenting:

1. **Authoritarian parenting.** The parents' word is law, not to be questioned. Misconduct brings strict punishment, usually physical, although authoritarian parents do not cross the line into physical abuse. Demands for maturity are high, and parent–child communication, especially about emotions, is low. Although they love and care about their children, authoritarian parents seem aloof, showing little affection or nurturance.
2. **Permissive parenting.** The parents make few demands on their children, hiding any impatience they feel. Discipline is lax because demands for maturity are low. Permissive parents are nurturant and accepting, and they communicate well with their offspring. They view themselves as available to help their children but not as responsible for shaping how their children turn out.
3. **Authoritative parenting.** Authoritative parents are similar in some ways to authoritarian parents, in that they set limits and enforce rules. However, they also listen to their children's requests and questions and discuss feelings and problems. Family rule is more democratic than dictatorial. The parents demand maturity of their offspring, but they are also nurturant and understanding, forgiving (rather than punishing) a child when demands for maturity are not met.

The characteristics of these three styles are summarized in Table 10.1.

authoritarian parenting Baumrind's term for a style of child rearing in which standards for proper behavior are high, misconduct is strictly punished, and parent–child communication is low.

permissive parenting Baumrind's term for a style of child rearing in which the parents seldom punish, guide, or control the child but are nurturant and communicate well with the child.

authoritative parenting Baumrind's term for a style of child rearing in which the parents set limits and provide guidance for their child but are willing to listen to the child's ideas and to make compromises.

TABLE 10.1 Characteristics of Baumrind's Parenting Styles

			Characteristics		
			Communication		
Style	Warmth	Discipline	Parent to Child	Child to Parent	Expectations of Maturity
Authoritarian	Low	Strict, often physical	High	Low	High
Permissive	High	Rare	Low	High	Low
Authoritative	High	Moderate, with much discussion	High	High	Moderate

All three styles of parenting reflect underlying love and concern. The authoritarian parent thinks it is important for the child to learn to behave properly; the permissive parent believes that learning happens best through conversation. In contrast, two other styles of parenting have been identified: **neglectful parenting,** in which the parents do not seem to care at all, and **indulgent parenting,** in which the parents accommodate the child's every whim. These two types are abusive and thus clearly harmful, unlike the three parenting styles that Baumrind described.

Baumrind and others have continued to study parenting styles, following the original 100 children as they grew and studying thousands of other children of various backgrounds and ages. Based on this research they have come to some basic conclusions:

■ *Authoritarian* parents raise children who are likely to be conscientious, obedient, and quiet; however, the children are not especially happy. They are more likely to feel guilty or depressed.
■ *Permissive* parents raise children who are even less happy and who lack self-control, especially within the give-and-take of peer friendships.
■ *Authoritative* parents raise children who are more likely to be successful, articulate, intelligent, happy with themselves, and generous with others.

Follow-up research has also found that, at least for middle-class families of European ancestry, the initial advantages of the authoritative approach are likely to grow even stronger over time, helping children to achieve in school, adolescents to avoid drug abuse, and young adults to have high self-esteem. Specifically in early childhood, researchers still find that authoritative strategies foster self-control and emotional regulation (Mauro & Harris, 2000). Other research finds that the best way to promote prosocial behavior and to limit aggression is to induce children to think through and verbalize the human consequences of their actions (Hoffman, 2001). This process is central to authoritative parenting.

Many studies have found the link between any one of the three basic parenting styles and the child's behavior to be less direct and inevitable than it appeared in Baumrind's original research. First, the child's temperament needs to be considered. A fearful child needs gentle parenting, and a bolder child needs more restrictive (but still warm) parenting (Bates et al., 1998; Kochanska et al., 1997). Second, community and cultural differences sometimes undercut, sometimes emphasize, and almost always influence the child's perception of the quality of parenting. Effective Asian- and African-American parents are often stricter than effective European-American parents (Darling & Steinberg, 1997; Wachs, 1999).

This last finding surprised developmentalists, who then hypothesized that, to some extent, more authoritarian parenting is required when families live in stressful, violent neighborhoods: Children need more guidelines in such places. However, non-European parents who are middle-class also tend to impose strict guidelines and occasional physical punishment, and they have more child-rearing success than do European-American parents who use the same strategies.

neglectful parenting An abusive style of child rearing in which the parents do not seem to care about their child at all.

indulgent parenting An abusive style of child rearing in which the parents accommodate the child's every whim.

Baumrind named two of her three parenting styles with almost the same word; only the last syllables differ. How will you remember them? One student said "authoritarian" *Is Awfully Negative (-ian),* but "authoritative" *Is Very Excellent (-ive).* Maybe this memory trick will work for you, too.

GEORGE GERSTER / PHOTO RESEARCHERS, INC.

What Kind of Parenting? The relationship between these two Botswana bushmen suggests authoritative, not authoritarian, parenting and serves as a reminder that parenting practices follow cultural and ethnic lines, not racial ones. In the largely democratic communities in the open areas of the Kalahari Desert, unlike urban neighborhoods, parents do not have to be strict.

The crucial factors seem to be parental warmth, support, and concern for the child, which are expressed in ways that vary with the family's cultural background and current circumstances.

Parents who seem authoritarian or permissive may raise well-adjusted children, depending on the child's personality and the circumstances. However, there is *no* evidence that abusive, indifferent, or neglectful parents are effective (Maccoby, 2000; McGroder, 2000).

Many parents today are raising young children while coping with extraordinary stresses of their own. Single parenthood, marital conflict, social prejudice, civil war, inadequate income—all of these can reduce a parent's patience, time, and warmth toward young children (McLoyd, 1998b). These factors are discussed in some detail in Chapter 13. One general point should be made here: No single one of these stresses always harms children. Some parents cope very well, and some children are quite resilient (Luthar et al., 2000). Low-income minority parents who are consistent and nurturant raise young children who can regulate their emotions and are ready for success in school and later life, just as can middle-income majority parents who are equally consistent and nurturant (Garner & Spears, 2000). One factor that contributes to nurturance is community support for parenting, evidence for which can be partly determined by looking at the percentage of children living in poverty (see Appendix A, Chapter 10)

Among the indicators of parental warmth are caressing or hugging the child, answering the child's questions, and asking the child to participate in a conversation between adults. Such warmth buffers the potentially harmful effects of strict standards of behavior (McLloyd & Smith, 2002).

Punishment

How a parent disciplines a child is an integral part of parenting style. No developmentalist would suggest that young children should do whatever they please; but, given what researchers have learned about cognition, it is apparent that proactive and preventive discipline is preferable to punishment after the misdeed. Four specific recommendations are listed in Table 10.2.

TABLE 10.2 Relating Discipline to Developmental Characteristics During Early Childhood

Remember theory of mind. Young children gradually understand things from other viewpoints. Hence involving empathy ("How would *you* feel if . . .?") will increase prosocial and decrease antisocial behavior.

Remember emerging self-concept. Young children are developing a sense of who they are and what they want, sometimes egocentrically. Adults should protect that emerging self: They should not force 3-year-olds to share their favorite toys, nor should they tell them, "Words will never hurt me." Relational aggression is painful, as young children know.

Remember the language explosion and fast mapping. Young children are eager to talk and think, but they are not always accurate in their verbal understanding. Hence a child who doesn't "listen" should not necessarily be punished, because a command might be misunderstood. However, conversation before and after an event helps the child learn.

Remember that young children are not yet logical. The connection between the misdeed and the punishment needs to be immediate and transparent. A child might learn nothing from waiting several hours to be spanked for deliberately breaking a dish but might learn a lot from having to pick up the pieces, mop the floor, and perhaps contribute some saved pennies toward a replacement.

Techniques of Disciplines

However, no disciplinary technique works quickly and automatically. Instead, over the years from 2 to 6, children gradually learn to reflect on the consequences of their actions, and their actions become more in line with expectations. Culture is a strong influence on disciplinary techniques. Japanese mothers, for example, use reasoning, empathy, and expressions of disappointment to control their children's social behavior more than North American mothers do. These techniques work quite well, partly because of the mother–child relationship referred to as *amae* (a very close interpersonal relationship, especially dependency on the mother), which is much stronger in Japan than in North America (Rothbaum et al., 2000). Parents in the United States are more likely than Japanese parents to allow and even encourage emotional expressions of all sorts, including anger. Perhaps as a result, in a series of experimental situations designed to elicit distress and conflict, American 4- to 5-year-olds were more aggressive than their Japanese counterparts (Zahn-Waxler et al., 1996).

One disciplinary technique often used in North America is the **time-out,** which involves requiring the child to stop all activity and sit in a corner or stay indoors for a few minutes. Other punishment practices are withdrawal of a privilege, such as television watching, and withdrawal of affection, as when the parent expresses disappointment or gives the child a stern "look." Each of these techniques may have unintended consequences. Developmentalists stress the need for parents to prevent misdeeds whenever possible and to choose punishments carefully, noting the effect on the child.

time-out A disciplinary technique in which the child is required to stop all activity and sit in a corner or stay indoors for a few minutes.

What About Spanking?

Many developmentalists wonder whether punishment in any form has a boomerang effect—whether children who are criticized develop low self-esteem, whether those who are shamed feel that they are not loved, whether those who are physically punished learn to be more aggressive. This question raises many cultural issues. In Sweden, for instance, physical punishment of children is against the law for parents as well as for teachers. By contrast, in some Caribbean nations, all parents are expected to physically punish their children and to be very sparing of praise (Durbrow, 1999). In the United States, physical punishment is more commonly accepted in the South than in the North.

More than 90 percent of today's adults in the United States were spanked when they were young, and most consider themselves none the worse for it. Indeed, most parents not only in North America but also throughout Asia, Africa, and South America believe that spanking is acceptable, legitimate, and necessary at times (Durrant, 1996; Levinson, 1989). They are especially likely to spank their children at ages 2 to 6, when the children are considered "old enough to know better" but "not old enough to listen to reason." Spanking is so common that parents of all types resort to it: permissive types in exasperation, authoritative types as a last resort after a series of warnings, and authoritarian types as a legitimate consequence of breaking a rule.

DAVID STRICKLER

Angela at Play Research suggests that being spanked is a salient and memorable experience for young children, not because of the pain but because of the emotions. Children seek to do what they have learned; they know not only how to place their hands but also that an angry person is able to do the hitting. The only part of the lesson they usually forget is what particular misdeed precipitated the punishment. Asked why she is spanking her doll, Angela will likely explain "She was bad."

However, many developmentalists are particularly concerned about spanking. Do children who are physically punished learn to be more aggressive? The answer is probably "yes." Domestic violence of any type—from spanking a child to letting siblings "fight it out" to exposing children to mutual insults or hitting between the parents—may make children aggressive with peers and, later on, with their own families (Straus, 1994).

Not every child in every family will learn to be aggressive from being spanked. Spanking poses that risk, but it is not a determining factor. It is to be avoided if possible, but it is not always destructive (McLloyd & Smith, 2002). For example, one research team (Strassberg et al., 1994) set out to study the relationship between punishment at home and aggression at school. They tracked 273 children aged 4 to 6 and their parents from many socioeconomic and cultural backgrounds. Roughly one-third were single parents; about three-fourths were European-Americans.

Before their children entered kindergarten, the parents were asked how frequently they had spanked, hit, or beaten their children over the past year. If the parents asked the difference between spanking and hitting, *spanking* was defined as "an open hand or an object on the child's buttocks in a controlled manner," whereas *hitting* was "the impulsive or spontaneous use of a fist or closed hand (or object) to strike the child more strongly than one would while spanking." (*Beating,* apparently, did not need to be defined.) Of the 408 parents surveyed, 9 percent never used physical punishment, 72 percent spanked but did not use more violent punishment, and 19 percent hit and/or beat, as well as spanked, their preschool children.

Six months later, observers, blind to the children's punishment history, recorded their behavior in kindergarten, taking particular note of acts of aggression. For an accurate snapshot of behavior, the observation phase was divided into 12 five-minute segments per child, occurring over several days. Within each segment, the observers recorded how many times each child engaged in instrumental, reactive, or bullying aggression.

Bullying aggression, as expected, was clearly associated with being violently punished (see Figure 10.1), particularly among "a few extremely aggressive children," mostly boys who were frequently hit or beaten as well as spanked by both of their parents. No surprise there.

The incidence of *instrumental aggression* was not surprising, either, since it is quite normal for young children to fight to get or keep hold of something, such as a toy. This type of aggression showed no correlation with the kind of

FIGURE 10.1 Punishment and Aggression
All the children, regardless of how their parents punished them, were about equally likely to exhibit instrumental aggression. The typical child did so once or twice an hour. By contrast, children who were severely punished by their parents were most often the bullies. The most interesting result involves reactive aggression. Children who were spanked interpreted such actions as hostile, and thus as requiring an aggressive response, twice as often as children who had not been physically punished.

?Observational Quiz (see answer, page 316): Could young children become bullies if their parents never spanked them?

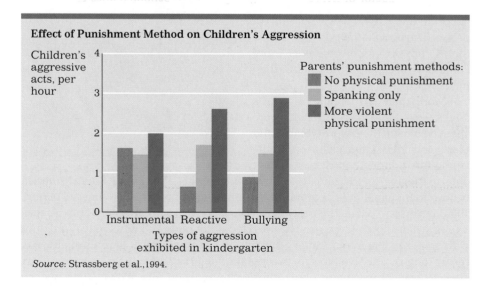

Effect of Punishment Method on Children's Aggression

Children's aggressive acts, per hour

Parents' punishment methods:
■ No physical punishment
■ Spanking only
■ More violent physical punishment

Types of aggression exhibited in kindergarten

Source: Strassberg et al.,1994.

punishment the children experienced at home. Children fought over posses-
sions and privileges whether they had been spanked, beaten, or not physically
punished at all.

However, *reactive aggression*—retaliation against another child for a real or
imagined wrong—was surprisingly common among children who were spanked.
Compared to children who were never spanked, those who were spanked retali-
ated more than twice as much. They angrily shoved, punched, or kicked at any
provocation, rather than asking the other child for an explanation, complaining
to the teacher, assuming it was an accident, or compromising their own actions.

The researchers point out that while violent punishment (hitting or beating)
seems to lead a child to be aggressive under all circumstances (to be a bully),
spanking does not. Rather, it seems to create a specific emotional-response
pattern—a quick physical reaction to a perceived attack—probably because
the child connects spanking to anger, a powerful emotion for a 4-year-old
(Strassberg et al., 1994). Generally, the gender of the child or the spanking parent or the frequency of spanking did not matter. Even a few spankings a year
by only one of the parents was still likely to make the child higher in reactive
aggression. There was one gender-related exception: Boys who were spanked
by their fathers reacted as if they had been hit as well as spanked; that is, they
tended to become bullies.

Although no single study proves a general point, the conclusions of this
study have been refined, not contradicted, by other research. For example, one
prospective, longitudinal study of adolescent mothers found that those who
controlled their children by yelling, grabbing, and spanking had children whose
aggressive and disruptive behavior increased between the ages of 3 and 6. The
correlation was more powerful for European-American than African-American
mothers, perhaps because the latter scored high on measures of warmth and affection as well as control (Spieker et al., 1999). As already pointed out, the overall
context of family support may be more powerful than any particular parental behavior. The general conclusion seems to be that although physical punishment
may be quick and effective at age 2 or 3, it may have negative repercussions later,
especially if the child experiences it as emotional rejection.

Further research clarifies the differences between families. Harsh discipline
was much more harmful to young children's development if it was accompanied
by parental anger and distress, especially if the parent's distress was related to
the child's negative emotions (such as the child's being upset at being teased or
scared of the doctor or nervous about going to a new school) (Fabes et al., 2001).
Children probably should be allowed to express anger, fear, or sorrow without
the parents themselves becoming upset. The physical impact of punishment is
only one part of a triad: The child's cognitive and emotional reactions are as important as the child's physical sensations.

Especially for Parents Suppose you agree that spanking is destructive, but you sometimes get so angry at your child's behavior that you hit him or her.

Boy or Girl: So What?

Male or female identity is an important feature of self-understanding during the
play years, as well as a particular concern of many parents. Social scientists distinguish between **sex differences,** which are the biological differences between
males and females, and **gender differences,** which are culturally imposed differences in the roles and behaviors of the two sexes. Curiously, although true *sex*
differences are far less apparent in childhood (when boys and girls are about the
same size and shape) than in adulthood (when physical differences become more
visible and anatomy becomes critical in sexual intercourse, pregnancy, and
birth), *gender* differentiation seems more significant to children than to adults.

sex differences Biological differences between males and females.

gender differences Culturally imposed differences in the roles and behavior of males and females.

(a)   (b)

Two Sets of Cousins Same day, same trampoline, and similar genes and culture, because these eight children are cousins. But sex or gender differences are quite apparent in the later preschool years. Of course, no one should read too much into a photograph. Nonetheless, this group, like any group of preschoolers, offers suggestive evidence of boy–girl differences, here including one specific aspect of their wearing apparel.

?Observational Quiz (see answer, page 320): What sex or gender differences can you see?

!Answer to Observational Quiz (from page 314): Yes, although bullies were three times as likely to be the product of a home in which physical punishment more violent than spanking was used.

Developmental Progression of Gender Awareness

Even at age 2, gender-related preferences and play patterns are apparent. Children already know whether they are boys or girls, can identify adult strangers as mommies or daddies, and apply gender labels (Mrs., Mr., lady, man) consistently. That simple cognitive awareness becomes, by age 3, a rudimentary understanding that male and female distinctions are lifelong (although some pretend, hope, or imagine otherwise). By age 4, children are convinced that certain toys (such as dolls and trucks) and certain roles (such as nurse and soldier) are appropriate for one gender but not the other (Bauer et al., 1998; Ruble & Martin, 1998). When given a choice, children play with children of their own gender, a tendency that is apparent at age 2 and is clear-cut by age 4, with children becoming more selective and exclusive as they mature (Martin & Fabes, 2001). Partly because of their largely gender-segregated play patterns, victims of physical aggression in preschool are more often boys, while most victims of relational aggression are girls (Crick et al., 1999).

A child who follows same-sex play patterns does not necessarily understand biological sex differences. A leading researcher of gender identity, Sandra Bem, described the day her young son Jeremy

> naively decided to wear barrettes to nursery school. Several times that day, another little boy insisted that Jeremy must be a girl because "only girls wear barrettes." After repeatedly asserting that "wearing barrettes doesn't matter; being a boy means having a penis and testicles," Jeremy finally pulled down his pants as a way of making his point more convincingly. The boy was not impressed. He simply said, "Everybody has a penis; only girls wear barrettes."
>
> *[Bem, 1989]*

As in this example, even though children confuse gender and sex throughout the play years, a child's awareness of differences is soon associated with what is good, bad, or simply wrong (Fagot & Leinbach, 1993). By age 6, children have well-formed ideas (and prejudices) and also know which sex is better (their own) and which sex is stupid (the other one) (Ruble & Martin, 1998).

Young children also insist on dressing in stereotypic ways: Shoes for preschoolers are often designed with such decorations as pink ribbons or blue footballs, and no child would dare wear the shoes meant for the other gender. Such dress codes become rigidly enforced by first grade, with some of the cruelest barbs of relational aggression used against children who dress oddly.

When they reach school age, a few children still may have a good friend of the other sex, but they rarely play with that friend when other children are around (Kovacs et al., 1996). Awareness that a person's sex is a biological characteristic that is not changed by clothing or activities develops gradually, not becoming solid until age 8 or so (Szkrybalo & Ruble, 1999).

Many young children also learn that sexual stereotyping is morally wrong, at least when other people do it. This was demonstrated in a study of 4-year-olds who were told several stories of sexual exclusion; for example: "A group of boys are playing with a truck. Sally comes over and asks if she can play. Two of the boys say that Sally cannot play because she is a girl. Is it all right or not all right for the boys to tell Sally she can't play?" Most of the girls (72 percent) and about half the boys (52 percent) said it was "not all right." Other types of examples elicited other responses, but noteworthy is that many children put aside their personal preferences (very few girls would actually try to join a group of boys in school) when moral judgments about sex discrimination must be made (Theimer et al., 2001).

Theories of Gender Differences

Experts disagree about what proportion of observed gender differences is biological—perhaps a matter of hormones, of brain structure, or of body size and musculature—and what proportion is environmental—perhaps embedded in centuries of cultural history or in the immediate, explicit home training each child receives (Beal, 1994). One reason for their disagreement is that the topic is so vast, individual experiences so varied, and the research so various that firm conclusions are difficult to reach. To develop a framework for analyzing the conflicting evidence, we need a theory. Fortunately, we have five theories, first described in Chapter 2.

Psychoanalytic Theory

Freud (1938) called the period from about age 3 to 6 the **phallic stage,** because he believed its central focus is the *phallus,* or penis. At about 3 or 4 years of age, said Freud, the process of maturation makes a boy aware of his male sexual organ. He begins to masturbate, to fear castration, and to develop sexual feelings toward his mother. These feelings make him jealous of his father—so jealous, according to Freud, that every son secretly wants to replace his dad. Freud called this the **Oedipus complex,** after Oedipus, son of a king in Greek mythology. Abandoned as an infant and raised in a distant kingdom, Oedipus later returned to his birthplace and, not realizing who they were, killed his own father and married his mother. When he discovered what he had done (after disaster struck the entire kingdom), he blinded himself in a spasm of guilt.

Freud believed that this ancient story still echoes through history because every man feels horribly guilty for the incestuous and murderous impulses that were buried in his youthful unconscious mind. Boys fear that their fathers will inflict terrible punishment if this evil secret is ever discovered, and therefore they hide their feelings, even from themselves. Specifically, boys cope with their guilt and fear through **identification,** a defense mechanism that allows a person to ally him- or herself with another person by symbolically taking on that person's behavior and attitudes. Since they cannot replace their fathers, young boys strive to become them, copying their fathers' masculine mannerisms, opinions, and actions.

Boys also develop, again in self-defense, a powerful conscience, called the **superego,** that is quick to judge and punish "the bad guys." According to Freud's

Response for Parents (from page 315): The worst time to spank a child is when you are angry, because you might seriously hurt the child and because the child will associate anger with violence and may follow your example. Better to learn to control your anger and develop other strategies for disciplining your child or preventing him or her from misbehaving in the first place.

phallic stage Freud's term for the third stage of psychosexual development, which occurs in early childhood and in which the penis becomes the focus of psychological concern as well as physiological pleasure.

Oedipus complex In the phallic stage of psychosexual development, the sexual desire that boys have for their mothers and the related hostility that they have toward their fathers.

identification A defense mechanism that lets a person symbolically take on the behaviors and attitudes of someone more powerful than him- or herself.

superego In psychoanalytic theory, the part of the personality that is self-critical and judgmental and that internalizes the moral standards set by parents and society.

theory, a young boy's fascination with superheroes, guns, kung fu, and the like comes directly from his unconscious urges to kill his father. An adult man's obsession with crime and punishment might be a product of an imperfectly resolved phallic stage. In this perspective, homosexuality, either overt or latent, is also evidence of a poorly managed phallic stage, as is homophobia.

Freud offered two overlapping descriptions of the phallic stage in girls. One form, the **Electra complex** (also named after a figure in classical mythology), is similar to the Oedipus complex: The little girl wants to eliminate her mother and become intimate with her father. In the other version, the little girl becomes jealous of boys because they have penises, an emotion Freud called *penis envy*. The girl blames her mother for this "incompleteness" and decides that the next best thing to having a penis is to become sexually attractive so that someone who does have a penis—preferably her father—will love her (Freud, 1933/1965). Her *identification* is with women her father finds attractive; her superego strives to avoid his disapproval.

Thus, the origins and consequences of the phallic stage are basically the same for girls as for boys. Biological impulses within a family context first produce lust and anger and then give rise to guilt and fear. By the end of the play years, these emotions have caused the development of a strict superego that mandates gender-appropriate behavior and harsh punishment for those who do not abide by the code. No wonder, then, that 5-year-olds seem obsessed by gender appropriateness; this is their best defense against unconscious urges.

Other psychoanalytic theorists agree that male–female distinctions are important to the young child's psychic development, although many disagree about the specifics.

Electra complex In the phallic stage of psychosexual development, the female version of the Oedipus complex: Girls have sexual feelings for their fathers and accompanying hostility toward their mothers.

In Person

Berger and Freud

As a woman, and as the mother of four daughters, I have always regarded Freud's theory of sexual development as ridiculous, not to mention antifemale. I am not alone. Psychologists generally agree that Freud's explanation of sexual and moral development is one of the weaker parts of his theory, reflecting the values of middle-class Victorian society at the end of the nineteenth century more than any universal developmental pattern. Many female psychoanalysts (e.g., Horney, 1967; Klein, 1957; Lerner, 1978) have been particularly critical of Freud's idea of penis envy. They believe that girls envy not the male sex organ but the higher status males are generally accorded. They also suggest that boys may experience "womb envy," wishing that they could have babies and suckle them. Virtually no contemporary psychologist or psychiatrist believes that homosexual urges are caused by problems during the phallic stage.

However, my own view of Freud's theory as utter nonsense has been modified somewhat by my four daughters. Our first "Electra episode" occurred in a conversation with my eldest, Bethany, when she was about 4 years old:

Bethany: When I grow up, I'm going to marry Daddy.
 Mother: But Daddy's married to me.
Bethany: That's all right. When I grow up, you'll probably be dead.
 Mother: *(Determined to stick up for myself)* Daddy's older than me, so when I'm dead, he'll probably be dead, too.
Bethany: That's OK. I'll marry him when he gets born again.

At this point, I couldn't think of a good reply, especially since I had no idea where she had gotten the concept of reincarnation. Bethany saw my face fall, and she took pity on me:

Bethany: Don't worry, Mommy. After you get born again, you can be our baby.

Our second episode was also in conversation, this time with my daughter Rachel, when she was about 5:

Rachel: When I get married, I'm going to marry Daddy.
Mother: Daddy's already married to me.
Rachel: *(With the joy of having discovered a wonderful solution)* Then we can have a double wedding!

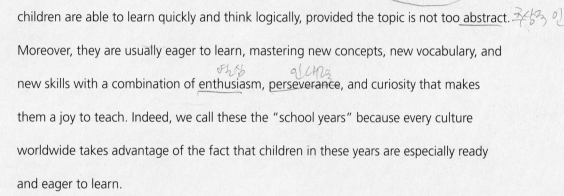

I f someone asked you to pick the best years of the entire life span, you might choose the years from about 6 to 11 and defend your choice persuasively. Physical development is usually almost problem-free, making it easy to master dozens of new skills. With regard to cognitive development, most children are able to learn quickly and think logically, provided the topic is not too abstract. Moreover, they are usually eager to learn, mastering new concepts, new vocabulary, and new skills with a combination of enthusiasm, perseverance, and curiosity that makes them a joy to teach. Indeed, we call these the "school years" because every culture worldwide takes advantage of the fact that children in these years are especially ready and eager to learn.

Finally, the social world of middle childhood seems perfect: Most school-age children think their parents are helpful, their teachers fair, and their friends loyal. The child's moral reasoning and behavior have reached that state where right seems clearly distinguished from wrong, without the ambiguities and conflicts that complicate morality during adolescence. As you will see, however, not every child escapes middle childhood unscathed.

The next three chapters celebrate the joys, and commemorate the occasional tragedies, of middle childhood.

Chapter Eleven

The School Years

The School Years: Cognitive Development

School-age children are primed to learn, and they can learn almost anything that is not too abstract. They can learn how to multiply and divide fractions, how to prepare a balanced and delicious meal, how to surf the Web to find an obscure fact. These skills take time to master—each day from age 7 to 11 is an occasion for small advances in knowledge—and reflect both the child's motivation and the culture's priorities. But all children can learn, each in a way that is unique, partly because of subtle differences in the intricate connections of their brains and partly because their experiences vary with family, culture, and historical context.

If the story ended with that, then adults might simply offer basic learning and let children choose. However, not only are children at this age primed to learn, but the specifics of *what* they learn are each culture's bridge to the future. Thus, adults decide exactly what children should learn and how best to teach them. Should every child learn calculus and chemistry, or is it enough that they know how to count and categorize? Should children be taught to be quiet and respectful of authority or to be creative and rebellious, questioning every rule? Should children learn to suspect any stranger or to accept everyone? What religion, what language, what principles must be passed on, and what standards, groupings, and measurements should schools use?

We begin this chapter by considering the universals of thinking, especially as described by Jean Piaget, Lev Vygotsky, and information-processing theorists. We then turn to some controversial topics: moral development, code-switching, bilingual education, educational standards, reading techniques, and national differences. Developmentalists know that all children must learn and that each child is different; getting from one of these certainties to the other is complicated.

Building on Piaget and Vygotsky

Both Piaget and Vygotsky, as you remember from Chapter 9, emphasize the structures or scaffolding that children develop in preparation for learning during middle childhood (Rogoff, 1998). Piaget, with his four major stages of development, explicitly differentiates the school-age child from the younger version. In Piaget's view, the most important cognitive achievement of middle childhood is the attainment of **concrete operational thought**, whereby children can reason logically about the things and events they perceive. Beginning at about age 7, children understand logical principles, and they apply

concrete operational thought Piaget's term for the ability to reason logically about the things and events that one perceives.

them in *concrete* situations, that is, situations that deal with visible, tangible, real things—things that are solid, just like the concrete poured to become a sidewalk or the foundation of a building. Children thereby become more systematic, objective, scientific—and educable—thinkers.

Vygotsky (1934/1994) believed that Piaget's attention to the actual thinking of the child was a marked improvement over the dull "meaningless acquisition" approach favored by the schools of his time. Such schools rendered the child "helpless in the face of any sensible attempt to apply any of this acquired knowledge" (pp. 356–357). However, Vygotsky was very critical of Piaget's view of the child as a socially isolated learner. To Vygotsky, instruction by others is crucial, with schools, peers, and teachers providing the bridge that is needed to connect the child's innate developmental potential with the skills and knowledge that formal education should provide.

Especially for Teachers: How might Piaget and Vygotsky help in teaching geography to a class of third-graders?

Logical Principles

To understand the place of logic in the development of concrete operational thought during middle childhood, consider three of the logical structures that Piaget describes: classification, identity, and reversibility. These ideas are difficult for younger children but are more easily grasped by school-age children.

Classifying Objects, Ideas, and People

classification The process of organizing things into groups (or categories or classes) according to some property they have in common.

Classification is the process of organizing things into groups (or *categories* or *classes*) according to some property they have in common. For example, a child's parents and siblings belong to the class called "family." Other categories include "toys," "animals," "people," and "food."

Classification leads to the related but more complicated concept of *class inclusion,* the idea that a particular object or person may belong to more than one class. For example, a baseball may be included in the classes of round objects, of sports equipment, and of small things, as well as in many other classes. Until school age, few children really understand class inclusion. As you remember, young children usually assume that each object has one and only one name and belongs to one and only one category (Inhelder & Piaget, 1958, 1964).

Consider the following experiment, similar to experiments conducted by Piaget. An examiner shows a child nine plastic dogs. Five of the dogs are collies; the others are a poodle, a Labrador retriever, and two German shepherds. First, the examiner makes sure that the child knows that all the plastic toys are types of dogs and that the child can name each breed. Then comes the crucial question: "Are there more collies or more dogs?" Until classification and class inclusion are firmly established (at about age 7), most children say "More collies." They do not understand that "dog" is the general category here and "collie" the subcategory, and that the general category includes (and so is greater than) the subcategory. So when they hear "collies" and realize that there are more collies than all the other breeds put together, they jump to the conclusion that there are more collies than dogs.

Once children do understand the relation between a category and its subcategories, they can understand the wide variety of relationships among people, objects, and events—all of which can, and usually do, belong to more than one class. They understand that categories or subcategories can be any of the following:

LEIF SKOOGFORS / WOODFIN CAMP & ASSOCIATES

Learning by Doing This science teacher and student are demonstrating the effects of static electricity. Such demonstrations bring out the logical abilities of concrete operational children much better than do abstract descriptions in textbooks.

- *Hierarchical.* A child is simultaneously a human, primate, mammal, animal, and living creature, with each category belonging to the higher categories, and each higher category including more members than the lower categories do. For example, all humans are primates, but not all primates are human.
- *Overlapping.* A child, within a family, can be an offspring, a sibling, one of the girls, and one of those with curly hair; other family members are likewise in some of those categories but not all of them.
- *Separate.* A child may be a member of the Lee family and simultaneously a member of Mr. Smith's fourth-grade class, but the other members of Mr. Smith's class are not members of the Lee family.

Obviously, a child who can consistently and thoughtfully apply logical principles is better equipped to analyze problems, derive correct solutions, and ask follow-up questions than an intuitive, haphazard thinker would be. The ability to think logically also makes older children more objective, enabling them to think analytically, not just to react emotionally.

Identity and Reversibility

Identity is the idea that certain characteristics of an object remain the same even if other characteristics change. Children who understand identity realize that superficial changes in an object's appearance do not alter that object's underlying substance or quantity. In conservation tests (see page 265), for example, identity tells us that pouring a liquid from one container into a different container does not change the amount of liquid present. "It's still the same milk," a 9-year-old might say. "You haven't changed that."

School-age children also come to understand **reversibility**, the idea that sometimes a thing that has been changed can be returned to its original state by reversing the process by which it was changed. A school-age child might prove that the amount of liquid has not changed by pouring it back into the first container, thus reversing the process.

Identity and reversibility are both relevant to mathematical understanding. Children need a firm grasp of identity to realize, for example, that the number 24 is always 24, whether it is obtained by adding 14 + 10, or adding 23 + 1, or adding 6 + 6 + 6 + 6. This logical principle of identity also enhances scientific understanding, whether that means grasping the underlying oneness of the tadpole and the frog or seeing that frozen water is still H$_2$O. Similarly, reversibility is essential to a school-age child's understanding of math and science. For example, subtraction is the reverse of addition (if 5 + 9 = 14, then 14 − 9 = the original 5).

Logical principles also apply to everyday social encounters. Identity enables a school-age child to understand—as most preschoolers cannot—that his mother was once a child and that her baby picture is, in fact, a picture of his mother. School-age children are even able to imagine their parents growing old—and to promise, as one child did, always to be around to push their wheelchairs. Similarly, a school-age child might say, "Let's start over and be friends again, OK?" (reversibility). Later, when we discuss moral development, we will note that school-age children understand the categories of sex and race well enough to know when relying on such categories amounts to prejudice.

identity The idea that certain characteristics of an object remain the same even if other characteristics change.

reversibility The idea that sometimes a thing that has been changed can be returned to its original state by reversing the process by which it was changed.

Measuring Soil Absorbency This science lesson in the fourth grade of a public school in New York City seems well designed for concrete operational thinking. The children analyze, investigate, and classify samples of soil by putting them in water, not by reading a textbook. Note also that each does his or her own work within a social setting—another sign of effective elementary education.

Logic and Culture

Piaget's basic idea about concrete operational thought—that children during middle childhood gradually come to comprehend and apply logical ideas that they did not understand before—remains valid. In math, in physics, and in explaining how people can or cannot catch physical or mental illnesses from someone else, children become more logical and less egocentric as they mature (Howe, 1998; Keil & Lockhart, 1999; Siegler & Jenkins, 1989). Indeed, in all these domains, the same research finds that sometimes older children make mistakes that younger children do not, again showing that school-age children apply their new logic even when it leads them astray.

Vygotsky's emphasis on the influence of the sociocultural context of learning adds to Piaget's ideas, illuminating why children learn and think as they do. According to Vygotsky, children are powerfully influenced by the people around them, who guide them in one direction or another, and by the cultural context. In physics, for instance, whether or not school-age children grasp certain concepts depends a great deal on the particulars of instruction and on the influence of their peers, as they learn within "a framework that was laid down by Piaget and embellished by Vygotsky" (Howe, 1998, p. 207).

Most of the research on children's cognition has been done in North America and England, but the same principles are apparent worldwide. In Zimbabwe, for example, children's understanding of the logical concept of classification was found to be influenced not only by their age but also by the particulars of their schooling and their family's socioeconomic status (Mpofu & van de Vijver, 2000). Japanese 4- to 11-year-olds' understanding of time, speed, and distance, as Piaget would predict, improved with age: Although younger children sometimes grasped the relationship between two of these three, they could not put all three together, as some of the oldest children could. However, comprehension of the reciprocity of time, speed, and distance varied much more than a straightforward stage theory would predict, suggesting that sociocultural factors were influential as well (Matsuda, 2001). Another study of Japanese children found that some mathematical skills closely followed Piaget (despite the mathematical advantages that some believe are conferred by Japanese families and language), but that other arithmetic strategies were definitely the result of specific school instruction (Naito & Miura, 2001).

The most detailed international example of the importance of culture and context comes from 6- to 15-year-old street children in Brazil, many of whom sell fruit, candy, and other products to earn their living. They have never attended school, but most become quite adept at pricing their wares, making change, and giving discounts for large quantities—a set of practices that must be recalibrated almost every day as inflation, wholesale prices, and demand change. These children calculate "complex markup computations and adjust for inflation in these computations by using procedures that were widespread in their practice but not known to children in school" (Saxe, 1999, p. 255). Thus, the demands of the situation, the social learning attained from other sellers, and their daily experience advance these children's cognitive performance in ways that neither maturation nor education could do alone. In short, learning is both developmental and sociocultural; both Piagetian and Vygotskyan.

Further research on Brazilian 4- to 14-year-olds confirms the special relationship of thinking and experience. The cognitive advantage of actually having dealt with money was greatest for children age 6 to 11, in middle childhood. Younger children were less able to understand the arithmetic problems as presented to them, even with experience,

Who Is the Smart One Here? Research on child street vendors in Brazil, such as this boy in São Paulo, reveals that few have attended school but that most have quite advanced arithmetic skills, allowing them to divide per-item cost, subtract to determine change, and even convert currency of another nation into the Brazilian equivalent— adjusted for inflation. Other research confirms that school-age children use their cognitive capacities to master whatever their culture values or requires, including the social skills needed—in this case, to convince tourists to buy lemons.

GEORGE ANCONA / INTERNATIONAL STOCK

Learning is both developmental & sociocultural,

and older ones could do just as well whether or not they had personal experience (Guberman, 1996).

Overall, Piaget constructed a valid sketch of cognitive development, but he underestimated the influence of context, instruction, and culture, and this, in turn, made him underestimate the variability from one child to another. Research inspired by Vygotsky and the sociocultural perspective fills in Piaget's outline with details of the actual learning situation.

Information Processing

A third approach to understanding cognition arises from *information-processing theory*. Like computers, people take in and store large amounts of information, then apply their mental processes to perform three functions: to search for specific items of information when they are needed, to analyze situations using the particular problem-solving strategies that are likely to yield correct solutions, and to express the best solution in a format that another person (or a networked computer) can understand.

Information-processing theory is useful precisely because people "can learn anything, sense or nonsense" (Simon, 2001, p. 205). Many 7- to 11-year-olds not only learn rapidly in school but also outscore their elders on computer games, repeat the rapid-fire lyrics of their favorite rap songs, and recognize out-of-towners by the clothes they wear. Some children, by age 11, beat their fathers at chess, play a musical instrument so well that adults pay to hear them, or write poems that get published. Other children that age run away from abusive homes and live by their wits on the street, and still others become soldiers in a civil war—having learned lessons that few adults want to know.

This enormous and impressive range of knowledge makes it clear that older school-age children are very different kinds of learners from, say, 4- or 5-year-olds. Not only do they know more, they also use their minds much more effectively, whether they must solve a problem or remember a piece of information to be retrieved easily when needed. As with a computer, greater efficiency means not simply having more information stored somewhere, but having better access strategies. This is the main reason 11-year-olds are better thinkers than 7-year-olds.

Memory

The **sensory register** is the first component of the information-processing system. It stores incoming stimulus information for a split second after it is received, to allow it to be processed. To use terms first explained in Chapter 5, *sensations* are retained for a moment while the person selects some sensations to become *perceptions*. This first step of information processing is quite good in early childhood and continues to improve slightly until about age 10. (For most people, hearing and vision are as sharp at age 10 as they will ever be, gradually declining from adolescence on.) Most sensations that come into the sensory register are lost or discarded, but meaningful information is transferred to working memory for further analysis.

It is in **working memory** (sometimes called *short-term memory*) that current, conscious mental activity occurs. Your working memory includes, at this moment, your understanding of this paragraph, any previous knowledge you recall that is related to it, and also, perhaps, distracting thoughts about weekend plans or the interesting person who sat next to you in class today. Working memory is constantly replenished with new information, so thoughts and memories are usually not retained for very long. Most are discarded, while a few are transferred to long-term memory, to be recalled later (as weekend plans were in this

Response for Teachers (from page 360): Here are two of the most obvious ways. First, use logic. Once children can grasp classification and class inclusion, they can understand cities within states, states within nations, and nations within continents. Organize your instruction to make logical categorization easier. Second, make use of children's need for concrete and personal involvement: You might have children learn first about their own location, then about the places where friends and family live, and finally about places beyond their personal experience via books, photos, guest speakers, and films.

sensory register The component of the information-processing system in which incoming stimulus information is stored for a split second to allow it to be processed.

working memory The component of the information-processing system in which current conscious mental activity occurs. Also called *short-term memory.*

long-term memory The component of the information-processing system in which virtually limitless amounts of information can be stored indefinitely.

Especially for Teachers: How might your understanding of memory help you teach 2,000 new words to a class of fourth-graders?

KAZ MORI / THE IMAGE BANK

Eye on the Ball This boy's concentration while heading the ball and simultaneously preparing to fall is a sign that he has practiced this maneuver enough times that he can perform it automatically. Not having to think about what to do on the way down, he can think about what to do when he gets up, such as pursuing the ball or getting back to cover his position.

knowledge base A broad body of knowledge in a particular subject area that makes it easier to master new learning in that area.

example). Working memory is one of the components that clearly improves in childhood (Meadows, 1993).

Finally, **long-term memory** stores information for minutes, hours, days, months, or years. The capacity of long-term memory—how much information can be crammed into one brain—is virtually limitless by the end of middle childhood. Together with the sensory register and working memory, long-term memory assists in organizing reactions to stimuli. Crucial here is not merely *storage* (how much material has been deposited in long-term memory) but also *retrieval* (how readily the material can be brought to the conscious mind to be used). Certain information is more readily retrievable (you remember your birth date more easily than your phone number), but all the information in long-term memory is stored somehow, unless something (such as a stroke) destroys it.

Speed of Processing

Older children are much quicker thinkers than younger children, and this greater speed benefits memory and a host of other cognitive skills (Williams et al., 1999). Speed directly increases mental capacity, because faster thinking makes it possible to hold and process more thoughts in one's conscious mind (working memory) at once. A sixth-grader can listen to the dinner-table conversation of her parents, respond to the interruptions of her younger siblings, think about her best friend, and still remember to ask for her allowance. In school, increased processing capacity means that she can answer a teacher's question with several relevant ideas rather than just one and, at the same time, monitor her words for accuracy and note her classmates' reactions to her answer.

Speed of thinking continues to increase throughout adolescence. In adulthood, it gradually slows down. Why does thinking speed increase even though adult brain size is reached by age 7? Neurological maturation, especially the ongoing myelination of neural axons and the development of the frontal cortex, partly accounts for these changes (Benes, 2001). But the advances seem more directly a matter of learning from experience than of simple maturation. Indeed, there is no evidence that the critical parts of the brain literally grow bigger during middle childhood. Instead, speed and capacity increase because as children learn to use their brains more efficiently, myelination increases and dendrites become more dense (Schneider & Pressley, 1997). As this happens, repetition makes many neurons fire in a coordinated and seemingly instantaneous way (Merzenich, 2001).

We saw in Chapter 11 that *automatization* is the process in which familiar, well-practiced mental activities become routine and automatic. As people use their intellectual skills, many processes that at first required hard mental labor now become automatic. This increases processing speed, frees up capacity, allows more to be remembered, and thus advances thinking in every way (Schneider & Pressley, 1997).

Progress from initial effort to automatization often takes years. Many children lose cognitive skills over the summer because the halt in daily schooling erases earlier learning (Huttenlocher et al., 1998). Not until something is overlearned does it become automatic.

Knowledge Base

Another aspect of thinking that takes years to develop is knowledge. Children know much more in the school years than in the play years. The more they know and remember, the more they can learn. That is, having an extensive **knowledge base,** a broad body of knowledge in a particular subject area, makes it easier to master new learning in that area. This fact is apparent not only in college classes but also in elementary school subjects, such as math and reading, and in psychological research. For example, one study compared fourth-graders of varied intelligence—some of whom were expert soccer players and others of whom were novices—on their ability to understand and remember a written passage about soccer (see Table 12.1). As expected, high-IQ children did somewhat better than low-IQ children—but this was true only for children who were at the same level of soccer expertise. When an expert soccer player with low intelligence was compared to a highly intelligent novice, the expert did better. In this experiment a larger knowledge base was sufficient to overcome slower thinking overall (Schneider et al., 1996).

Further research emphasizes that the connections between bits of information improve as the knowledge base expands. When people learn more about a particular topic, they remember how the new knowledge relates to the previous knowledge. This explains why learning by rote is fragile, while learning by comprehension of ideas endures.

Control Processes

The mechanisms that put memory, processing speed, and knowledge together are the **control processes**, which regulate the analysis and flow of information within the system. Control processes include selective attention, emotional regulation, and metacognition. When someone wants to concentrate on only one part of all the material in the sensory register, or summon a rule of thumb from long-term memory to working memory in order to solve a problem, control processes assume an executive role in the information-processing system.

If this sounds familiar, it is because you read in Chapter 8 about the maturation of the prefrontal cortex, where the brain regulates and coordinates emotions and thoughts. This part of the brain (actually several parts, including the medial prefrontal cortex, the orbital prefrontal cortex, the anterior cingulate, and the hypothalamus) is sometimes called the *executive function* precisely because it controls the other parts. The underlying problem of children with AD/HD (as we saw in Chapter 11) may well be that an underdeveloped prefrontal cortex reduces their ability to control their impulses; without control processes, a child blurts out words and is easily distracted (Karatekin, 2001).

Selective Attention

One of the most important control processes is the ability to focus one's thoughts on what is important. If you were to observe children learning in a kindergarten classroom and a fifth-grade classroom, you would see many differences in attention. Kindergartners are easily distracted, whether they are listening to a story or printing letters of the alphabet. While they are working, they chatter to each other, look around, fidget, call out to the teacher, and sometimes get up to visit friends or just wander around. Their curriculum is designed to be highly varied, with plenty of changes of activity, because the teachers know the nature of their 5-year-old charges.

By contrast, fifth-graders might work independently at desks or in groups around a table, managing to read, write, discuss, and seek assistance without distracting, or being distracted by, other students. Or they might all quietly follow a demonstration at the chalkboard, raising their hands to be called on rather than shouting out. Remember Billy, the boy with AD/HD, from Chapter 11, as he sat in class? The problem was not that he didn't know the right answer; in fact, he got angry precisely because he was right. The problem was that he could not wait quietly, with his hand raised, to be called on. As this example demonstrates,

TABLE 12.1 Who Remembers Most After Reading a Passage About Soccer?

	Intelligence	
	High IQ	Low IQ
Expert soccer players	Most	Second most
Novice soccer players	Third most	Least

Experts Versus Novices That intelligent children who are experienced soccer players remember the most, or that their opposites remember the least, about a written passage concerning soccer is not surprising. What is surprising is the group that came in second: those children who were not very intelligent overall but who happened to know a lot about soccer. Given a passage they had never seen before, both their comprehension and their memory were better than those of smarter children with less knowledge about the subject.

control processes The mechanism—selective attention, emotional regulation, and strategic thinking—that put memory, processing speed, and knowledge together in order to regulate the analysis and flow of information within the information-processing system.

selective attention The ability to screen out distractions and to focus on the details that will help in later recall of information.

metacognition "Thinking about thinking," or the ability to evaluate a cognitive task to determine how best to accomplish it, and then to monitor and adjust one's performance on that task.

They've Read the Book Acting in a play based on *The Lion, the Witch, and the Wardrobe* suggests that these children have metacognitive abilities beyond almost any preschooler. Indeed, the book itself requires a grasp of the boundary between reality (the wardrobe) and fantasy (the witch). "Thinking about thinking" is needed in order to appreciate the allegory.

? *Observational Quiz* (see answer, page 368): Beyond the book, what are three examples of metacognition implied here? Specifically, how does the ability to memorize lines, play a part, and focus on the play illustrate metacognition?

toward the end of middle childhood, academic tasks are more difficult and take longer to complete, but teachers expect students to persist in the face of challenge, waiting and thinking.

Selective attention, the ability to screen out distractions and concentrate on relevant information, is the critical difference between the kindergartners and fifth-graders. Selective attention improves throughout middle childhood and beyond (Goldberg et al., 2001). Memory and thought depend on the improved ability to ignore most of the information that bombards the senses and to focus on details that will help in later recall—perhaps using an already-memorized address to remember a historical date. Focusing on what should be remembered and ignoring what should be forgotten are equally important components of selective attention (Cowan, 1997).

Improved Control

The ability to control one's mental processes begins during the preschool years, as children show signs of *emotional regulation*—holding their anger instead of hitting their friends, distracting themselves instead of crying at the dentist, and so on. This works in the opposite direction, too: Overly inhibited children become less shy and fearful. As you saw in Chapter 10, these processes are powerfully influenced by the responses within the family and by the values of the child's culture.

Metacognition

During the school years, control processes become markedly better, especially in regard to intellectual, not just emotional, efforts, which are reinforced by the school. Children develop **metacognition**, which means "thinking about thinking," the ability to evaluate a cognitive task to determine how best to accomplish it, and then to monitor and adjust one's performance on that task. For example, experimenters first tested 6- to 10-year-old children's knowledge base about animals, including their knowledge that woolly animals live in cold places. The experimenters then gave the children examples from a mythical planet that contradicted their previous knowledge. The older children were better able to alter their prior knowledge to accommodate the new information, even though they had a firmer knowledge base and hence required more adjustment than the younger children (Carmichael & Hayes, 2001). Thus, as middle childhood proceeds, children become better able to control their knowledge, changing their assumptions if necessary.

Much other research provides evidence for the marked advances in control processes and metacognition that take place over the school years (Case, 1998; Ferrari & Sternberg, 1998). For example, preschool children find it difficult to judge whether a problem is easy or difficult, or whether or not they remember a particular fact. Thus, when they try to study something, they cannot monitor or judge what they need to know, so they wastefully devote equal effort to the easy and the hard, to what is already known and what is not yet known. Children at the start of middle childhood still make this mistake; consequently, "young grade school children have enormous problems responding appropriately to monitoring activities" (Schneider, 1998).

By around age 8 or 9, children realize that they must identify challenging tasks. They become much more accurate about what they already know and thus more efficient when they study. They can evaluate their learning progress, judging whether they have learned a set of spelling words or science principles, rather than simply asserting (as many younger children do) that they know it all (Harter, 1999). In short, older children approach cognitive tasks in a more strategic and analytical manner. Storage and retrieval strategies improve as they learn how to pluck something from memory, when to use mnemonic devices (memory aids, such as "*i* before *e* except after *c*"), and when something is not worth learning. All this is part of metacognition, including both control processes and memory strategies (Meadows, 1993).

Language

To understand the thinking of the school-age child, it is vital to examine language, which is a cause, a consequence, and the best evidence, of cognitive development from ages 7 to 11. For example, younger children tend to use intuition and subjective impressions to interpret the results of a classroom science experiment ("Maybe the caterpillar just felt like becoming a butterfly"); in contrast, school-age children seek verbal explanations that are rational, consistent, and generalizable ("Does the caterpillar use the air temperature to know when it's time to start spinning a cocoon?"). Preoperational thinkers ask "Why?" but reject answers that are not to their liking; concrete operational thinkers ask "Why?" and then want to know more facts.

Similarly, 5-year-olds on the playground may argue over the rules of a game by using increasingly loud and assertive protests ("Is!" "Is not!" "Is!" "Is not!"), whereas 10-year-olds temper their arguments with reason and justification ("That can't be right, because if it was, we'd have to score points differently"). In both academic and nonacademic contexts, school-age children's logical thinking and precise use of language are crucial to their understanding, knowledge, and communication. How, and how much, language is learned often differentiates the cognitive achievements of school-age children.

Learning Vocabulary

Both Piaget and Vygotsky stress that the school years are the ideal time for teaching language. By some estimates, school-age children's rate of vocabulary growth exceeds that of younger children. Some children learn as many as 20 words a day during elementary school, reaching a vocabulary of nearly 40,000 words by the fifth grade. However, variation is enormous: 6-year-olds' vocabulary ranges between 5,000 and 20,000 words—a 400 percent difference (Moats, 2001). Children from low-income families are usually at the low end of this range, not only in vocabulary but also in syntax and sentence length (Hart & Risley, 1995). This means that, even if vocabulary doubles in size between ages 5 and 11, disadvantaged children know an average of only 10,000 words, compared to 40,000 words for more advantaged children.

The size of the child's vocabulary at the start of middle childhood depends on how much he or she has been exposed to

Response for Teachers (from page 364): Children can be taught strategies for remembering at this age, making links between working memory and long-term memory. Accordingly, you might break down the vocabulary list into word clusters, looking for root words, connections to the children's existing knowledge, applications, or (as a last resort) by first letters or rhymes. Active, social learning is useful; perhaps in groups the students could write a story each day that incorporates 15 new words. Each group could read its story aloud to the class. Four days a week, 15 new words a day, would be appropriate for this activity.

Connections Basic vocabulary is learned by age 4 or so, but the school years are best for acquiring expanded, derivative, and specialized vocabulary, especially if the child is actively connecting one word with another. With his father's encouragement, this boy in San Jose, California, will remember *Jupiter, Mars,* and the names of the other planets and maybe even *orbit, light years,* and *solar system.*

RACHEL EPSTEIN / THE IMAGE WORKS

new words that label experiences, which is not necessarily correlated with socioeconomic status (SES). For example, in one study researchers recorded 44 hours of conversations between 53 low-income mothers and their 5-year-olds during mealtime, playtime, and reading time. Despite their similar SES, these mothers varied widely in the amount of linguistic encouragement they gave their children. Some mothers simply told their children "eat"; other mothers used mealtime as an occasion for informal language instruction. For example:

> **Child:** [makes gulping noise in throat]
> **Mother:** Please stop.
> **Child:** Okay.
> **Mother:** Were you planning to eat more?
> **Child:** No.
> **Mother:** We kinda wasted some of that first piece of chicken there. Don't you think?
> **Child:** No. [makes noise again]
> **Mother:** Stop it now.
> **Child:** Okay.
> **Mother:** Now you're gonna have to roll up your sleeves and wash your hands and your face. Try not to get your pajama top wet. See how you do. You can wash your face with the face cloth.
> **Child:** Okay.
> **Mother:** Don't you make that gulping noise.
> **Child:** [laughs for a while]
>
> *[adapted from Weizman & Snow, 2001, p. 269]*

This child said only "okay" and "no," but the mother employed a fairly extensive vocabulary, including "planning," "wasted," "gulping," "roll up," and "face cloth," using each term in the immediate context so that it had concrete meaning for the child. Poverty put all the children in this study "at risk," but those 5-year-olds with mothers like this one became school-age children with large vocabularies, as measured on standardized tests (see Table 12.2). These findings "demonstrate that there is a powerful linkage between early exposure to sophisticated vocabulary—even if it constitutes as little as 1% of total maternal input—during

TABLE 12.2 Variability in Maternal Talking

During All Five Interactions	Average	Least	Most
Time spent by mother in interaction with child	50 minutes	28 minutes	90 minutes
Number of different words used by mother	1,073 words	381 words	1,636 words
Percentage of words not in child's basic vocabulary	1.8%	Less than 0.3%	More than 4.0%
During Mealtime Interactions Only			
Time spent by mother in interaction with child	20 minutes	1 minute	47 minutes
Number of different words used by mother	259 words	3 words	595 words
Percentage of words not in child's basic vocabulary	3.5%	None	More than 8%

Source: Weizman & Snow, 2001.

Talk to Me! In a detailed study of low-income mothers in the Boston area and their 5-year-old children, five interactions were recorded for each pair: two reading, two playing, and one mealtime. Despite their similar economic and geographic status, the mothers varied enormously in how much time they spent interacting with their child (by a factor of 3), how much they said (by a factor of 5), and, especially, how many words they used that were not part of a child's expected basic vocabulary (by a factor of 12). Note that the percentage of new words used by the mothers at mealtime—the only one of these five interactions that is always part of each child's day—was greater than the average (mean) percentage for all five interactions. By the time they reached second grade, the children who had heard the most varied maternal talk were ahead of their peers in vocabulary acquisition.

This research method is cumbersome, time-consuming, and susceptible to scoring bias. The focus on logical, expressed explanations favors articulate respondents over those who may be equally moral but less verbal.

To avoid this methodological problem, James Rest, another prominent researcher, developed an alternate measure of moral thinking that asks people to read various dilemmas and then to rank 12 statements as possible resolutions for each situation. This questionnaire, called the **Defining Issues Test (DIT),** has been used widely, comparing people of various ages and backgrounds (Rest et al., 1999a). Answers are easier to collect, tabulate, and compare than with Kohlberg's original method. Results from the DIT show that Kohlberg's three levels (self-centered, community-centered, and principle-centered) are valid. They also show that cultural differences affect moral judgments—a finding that leads to the second criticism.

Defining Issues Test (DIT) A questionnaire devised by James Rest that measures moral thinking by asking people to read various dilemmas and then to rank 12 statements as possible resolutions for each situation.

Cultural Differences

It is now well established that every culture has distinctive values and morals, which are sometimes connected to a particular religion, sometimes not. For example, children may hold the belief that eating beef (or pork, whale, or dog) is immoral; such a value is not universal but very culture-specific. Kohlberg was from a Western intellectual background. Did this influence his hierarchy?

To be specific, some critics of Kohlberg believe that his level III (stages 5 and 6) reflects only liberal, Western intellectual values. In many non-Western nations and among many non-Western ethnic groups within Western cultures, the good of the family, the well-being of the community, or adherence to religious tradition takes moral precedence over all other considerations (Wainryb & Turiel, 1995). This makes it harder for non-Westerners to score at Kohlberg's postconventional level or even to move up the hierarchy as fast as others. For example, in a study of teenagers in the Netherlands, Moroccan and Turkish students were significantly behind Dutch and Surinamese adolescents in Kohlberg's hierarchy (De May et al., 1999). The Moroccan and Turkish emphasis on family and community, taken as a handicap in Kohlberg's scheme, can be considered a higher form of moral thinking than the individualism and rationality enshrined by Kohlberg. It may be that Kohlberg's "philosophical emphasis on justice and psychological emphasis on reasoning" are too narrow and restrictive (Walker et al., 1995).

In contrast, Kohlberg's hierarchy may underestimate the reasoning capacity of some school-age children in some cultures. Canadian 6- to 10-year-olds, who were presumably too young to think past level I or II, were able to judge whether laws were just and to condone disobedience when a law was unjust—a stage-five reaction. These issues are not discussed in elementary school, presumably because they are thought to be beyond young children (Helwig & Jasiobedzka, 2001).

Morality and Gender

Carol Gilligan (1982) raised the third criticism, that Kohlberg overlooked significant gender differences, in part because his original research used only boys as subjects. Gilligan explains that females develop a **morality of care** more than a **morality of justice.** The morality of care makes girls and women reluctant to judge right and wrong in absolute terms (justice) because they are socialized to be nurturant, compassionate, and nonjudgmental (caring).

As an example, Gilligan cited the responses of two bright 11-year-olds, Jake and Amy, to the Heinz story. Jake considered the dilemma "sort of like a math

morality of care In Gilligan's view, the tendency of females to be reluctant to judge right and wrong in absolute terms because they are socialized to be nurturant, compassionate, and nonjudgmental.

morality of justice In Gilligan's view, the tendency of males to emphasize justice over compassion, judging right and wrong in absolute terms.

Carol Gilligan Gilligan is best known for comparing moral logic to real-life dilemmas. She pointed out that because females are often inclined to consider human relationships, they are less abstract and less dogmatic than men—and less advanced in Kohlberg's hierarchy of moral development. .

Gilligan
= nurturant
+ compassionate,
non judgmental

problem with humans," and he set up an equation that showed that life is more important than property. Amy, in contrast, seemed to sidestep the issue, arguing that Heinz "really shouldn't steal the drug—but his wife shouldn't die either." She tried to find an alternative solution (a bank loan, perhaps) and then explained that stealing wouldn't be right because Heinz "might have to go to jail, and then his wife might get sicker again, and he couldn't get more of the drug."

Amy's response may seem just as ethical as Jake's, but Kohlberg would score it lower. Gilligan argues that this is unfair, because what appears to be females' moral weakness—their hesitancy to take a definitive position based on abstract moral premises—is, in fact,

> inseparable from women's moral strength, an overriding concern with relationships and responsibilities. The reluctance to judge may itself be indicative of the care and concern that infuse the psychology of women's development.
>
> *[Gilligan, 1982]*

Many researchers have tested Gilligan's ideas with children, by looking for a morality of care or a morality of justice. In one study, the moral dilemma presented was not Kohlberg's but a fable about a family of moles who invite a lonely and cold porcupine to share their underground home for the winter. He accepts, but then the moles realize that the porcupine's size and sharp quills make them very uncomfortable. They politely ask him to leave, but he refuses. What to do? One 8-year-old was very caring:

> They should all go on an expedition for marshmallows and stick the marshmallows on the porcupine's quills and then the moles will really, really, really not get pricked. Then the porcupine would be happy because he could live in the moles' house that suited him just fine and the moles could have tasty tidbits as well as a warm home because of the porcupine's body heat . . . and all would be happy.
>
> *[Garrod, 1993]*

This version of "the morality of care" found a way for everyone to be happy. By contrast, law and order were evident in another child's response, which is a good example of "the morality of justice":

> The central problem, as I see it, is that the moles want the porcupine to leave and he's refusing. I think that they should kick him out. They were nice to let him in in the first place. And it's not their fault that he has quills. They have a right to be comfortable in their own home . . . they can do what they want in their cave. It's like if a homeless man moved into my home while my family was vacationing in Florida. We'd definitely call the police.
>
> *[Garrod, 1993]*

Both these respondents were boys. Thus, in this research (and in other research involving the actual responses and actions of school-age children) there is no clear gender distinction regarding the morality of justice or the morality of care. Gilligan may have articulated an important difference in the way males and females are encouraged to respond in ethical situations, but the evidence from hypothetical dilemmas does not support a gender divide between a morality of care and a morality of justice (Walker, 1988). From all the cross-cultural research on moral development, however, researchers find that moral dilemmas are provocative issues for school-age children—who have opinions and like to express them.

Another conclusion about morality is also widely held: Abstract reasoning about the justice of hypothetical situations is not the only, or necessarily the best, way to measure moral judgment (Emler, 1998). What children actually do when they personally care about an issue is more reflective of morality than what they might say about Heinz, or porcupines, or any other hypothetical situation.

Prosocial Behavior: Two versions School-age children, such as these Habitat for Humanity builders and this Girl Scout, are able to perform many useful prosocial tasks. Although prosocial acts are performed without expectation of rewards, they can result in a very important benefit: a sense of connection. The adults' role is to find suitable prosocial activities for school-age children—not always an easy task because children don't always feel comfortable "helping." These boys, for instance, might not enjoy wearing a uniform and chatting with the elderly, but they certainly take pride in pounding nails with their friends.

Children's Actual Moral Behavior

As we have seen, during middle childhood children are passionately concerned with issues of right and wrong. Overall, these are the

> years of eager, lively searching on the part of children, whose parents and teach-
> ers are often hard put to keep up with them as they try to understand things, to
> figure them out, but also to weigh the rights and wrongs of this life. This is the
> time for growth of the moral imagination, fueled constantly by the willingness,
> the eagerness of children to put themselves in the shoes of others.
>
> *[Coles, 1997]*

The specifics depend heavily on the values of the child's parents and society. If a family and culture are conscientious about providing children with guided participation in their set of values, with both adult and child undertaking moral actions, school-age children learn and, eventually, behave accordingly (Goodnow, 1997). As you saw in Chapter 10, prosocial behavior—acts of sharing, helping, and caring—is learned in much the same way that antisocial behavior is—from parents, schools, and peers (Eisenberg et al., 1996).

Few children *always* follow their parents' moral standards, their culture's conventions, or their own best moral thinking; yet moral thought has a decided influence on children's actions (Eisenberg, 1986; Rest, 1983). Increasingly, as they grow older, children try to figure out their own standards of what the "right" thing to do is, and they feel guilty and ashamed when they do "wrong," even if no one else knows (Harter, 1996). For example, when children were asked whether they would break a law to help their siblings or peers, the answer was almost always "yes." In general, school-age children considered loyalty to siblings or peers—especially to a close friend—a compelling reason to ignore community standards of proper action. Many children said they would cheat, lie, or steal to help a needy friend (Smetana et al., 1991; Turiel et al., 1991). Further, authority figures—parents, teachers, police officers, store owners—are not necessarily seen as right, as the In Person feature illustrates.

Especially for Parents: Suppose you and your school-age children move to a new community that is 50 miles from the nearest location that offers instruction in your religious faith or secular value system. Your neighbor says, "Don't worry, they don't have to make any moral decisions until they are teenagers." What do you do?

In Person

Challenging the Adults

As a mother of four, teaching moral thinking and behavior is very important to me. I have often said that I would rather have my children become loving and caring adults than become successful and rich—although I take great pride in their successes. It is not surprising, then, that they also care about moral issues, sometimes taking actions that are not the ones I would choose.

For example, my daughter Sarah regularly gives her pocket money to homeless people and is quick to criticize me for rudely (her word) passing them by. The strength of her conviction was illustrated years ago when her fourth-grade class visited the local police precinct in New York City to hear an officer instruct them on street safety. Most of his talk was accepted without protest, until:

Officer: Never take money out of your pocket while you are on the street—

(At this point, according to the mother who helped chaperone the school trip, Sarah raised her hand insistently, "the way children do who have to go to the bathroom right away.")

Officer: *(Interrupting his speech.)* Yes?

Sarah: But what if a homeless man wants money?
Officer: Your parents give you money for lunch, not to give away.
Sarah: But what if you decide you don't need lunch?
Officer: You should not give money to beggars; you don't know how they will spend it.
Sarah: But what if you decide he really really needs it?
Officer: Don't give it. Adults are taking care of the homeless people who really need help.
Sarah: *(Shaking her head.)* Well, you aren't doing a very good job.

That incident made me proud, as the mother who telephoned me to report it knew it would.

Although I still disagree with Sarah about the most moral response to street beggars, I appreciate at least one aspect of this incident. Sarah's active sense of morality bodes well. Children who engage in moral discussion and feel personally responsible for their ethical behavior tend to be more accomplished than others, socially as well as academically (Bandura et al., 1996). Active reflection is much more likely to lead to moral action than is merely accepting social conventions and laws.

Because cultural and religious values shape moral perception, what is merely conventional in one culture may take on moral significance in another. Children behave in accord with their moral beliefs, nurtured by family, school, and, especially, the peer group. As they grow older, their actions become more ethical and less self-interested, because they have the social experiences, the cultural awareness, and the cognitive capacity to generate more persuasive arguments—both in convincing themselves to do the right thing and in justifying their actions to others (Emler, 1998). They maintain these patterns and values when they are fully grown, becoming better at recognizing true moral dilemmas.

One team of researchers asked third-graders, seventh-graders, and college students "whether it is all right" for other people to hold beliefs that they themselves did not hold (Wainryb et al., 2001). The beliefs tested were of four kinds: moral, conventional, psychological, and metaphysical. (In pretesting, the examiners determined that these subjects did not hold these particular beliefs.) Here are examples of the four kinds of beliefs tested:

■ *Moral.* "It is all right to hurt children just because one wants to hurt them."
■ *Conventional.* "The way to get a waiter's attention is to put one's fork in a glass."
■ *Psychological.* "The way to be really good friends with someone is never to tell them how you feel about anything."
■ *Metaphysical.* "Only people who die on Tuesday become angels."

GARY LANGLEY

Give Peace a Chance The setting is Israel; the sheep washers include Jews and Muslims. In all probability, these boys are aware that their cooperative efforts are in accord with moral values but are contrary to the social customs prevailing around them. The school years are a good time to teach children about other races and cultures, a lesson best learned through personal experience.

Not surprisingly, subjects were likely to judge moral beliefs that were divergent from their own to be "not all right" and divergent *metaphysical* beliefs to be "all right." Third graders were already quite similar to adolescents and adults in their moral judgments, particularly about what is tolerable (although odd) and what is beyond acceptance.

In two important ways, however, the third-graders differed from the older subjects. First, they more strongly believed that disagreements with conventional beliefs (putting a fork in a glass) were "not all right," especially when the person not only held the unconventional idea but also acted on it, even if that person's culture approved of such behavior. Second, they were more likely to judge someone who held any of these four types of divergent beliefs "insane" compared to the seventh-graders and college students, who more often thought such a person was merely "immature" or "uninformed." In other words, compared to adolescents and adults, school-age children were more critical and dismissive of people who thought differently from themselves. Likewise, another study found that, compared to college students, school-age children judged liars more harshly, especially liars who personally benefited from their lies (Barnett et al., 2000).

This tendency to be critical of other people who disagree is apparent in school-age children's everyday behavior: They increasingly want to dress, talk, and think like their peers, even if adults have other preferences. Does this conformity mean that children prefer other children who are just like them, including their own sex and ethnicity? Yes! However, when asked, they oppose exclusion based on race or sex. In one study, children in the first, third, and seventh grades were adamant that it was *not* all right to exclude a child just because he or she was different from other members of an after-school club. This moral judgment was made by 94 percent of the children when the difference was sex and 97 percent when the difference was race (Killen & Stangor, 2001). The third-graders were slightly more inclusive than the others. Other research suggests that school-age children come to their beliefs as a result of their thoughts and experiences, not just of an innate moral sensibility. In fact, by about age 11 almost all children have well-formed ideas of justice and fairness, and can think of instances when they themselves have been wronged (Evans et al., 2001). The advanced control processes that we have described mean that 11-year-olds are less likely to react to their feelings in a harmful way; nevertheless, they are well aware of immoral behavior in adults.

Response for Parents (from page 377): Your neighbor is mistaken: These are prime years for moral education. You might travel those 50 miles once or twice a week or recruit other parents to organize a local program. Whatever you do, don't skip moral instruction. Discuss and demonstrate your moral and religious values, and help your children meet other children who share those values.

selective attention

Schools, Values, and Research

Worldwide, many ideological debates swirl around the content and the practice of elementary education. A review of educational practices in five cultures found that there is often a discrepancy between "expressed claim and observed reality," because "not uncommonly school structures are at variance with educational goals, frustrating or even contradicting them" (Alexander, 2000, p. 176). Virtually no nation has good information on the extent to which reforms and policies are actually implemented in the classroom. As a result, moving from what is known about the psychology and brain of the school-age child to what happens in the classroom is a hazardous journey.

Sometimes answers are not clearly established or well understood by scholars or the public. For that reason, developmentalists advocate large-scale outcome evaluations for every new or old educational practice, in which children from many cultures are compared. At other times the research leads in one direction but ideology seems disconnected from the research (Rayner et al., 2001). Developmental principles and research provide some guidance through the thicket of ideology, politics, and culture that surrounds educational controversies.

Deciding How Children Should Learn

Children can learn anything if it is "packaged" properly—but not everything all at once. Our understanding of cognition suggests that learning is easiest and most efficient if it is concrete, not abstract (Simon, 2001); builds on an established knowledge base; is connected to other material; and is taught directly and sequentially, with explicit goals and demands. What does this mean for school curricula?

Internationally and across the decades, adults have agreed that schools should teach reading, writing, and arithmetic. The school years are the best time for that academic learning, although about a fifth of the world's people never learn the basics and remain illiterate (United Nations, 2001). Beyond these three subjects, curricula vary. For example, in Russia and France, oral expression and reasoned argument are central to the elementary school curriculum; this is not so in India and the United States (Alexander, 2000). Specific national history is sometimes emphasized, sometimes not. In the United States, some observers point out that children do not know American history (one report found that only 32 percent of fourth-graders could name even one of the 13 original colonies [Hitchens, 1998]); other observers note that knowledge of science lags behind that of children in other nations (see Appendix A); and others report that health, or sports, or second-language learning are not part of every child's school day.

The much-publicized achievement of Japanese, Chinese, and Korean children in math and science, which is far superior to the achievement of children in the United States and Canada, led to pressure to have North American children spend more time learning and less time playing. This shift has indeed happened since the early 1980s (see Appendix A).

The debate about what specific skills to stress in elementary education is ongoing. School-age children are able and eager to learn almost anything, but they cannot learn everything at once. Comparing nations, comparing schools, and comparing children can show which educational strategies and curricula succeed, as we have seen. However, another set of criteria is needed to measure what should be valued. For example, the need "to ensure a competitive workforce . . . to fill the jobs of the future and compete in a global economy" led the United States to set the goal of being first worldwide in math and science by the year 2000. At that point, most Americans probably agreed that this was a desirable aim (National Endowment Goals Panel, 1997). But if math and science become priorities, and scores continue to rise, what will happen in literacy and creativity, areas in which the United States has traditionally excelled? Music, art, and physical education programs have been cut back in almost every public school. Emotional regulation and community values may be even more important. As one teacher said, "My trouble is too many children are sad, or mad, or bad; not that they can't add" (quoted in Thompson, 2001).

The Reading Wars

Two distinct approaches to teaching reading are used in the United States and in many other nations: phonics and whole language (Rayner et al., 2001). Clashes over the two approaches have been called the Reading Wars; these battles have sometimes been waged without concern for scientific evidence, developmental changes, or children's needs (Adams et al., 1998).

Traditionally, the **phonics** approach (from the root word for "sound") meant requiring children to learn the sounds of each letter before they began to decipher simple words. This works well in learning to read languages such as Italian, where the sound–letter connections are clear, but not as well in English, where there are many exceptions. In the first half of the twentieth century, schools in the United States were characterized by:

> drill and more drill . . . instruction in letter–sound relationships and pronunciation rules. . . . Children had to learn so much abstract material by rote before doing any significant amount of reading.
>
> *[Diederich, 1973, p. 7]*

By contrast, the **whole-language** approach begins by recognizing that language is an entire set of skills—talking and listening, reading and writing—all with the goal of communication. Children are encouraged to write on their own, inventing the spelling according to how the words sound. For example, one 4-year-old boy tried to keep others out of his room with this sign on his door: GNYS AT WRK (Bissex, 1980); a school girl named Karla wrote a stern note to her mother (see Figure 12.2). These demonstrate the whole-language idea that children can communicate their emotions in writing long before they have mastered standard spelling.

Both these approaches have merit. First, both maintain that motivation matters: Children learn best when they understand why they are learning. Abstract, decontextualized memorization is difficult—no wonder traditional phonics did not always succeed. Second, unlike talking, which is experience-expectant, reading is experience-dependent. Most children will not be able to figure it out on their own without explicit instruction in the relationship among sounds, letters, and words. Beginning readers often need to be taught how to translate spoken words into printed ones. Instruction in phonics and then practice with standard spelling are needed for children to be able to break the code and decipher words. Until then, children will not practice reading on their own. Without practice, automatization in reading will not occur, because brain patterns are established only through extensive repetition (Rayner et al., 2001; Stanovich, 2000).

Third, research emphasizes that each step of development, each component of language learning, and each child's learning style and maturation level are unique in crucial ways. In practical terms, this means that phonics is particularly useful for children who are just beginning to read and for the many children who need help with learning to decipher new words. If children speak another language or do not already have strong listening and speaking skills, they also need explicit vocabulary-building and pronunciation practice. In fact, every teacher

FIGURE 12.2 "You Wud Be Sad Like Me" Although Karla, a first-grader, uses invented spelling, her arguments show that she is reasoning quite logically; her school-age mind is working quite well. (If you have trouble deciphering Karla's note, turn the book upside down for a translation.) *Source:* Lerner, 2000, p. 462.

"From Karla to my mom. It's no fair that you made me let my lady bug go. What if I was your mom and I made you take your lady bug. I am sure you would be sad like me. That lady bug might have been an orphan. So you should have let me have it anyway.

phonics approach The teaching of reading by requiring children to learn the sounds of each letter before they begin to decipher simple words.

whole-language approach The teaching of reading by encouraging children to develop all their language skills—talking and listening, reading and writing—all with the goal of communication.

should use many methods and strategies, for there are "alternate pathways in learning to read" (Berninger et al., 2002, p. 295). Phonics should be part of instruction, but other aspects of literacy, taught in other ways, are important as well (Adams & Bruck, 1995; Rayner et al., 2001).

Teaching Math

In the United States, math was traditionally taught through rote learning; children memorized number facts, such as the multiplication tables, and filled page after page of worksheets. As a result, many children came to hate math and did poorly in it. In response, the U.S. government supported research devoted to improving the math curriculum, and experts, inspired by Vygotsky, found ways to make math a more active, engaging subject (Ginsburg et al., 1998).

One notable set of standards and practices came from the National Council of Teachers of Mathematics (1989), which developed a new curriculum emphasizing concepts and problem solving, estimating and probability. Recommended pedagogical techniques included social norms: "Students are obligated to explain and justify solutions, to attempt to make sense of solutions given by others . . . and to ask clarifying questions or challenge alternatives" (Cobb, 2000, pp. 464–465). The focus is on the process, not the product. One teacher asked the class how many runners were in a race that had two teams of six runners each. The children had already worked in pairs to come up with the process for answering, called the "answer solution."

> **Teacher:** Jack, what answer solution did you come up with?
> **Jack:** Fourteen.
> **Teacher:** Fourteen. How did you get that answer?
> **Jack:** Because 6 plus 6 is 12. Two runners on two teams . . .

(Jack stops talking, puts his hands to the side of his face and looks down at the floor. Then he looks at the teacher and at his partner, Ann. He turns and faces the front of the room with his back to the teacher and mumbles inaudibly.)

> **Teacher:** Would you please say that again. I didn't quite get the whole thing. You had—say it again please.
> **Jack:** *(Softly, still facing the front of the room)* It's six runners on each team.
> **Teacher:** Right.
> **Jack:** *(Turns to look at the teacher)* I made a mistake. It's wrong. It should be twelve. *(He turns and faces the front of the room again.)*

(Jack's acute embarrassment . . . confounded the teacher's intention that the children should publicly express their thinking and, more generally, engage in mathematical practice characterized by conjecture, argument, and justification.)

> **Teacher:** *(Softly)* Oh, okay. Is it okay to make a mistake?
> **Andrew:** Yes.
> **Teacher:** Is it okay to make a mistake, Jack?
> **Jack:** Yeah.
> **Teacher:** You bet it is. As long as you're in my class it is okay to make a mistake. Because I make them all the time, and we learn from our mistakes— a lot. Jack already figured out, "Ooops, I didn't have the right answer the first time" *(Jack turns and looks at the teacher and smiles),* but he kept working at it and he got it.
>
> [Cobb et al., 1993]

Nevertheless, changes in educational practice remain controversial: "Even mathematics—that cold, rational, neutral, nerdy subject matter—can become embroiled in political dispute, at least when hot issue of values are introduced" (Ginsburg et al., 1998, p. 437). The primary problem is that parents (and some teachers) disagree with the recommendation that children work in groups to find solutions to difficult problems on their own, without the textbooks, worksheets, or homework that parents understand.

Teacher practice seems more strongly influenced by culture than by research, as illustrated by an international study in which hundreds of math lessons were videotaped (Stigler & Hiebert, 1999). The researchers found that math instructors in Japan require children to collaborate on developing math solutions and proofs, after the teachers ensure step-by-step learning that makes such challenges surmountable. The same study found that, even though schools in the United States are diverse in population and structure, most math teachers stress basic procedures for solving simple problems, and these procedures are often presented in a scattered, repetitive way (Stigler & Hiebert, 1999). Math classes in the United States were found to be less difficult than those in the other parts of the world, but the children learned less. Children progress faster when they are taught strategies, not mere facts, and when they learn through teacher guidance and peer collaboration, not on their own. When the group problem solving that is the usual mode in Japan is tried in North America, it seems to work effectively (Johnson & Johnson, 1994).

Popular beliefs and actual learning are not necessarily connected. For example, children and parents in the United States are more satisfied with their math achievements, even though it is lower than are children and parents in Japan (Stigler & Hiebert, 1999). Similar discrepancies between cultural norms and real learning seem to exist in many nations, in math and in other subjects (Alexander, 2000).

Learning a Second Language

Learning a second language is required in some nations (such as India and Canada) but not in others (such as the United States) (Alexander, 2000). As we saw in Chapter 9, learning two languages is easiest in early childhood. However, many children arrive in kindergarten speaking only one language, which makes schooling a crucial path toward bilingualism.

Almost every nation has a sizable minority whose members speak a non-majority language; for them, learning the majority language is a necessity. In fact, most of the estimated 6,000 languages of the world are never used in formal educational settings. Consequently, most of the world's children are educated in a language other than their mother tongue (Tucker, 1998).

While the best time to *learn* a second language by listening and talking is during early childhood, the best time to *teach* a second language seems to be during middle childhood. Because of their readiness to understand code-switching, their eagerness to communicate, their wish to be good students, their grasp of

Especially for Parents: You are tired but are setting out to buy groceries. Your 7-year-old son wants to go with you. Should you explain that you are too tired to take him?

[handwritten notes] middle childhood. children's joy with language → poetry Jokes secret language

BOB DAEMMRICH / THE IMAGE WORKS

Maintaining Tradition Some would say that these Vietnamese children in Texas are fortunate. They are instructed in two languages by a teacher who knows their culture, including the use of red pens for self-correction as well as teacher correction. Others would say that these children would be better off in an "English-only" classroom.

total immersion An approach to teaching a second language in which instruction occurs entirely in that language and the learner's native language is not used at all.

Response for Parents (from page 383): Your son would understand your explanation, but you should take him along. Any excursion is a learning opportunity. You wouldn't ignore his need for food or medicine; don't ignore his need for learning. While shopping, you can teach vocabulary (does he know *pimientos, pepperoni, polenta?*), categories ("root vegetables," "freshwater fish"), and math (which size is cheaper?). Explain in advance that you need him to help you find things and carry them, and that he can choose only one item that you wouldn't normally buy. Seven-year-olds can understand rules, and they enjoy being helpful.

logic, and their ear for nuances of pronunciation, children aged 7 to 11 are at their prime for being taught a second language.

No single approach to teaching a second language has yet been recognized as best for all children in all contexts (Bialystok, 2001). Strategies include both extremes—from **total immersion,** in which instruction occurs entirely in the second (majority) language, to *reverse immersion,* in which the child is taught in his or her first (native) language for several years, until the second language can be taught as a "foreign" language. Variations between these extremes include presenting some topics of instruction in one language and other topics in the other; presenting every topic in both languages; or conducting separate after-school classes in a "heritage language" to allow children to connect with their culture while learning all academic subjects in the dominant tongue. In the United States, three approaches attempt to avoid the shock of complete immersion in English for non-English-speakers (see Table 12.4).

Which teaching strategy is best? In Canada, immersion has succeeded with more than 300,000 English-speaking children who were initially placed in French-only classrooms. These children showed no decline in English skills (learned at home) or in other academic achievement (Edwards, 1994; Lambert et al., 1993). Indeed, even when Canadian children whose native language is English are immersed in two other languages—French and Hebrew—from the first to the sixth grade, they do well on achievement tests in all three languages (Genesee, 1998). Note, however, that this was a six-year program.

By contrast, reverse immersion works best in Guatemala, where children learn the second language (Spanish) only after they have already been well taught in their native Mayan language (Tucker, 1998). In Belgium, biculturalism

TABLE 12.4 Three Strategies for Teaching English as a Second Language

English as a Second Language (ESL)
Requires all non-English-speaking students to undergo an intensive instructional period together, with the goal of mastering the basics of English in six months or so. In classes using ESL, the teacher neither speaks in the child's native language nor allows the children to talk to each other in any language except English.

Bilingual Education
Requires that the teacher instruct the children in school subjects using their native language as well as English. In the early years, children are greeted, instructed, and (when necessary) disciplined in the two languages, in the hope that they will progress in both. Informal talk between one child and another is almost always in the native language, as is much of the teacher's informal conversation.

Bilingual–Bicultural Education
Recognizes that non-English-speaking children come to school with non-Anglo values, traditions, and perceptions that may need to be preserved. Implementation of the strategy may be as simple as celebrating special holidays (such as, for Mexican-American children, Three Kings Day, Cinco de Mayo, and the Day of the Dead), or it may be as complex as instituting new classroom strategies (such as cooperative learning or special discipline). Practically as well as politically, bilingual–bicultural education requires a large concentration of children whose parents value the native language. In the United States, bilingual–bicultural programs during school usually involve Hispanic children, and bilingual–bicultural after-school programs more commonly serve Asian children, if enough Koreans, Vietnamese, Hmong, or other groups live in the same area. In fact, one reason immigrants to the United States tend to settle near other people from the same area is to preserve the culture of the homeland for the children. Bicultural education thus happens naturally in the community, because parents fear that their children will become "Americanized" as well as English-speakers (Suarez-Orozco & Suarez-Orozco, 2001).

works with children of Italian ancestry, if Belgian-born and Italian-born teachers each teach the students for half a day (Byram, 1998). Thus, all three strategies can succeed—sometimes.

Immersion tends to fail if children are made to feel shy, stupid, or socially isolated because of their language difference. In such cases, this educational approach might more aptly be called *submersion,* because children are more likely to sink than swim (Edwards, 1994). Immersion that occurs after puberty, even if the children already have some knowledge of the second language, also impedes education (Marsh et al., 2000).

In the United States, many school systems use none of the three approaches outlined in Table 12.4. For most of the twentieth century, Native American children were sent to boarding schools to learn white ways. Many of them became sick, ran away, or became alienated from their families, victims of an attempt at cultural obliteration that has only recently been recognized (Coontz, 1998). Even today, many Spanish-speaking children who are instructed only in English become slow learners who repeat a grade or two until they are old enough to drop out of school. Unfortunately, the main alternative—bilingual education—does not necessarily produce children who are sufficiently fluent in English to perform well in an English-only high school. In both cases, their poor performance is blamed on their deficiency in English rather than on the teachers and educational programs that failed to take into account the special needs of such children (Romo & Falbo, 1996).

Success or failure in second-language learning seems to lie in the attitudes of the parents, the teachers, and the larger community. If both languages are valued as well as used extensively, then *additive bilingualism* occurs, with fluency in the second language added to fluency in the first. Sometimes, however, neither language is learned well, and the child is *semilingual,* not even monolingual—literally possessing only part of one language (Swain & Johnson, 1997). As one review regarding the need for well-trained language teachers explained, "Whether policies are overtly articulated, covertly implied, or invisibly in the making, the central concern in multilingual education appears to be how much status and recognition within the educational system should be given to the languages of the minority group" (Nunan & Lam, 1998). This is a political question more than a developmental one.

Teaching Moral and Civic Values

Some parents criticize or praise "godless schools," but actually all schools teach moral and civic values. The true controversy is over whose moral code and which values should be taught. In some schools, memorized prayers and recited commandments are part of each school day. For example, in many Islamic countries a major reason for schooling is to learn the Koran; in the United States, the Constitution prohibits the teaching of any particular religion in public schools, which 90 percent of young children attend. Religious tolerance is itself a national value in the United States (Marshall, 2001).

Developmental research indicates that middle childhood is a prime time for incorporating values as well as for memorizing texts—if not the Ten Commandments or a particular prayer, then the Pledge of Allegiance, the Bill of Rights, or a Shakespeare monologue. Language—the words in which a particular code is expressed—is a joy to school-age children. In middle childhood, moral and behaviorial rules are understood and often rigidly interpreted, whether they are the rules of the school administration (requiring school uniforms, for example), of the political culture (as in elections for student council representatives), or of the children themselves (forbidding them to rat on their friends). Adults should ensure that whatever values and principles their children learn are the ones they

Friendly Immersion The poster is in English, because this Toronto teacher is explaining a sign in the city, but all the instruction occurs in French, even though none of these children are native French speakers. Their parents chose it not only because French immersion works successfully in Canada but also because such programs have a reputation for academic rigor, including high standards for conduct and achievement. Attitudes, not just instruction, facilitate learning a second language.

themselves believe in. Given the concrete nature of school-age children's minds and their concern about fairness, adults need to teach morality not only by words but also by example.

Educational Structures and Policies

The importance of explicit practices is reflected in the need for instructional practices and school organization to reflect the goals of the educators or of the broader community. In addition to its academic curriculum, each school has a **hidden curriculum**, which is not published in any curriculum guide or even articulated by the staff but which influences every aspect of school learning. The hidden curriculum affects school structures and teacher actions. It is manifest in discipline tactics, in grades and teacher comments on report cards, in salaries, in school schedules, in the assignment of children to particular classes, and so on. Every culture creates its own hidden curriculum, usually without being aware of it until a change is suggested (Alexander, 2000). We will look now at two aspects of the hidden curriculum—class size and testing—that illustrate its complex relationship to our understanding of development.

hidden curriculum The unofficial, unstated, or implicit rules and priorities that influence the academic curriculum and every other aspect of school learning.

Class Size

It seems obvious to every parent and teacher, and to many politicians, that children learn better when there are fewer children in each class. Smaller class size is one reason some parents send their children to private schools, some politicians advocate charter schools or vouchers, and some teachers go on strike.

Surprisingly, the research supporting this popular assumption is weak. In fact, some data suggest that class size makes no difference in children's performance (Betts, 1995; Hanushek, 1999). The pupil/teacher ratio is far lower in the United States than in almost any other nation, having declined from 25 to 18 between 1969 and 1997 (Alexander, 2000), with no comparable advance in learning. Schools in the United States have more low-income and immigrant children and fewer qualified teachers than they had in the 1960s, so educational gains caused by reduced class size may be offset by losses resulting from other factors (Ehrenberg et al., 2001).

Advocates have looked for experimental (not correlational, as in the example above) evidence that smaller class size results in better learning. A massive experiment in Tennessee, involving 12,000 children in 70 schools, began in 1985 and continued for four years. Kindergarten children and teachers were randomly assigned to one of three classroom conditions: regular (22–26 children), regular with aid (22–26 children with a full-time teacher's assistant), or small (13–17 children). Children (especially nonwhite children) in the small classes learned more, and those in the regular classes with an aide did no better than those in regular classes without an aide. Follow-up research shows that even after the children had been in regular classes for years, those who once had small classes still outperform their peers (Finn et al., 2001).

Although smaller class size made some difference, there is disagreement about how substantial the benefits were, why they occurred, and whether the gains were worth the expense (Rayner et al., 2001). California, inspired by Tennessee, reduced class sizes in the early grades—but, unlike Tennessee, California had neither enough qualified teachers nor suitable classrooms for this expansion, and the average class-size reduction was only from 30 to 20, not 24 to 15. The California results were "disappointing"—statistically significant, but very small (Stecher & Bohrnstedt, 2000). During the same years California public schools reinstated the teaching of phonics and basic math and reduced bilingual education, so solid conclusions from California are elusive.

A review of all the research leaves many questions unanswered. The early grades may be crucial, but another year may be equally important—perhaps sixth grade, when puberty hits, or twelfth grade, when high school graduation should occur. Other reforms in the hidden curriculum—raising teacher salaries, improving professional education, extending school hours until 6 P.M., expanding the school year to 11 months a year, or including more sports, music, more reading—might have a great impact, or might be neutral, or might be destructive.

These questions are not yet answered because the connection between developmental research and practical policy is problematic (Thompson & Nelson, 2001). As one review explains:

> . . . reductions in class size are but one of the policy options that can be pursued to improve student learning. Careful evaluations of the impacts of other options, preferably through the use of more true experiments, along with an analysis of the costs of each option, need to be undertaken. However, to date there are relatively few studies that even compute the true costs of large class-size reduction programs, let alone ask whether the benefits . . . merit incurring the costs.
>
> *[Ehrenberg et al., 2001]*

Merely raising the question alerts us to the hidden assumption about class size. If Piaget is correct and learning happens individually, then smaller class sizes would be beneficial because the teacher could give each child more personal attention. However, if Vygotsky is right and learning is a social process that may include learning from peers, then reducing class size would be counterproductive.

Educational Standards and Testing

National and statewide standardized tests of children's academic achievement are popular in the United States; 98 percent of children are tested in both math and English at least once in elementary, middle, and high school. Many states require more frequent tests (usually beginning in third grade), and most states test achievement in science and social studies as well.

Learning to Learn These two classes, in Somalia *(left)* and Japan *(right)*, are different from each other in many ways. However, they both share several characteristics that are rare in most nations where this textbook is used.

Experts disagree about what educational standards should be and how they should be measured. Flawed standards—too high, too low, too vague—undermine learning and increase stress. Even worse are standards that differ from what the tests assess, because then no one knows if the children are reaching the standards or not.

Few developmentalists oppose periodic assessment of educational achievement, since accurate longitudinal data are essential for science. However, many criticize specific testing practices, since tests are not necessarily accurate, valid, or aligned to standards, curricula, or learning. Too-difficult tests may lead to failure, with many children repeating grades and then dropping out; too-easy tests are useless; irrelevant or rigid tests crowd out creative and individualized learning and teaching. Teachers may begin "teaching to the test" in an effort to raise their students' scores so they will be rated as good teachers and perhaps earn merit pay. If the goal of a test is not to measure past teaching accomplishments but to reveal what children need to learn, then the testing process should occur within a zone of proximal development, with children offered assistance by friends and teachers as needed (Meijer & Elshout, 2001). This approach is taken in some European nations and in some informal assessments in the United States, but the usual practice is for children to take tests in a large group, sometimes without their own teachers present. The tests are scored elsewhere, so that teachers are unable to use the results to improve their instruction of each child. Most developmentalists would probably agree that "standards and assessment, though necessary, are not enough. . . . Standards set the course, and assessments provide the benchmarks, but it is teaching that must be improved to push us along the path to success" (Stigler & Hiebert, 1999, p. 2).

Testing and standards can alert us to hidden assumptions about how children learn. Frequent testing, high and measurable standards that must be met before promotion or graduation, and an overall emphasis on individual academic accomplishments seem to undermine an appreciation of every child's learning strength and style, of every teacher's professional judgment, and of cooperative learning. These two versions of how teaching and learning should be done reflect two hidden curricula whose supporters sometimes clash openly, as in British Columbia, Canada, when some parents wanted the school board to create a traditional school that would presumably have higher academic and behavioral standards than a more progressive school. Here are excerpts from three letters to the editor of the local newspaper (quoted in Mitchell, 2001, pp. 64–65). One mother wrote in favor of a traditional school:

> Our children's performances are much lower both in academic and moral areas. I noticed the children have learnt very little academically. They learned to have self-confidence instead of being self-disciplined; learned to speak up instead of being humbled; learned to be creative instead of self-motivated; and learned to simplify things instead of organizing. All of these characteristics were not balanced, and will be the source of disadvantage and difficulties in children in this competitive society.

Two other parents disagreed:

> These characteristics she disapproves of are the very characteristics I encourage in my children, as do their teachers and the public schools. Self-confidence, creativity, and individuality are wonderful qualities, which in no way detract from a child being respectful and pleasant, and achieving academic success.

> She wants her children to be self-disciplined, humble, self-motivated and organized, instead of being self-confident, assertive, creative and analytic. . . . These repressive, authoritarian, "traditional" parents who hanker for the days of yore, when fresh-faced school kids arrived all neatly decked out in drab-grey uniforms and shiny lace-up leather shoes, are a menace to society. They desire their kids to sit quietly in tidy serried ranks . . . should they err in any way, a thousand lines or a good beating will learn 'em real good.

Conclusion

This chapter has demonstrated the remarkable ability of children aged 7 to 11 to learn, not only grasping logic and accumulating facts but adding tens of thousands of words to their vocabulary, using dozens of strategies for learning, incorporating moral values that last a lifetime, generalizing concepts, and refining habits of thought and action.

We will close this chapter by reminding you of an example that stresses the strong intellectual capacity of the school-age child, if experience and motivation are in place. The young Brazilian street vendors whom we mentioned earlier in this chapter—all in middle childhood, with little formal education—do very poorly when given standard problems presented the way achievement tests usually present them (such as 420 + 80). However, when given oral problems involving fruit purchases and making change for a customer ("I'll take three coconuts. Here's a 10-real [the basic Brazilian unit of money] bill. How much do I get back?"), they solve the problems far more quickly and successfully, often using unconventional but effective math strategies (Carraher et al., 1985, 1988). In other words, although they seem to lack the cognitive strategies necessary to solve arithmetic problems, these children have developed sophisticated math abilities. In fact, the prices of the fruit they sell must be recalculated often, as wholesale prices vary with supply and as inflation changes the value of the currency. These unschooled children have mastered that math very well; their survival depends on it (Saxe, 1999).

To repeat the theme of this chapter: Children in the school years can and do learn whatever their culture and context teach. Parents, peers, and community leaders must decide what that should be.

SUMMARY

Building on Piaget and Vygotsky

1. According to Piaget, children enter the stage of concrete operational thought at about age 6 or 7. Egocentrism diminishes and logical ideas, including identity and irreversibility, are applied to every aspect of experience.

2. Their new logical abilities enable school-age children to understand classification, conservation, and many other concepts. This concrete operational understanding advances all forms of academic thinking, particularly in math, as well as social relationships.

3. Vygotsky stressed the social context of learning, including the role of teachers and peers in guiding each child's education. International research finds that maturation is one factor in the cognitive development of school-age children (as Piaget predicted) and that cultural and economic forces are also influential (as Vygotsky predicted).

Information Processing

4. An information-processing approach examines each step of the thinking process, from input to output, using the computer as a model. Humans are more creative than computers, but this approach is a useful guide to memory, perception, and expression.

5. Memory begins with the sensory register, which briefly stores information that reaches the brain from the sense organs. The information proceeds to working memory, where perceptions are processed for a short time in active consciousness. Some images and ideas are stored indefinitely in long-term memory.

6. Advances in memory during middle childhood occur primarily because of improvement in working memory, aided by selective attention and logical retrieval. Long-term memory increases as well, as more material in the knowledge base makes more learning possible.

7. Speed of thought accelerates with continued brain myelination. Faster processing advances every aspect of cognition, including working memory. Repeated practice makes thought patterns and skill sets almost automatic, requiring little time or conscious effort.

8. Children become better at controlling and directing their thinking as the prefrontal cortex matures. Consequently, metacognition advances and children learn better, particularly in school.

Language

9. Language becomes more logical and extensive as children move through middle childhood. Children who are exposed to a rich vocabulary at home and in school are likely to become very adept at articulating their thoughts and ideas.

10. By the end of middle childhood, children can interpret vocal tones and can comprehend nuances of meaning that they could not grasp earlier. Children also recognize that certain forms of speech are more appropriate in one context or another. Recognition of the difference between informal and formal speech codes leads to code-switching, which means that children speak informally with friends and formally at school.

Moral Development

11. School-age children are passionately concerned about moral questions. Kohlberg described three levels of moral reasoning, from preconventional (self-concerned) to conventional (community-centered) to postconventional (centered on moral principles). Individual responses to Kohlberg's moral dilemmas are sometimes difficult to score; another measure, the Defining Issues Test, uses a questionnaire to indicate moral development.

12. Kohlberg's stages have been criticized for being too abstractly rational, downgrading the morals of people from traditional, non-Western communities. In addition, he ranked the "morality of justice" higher than the "morality of care," although the latter may be preferred by those who are more concerned with human relationships than with absolute rules. Although some claim the "morality of care" to be more representative of females, research evidence does not support this assertion.

13. During the school years, children tend to value loyalty to their friends over adult standards. They can be quite rigid in their judgments of right and wrong, with a strong personal belief in justice and fairness.

Schools, Values, and Research

14. Many issues regarding education are hotly debated. Developmental research provides some answers, but most of the core issues require social choice, not just better research. Concern about education in the United States has led to more time spent in educating school-age children.

15. Internationally, all agree that children should learn to read and compute, but experts and nations disagree as to how that learning should occur and what else should be taught in schools. The arguments of both sides in the "Reading Wars" and math debates have merit. Nevertheless, some phonics instruction in reading and some group learning in math seem advisable.

16. During the school years, children are particularly open to learning a second language and absorbing moral and civic values. The specifics of second-language instruction and moral education remain controversial, with marked variations from nation to nation.

17. Smaller class size does not necessarily advance achievement, although a massive experiment in Tennessee that reduced class size to about 15 in kindergarten through the third grade resulted in higher achievement. It is not clear whether the Tennessee experiment is generalizable and cost-effective.

18. Over the past decade or so, the United States has moved toward higher standards of academic achievement and more frequent testing. Most scholars agree with the basic philosophy behind these trends, but many criticize the specifics.

19. Every decision about school-age children's cognition raises deep moral, political, and sociocultural issues. These children can and do learn a great deal; their families and communities must choose what to teach them.

KEY TERMS

concrete operational thought (p. 359)
classification (p. 360)
identity (p. 361)
reversibility (p. 361)
sensory register (p. 363)
working memory (p. 363)
long-term memory (p. 364)

knowledge base (p. 364)
control processes (p. 365)
selective attention (p. 366)
metacognition (p. 366)
code-switching (p. 371)
formal code (p. 371)
informal code (p. 372)

preconventional moral reasoning (p. 373)
conventional moral reasoning (p. 373)
postconventional moral reasoning (p. 373)
Defining Issues Test (DIT) (p. 375)

morality of care (p. 375)
morality of justice (p. 375)
phonics approach (p. 381)
whole-language approach (p. 381)
total immersion (p. 384)
hidden curriculum (p. 386)

KEY QUESTIONS

1. According to Piaget, what are the distinctive characteristics of cognition in middle childhood?

2. How might concrete operational thought aid in learning multiplication?

3. What does international research on school-age children find regarding Piaget's and Vygotsky's views?

4. Which step of memory improves most during middle childhood and why?

5. How are selective attention and speed of processing related?

6. How does an expanded knowledge base improve learning?

7. What would signify better control processing during middle childhood?

8. Why do children need both formal and informal speech codes?

9. How do jokes reflect children's understanding of language?

10. What are the three major criticisms of Kohlberg's stages of moral development?

11. What differences would you expect between 8-year-olds' moral values and adult moral actions?

12. What are the arguments for and against the phonics approach to teaching reading?

13. Which method of teaching a second language seems most effective?

14. What does research reveal about reductions in class size?

Chapter Thirteen

The School Years: Psychosocial Development

latency Freud's term for middle childhood, during which children's emotional drives are quieter, their psychosexual needs are repressed, and their unconscious conflicts are submerged.

industry versus inferiority The fourth of Erikson's eight crises of psychosexual development, in which school-age children attempt to master many skills and develop a sense of themselves as either industrious and competent or incompetent and inferior.

In middle childhood, children break free from the closely supervised and limited arena of the younger child. Usually with their parents' blessing but sometimes breaking the rules, school-age children explore the wider world of neighborhood, community, and school. They experience new vulnerability, increasing competence, ongoing friendships, troubling rivalries, and deeper social understanding. Although often beyond direct adult supervision, their lives are still shaped by family structures and community values.

Our goal in this chapter is to examine the interplay between expanding freedom and guiding forces. We will look first at emotional growth, then at peer and family influences that direct and propel that growth, and, finally, at strategies and strengths that enable most children to move forward, ready for adolescence. In tackling this topic, there is a danger of overloading the discussion by including every perspective and opinion from every pupil, teacher, or political leader—all of whom care about children. Indeed, adults from many professions—educators, sociologists, anthropologists, politicians, economists, and others—are concerned about how children develop during these years. To anchor our analysis, we begin with the perspectives on development in middle childhood that have been offered by the five major theories that were introduced in Chapter 2.

Theories of School-Age Development

Throughout the world, school-age children are noticeably more independent, more responsible, and more capable than younger children. This increased competence is recognized by parents and schools, in research results, and in every developmental theory.

Sigmund Freud described middle childhood as the period of **latency**, during which children's emotional drives are quieter, their psychosexual needs are repressed, and their unconscious conflicts are submerged. This makes latency "a time for acquiring cognitive skills and assimilating cultural values as children expand their world to include teachers, neighbors, peers, club leaders, and coaches. Sexual energy continues to flow, but it is channeled into social concerns" (Miller, 2002, p. 131).

Erik Erikson (1963) agreed with Freud that middle childhood is a quiet period emotionally, a period in which the child "becomes ready to apply himself to given skills and tasks." During Erikson's crisis of **industry versus inferiority**, children busily try to master whatever abilities their culture values. On the basis of their degree of success, they judge themselves as either *industrious* or *inferior*—that is, competent or incompetent, productive or failing, winners or losers.

Industry on Display One characteristic of school-age children is their obsession with collecting, whether their interest is stamps or insects, Harry Potter paraphernalia or, as shown here, Yu-Gi-Oh cards, which are the latest collecting fad in Japan. Children are much more industrious than adult collectors, busily counting, organizing, and trading their treasures.

social cognitive theory A perspective that highlights how the school-age child advances in learning, cognition, and culture, building on maturation and experience to become more articulate, insightful, and competent.

Developmentalists influenced by two other grand theories—behaviorism and cognitive theory—are concerned with the acquisition of new skills and self-understanding, respectively. The overview from these two theories is quite similar to that of psychoanalytic theory. School-age children meet the challenges of the outside world with an openness, insight, and confidence that few young children possess.

One offshoot of the grand theories, **social cognitive theory,** is particularly relevant to middle childhood because it highlights how the school-age child advances in learning, cognition, and culture (Bandura, 2001). Social cognitive theory stresses the combination of maturation and experience that allows school-age children to become much more articulate, reflective, and active, able to understand themselves and to be effective and competent. They think logically, as we saw in Chapter 12, and they apply their new learning ability to their expanding social world. In practical terms, 10-year-olds can explain their emotions to their parents, or decide to wake up early to study for a test, or choose which friend to phone for the homework assignment. All these actions make the older child more active than passive in the social world, displaying what Albert Bandura (1997) calls "social efficacy" and what the proud smile of any 10-year-old who has just won a race, earned a perfect grade, or finished a work of art conveys.

The two emergent theories, sociocultural and epigenetic systems, also acknowledge the new independence of school-age children but go further: Considering both current context and genetic factors, sociocultural theory looks not only at children from widely separated parts of the world—for instance, rural China versus urban Canada—but also at various subcultures within one nation or even on one city block. Yolanda and Paul, the children whom you met at the beginning of Chapter 11, were from the same nation (United States), state (California), region (Los Angeles area), and heritage (Mexican-American), yet their differences are apparent. Consider their opinions about education:

Yolanda: I feel proud of myself when I see a [good] grade. And like I see a C, I'm going to have to pull this grade up. . . . I like learning. I like really getting my mind working. . . . [Education] is good for you. . . . It's like when you eat. It's like if you don't eat for the whole day, you feel weird.

Paul: I try not to get influenced too much, pulled into what I don't want to be into. But mostly, it's hard. You don't want people to be saying you're stupid. "Why do you want to go to school and get a job? . . . Drop out." . . . They try to pull you down and then you just got to be strong enough to try to pull away.

[quoted in Nieto, 2000, pp. 220, 221, 252]

Both these children have been affected by family and cultural influences that were radically different during middle childhood. Consequently, they are different from each other, as sociocultural theory would anticipate.

Finally, epigenetic systems theory considers how inherited impulses that mature during middle childhood have enabled families over the centuries to raise their children. Thus, genes within each human lead to maturation—not only biological but also social. For instance, during these middle-childhood years, to ensure survival of the next generation, children need to reach out to peers and adults, developing a social network that will guide them toward adulthood.

The human species still responds to the ancient genetic mechanisms: The 7- to 11-year-old develops a body and a brain that allow greater intellectual focus (selective attention), rationality (concrete operational thought), and physical hardiness (slowed growth and increased control). In prior centuries, these protected the child when parents typically had younger children who needed close attention. Indeed, among all primate species, it seems that normal maturation pulls developing children to become more independent of their mothers and more dependent on their peers in middle childhood (Suomi, 2002). At the same time, genetic impulses are shaped by the social environment, which is why epigenetic systems theorists study "the role of the environment in bringing about species-typical behavior" (Dent-Read & Zukow-Goldring, 1997, p. 11).

Notice that all five major theories describe the child from ages 7 to 11 in similar ways, as competent, eager, and manageable outside the home. Worldwide, cultures recognize the wonderful characteristics of this stage by selecting these years as the time to give the child more independence and responsibility, from attending first grade to making one's First Communion, from doing significant chores at home to facing major challenges at school. In the twenty-first century, even in the poorest nations, most school-age children are, in fact, in school (Alexander, 2000).

Celebrating Spring No matter where they live, 7- to 11-year-olds seek to understand and develop whatever skills are valued by their culture. They do so in active, industrious ways, as described in behaviorism as well as cognitive, sociocultural, psychoanalytic, and epigenetic systems theories. This universal truth is illustrated here, as four friends in Assam, northeastern India, usher in spring with a Bihu celebration. Soon they will be given sweets and tea, which is the sociocultural validation of their energy, independence, and skill.

Understanding Self and Others

Social scientists once categorized cultures, societies, and even individuals into two opposite groups: individualistic/collective, independent/dependent, self-oriented/other-oriented, introverted/extroverted (Triandis, 1989). This distinction was applied to entire regions of the world; for example, North America and Western Europe would be categorized as individualistic and Asia, Africa, and South America as collective. Today, such broad distinctions may still be made, but most scholars agree that every successful person and culture must find a balance, an interdependence, and that both autonomous and social forces are at work in every society (Harter, 1999; Oyserman et al., 2002).

Similarly, human development from birth to age 20 can be depicted as a progression from total dependence in infancy to self-determination in adolescence. Middle childhood is the time when children learn whatever skills they will need as adults, concretely (Piaget's word) or industriously (Erikson's word) going their own, self-centered way and shedding their dependence on parents during latency (Freud's word). However, research finds that self-development occurs in harmony with connection to parents and peers, no less in middle childhood than earlier. The following self-description could have been written by many 10-year-olds:

> I'm in the fourth grade this year, and I'm pretty popular, at least with the girls. That's because I'm nice to people and can keep secrets. Mostly I am nice to my friends, although if I get in a bad mood I sometimes say something that can be a little mean. I try to control my temper, but when I don't, I'm ashamed of myself. I'm usually happy when I'm with my friends, but I get sad if there is no one to do things with. At school, I'm feeling pretty smart in certain subjects like Language Arts and Social Studies. I got A's in these subjects on my last report card and was really proud of myself. But I'm feeling pretty dumb in Math and Science, especially when I see how well a lot of the other kids are doing. Even though I'm not doing well in those subjects, I still like myself as a person, because Math and Science just aren't that important to me. How I look and how popular I am are more important. I also like myself because I know my parents like me and so do other kids. That helps you like yourself.
>
> *[Harter, 1999, p. 48]*

It is evident that both children and their social contexts develop during the school years.

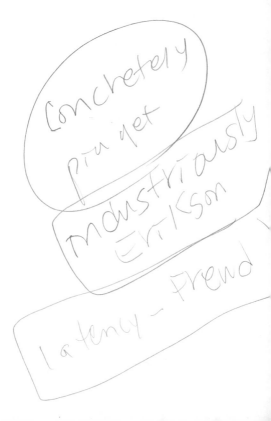

ELLIS HERWIG / STOCK, BOSTON

Read Their Expressions This girl seems hesitant to proceed, perhaps in anticipation of getting a cold shock. However, because of the expanded emotional understanding that is typical of school-age children, she probably realizes that if she stalls much longer, she is bound to get teased. This greater emotional understanding may also help her to control her anxiety long enough to take the plunge.

?Observational Quiz (see answer, page 398): What gender differences do you see?

social cognition A person's awareness and understanding of human personality, motives, emotions, intentions, and actions.

Social Understanding

The development of school-age children depends on advances in **social cognition**, that is, in understanding the social world. At younger ages, in their simple theory of mind, children began to realize that other people are motivated by thoughts and emotions that differ from their own. But preschoolers' early theorizing is prone to error, because their grasp of other viewpoints is quite limited and fragile.

During the school years, theory of mind evolves into a complex, multifaceted perspective. Cognitive advances allow children to understand that human behavior is not simply a response to specific thoughts or desires. Instead, they see behavior as actions that are influenced—simultaneously—by a variety of needs, emotions, relationships, and motives. The ability to regulate their own emotions improves (Eisenberg, 2000). For example, a preschooler who was told to stop getting into fights with his friends said he couldn't help it because sometimes the fight "just crawled out of me." By contrast, school-age children know what leads to the fights—and what might follow if they choose to fight back. They usually judge where, when, why, and with whom to fight according to this new, deeper understanding (but not always; see the discussion of bullying, page 402).

The development of social understanding was demonstrated in a simple study in which 4- to 10-year-olds were shown pictures and asked how the mother might respond and why (Goldberg-Reitman, 1992). In one picture, a child curses while playing with blocks. As you can see in the following typical responses, the 4-year-olds focused only on the immediate behavior, whereas the older children recognized the implications and possible consequences:

4-year-old: "The mother spanks her because she said a naughty word."
6-year-old: "The mother says 'Don't say that again' because it's not nice to say a bad word."
10-year-old: "The mother maybe hits her or something because she's trying to teach her . . . because if she grew up like that she'd get into a lot of trouble . . . she might get a bad reputation."

[Goldberg-Reitman, 1992]

Similar research and everyday experience tell us that younger children are likely to focus solely on observable behavior—not on motives, feelings, or social consequences. They know when an adult might protect, nurture, scold, or teach a child, but not why. Older children add three more elements:

■ They understand the motivation and origin of various behaviors.
■ They can analyze the future impact of whatever action a person might take.
■ They recognize personality traits and use them to predict a person's future reactions.

Developmental progression builds on these elements as children mature, a maturation evident in research on children's psychosocial understanding. For example, younger children recognize basic personality traits; they can say whether it is good or bad to have a particular characteristic. However, they are much less able than slightly older children to predict how having a particular personality trait might affect future actions (Alvarez et al., 2001). Overall, from ages 5 to 11, a "developmental sequence reflects children's growing understanding of the multiple or changing representations of emotional situations" (Terwogt & Stegge, 1998).

As a result of their new social cognition, children manage their own emotions better. They can mentally distract themselves to avoid becoming fidgety during a boring concert, for example, or can look attentive in class even when they are not paying attention. They can even mask or alter inborn tendencies. When a group of 7-year-olds looked at videotapes of themselves being shy at age 2, most were distressed to see how timid they had once been, but only a few still acted shy. Many said they had learned to understand themselves and adjust their timidity. As one explained, "I was a total idiot then [but] I learned a lot of new stuff, so now I'm not as scared as I was when I was a baby . . . I've gotten older and I don't want to be embarrassed" (quoted in Fox et al., 1996). This new self-understanding leads directly to better social skills, with children less fearful, less likely to start fights, and better able to concentrate as they mature (Brendgen et al., 2001; Nagin & Tremblay, 1999). Another consequence of maturing social cognition is more nuanced self-evaluation.

Self-Understanding

School-age children begin to make measurements of themselves, comparing quite specific abilities to those of their peers—as did the fourth-grader quoted on page 395. Nonacademic skills are also compared. A boy might, for example, realize that he is weak at playing the piano, OK at basketball, and a whiz at Nintendo.

Increased self-understanding comes at a price. Self-criticism rises and self-esteem dips, especially when children are asked general questions, such as "Are you smart?" and "Are you good?" Instead of simply answering "yes," as a younger child might, older children accept and use the specific standards set by their parents, teachers, and peers. This also means that they use **social comparison**, the ability to compare themselves with other people even when no one else explicitly makes the comparison. Then children examine their own actual behavior, abandoning the imaginary, rosy self-evaluation of preschoolers (Grolnick et al., 1997).

Older children feel personally at fault for their shortcomings and are less likely to blame luck or someone else. Further, as they compare themselves to others, "children become increasingly concerned about self-presentation" (Merrell & Gimpel, 1998). Other children are more important as both critics and commentators than they once were, and the opinions of parents or teachers (who are likely to say, in ignorance, "You are fine, stop worrying") are now discounted.

The Peer Group

In general, the most influential system for developing the self-concept is the **peer group,** a group of individuals of roughly the same age and social status who play, work, or learn together. It is almost impossible to overstate the importance of peers. As one group of researchers who did an extensive study of children during the school years reported, "Friends and being part of a peer group were central to living a full life and feeling good" (Borland et al., 1998, p. 28).

Most developmentalists consider getting along with peers to be crucial during middle childhood (although parents and teachers do not always agree) (Merrell & Gimpel, 1998). Indeed, some psychologists think peers are the deciding influence during the school years, far more important in determining personality and self-concept than parents (Harris, 1998). That position is extreme, but "ample evidence exists that difficulties with peers place a child at risk for developing subsequent problems of a psychological nature" (K.H. Rubin et al., 1998, p. 674). Being rejected by peers is a precursor to serious developmental

social comparison The tendency to assess one's abilities, achievements, social status, and other attributes by measuring them against those of other people, especially one's peers.

peer group An aggregate of individuals of roughly the same age and social status who play, work, or learn together.

problems later on, including juvenile delinquency, depression, and drug abuse (Laird et al., 2001). Conversely, even children who were harshly treated by their parents, and thus more likely to be victimized by their peers, are protected from victimization if they have a friend (Schwartz et al., 2001).

There is an important developmental progression here. Preschool children have friends and learn from playmates, of course, but they are more egocentric and therefore less needy of friends. In middle childhood, however, children tend to be concerned with the opinions and judgment of the entire group of classmates. They become more dependent on each other, not only for companionship but also for self-validation and advice. One reason for this dependence is that peer relationships, unlike adult–child relationships, involve partners who must learn to negotiate, compromise, share, and defend themselves as equals (Hartup, 1996). Children learn lessons from each other that adults cannot teach.

Because peers are so important to children, developmentalists are troubled if children have no free time to spend with each other. Many protective parents insist that their children come home immediately after school. In school, the push for higher standards and international competitiveness has reduced the time set aside for recess, for lunch, and, as we saw in Chapter 12, for playing outdoors, which often meant playing with neighborhood children. In addition, most parents are now employed outside the home, so after-school supervision sometimes means enrolling the children in organized programs. Children themselves, however, generally prefer the freedom to choose their own activities with their own friends (Belle, 1999).

This is not the only example of parents misperceiving what their children need. A study comparing parents' and children's perceptions of middle childhood found that parents worried most about predatory strangers and illicit drug use. The children were much more concerned about peer relationships, family conflicts, and parental use of alcohol or cigarettes (Borland et al., 1998). Thus, the peer group, which is often feared by the parents, can be very helpful to the children. The family's influence also remains strong, for good or ill. Fortunately, parents' influence is positive, for the most part, in preparing children to have close friends (Parke & Buriel, 1998; Updegraff et al., 2002).

society of children The social culture of children, consisting of the games, vocabulary, dress codes, and rules of behavior that characterize their interactions.

The Society of Children

When school-age children play together, they develop patterns of interaction that are distinct from those of adult society and culture. Accordingly, some social scientists call the peer group the **society of children,** highlighting the fact that children create their own subculture, which is firmly in place by age 10 or so.

The society of children typically has special norms, vocabulary, rituals, and rules of behavior that flourish without the approval, or even the knowledge, of adults. Its slang words and nicknames are often ones adults would frown on (if they understood them), and its activities—such as (in the United States) hanging out at the mall, playing games at the playground, and having long, meandering phone conversations—do not invite adult participation (Opie, 1993; Zarbatany et al., 1990). Its dress codes become known to parents only when they try to get their son or daughter to wear something that violates those codes—as when a perfectly fine pair of hand-me-down jeans is something the child "would not be caught dead in" because, by the norms of the society of children, they are an unfashionable color, have the wrong label, are too loose or too tight. In some nations, including Brazil, Romania, and India, the society of children functions as the only social-

The Rules of the Game These young monks in Burma are playing a board game that adults also play, but they have some of their own refinements of the general rules. The society of children often modifies the dominant culture, as is evident in everything from superstitions to stickball.

KYUYA KAMAZAWA / HAGA / THE IMAGE WORKS

izing influence on homeless children whose parents or circumstances have forced them to live on their own.

Throughout the world, many of the norms and rules of the peer group implicitly encourage independence from adults, and some go even further, demanding distance from adult society. By age 10, if not before, the peer group pities children (especially boys) whose parents kiss them in public ("momma's boy"), teases children whose teachers favor them ("teacher's pet"), and despises those who betray other children to adults ("tattletale," "snitch," "rat"), especially adults in authority such as teachers or the police.

Close friends and the society of children are always powerful but not always positive (Hartup & Stevens, 1999). Children tend to take on the characteristics and values of those in their group. This makes the society of children one of the best sources of language learning—which is essential if a child needs to learn a second language, but less benign if the new code includes a marked regional accent and unacceptable slang and cursing, or if the values of the group include petty delinquency and antagonism to school. By age 9, Paul, the California boy you met in Chapter 11, believed that "I got in just to be in a gang, be somewhere, be known from somewhere." In elementary school he was already breaking rules, fighting, and getting suspended; by junior high he had a tattoo and a gang identity, which led him to drugs and crime by the end of adolescence.

By age 10 or 11, a circle of deviant, antisocial friends may make a child deviant and antisocial, ready to gang up on an outsider or to scorn one of the group. In sum, whether or not friends and the society of children are beneficial depends partly on who those children are.

Friendship

While acceptance by the entire peer group is valued, personal friendship is even more important (Erwin, 1998). Indeed, if they had to choose between being popular but friendless and having close friends but being unpopular, most children would take the friends. Such a choice is consistent with developmentalists' view of the close relationship between friendship and psychosocial development (Hartup & Stevens, 1999; Ladd, 1999). For example, one study found that children from violent and nonviolent homes said they had similar numbers of acquaintances, but the children from conflicted homes were less likely to have close friends and more likely to be lonely. The authors explained, "Skill at recruiting surface acquaintances or playmates is different, therefore, from the skill required to sustain close relationships," and the latter is needed if the child is to avoid loneliness, isolation, and rejection (McCloskey & Stuewig, 2001, p. 93).

CAROL BECKWITH & ANGELA FISHER / HAGA / THE IMAGE WORKS

Friends and Culture Like children everywhere, these children—two 7-year-olds and one 10-year-old—of the Surma people in southern Ethiopia model their appearance after slightly older children, in this case adolescents who apply elaborate body paint for courtship and stick-fighting rituals.

? *Observational Quiz* (see answer, page 400): Are these boys or girls, and which two are best friends?

As friendships become intense and more intimate, older children demand more of their friends, change friends less often, find it harder to make new friends, and are more upset when a friendship breaks up (Erwin, 1998). They are also pickier: They tend to choose best friends whose interests, values, and backgrounds are similar to their own. In fact, from ages 3 to 13, close friendships increasingly involve children of the same sex, age, ethnicity, and socioeconomic status (Aboud & Mendelson, 1996). When friendships across age, sex, ethnic, or SES lines flourish, they are based on a common need, interest, or personality trait (Hartup, 1996). Generally, however, having a best friend who is not the same age or sex correlates with being rejected or ignored by one's classmates and being unhappy (Kovacs et al., 1996). Having no friend at all is even worse.

Whereas most 4-year-olds say they have many friends (perhaps everyone in their nursery school class, with one or two exceptions), most 8-year-olds have a

! *Answer to Observational Quiz* (from page 399): They are girls. The short hair and necklaces give conflicting signals, from a Western perspective, but the unmistakable sign is that two of them have outlined their future breasts, in imitation of their older sisters. They are all friends, but the two younger girls are especially close: The photographer reports that they decorated their bodies in similar ways to show their affection for each other.

aggressive-rejected Referring to children who are actively rejected by their peer group because of their aggressive, confrontational behavior.

withdrawn-rejected Referring to children who are actively rejected by their peer group because of their withdrawn, anxious behavior.

small circle of friends. And by age 10, children often have one "best" friend to whom they are quite loyal. This trend toward fewer but closer friends is followed by both sexes, but it is more apparent among girls. Boys tend to emphasize group identity and loyalty, "using the group in their quest for recognition and self-esteem while they jockey for position within the group." By contrast, girls form smaller, more intimate networks and then are more concerned about being excluded from the small circle (Borland et al., 1998; Buhrmester, 1996; Erwin, 1998). By the end of middle childhood, many girls have one, and only one, best friend on whom they depend.

Rejected Children

All children occasionally feel left out or unwelcome by their peers, but only a small minority are spurned most of the time. For instance, in one study, for six consecutive years (from the first through the sixth grade), researchers asked 299 children which classmates they particularly wanted or did not want as playmates. Each year, the rankings were tabulated and clustered into three groups: popular, or often chosen (36 percent of the children fell into this category); average, or sometimes chosen (47 percent); and unpopular, or often rejected (17 percent). Almost all of the children (89 percent) changed from one category to another over the six years. Only 2 percent of the children were consistently unpopular (Brendgen et al., 2001).

Three distinct categories of unpopular children can be identified. One group consists of neglected, not really rejected, children. No classmate picks them as friends, but nobody avoids them, either. This lack of friends is far from ideal, but it may not be harmful to long-term psychosocial development. Two buffers that sometimes protect the self-esteem of neglected children are good family relationships and outstanding talents (such as the ability to play a musical instrument very well).

The other two types of unpopular children are not just neglected; they are actively rejected. They may be either **aggressive-rejected**—that is, disliked because of their antagonistic, confrontational behavior—or **withdrawn-rejected**—disliked because of their timid, anxious behavior. These seemingly opposite types of rejected children are similar in many ways: Both have problems regulating their emotions, and both are likely to come from homes where they have been mistreated in some way (Pollak et al., 2000).

In contrast, well-liked children are typically helpful and willing to assume the best about other children (Ladd, 1999). This is particularly true as regards

Following Social Rules This argument in a schoolyard is not just a fight between two boys but a sociocultural event.

? *Observational Quiz* (see answer, page 402): What can you see in the behavior of these four boys that suggests that they are aware of the rules of such confrontations?

BOB DAEMMRICH / THE IMAGE WORKS

TABLE 13.1 Examples of the Perceptions and Reactions of Popular and Unpopular Children

Situation	Child B's Type	Typical Interpretation	Typical Response
Child A spills a glass of milk on child B during lunch.	Aggressive-rejected	It was on purpose.	Pour milk on child A, or say something mean.
	Withdrawn-rejected	It was on purpose, or it was accidental.	Ignore it, or leave the table.
	Well-liked	It was accidental.	Get a towel, or ask how it happened.

emotional interpretations. Well-liked children assume that social slights, from a push to an unkind remark, are accidental and not intended to harm, and therefore they do not react with fear (as withdrawn children do) or anger (as aggressive children do) (see Table 13.1). In ambiguous situations, well-liked children try to solve the problem, perhaps by first asking the other child for an explanation (Erdley & Asher, 1996). Given a direct conflict between themselves and another, they seek not revenge, but rather a compromise that maintains the friendship (Rose & Asher, 1999).

These prosocial skills—benign social perceptions, insight into human relationships, and the tendency to help rather than to attack others—are rare in rejected children of either type (Ladd, 1999). Both aggressive-rejected and withdrawn-rejected children misinterpret other people's words and behavior, are poor listeners, and avoid social situations. They tend to be clumsy, awkward, and inept around other children.

Can I Play? If she dares to ask, she is likely to be rejected, because the rules of bonding at this age tend to exclude as well as include. The ability to deal with such situations is one of the most difficult skills taught by the society of children.

Teaching Social Skills

Since the school years are prime time for education, and since rejected children have apparently not learned how to get along with other children, it seems logical simply to teach them how to do so. However, efforts to teach social skills to rejected children have met with mixed success (Merrell & Gimpel, 1998; Sridher & Vaughn, 2001), as have all attempts to intervene by somehow "fixing" the child. As one review candidly reports, "Although intervention has been praised extensively by the teachers and parents involved and it is in great demand, it has been hard to show that . . . changes in aggressive behavior followed from the intervention" (Huesmann & Reynolds, 2001, p. 265).

There are three reasons why aggressive and withdrawn children do not learn better social skills:

- Defensive and destructive social responses are usually learned from the parents during early childhood; such lessons from home are hard to unlearn.
- Peer attitudes and actions resist change. For instance, even if rejected children learn how to start a friendly conversation, their efforts may fail because the other children fear that befriending an unpopular child will jeopardize their own social standing.
- Children sometimes say one thing and do another. A rejected child might verbalize what he or she should do in a given social situation but not actually do it when the time comes; emotions take over, and fear or aggression replaces logic.

In trying to remedy the rejection of withdrawn children, one must acknowledge the power of parents and peers by teaching the parents and training popular peers. Intervention before the third grade (when patterns are set and problems

bullying A child's repeated, systematic efforts to inflict harm on another, particular child through physical, verbal, or social attacks.

typically emerge) and helping all the children to accept themselves and appreciate others are more effective than targeting the older rejected child for special assistance. Sometimes the best intervention is academic: Contrary to the popular misconception, school-age children who are accomplished students are less, not more, likely to be rejected by peers (Stipek, 2001).

It is even harder to turn around the rejection of aggressive children, partly because most 7- to 11-year-old aggressive-rejected children have a few awed and cowed friends (Brendgen et al., 2001; Ladd, 1999). As a result, they overestimate their acceptance and are oblivious of their unpopularity. When another child rejects them, they blame that child rather than themselves. Accordingly, they have no motivation to learn new social skills.

Ironically, these aggressive children often display a "veneer of self-satisfaction and invulnerability [that] may further decrease the likelihood that others will offer encouragement, warmth, and support" (Hughes et al., 1997). If an aggressive child makes an awkward attempt to do a good deed, other children will be wary; the aggressive child will be pushed back toward the familiar, hostile ways. The best solution for both types of rejected children is to change the entire social context.

Bullies and Their Victims

Any discussion of aggressive and withdrawn children is likely to bring to mind bullies and their victims. (The behavior of bullies and victims occurs when these children are in a social context that allows active expression of aggressive and withdrawn temperaments.)

Researchers define **bullying** as repeated, systematic efforts to inflict harm through physical attack (such as hitting, pinching, or kicking), verbal attack (such as teasing, taunting, or name-calling), or social attack (such as deliberate shunning or public mocking). Bullies are actively aggressive, and victims of bullying are "cautious, sensitive, quiet, . . . lonely and abandoned at school. As a rule, they do not have a single good friend in their class" (Olweus, 1999, p. 15). Victims are no more likely to be fat or homely or to speak with an accent than nonvictims are. However, victims are usually withdrawn-rejected children—anxious and insecure, unable or unwilling to defend themselves—and bullies are described as mean by other children (Boulton, 1999; Poulin & Boivin, 2000). Such characterizations are probably universal. For example, Chinese and Japanese children who are victims of bullying show the same characteristics as their Western counterparts (Rios-Ellis et al., 2000; Schwartz et al., 2001).

Bullying was once thought to be a normal part of children's play—not to be encouraged, of course, but of little consequence in the long run. However, developmental researchers who have looked closely at the society of children now realize that bullying is a serious problem, harming both the victim and the aggressor (Bukowski & Sippola, 2001; Garrity & Baris, 1996).

The leading researcher in this area is Dan Olweus, who has studied bullying for 30 years. The cruelty, pain, and suffering that he has documented are typified by the details of two cases (Olweus, 1993a):

> Linda was systematically isolated by a small group of girls, who pressured the rest of the class, including Linda's only friend, to shun her. Then the ringleader of the group persuaded Linda to give a party and invite everyone. She did. Everyone accepted, but, following the ringleader's instructions, no one came. Linda was devastated, her self-confidence "completely destroyed."

> Henry's experience was worse. Daily, his classmates called him "Worm," broke his pencils, spilled his books on the floor, and mocked him whenever he answered a teacher's questions. Finally, a few boys took him to the bathroom and made him lie, face down, in the urinal drain. After school that day he tried to kill himself. His parents found him unconscious, and only then learned about his torment.

Boys versus Girls

Children of both sexes can be bullies or victims, although gender differences exist. Boys who are bullies are often above average in size, whereas girls who are bullies are often above average in verbal assertiveness. Bullies' victims tend to be less assertive; boy victims are often physically weaker, whereas girl victims are more shy.

These gender differences are reflected in bullying tactics: Boys typically use force or the threat of force; girls often mock or ridicule their victims, making fun of their clothes, behavior, or appearance, revealing their most embarrassing secrets, or spreading destructive rumors about them. This gender-related difference in tactics reflects the difference between *physical* aggression and *relational* aggression. Physical aggression, as you remember from Chapter 10, involves punching, kicking, and causing the victim other physical pain; relational aggression involves undercutting the victim's friendships and self-esteem.

To some extent, gender norms condone bullying. As we have already noted, children are shunned by their peers if they complain to adults, so most children suffer bullying in silence. These norms allow bullies of both sexes to believe they are doing nothing wrong when the boys act tough or the girls gossip maliciously. They also mean that boys, in particular, become bullies because they consider it a sign of strength—a belief shared by many peers and even by some adults. Fewer girls become bullies, except in Japan, where social cooperation is so crucial that exclusion and the spreading of false rumors (two forms of relational aggression) are especially potent bullying weapons for girls (Morita et al., 1999).

Especially for Former Victims of Bullying: How can you overcome the psychic scars of having been a victim?

Bullying Around the World

Following the suicides of three victims, the Norwegian government asked Dan Olweus to determine the extent and severity of bullying. After concluding a confidential survey of nearly all of Norway's 90,000 school-age children, Olweus reported that bullying was widespread and serious (see Figure 13.1 on page 404); that teachers and parents were "relatively unaware" of specific incidents; and that even when adults noticed, they rarely intervened. Of all the children Olweus surveyed, 9 percent said they were bullied "now and then"; 3 percent were victims once a week or more; and 7 percent admitted that they themselves sometimes deliberately hurt other children, verbally or physically (Olweus, 1993b).

These numbers are equaled or exceeded in many other countries (Smith et al., 1999). For instance, confidential surveys found that 10 percent of British children bullied another child at least once a week (Smith et al., 1999), as did 18 percent of Italian and Australian children and 13 percent of Japanese children (Fonzi et al., 1999; Morita et al., 1999; Rigby & Slee, 1999). A study of a multiethnic, multi-income group of children in Los Angeles found that 10 percent (three-quarters of them boys) were teased and picked on and another 17 percent (most of them girls) were socially rejected (Graham & Juvonene, 1998).

Research in many nations finds wide variation among schools within the same community and much higher rates in locations where many adults are engaged in violence, such as the Palestinian territory, Ethiopia, and South Africa (Ohsako, 1999). Bullying is never completely absent, however. It occurs in every nation, in small rural schools and large urban ones, among well-to-do majority children and poor immigrant ones, among children of every race and religion (Smith et al., 1999).

A child's social status and behavior often change from year to year. For example, in the United States, when children from kindergarten through third grade were asked every year whether they had been the target of physical or relational aggression, only 4 percent said "yes" for all four years, but 60 percent said "yes" for at least one year (Kochenderfer-Ladd & Wardrop, 2001). The first years of elementary school are the time of greatest change, as some children learn to act in

FIGURE 13.1 Every Country Has Bullies
The rates of being bullied in the various grades as reported by Norwegian schoolchildren are typical of the rates in many other countries. This chart shows physical bullying only; relational bullying may increase with age. Although physical bullying is less common among older children, relational bullying becomes more devastating, because older children depend much more on peers for self-esteem.

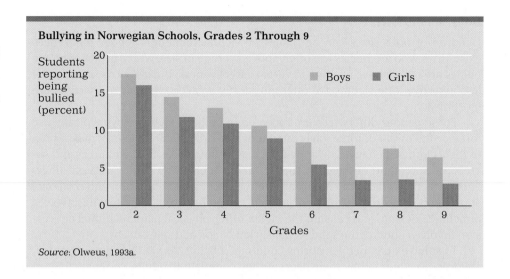

Bullying in Norwegian Schools, Grades 2 Through 9

Source: Olweus, 1993a.

Response for Former Victims of Bullying (from page 403): Realize that it was not your fault; the bully was in the wrong and should have been stopped by adults at home and at school. Make sure your self-esteem is not still damaged. Write about the situation, see a psychotherapist, or talk it over with a supportive friend.

Especially for the Parents of a Bully: Another parent has told you that your child is bullying his or her child, but your child denies it and explains that the other child doesn't mind being teased.

prosocial rather than antisocial ways and thus achieve more social acceptance (Haselager et al., 2002). To assess the cumulative frequency of bullying, other researchers asked older children if they *ever* were bullies or victims. Among U.S. middle-school students, 80 percent said they had engaged in bullying (Bosworth et al., 1999) and 77 percent said they had been victims (Hoover et al., 1992).

The Consequences of Bullying

A key word in the definition of bullying is *repeated*. Most children experience isolated attacks or social slights from other children and come through unscathed; and when the social play described in Chapter 10 turns hurtful, both the aggressor and the injured usually learn how to stop and repair the friendship. But when a child endures shameful experiences again and again—being forced to hand over lunch money, or to drink milk mixed with detergent, or to lick someone's boots, or to be the butt of insults and practical jokes, with everyone watching and no one defending—the effects can be deep and long-lasting. Bullied children are anxious, depressed, and underachieving during the months and years of their torment. To make matters worse, longitudinal studies show that a drop in self-esteem and an increase in loneliness follow the bullying experiences; even if the child is no longer bullied, negative effects linger (Kochenderfer-Ladd & Wardrop, 2001).

The picture is also ominous for bullies. As we have noted, in middle childhood bullies usually have friends who abet, fear, and admire them. They are brashly unapologetic about the pain they have inflicted "all in fun." Their parents do not stop them but instead are part of the problem, treating their children with a combination of neglect and hostility and using physical punishment, verbal criticism, and dominance to control and demean them (Olweus, 1993a).

However, bullies' popularity and school success fade over the years, as their peers become increasingly critical of their behavior. In reaction, bullies become more hostile, getting into trouble not only with peers and teachers but also with the police. In one longitudinal study, by age 24 two-thirds of boys who were bullies in the second grade had been convicted of at least one felony, and one-third of those who were bullies in the sixth through ninth grades had been convicted of three or more crimes, usually violent ones, and had already done prison time (Olweus, 1993b). This particular study came from Norway, but international research confirms that children who regularly victimize other children and challenge authority often become violent criminals (Moffitt et al., 2002).

Bullying is difficult to change. The origins of all kinds of antisocial behavior, including bullying, predate middle childhood and may lie in brain abnormalities that are present at birth and that are then strengthened by insecure attachment, poor emotional regulation, and other deficits (Cairns & Cairns, 2001; Holden, 2000). In fact, aggression may be natural to all children. As one researcher quipped, "Babies do not kill each other because we do not give them access to guns" (Tremblay, 2000, p. 581).

Fortunately, there are two hopeful notes. First, children *do* change if family, school, and the society of children encourage them to. A longitudinal study found that about one-fourth of a group of 51 high-risk children who were unusually aggressive and uncontrolled in the first grade improved as time went on. By adolescence they were not delinquents, not bullies, and not particularly stressed, even though they still lived in low-income, violence-prone neighborhoods. The other three-fourths remained antisocial, with numerous signs that they had criminal futures (Aguilar et al., 2000). The researchers suspect that psychosocial influences, such as those provided by families and schools, are more powerful than biological ones, such as genetic inheritance and brain damage, which are difficult to change.

A second reason for hope is that careful research has shown how bullying can be reduced, as discussed in the Thinking Like a Scientist feature.

Jimmy, Sixth-Generation Pain in the Ass

Like Father, Like Son If parents and grandparents use their greater physical power to punish and criticize their offspring, the children (especially the boys) are often hostile to everyone they know.

Thinking Like a Scientist

Don't Suffer Bullying in Silence

Bullies and victims share one firm cognitive assumption: Adults will not intervene. Robert Coles (1997) describes a 9-year-old boy who reported that one of his classmates, a girl, was cheating. The boy was then victimized, not only by the girl and her friends but more subtly by the teacher and the principal, who made excuses for the girl (her grandfather had died several months earlier). Coles believes the overall moral climate teaches many children to ignore the actions of bullies and the feelings and needs of victims of bullying.

A recent study in Ontario, Canada, that unobtrusively recorded playground bullying (verbal and physical) found that girls were as involved as boys, teachers intervened in only 4 percent of the situations, other children stopped 12 percent of the incidents, and the principal of the school with the most bullying denied that his school had any bullying at all (Pepler et al., 1999). Most children are sympathetic to victims, are afraid of bullies, and believe that teachers could stop the bullies but are "too soft. . . . The most she'll do is, like, go 'Don't do it again'" (quoted in Borland et al., 1998).

One 8-year-old explained how a bully in his class operated:

He sits across the aisle from me, and he doesn't give me any trouble, because I'm able to defend myself, and he knows it, but he's a bully, that's what he is, a real meanie. He tries to get his way by picking on kids who he's decided are weaker than him. They help him with his homework—they give him answers. They give him candy from their lunches. They take orders from him. He cheats—I see him. I think the teacher knows, but the kid's father is a lawyer, and my dad says the teacher is probably afraid—she's got to be careful, or he'll sue her.

[quoted in Coles, 1997]

The children who made these observations may be right about the influence of teachers, and they are certainly right about the perception of children. This also can change. In England, when a pamphlet entitled "Don't Suffer in Silence" was distributed to all schoolchildren and teachers were trained in ways of responding to bullying incidents, bullying in primary schools was reduced by almost 50 percent (Smith et al., 1999).

Researchers now realize that intervention must change the social climate so that bully–victim cycles no longer spiral out of control. A "whole-school" approach is needed, as was first demonstrated in Norway. Dan Olweus had been studying bullying for many years when the Norwegian government asked him to design an intervention effort. Olweus first collected data from all the children and then, using an ecological approach, began to change the school culture. All parents received pamphlets that described signs of victimization (such as a child's having bad dreams, no real friends, damaged clothes, torn books, or unexplained bruises). All students saw videotapes intended to evoke sympathy for victims. All teachers were given special training in intervention.

The second phase was more direct. In every classroom, students discussed reasons to stop bullying, ways to mediate peer conflicts, and how to befriend lonely children. The last action is particularly crucial: Having at least one protective peer "watching your back" not only prevents the escalation of bullying but reduces its emotional sting (Hodges et al.,

Shake Hands or Yell "Uncle" Many schools, such as this one in Alaska, have trained peer mediators who intervene in disputes, hear both sides, take notes, and seek a resolution. Without such efforts, antagonists usually fight until one gives up, giving bullies free rein. Despite Alaska's higher rate of alcohol abuse, the state's adolescent homicide rate is lower than the national average.

? *Observational Quiz* (see answer, page 408): Could this be one reason?

1999). Therefore, teachers organized cooperative learning groups within classes so that no child could be isolated and then bullied, and teachers halted each incident of name-calling or minor assault, recognizing the undercurrent beneath the bully's excuses and the terror behind the victim's silence or nervous laughter. Principals learned that adult supervision in the lunchroom, bathroom, and playground was pivotal, and they redeployed staff to keep watch and intervene.

If bullying occurred despite these preventive steps, counselors used very direct measures: conducting intensive family therapy with the bully and parents; removing the bully to a different class, grade, or even school; and helping the victim strengthen social and academic skills. (Note that bullies and their families bore the major burden. If the victim were to change school and the bully were to stay, the wrong child would be punished.)

Twenty months after this campaign began, Olweus resurveyed the children. Bullying had been reduced overall by more than 50 percent, with dramatic improvement for both boys and girls at every grade level (Olweus, 1992). These results are thrilling to developmentalists because they show that research can lead to an inexpensive, widespread intervention that effectively reduces a serious problem. Especially noteworthy is that the intervention did not attempt to change the children's nature—no drugs, no suspensions, no expulsions—but used children's normal desires to be friends and to do well in school. Adult guidance made prosocial behavior the norm, changing the school climate—which, again, is much easier at the beginning of middle childhood than at the end of adolescence. Olweus (1993a) concludes:

> It is no longer possible to avoid taking action about bullying problems at school using lack of awareness as an excuse . . . it all boils down to a matter of will and involvement on the part of adults.

Unfortunately, many school systems throughout the world have not yet even acknowledged the harm caused by bullying. A research team from Finland complains:

> It is somewhat strange that society provides education in a large variety of subjects of a scholarly nature, but when it comes to human relations, which is the source of both the greatest misery and the greatest joy in life, we do not consider it worth covering in our educational system.
>
> *[Bjorkqvist & Osterman, 1999]*

Many educators in many nations are beginning to address bullying, although some efforts are scattershot, some ineffective, and some (particularly in high school) self-defeating (Olewus, 2001; Smith et al., 1999). A whole-school approach, with involvement by all concerned over a period of years, can be very successful in middle childhood, if the "will and involvement" are present.

Family Influences

A debate rages between those who believe that parenting styles and processes are very influential and those who believe that a child's genes and peers are much more powerful than anything the parents might do (Maccoby, 2000). Putting it strongly, those who advocate the supremacy of parenting say:

> The vulnerabilities of older children may differ substantially in kind from those of young ones, but the potential consequences of risks remain equally great throughout the developmental period. The extent to which parents provide healthy and supportive environments for their developing children is a critical component in their lifelong well-being.
>
> [Ramey, 2002, p. 48]

And those who assert that heredity predominates contend:

> Children somewhat resemble their biological parents and siblings in personality, but the genes they have in common can account for almost all of the resemblance. These results indicate that being reared by conscientious parents does not, on average, make children more (or less) conscientious, that being reared by social parents does not, on average, make children more (or less) sociable, and that being reared by open-minded parents does not, on average, make children more (or less) open-minded.
>
> [Harris, 2002, p. 5]

All researchers agree that both nature and nurture are important. All agree that the interaction between the two is crucial and that nurture—the environment—involves not simply parenting practices but also other influences, such as school and friendships. These aspects of the environment are called "nonshared" because children in the same family do not share them. When researchers calculate the correlation between various genetic traits among parents and siblings (including twins, adoptees, and stepchildren), they find that roughly half of the traits seem genetic and half seem environmental, with most environmental effects "nonshared"— a blow to parents who thought they could mold their children's personalities (Plomin et al., 2001). But, as you remember from Chapters 1–3, exactly how scientists should quantify and interpret variables can be disputed. Moreover, developmentalists disagree about the meaning of nonshared influences. Do they mean that school and friends combined with genes determine a child's personality?

Most developmentalists answer "no", for two reasons. First, differences between siblings from the same family are much less than differences between children from extremely diverse families, such as between a well-educated, well-to-do suburban couple and an impoverished, illiterate single parent. Studies of adopted children, who share no genes with their adoptive parents, reveal that nonfamilial contextual factors are as powerful as genetic influences. Because parents choose neighborhoods and schools, they determine contexts. Thus, indirectly, they have a powerful effect. Second, virtually all the research is correlational and therefore static, from one moment in time, even though parent–child interaction is a dynamic, ever-changing system.

> As every parent knows, parents continually try to make up for their past errors with their children, and they are generally fairly successful at mid-life correction. They are constantly responsive to their past actions and to their child's current level of adaptation. A child who is getting into trouble will be met with a parent who intensifies her monitoring and restriction of the child, whereas a child's demonstration of responsibility will be met with a parent who grants greater freedom. Because of this responsivity, simple-minded correlational studies will misrepresent the relation between parenting behavior and child behavior. . . . The point is that the parent will titrate her actions in an exquisite manner when the child's behavior begins to deviate. So, too, the child's behavior is just as exquisitely responsive to changes in parenting.
>
> [Dodge, 2002, p. 218]

Response for the Parents of a Bully (from page 404): The future is ominous if the charges are true, and your child's denial is a symptom of a problem. (If your child were not a bully, he or she would be worried about the other child's misperception instead of categorically denying that any problem exists.) You might ask the teacher and guidance counselor what they are doing about bullying in the school. Since bullies often learn behavior at home, perhaps family counseling would help you to become less punitive and your child to become less aggressive. Because bullies often have a few friends who encourage them, you may need to monitor your child's friendships and perhaps even befriend the victim. Talk matters over with your child, as often as necessary. Ignoring the situation may lead to heartache later on.

!Answer to Observational Quiz (from page 406): Yes. Children learn their conflict-resolution patterns in elementary school and then tend to use them in adolescence

family function The ways in which a family operates to nurture the development of its children's potential: meeting their physical needs for food, clothing, and shelter; encouraging them to learn; developing their self-esteem; nurturing their friendships with peers; and providing harmony and stability at home.

family structure The legal and genetic relationships among the members of a particular family.

You may find one or another of the three quotations above more persuasive than the others, but the controversy is not yet settled. All developmentalists agree that genes, peers, and families are influential in middle childhood, and that dynamic, longitudinal, experimental studies are too scarce to be definitive (Demo & Cox, 2000). Keep this in mind as you read about family functions and structures. Decide for yourself the impact of parents during the school years.

Family Function

Families may be classified in two ways; by function and by structure. **Family function** refers to how a family works to meet the needs of its members; **family structure** refers to how a family is legally constructed and how its members are genetically connected. Some family structures tend to function better than others, as we will see.

Although the details vary, families serve five essential functions for school-age children:

1. *Meet physical needs by providing food, clothes, and shelter.* In middle childhood, children are old enough to dress, wash, and put themselves to bed, but they cannot yet obtain the basic necessities of life without their families' help.
2. *Encourage learning.* A critical task during middle childhood is to master academic skills. Families must get their children to school and then guide and motivate their education.
3. *Develop self-esteem.* As they become more cognitively aware, children become more self-critical. Families need to make their children feel competent, loved, and appreciated.
4. *Nurture peer friendship.* Families can provide the time, space, opportunity, and skills needed to develop peer relationships.
5. *Provide harmony and stability.* Children need to feel safe and secure, confident that family routines are protective and predictable.

Thus, a family that functions well provides material and cognitive resources as well as emotional security, so that the children grow in body and mind. No family functions perfectly for every child. Recurrent unresolved conflict between the adults is common but harmful, whether or not the child is directly involved in it and whether or not it leads to divorce (Cox & Brooks-Gunn, 1999; Cummings et al., 2002).

Mom Urges Fit Over Fashion The basic function of families is to provide children with basic necessities, such as clothing. When middle-class school-age children are involved, this is more difficult than it seems. The society of children is often quite specific about the most desirable brand, color, and design of every item of clothing, especially shoes.

JOHN BOYKIN / PHOTOEDIT

Styles of Parenting

You read in Chapter 10 about Diana Baumrind's (1967, 1971) classification of parenting styles: authoritarian, authoritative, and permissive. Think about how each of these three parenting styles relates to the five family functions just listed. If parents with a permissive style simply accept whatever their child does, they fail at all but the first function. The child needs both warmth and discipline, both encouragement and direction, as typified by the authoritative style. Research suggests that parents who actively promote education, self-esteem, and social skills have children who are more likely to achieve in school and to have solid friendships. Organization of family life is key; chaos is destructive (Maccoby, 2000).

Although authoritative families (warm, communicative, and demanding) generally raise more successful and self-confident children, a diversity of family styles can function well for children (Dishion & Bullock, 2002). For example, it is important that

This realization can guide adults who seek to be of help. If the home situation is difficult, for instance, any adult, from a caring teacher to a loving grandparent, can step in and make a critical difference. If parents decide to divorce, they should first figure out how to ensure that their children will receive the necessary material and emotional resources. Grandparents can take over, quite successfully, if a parent is incapable. Or if a child has a severe reading difficulty, helping the child develop talents in some other area—math or baseball or music—may be as important to the child's overall well-being as tutoring to overcome the learning disability.

Within neighborhoods, the attitude that everyone is responsible for all the children's behavior can also improve life for individuals (Sampson et al., 1997). More broadly, measures designed to enhance the social context, perhaps by making violent neighborhoods safer or improving job opportunities in impoverished communities, can benefit school-age children substantially.

> Successful children remind us that children grow up in multiple contexts—in families, schools, peer groups, baseball teams, religious organizations, and many other groups—and each context is a potential source of protective factors as well as risks. These children demonstrate that children are protected not only by the self-righting nature of development, but also by the actions of adults, by their own actions, by the nurturing of their assets, by opportunities to succeed, and by the experience of success. The behavior of adults often plays a critical role in children's risks, resources, opportunities, and resilience. Development is biased toward competence, but there is no such thing as an invulnerable child. If we allow the prevalence of known risk factors for development to rise while resources for children fall, we can expect the competent individual children and the human capital of the nation to suffer.
>
> *[Masten & Coatsworth, 1998]*

As you will see in the next three chapters, adolescence is a continuation of middle childhood as well as a radical departure from it. Stresses and strains continue to accumulate, and "known risk factors," including drug availability and sexual urges, become more prevalent. Fortunately, for many young people protective resources and constructive coping also increase. Personal competencies, family support, and close friends get most children through childhood and adolescence undamaged. Indeed, the same factors help each of us throughout our development, as we overcome the problems, and build on the strengths, that characterized the first years of our lives.

SUMMARY

Theories of School-Age Development

1. All three grand theories acknowledge that school-age children become more independent and capable in many ways. In psychoanalytic theory, Freud described latency, when sexual needs are quiet; Erikson emphasized industry, when children are busy mastering various tasks. Behaviorism and cognitive theory stress the new skills that maturation and wider social opportunities afford.

2. Social cognitive theory combines these grand theories to describe how children begin to think more deeply about their social context and to act effectively within it. The sociocultural and epigenetic systems theories also describe an increase in independence in middle childhood.

Understanding Self and Others

3. Research confirms these theories. The interplay of self-understanding and social perception is increasingly evident during the school years. Children figure out who they are partly by comparing themselves to others.

The Peer Group

4. Peers are crucial. Rejection by peers is devastating; intimacy with at least one good friend makes school and other challenges surmountable. Children typically group themselves together, forming their own subculture, with slang, rituals, and taboos that change from one community or nation to another.

5. Friendships become increasingly close and influential. Usually friends provide needed companionship and allow development of social skills, but sometimes they encourage deviant, antisocial behavior.

6. Rejected children may be neglected, withdrawn, or aggressive. All three types have difficulty interpreting the normal give-and-take of childhood. Usually rejection is temporary, but it is difficult to teach a rejected child to become more popular without also teaching parents and peers, because social skills are not learned in isolation.

7. Aggressive children can become bullies, who do obvious damage over the years to themselves and to their victims. Unless they change, many bullies become delinquent and then criminal, and many victims develop persistent feelings of mistrust and anxiety.

8. In most nations, boys are often bullies and tend to use physical attacks. Girls are more likely to use relational aggression, involving social exclusion and rumor spreading, which can be very destructive.

9. Adults can prevent most bullying. Because of various policies and attitudes, some schools have four times more bullying than others. There are international variations as well, but bullying is common worldwide—usually more than 10 percent of school-age children do it.

Family Influences

10. Families influence children in many ways, as do genes and peers. The five functions of a supportive family are to help the child meet physical needs; learn; develop friends; protect self-esteem; and live in a safe, stable, and harmonious home. This last function is crucial, but many families find it difficult, because adults fight, neighborhoods change, and violence is prevalent.

11. Generally, authoritative families balance support and discipline effectively. However, there are many variations: No one parenting style always functions best. Impoverished families find all five functions difficult to fulfill; poor children are at greater risk for emotional and behavioral problems.

12. Family structures that are common today include nuclear, extended, blended, grandparent, adoptive, and foster families. Less than half of all children born in the United States today will live in a nuclear family from birth to age 18. No one of these structures guarantees good—or bad—child development.

13. Nuclear families have natural advantages, including more stability and higher income. Divorce impedes child development, at least for a few years, particularly reducing school achievement.

14. The most difficult family structure may be foster families. Children enter such families with many problems, and foster parents are not guaranteed a permanent connection to their foster children. This is a particular problem in middle childhood, when stability and continuity are crucial.

Coping with Problems

15. School-age children tend to be resilient. Many cope well with major problems—learning disabilities, immigration, social rejection, families that are not supportive, poverty, violence.

16. In general, children benefit from social support (perhaps a best friend or a grandparent), natural assets (intelligence, a winning personality, a special skill), personal strengths (religious faith, a stable early childhood), and few stresses. The innate drive toward competence and independence keeps most school-age children from being overwhelmed by problems.

KEY TERMS

latency (p. 393)	social comparison (p. 397)	bullying (p. 402)	single-parent family (p. 410)
industry versus inferiority (p. 393)	peer group (p. 397)	family function (p. 408)	blended family (p. 410)
social cognitive theory (p. 394)	society of children (p. 398)	family structure (p. 408)	grandparent family (p. 410)
social cognition (p. 396)	aggressive-rejected (p. 400)	nuclear family (p. 410)	adoptive family (p. 410)
	withdrawn-rejected (p. 400)	extended family (p. 410)	foster family (p. 410)

KEY QUESTIONS

1. How do the five major theories differ in describing middle childhood?

2. How does a school-age child develop a sense of self?

3. The society of children strongly disapproves of tattletales. How does this affect child development?

4. Why is social rejection particularly devastating during middle childhood?

5. Describe the personal characteristics of a bully and a victim.

6. How do schools, families, and cultures contribute to the incidence of bullying?

7. What is the difference between family function and family structure?

8. Why is a safe, harmonious home particularly important during middle childhood?

9. What are the special advantages and disadvantages of adoption?

10. Compare the child-rearing advantages of never-married parents with those of divorced parents.

11. Why is coping with family problems easier during middle childhood than earlier?

BIOSOCIAL

Growth and Skills During middle childhood, children grow more slowly than they did during infancy and toddlerhood or than they will during adolescence. Increased strength and lung capacity give children the endurance to improve their performance in skills such as swimming and running. Slower growth contributes to children's increasing bodily control, and children enjoying exercising their developing skills of coordination and balance. Which specific skills they master depends largely on culture, gender, and inherited ability.

Special Needs Many children have special learning needs that may originate in brain patterns but that express themselves in educational problems. Early recognition, targeted education, and psychological support help all children, from those with autism to the much milder instance of a specific learning disability or ADHD.

COGNITIVE

Thinking During middle childhood, children become better able to understand and learn, in part because of growth in their processing capacity, knowledge base, and memory capacity. At the same time, metacognition techniques enable children to organize their learning. Beginning at about age 7 or 8, children also develop the ability to understand logical principles, including the concepts of identity, reciprocity, and reversibility.

Language Children's increasing ability to understand the structures and possibilities of language enables them to extend the range of their cognitive powers and to become more analytical in their use of vocabulary. Most children develop proficiency in several language codes, and some become bilingual.

Education Formal schooling begins worldwide, with the specifics of the curriculum depending on economic and societal factors. An individual child's learning success depends on the time allotted to each task, specific guided instruction from teachers and parents, and the overall values of the culture. Curricula and goals vary, and some variations are more crucial than others.

PSYCHOSOCIAL

Emotions and Personality Development School-age children come to understand themselves, as well as what is right in their relations with others. The peer group becomes increasingly important as children become less dependent on their parents and more dependent on friends for help, loyalty, and sharing of mutual interests. Rejection and bullying become serious problems.

Parents Parents continue to influence children, especially as they exacerbate or buffer problems in school and the community. During these years, families need to meet basic needs, encourage learning, develop self-esteem, nurture friendship, and—most important—provide harmony and stability. Parents in the midst of divorce may be deficient in all of these. Most single-parent, foster, or grandparent families are better than families in open conflict, but a family with two biological parents, both of whom are cooperative with each other and loving to the child, is generally best. Fortunately, school-age children often develop competencies and attitudes to defend against the stress that most experience. Friends, family, school, and community can all be helpful.

Appendix A
Supplemental Charts, Graphs, and Tables

Often, examining specific data is useful, even fascinating, to developmental researchers. The particular numbers reveal trends and nuances not apparent from a more general view. For instance, many people mistakenly believe that the incidence of Down syndrome babies rises sharply for mothers over 35, or that even the tiniest newborns usually survive. Each chart, graph, or table in this appendix probably contains information not generally known.

Children as a Proportion of a Nation's Population

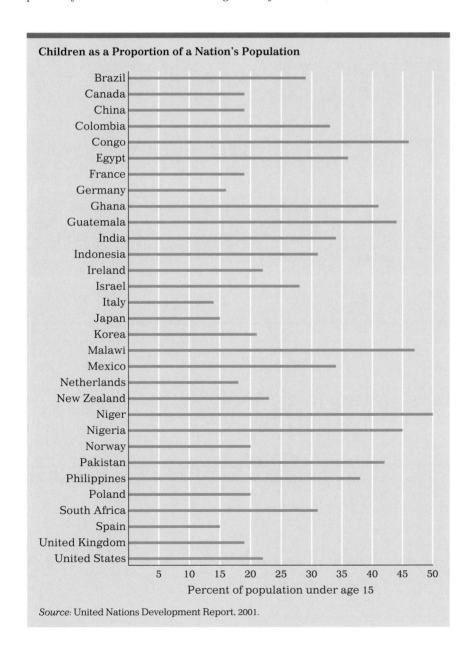

Percent of population under age 15

Source: United Nations Development Report, 2001.

More Children, Worse Schools? (Chapter 1)

Nations that have high birth rates also have high death rates, short life spans, and more illiteracy. A systems approach suggests that these variables are connected: For example, the Montessori and Reggio-Emilio early-childhood education programs, said to be the best in the world, originated in Italy, and Italy has the lowest proportion of children under 15 of all the countries in this graph.

Ethnic Composition of the U.S. Population (Chapter 2)

Thinking about the ethnic makeup of the U.S. population can be an interesting exercise in social comparison. If you look only at the table, you will conclude that not much has changed over the past 30 years: Whites are still the majority, Native Americans are still a tiny minority, and African-Americans are still about 11 percent of the population. However, if you look at the chart, you can see why every group feels that much has changed. Because the proportions of Hispanic-Americans and Asian-Americans have increased dramatically, European-Americans see the current nonwhite population at almost one-third of the total, and African-Americans see that Hispanics now outnumber them.

? *Observational Quiz* (see answer, page A-4): Which ethnic group is growing most rapidly?

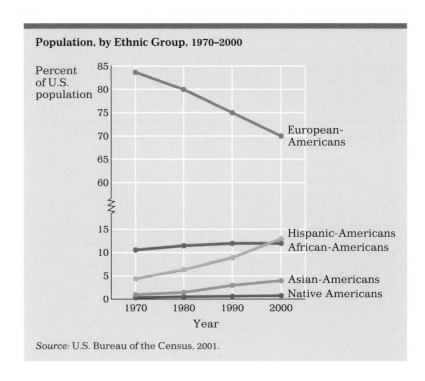

Population, by Ethnic Group, 1970–2000

Source: U.S. Bureau of the Census, 2001.

	PERCENT OF U.S. POPULATION			
ETHNIC ORIGIN	**1970**	**1980**	**1990**	**2000**
European (white)	83.7	80	75	70
African (black)	10.6	11.5	12	12
Latino (Hispanic)	4.5	6.4	9	13
Asian	1.0	1.5	3	4
Native American	.4	.6	.7	.8

The Genetics of Blood Types (Chapter 3)

Blood types A and B are dominant traits, and type O is recessive. The percentages given in the first column of this chart represent the odds that a child born to the parents with the various combinations of genotypes will have the genotype given in the second column.

Genotypes of Parents*	Genotype of Offspring	Phenotype	Can Donate Blood To (Phenotype)	Can Receive Blood From (Phenotype)
AA + AA (100%) AA + AB (50%) AA + AO (50%) AB + AB (25%) AB + AO (25%) AO + AO (25%)	AA (inherits one A from each parent)	A	A or AB	A or O
AA + OO (100%) AB + OO (50%) AO + AO (50%) AO + OO (50%) AB + AO (25%) AB + BO (25%)	AO	A	A or AB	A or O
BB + BB (100%) AB + BB (50%) BB + BO (50%) AB + AB (25%) AB + BO (25%) BO + BO (25%)	BB	B	B or AB	B or O
BB + OO (100%) AB + OO (50%) BO + BO (50%) BO + OO (50%) AB + AO (25%) AB + BO (25%)	BO	B	B or AB	B or O
AA + BB (100%) AA + AB (50%) AA + BO (50%) AB + AB (50%) AB + BB (50%) AO + BB (50%) AB + BO (25%) AO + BO (25%)	AB	AB	AB only	A, B, AB, O ("universal recipient")
OO + OO (100%) AO + OO (50%) BO + OO (50%) AO + AO (25%) AO + BO (25%) BO + BO (25%)	OO	O	A, B, AB, O ("universal donor")	O only

*Blood type is not a sex-linked trait, so any of these pairs can be either mother-plus-father or father-plus-mother.
Source: Adapted from Hartl & Jones, 1999.

Odds of Down Syndrome by Maternal Age and Gestational Age (Chapter 4)

The odds of any given fetus, at the end of the first trimester, having three chromosomes at the 21st site (trisomy 21) and thus having Down syndrome is shown in the 10-weeks column. Every year of maternal age increases the incidence of trisomy 21. The number of Down syndrome infants born alive is only half the number who survived the first trimester. Although obviously the least risk is at age 20 (younger is even better), there is no year when the odds suddenly increase (age 35 is an arbitrary cut-off). Even at age 44, less than 4 percent of all newborns have Down syndrome. Other chromosomal abnormalities in fetuses also increase with mother's age, but the rate of spontaneous abortion is much higher, so births of babies with chromosomal defects is not the norm, even for women over age 45.

AGE (YRS)	GESTATION (WEEKS)		LIVE BIRTHS
	10	35	
20	1/804	1/1,464	1/1,527
21	1/793	1/1,445	1/1,507
22	1/780	1/1,421	1/1,482
23	1/762	1/1,389	1/1,448
24	1/740	1/1,348	1/1,406
25	1/712	1/1,297	1/1,352
26	1/677	1/1,233	1/1,286
27	1/635	1/1,157	1/1,206
28	1/586	1/1,068	1/1,113
29	1/531	1/967	1/1,008
30	1/471	1/858	1/895
31	1/409	1/745	1/776
32	1/347	1/632	1/659
33	1/288	1/525	1/547
34	1/235	1/427	1/446
35	1/187	1/342	1/356
36	1/148	1/269	1/280
37	1/115	1/209	1/218
38	1/88	1/160	1/167
39	1/67	1/122	1/128
40	1/51	1/93	1/97
41	1/38	1/70	1/73
42	1/29	1/52	1/55
43	1/21	1/39	1/41
44	1/16	1/29	1/30

Source: Snijders & Nicolaides, 1996.

Saving Young Lives: Childhood Immunizations (Chapter 5)

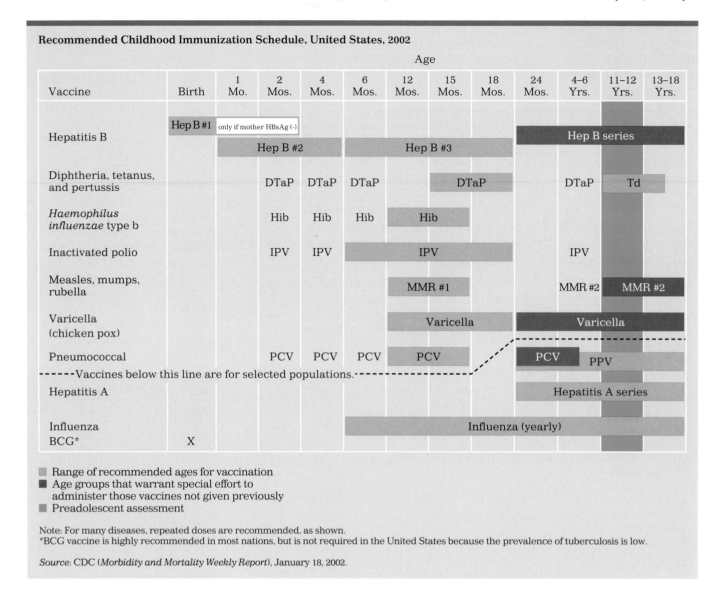

Recommended Childhood Immunization Schedule, United States, 2002

Vaccine	Birth	1 Mo.	2 Mos.	4 Mos.	6 Mos.	12 Mos.	15 Mos.	18 Mos.	24 Mos.	4–6 Yrs.	11–12 Yrs.	13–18 Yrs.
Hepatitis B	Hep B #1 only if mother HBsAg (–)	Hep B #2				Hep B #3				Hep B series		
Diphtheria, tetanus, and pertussis		DTaP	DTaP	DTaP		DTaP				DTaP	Td	
Haemophilus influenzae type b		Hib	Hib	Hib	Hib							
Inactivated polio		IPV	IPV		IPV					IPV		
Measles, mumps, rubella						MMR #1				MMR #2	MMR #2	
Varicella (chicken pox)						Varicella			Varicella			
Pneumococcal		PCV	PCV	PCV	PCV				PCV	PPV		

-----Vaccines below this line are for selected populations.-----

Hepatitis A										Hepatitis A series		
Influenza					Influenza (yearly)							
BCG*	X											

- Range of recommended ages for vaccination
- Age groups that warrant special effort to administer those vaccines not given previously
- Preadolescent assessment

Note: For many diseases, repeated doses are recommended, as shown.
*BCG vaccine is highly recommended in most nations, but is not required in the United States because the prevalence of tuberculosis is low.

Source: CDC (*Morbidity and Mortality Weekly Report*), January 18, 2002.

First Sounds and First Words: Similarities Among Many Languages (Chapter 6)

	BABY'S WORD FOR:	
LANGUAGE	Mother	Father
English	mama, mommy	dada, daddy
Spanish	mama	papa
French	maman, mama	papa
Italian	mamma	babbo, papa
Latvian	mama	tēte
Syrian Arabic	mama	baba
Bantu	ba-mama	taata
Swahili	mama	baba
Sanskrit	nana	tata
Hebrew	ema	abba
Korean	oma	apa

!Answer to Observational Quiz (from page A-2): Asian-Americans, whose share of the U.S. population has quadrupled in the past 30 years.

Mothering: Knowledge Over Instinct (Chapter 7)

Differentiating excellent from destructive mothering is not easy, once basic needs for food and protection are met. However, as the Toni and Jacob examples in Chapter 7 make clear, psychosocial development depends on responsive parent–infant relationships. Breast-feeding is one sign of intimacy between mother and infant. Regions of the world differ dramatically in rates of breast-feeding, with the highest worldwide in Southeast Asia, where half of all 2-year-olds are still breast-fed.

In the United States, the South is lowest and the West is highest in rate of breast-feeding at one month. The overall rate increased from 39 percent in 1993 to 52 percent in 1999. In the United States, other factors that affect the likelihood of breast-feeding (not shown here) are ethnicity (Latinas are more likely, and African-Americans less likely, to breast-feed than European-Americans); maternal age (a positive correlation between age and breast-feeding); and newborn weight (low-birthweight babies are less likely to be breast-fed). The most marked influence of all is the mother's education.

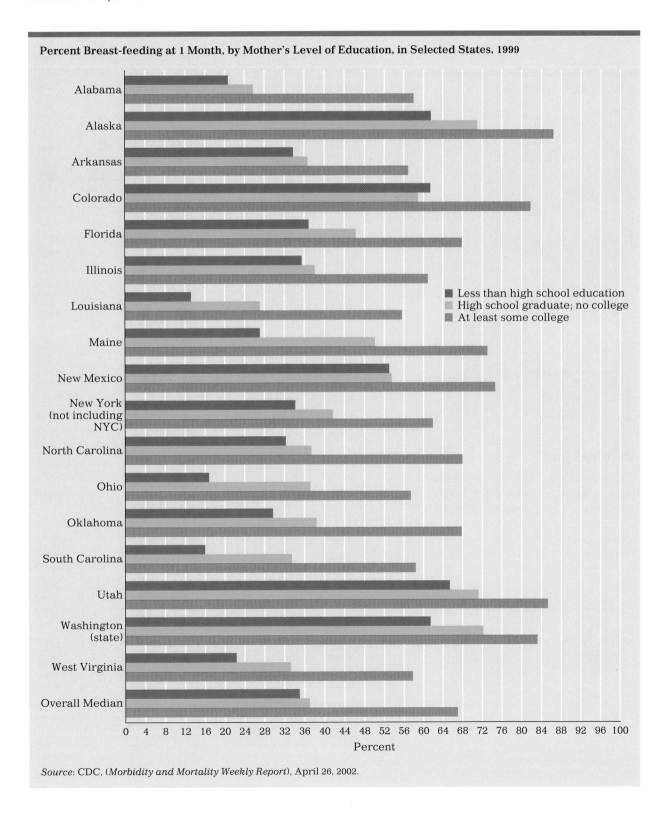

Percent Breast-feeding at 1 Month, by Mother's Level of Education, in Selected States, 1999

Legend:
- Less than high school education
- High school graduate; no college
- At least some college

States: Alabama, Alaska, Arkansas, Colorado, Florida, Illinois, Louisiana, Maine, New Mexico, New York (not including NYC), North Carolina, Ohio, Oklahoma, South Carolina, Utah, Washington (state), West Virginia, Overall Median

Percent (x-axis): 0 4 8 12 16 20 24 28 32 36 40 44 48 52 56 60 64 68 72 76 80 84 88 92 96 100

Source: CDC, (*Morbidity and Mortality Weekly Report*), April 26, 2002.

Height Gains from Birth to Age 18 (Chapter 8)

The range of height (on this page) and weight (see page A-7) of children in the United States. The columns labeled "50th" (the fiftieth percentile) show the average; the columns labeled "90th" (the ninetieth percentile) show the size of children taller and heavier than 90 percent of their contemporaries; and the columns labeled "10th" (the tenth percentile) show the size of children who are taller than only 10 percent of their peers. Note that girls are slightly shorter, on average, than boys.

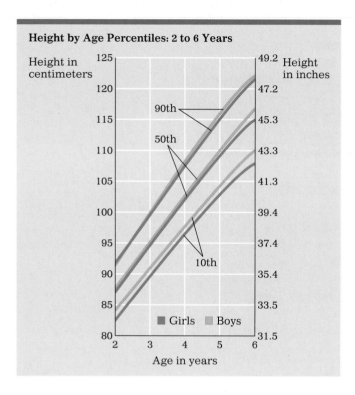

Height by Age Percentiles: 2 to 6 Years

Same Data, Different Form

The columns of numbers in the table at the right provide detailed and precise information about height ranges for every year of childhood. The illustration above shows the same information in graphic form for ages 2–6. The same is done for weight ranges on page A-7. Ages 2–6 are singled out because that is the period during which a child's eating habits are set. Which form of data presentation do you think is easier to understand?

Length in Centimeters (and Inches)

AGE	BOYS: PERCENTILES			GIRLS: PERCENTILES		
	10th	50th	90th	10th	50th	90th
Birth	47.5 (18¾)	50.5 (20)	53.5 (21)	46.5 (18¼)	49.9 (19¾)	52.0 (20½)
1 month	51.3 (20¼)	54.6 (21½)	57.7 (22¾)	50.2 (19¾)	53.5 (21)	56.1 (22)
3 months	57.7 (22¾)	61.1 (24)	64.5 (25½)	56.2 (22¼)	59.5 (23½)	62.7 (24¾)
6 months	64.4 (25¼)	67.8 (26¾)	71.3 (28)	62.6 (24¾)	65.9 (26)	69.4 (27¼)
9 months	69.1 (27¼)	72.3 (28½)	75.9 (30)	67.0 (26½)	70.4 (27¾)	74.0 (29¼)
12 months	72.8 (28¾)	76.1 (30)	79.8 (31½)	70.8 (27¾)	74.3 (29¼)	78.0 (30¾)
18 months	78.7 (31)	82.4 (32½)	86.6 (34)	77.2 (30½)	80.9 (31¾)	85.0 (33½)
24 months	83.5 (32¾)	87.6 (34½)	92.2 (36¼)	82.5 (32½)	86.5 (34)	90.8 (35¾)
3 years	90.3 (35½)	94.9 (37¼)	100.1 (39½)	89.3 (35¼)	94.1 (37)	99.0 (39)
4 years	97.3 (38¼)	102.9 (40½)	108.2 (42½)	96.4 (38)	101.6 (40)	106.6 (42)
5 years	103.7 (40¾)	109.9 (43¼)	115.4 (45½)	102.7 (40½)	108.4 (42¾)	113.8 (44¾)
6 years	109.6 (43¼)	116.1 (45¾)	121.9 (48)	108.4 (42¾)	114.6 (45)	120.8 (47½)
7 years	115.0 (45¼)	121.7 (48)	127.9 (50¼)	113.6 (44¾)	120.6 (47½)	127.6 (50¼)
8 years	120.2 (47¼)	127.0 (50)	133.6 (52½)	118.7 (46¾)	126.4 (49¾)	134.2 (52¾)
9 years	125.2 (49¼)	132.2 (52)	139.4 (55)	123.9 (48¾)	132.2 (52)	140.7 (55½)
10 years	130.1 (51¼)	137.5 (54¼)	145.5 (57¼)	129.5 (51)	138.3 (54½)	147.2 (58)
11 years	135.1 (53¼)	143.33 (56½)	152.1 (60)	135.6 (53½)	144.8 (57)	153.7 (60½)
12 years	140.3 (55¼)	149.7 (59)	159.4 (62¾)	142.3 (56)	151.5 (59¾)	160.0 (63)
13 years	145.8 (57½)	156.5 (61½)	167.0 (65¾)	148.0 (58¼)	157.1 (61¾)	165.3 (65)
14 years	151.8 (59¾)	63.1 (64¼)	173.8 (68½)	151.5 (59¾)	160.4 (63¼)	168.7 (66½)
15 years	158.2 (62¼)	169.0 (66½)	178.9 (70½)	153.2 (60¼)	161.8 (63¾)	170.5 (67¼)
16 years	163.9 (64½)	173.5 (68¼)	182.4 (71¾)	154.1 (60¾)	162.4 (64)	171.1 (67¼)
17 years	167.7 (66)	176.2 (69¼)	184.4 (72½)	155.1 (61)	163.1 (64¼)	171.2 (67½)
18 years	168.7 (66½)	176.8 (69½)	185.3 (73)	156.0 (61½)	163.7 (64½)	171.0 (67¼)

Source: These data are those of the National Center for Health Statistics (NCHS), Health Resources Administration, DHHS. They were based on studies of The Fels Research Institute, Yellow Springs, Ohio. These data were first made available with the help of William M. Moore, M.D., of Ross Laboratories, who supplied the conversion from metric measurements to approximate inches and pounds. This help is gratefully acknowledged.

Weight Gains from Birth to Age 18 (Chapter 8)

These height and weight charts present rough guidelines; a child might differ from these norms and be quite healthy and normal. However, if a particular child shows a discrepancy between height and weight (for instance, at the 90th percentile in height but only the 20th percentile in weight) or is much larger or smaller than most children the same age, a pediatrician should see if disease, malnutrition, or genetic abnormality is part of the reason.

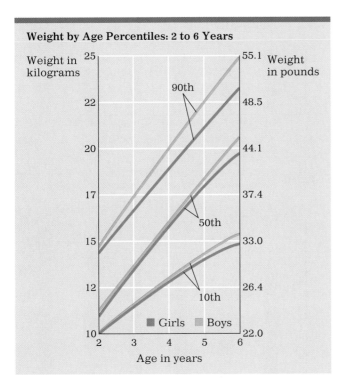

Weight by Age Percentiles: 2 to 6 Years

Comparisons

Notice that the height trajectories in the graph on page A-6 are much closer together than the weight trajectories shown in the graph above. By age 18, the height range amounts to only about 6 inches, but there is a difference of about 65 pounds between the 10th and the 90th percentiles.

❓ Critical Thinking Question (see answer, page A-8): How can this discrepancy between height and weight ranges be explained?

Weight in Kilograms (and Pounds)

AGE	BOYS: PERCENTILES			GIRLS: PERCENTILES		
	10th	50th	90th	10th	50th	90th
Birth	2.78 (6¼)	3.27 (7¼)	3.82 (8½)	2.58 (5¾)	3.23 (7)	3.64 (8)
1 month	3.43 (7½)	4.29 (9½)	5.14 (11¼)	3.22 (7)	3.98 (8¾)	4.65 (10¼)
3 months	4.78 (10½)	5.98 (13¼)	7.14 (15¾)	4.47 (9¾)	5.40 (12)	6.39 (14)
6 months	6.61 (14½)	7.85 (17¼)	9.10 (20)	6.12 (13½)	7.21 (16)	8.38 (18½)
9 months	7.95 (17½)	9.18 (20¼)	10.49 (23¼)	7.34 (16¼)	8.56 (18¾)	9.83 (21¾)
12 months	8.84 (19½)	10.15 (22½)	11.54 (25½)	8.19 (18)	9.53 (21)	10.87 (24)
18 months	9.92 (21¾)	11.47 (25¼)	13.05 (28¾)	9.30 (20½)	10.82 (23¾)	12.30 (27)
24 months	10.85 (24)	12.59 (27¾)	14.29 (31½)	10.26 (22½)	11.90 (26¼)	13.57 (30)
3 years	12.58 (27¾)	14.62 (32¼)	16.95 (37¼)	12.26 (27)	14.10 (31)	16.54 (36½)
4 years	14.24 (31½)	16.69 (36¾)	19.32 (42½)	13.84 (30½)	15.96 (35¼)	18.93 (41¾)
5 years	15.96 (35¼)	18.67 (41¼)	21.70 (47¾)	15.26 (33¾)	17.66 (39)	21.23 (46¾)
6 years	17.72 (39)	20.69 (45½)	24.31 (53½)	16.72 (36¾)	19.52 (43)	23.89 (52¾)
7 years	19.53 (43)	22.85 (50¼)	27.36 (60¼)	18.39 (40½)	21.84 (48¼)	27.39 (60½)
8 years	21.39 (47¼)	25.30 (55¾)	31.06 (68½)	20.45 (45)	24.84 (54¾)	32.04 (70¾)
9 years	23.33 (51½)	28.13 (62)	35.57 (78½)	22.92 (50½)	28.46 (62¾)	37.60 (83)
10 years	25.52 (56¼)	31.44 (69¼)	40.80 (90)	25.76 (56¾)	32.55 (71¾)	43.70 (96¼)
11 years	28.17 (62)	35.30 (77¾)	46.57 (102¾)	28.97 (63¾)	36.95 (81½)	49.96 (110¼)
12 years	31.46 (69¼)	39.78 (87¾)	52.73 (116¼)	32.53 (71¼)	41.53 (91½)	55.99 (123½)
13 years	35.60 (78½)	44.95 (99)	59.12 (130¼)	36.35 (80¼)	46.10 (101¾)	61.45 (135½)
14 years	40.64 (89½)	50.77 (112)	65.57 (144½)	40.11 (88½)	50.28 (110¾)	66.04 (145½)
15 years	46.06 (101½)	56.71 (125)	71.91 (158½)	43.38 (95¾)	53.68 (118¼)	69.64 (153¼)
16 years	51.16 (112¾)	62.10 (137)	77.97 (172)	45.78 (101)	55.89 (123¼)	71.68 (158)
17 years	55.28 (121¾)	66.31 (146¼)	83.58 (184¼)	47.04 (103¾)	56.69 (125)	72.38 (159½)
18 years	57.89 (127½)	68.88 (151¾)	88.41 (195)	47.47 (104¾)	56.62 (124¾)	72.25 (159¼)

Source: Data are those of the National Center for Health Statistics, Health Resources Administration, DHHS, collected in its Health Examination Surveys.

Day Care and Family Income (Chapter 9)

Note that, in both years, the wealthier families were less likely to have children exclusively in parental care and more likely to have children in center-based care.

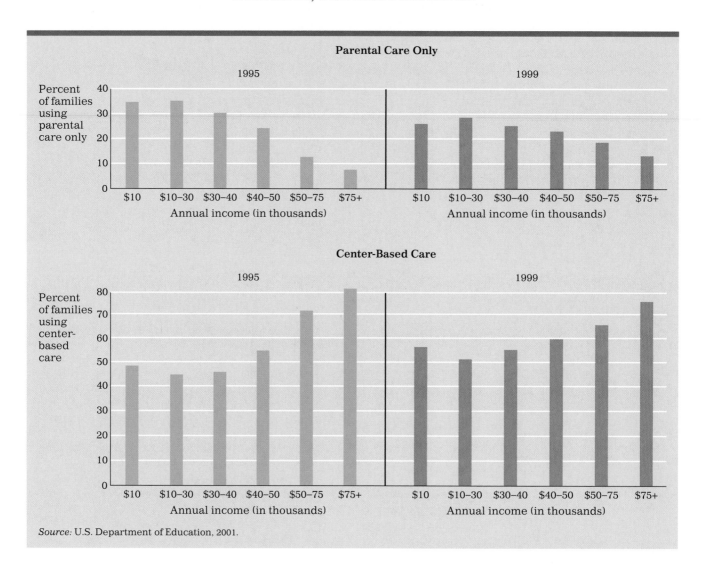

Parental Care Only

Source: U.S. Department of Education, 2001.

! *Answer to Critical Thinking Question*
(from page A-7): Nutrition is generally adequate in the United States, and that is why height differences are small. But as a result of the strong influence that family and culture have on eating habits, almost half of all North Americans are overweight or obese.

grandparent family A family that consists of children living with their grandparents instead of with their parents. (p. 410)

graspability The perception of whether or not an object is of the proper shape, size, texture, and distance to afford grasping. (p. 178)

gross motor skills Physical abilities involving large body movements, such as waving the arms, walking, and jumping. (p. 150)

guided participation In sociocultural theory, the process by which a skilled person helps a novice learn by providing not only instruction but also a direct, shared involvement in the learning process through social experiences and exploration. (pp. 49, 266)

H

habituation The process of getting used to an object or event through repeated exposure to it. (p. 176)

head-sparing A phenomenon by which the brain continues to grow even though the body stops growing as a result of malnutrition. (p. 136)

hidden curriculum The unofficial, unstated, or implicit rules and priorities that influence the academic curriculum and every other aspect of school learning. (p. 386)

high risk Term used by educators to refer to a child whose chances of poor achievement are notably higher than average. More generally, high risk refers to someone with an increased likelihood of some negative experience, such as catching a disease or dropping out of school. (p. 288)

holophrase A single word that is used to express a complete, meaningful thought. (p. 188)

Human Genome Project An international effort to map the complete human genetic code. (p. 70)

human immunodeficiency virus (HIV) A virus that gradually overwhelms the body's immune responses, leaving the individual defenseless against a host of pathologies that eventually manifest themselves as AIDS. (p. 114)

hypothesis A specific prediction that is stated in such a way that it can be tested and either confirmed or refuted. (p. 20)

I

identification A defense mechanism that lets a person symbolically take on the behaviors and attitudes of someone more powerful than him- or herself. (p. 316)

identity In Piaget's theory, the idea that certain characteristics of an object remain the same even if other characteristics change. (p. 361)

imaginary companion A make-believe person or other creature that a young child talks to and plays with. (p. 277)

immunization A process that stimulates the body's immune system to defend against attack by a particular contagious disease. (p. 155)

implantation Beginning about a week after conception, the burrowing of the organism into the lining of the uterus, where it can be nourished and protected during growth. (p. 104)

implicit memory Memory of events, objects, and experiences that can be recognized when certain cues are present but cannot be recalled without reminders. (p. 184)

inclusion A policy under which learning-disabled children are included in the regular class, as in mainstreaming, but are supervised by a specially trained teacher or paraprofessional for all or part of the day. (p. 354)

independent variable In an experiment, the variable that is introduced or changed to see what effect it has on the dependent variable. (p. 23)

indulgent parenting An abusive style of child rearing in which the parents accommodate the child's every whim. (p. 310)

industry versus inferiority The fourth of Erikson's eight crises of psychosexual development, in which school-age children attempt to master many skills and develop a sense of themselves as either industrious and competent or incompetent and inferior. (p. 393)

infantile amnesia The inability, hypothesized by Freud, to remember anything that happened before the age of 2 or anything except very important events before the age of 5. (p. 182)

infertile Referring to a couple who are unable to produce a baby after at least a year of trying. (p. 76)

informal code Speech that is characterized by the use of relatively few words and simpler syntax and by reliance on gestures and intonation to convey meaning. Also called *restricted code*. (p. 372)

information-processing theory A perspective that compares human thinking processes, by analogy, to computer analysis of data, from sensory input through brain reactions, connections, and stored memories to output. (p. 176)

initiative versus guilt The third of Erikson's eight stages of psychosocial development, in which the young child eagerly begins new projects and activities and feels guilt when his or her efforts result in failure or criticism. (p. 300)

injury control/harm reduction The idea that accidents are not random but can be made less harmful with proper control. In practice, this means anticipating, controlling, and preventing dangerous activities. (p. 248)

insecure attachment A relationship that is unstable or unpredictable; in infancy such relationships are characterized by the child's fear, anxiety, anger, clinging, or seeming indifference toward the caregiver. (p. 219)

insecure-avoidant Referring to a pattern of attachment in which one person tries to avoid any connection with another, as an infant who is uninterested in the caregiver's presence or departure and ignores the caregiver on reunion. (p. 219)

insecure-resistant/ambivalent Referring to a pattern of attachment in which anxiety and uncertainty keeps one person clinging to another, as an infant who resists active exploration, is very upset at separation, and both resists and seeks contact on reunion. (p. 219)

instrumental aggression Aggressive behavior that is aimed at getting or keeping an object desired by another. (p. 303)

interaction effect The phenomenon in which a teratogen's potential for causing harm increases when it is combined with another teratogen or another risk factor. (p. 113)

internalizing problems Difficulties that arise from a person's tendency to internalize emotions, or to inhibit their expression, being fearful and withdrawn or inflicting harm on themselves. (p. 295)

in vitro fertilization (IVF) A technique for helping couples conceive in which ova are surgically removed from a woman, mixed with sperm, and inserted into the woman's uterus once viable zygotes have formed. (p. 76)

IQ tests Aptitude tests designed to measure a person's intellectual aptitude, or ability to learn in school. This aptitude was originally defined as mental age divided by chronological age, times 100—hence, intelligence quotient, or IQ). An example:
Actual age of three children: 12, 12, 12
Mental ages of the three: 15, 12, 8
IQ of each of these three:
$15/12 = 1.25 \times 100 = 125$ (superior)
$12/12 = 1 \times 100 = 100$ (average)
$8/12 = .75 \times 100 = 75$ (slow learner)
(p. 346)

irreversibility A characteristic of preoperational thought in which the young child fails to recognize that reversing a process can restore whatever existed before the transformation occurred. (p. 265)

K

kinship care A form of foster care in which a relative of the maltreated child becomes the approved caregiver. (p. 257)

knowledge base A broad body of knowledge in a particular subject area that makes it easier to master new learning in that area. (p. 364)

kwashiorkor A disease of chronic malnutrition in which a deficiency of protein causes the child's face, legs, and abdomen to bloat, or swell with water, and makes the child more vulnerable to other diseases, such as measles, diarrhea, and influenza. (p. 161)

L

language acquisition device (LAD) Chomsky's term for a hypothesized brain structure responsible for the innate human ability to learn language, including the basic aspects of grammar. (p. 192)

latency Freud's term for middle childhood, during which children's emotional drives are quieter, their psychosexual needs are repressed, and their unconscious conflicts are submerged. (p. 393)

lateralization Literally, "sidedness," here referring to the differentiation of the two sides of the body or brain so that one side specializes in a certain function; brain later-

alization means that the left side of the brain controls the right side of the body, and vice versa. (p. 240)

learning-disabled Having a marked delay in a particular area of learning that is not associated with any obvious physical handicap, overall mental retardation, or unusually stressful home environment. (p. 346)

least restrictive environment (LRE) A legally required school setting that offers children with special needs as much freedom as possible to benefit from the instruction available to other children; often, in practice, the general classroom. (p. 353)

life-span perspective A view of human development that takes into account all phases of life, not just childhood or adulthood. (p. 5)

linear change A process in which change occurs in a gradual, regular, predictable sequence. (p. 2)

"little scientist" Piaget's term for the stage-five toddler (age 12 to 18 months), who actively experiments with objects to learn about their properties. (p. 174)

long-term memory The component of the information-processing system in which virtually limitless amounts of information can be stored indefinitely. (p. 364)

longitudinal research A research method in which the same individuals are studied over a long period of time. (p. 28)

low birthweight (LBW) A birthweight of less than $5\frac{1}{2}$ pounds (2,500 grams). (p. 119)

M

mainstreaming A policy (mandated by the Education of All Handicapped Children Act in 1975) under which children with special needs must be taught in "the least restrictive environment" available, which usually means that they are taught with other children in the general classroom. (p. 353)

marasmus A disease of severe protein–calorie malnutrition in which growth stops, body tissues waste away, and the infant eventually dies. (p. 161)

mental combinations Sequences of actions that the toddler in Piaget's stage six of sensorimotor intelligence (age 18 to 24 months) develops intellectually before actually performing them. (p. 174)

mentally retarded Having severe delays in all areas of mental development. (p. 346)

metacognition "Thinking about thinking," or the ability to evaluate a cognitive task to determine how best to accomplish it, and then to monitor and adjust one's performance on that task. (p. 366)

middle childhood The period from age 7 to 11. (p. 331)

minitheories Theories that focus on some specific area of development but are less general and comprehensive than the grand theories. (p. 36)

modeling In social learning theory, the process in which people observe and then copy the behavior of others. (p. 43)

molecular genetics The study of genetics at the molecular level, including the study of the chemical codes that constitute a particular molecule of DNA. (p. 83)

monozygotic twins Twins who have identical genes because they were formed from one zygote that split into two identical organisms very early in development. (p. 75)

morality of care In Gilligan's view, the tendency of females to be reluctant to judge right and wrong in absolute terms because they are socialized to be nurturant, compassionate, and nonjudgmental. (p. 375)

morality of justice In Gilligan's view, the tendency of males to emphasize justice over compassion, judging right and wrong in absolute terms. (p. 375)

multicontextual A characteristic of development, referring to the fact that each human life takes place within a number of contexts—historical, cultural, and socioeconomic. (p. 5)

multicultural A characteristic of development, referring to the fact that it takes place within many cultural settings worldwide and thus reflects a multitude of values, traditions, and tools for living. (p. 5)

multidirectional A characteristic of development, referring to its nonlinear progression—gains and losses, compensations and deficits, predictable and unexpected changes. (p. 5)

multidisciplinary A characteristic of development, referring to the fact that many academic fields contribute data and insight to the science of development. (p. 5)

Maccoby, Eleanor E. (2000). Parenting and its effects on children: On reading and misreading behavior genetics. *Annual Review of Psychology, 51,* 1–27.

Maccoby, Eleanor E. (2002). Parenting effects: Issues and controversies. In John G. Borkowski, Sharon Landesman Ramey & Marie Bristol-Power (Eds.). *Parenting and the child's world: Influences on academic, intellectual, and social-emotional development.* Mahwah, NJ: Erlbaum. 35–46.

Macfie, Jenny, Cicchetti, Dante, & Toth, Sheree L. (2001). The development of dissociation in maltreated preschool-aged children. *Development and Psychopathology, 13,* 233–254.

Macpherson, Alison, Roberts, Ian, & Pless, I. Barry. (1998). Children's exposure to traffic and pedestrian injuries. *American Journal of Public Health, 88,* 1840–1845.

Maddox, John. (1993). Willful public misunderstanding of genetics. *Nature, 364,* 281.

Magnusson, David. (1996). *The life-span development of individuals: Behavioral, neurobiological, and psychosocial perspectives.* Cambridge, England: Cambridge University Press.

Magnusson, David. (2000). The individual as the organizing principle in psychological inquiry: A holistic approach. In Lars R. Bergman, Robert B. Cairns, Lars-Goran Nilsson, & Lars Nystdt (Eds.), *Developmental science and the holistic approach* (pp. 34–48). Mahwah, NJ: Erlbaum.

Mahady Wilton, Melissa M., Craig, Wendy M., & Pepler, Debra J. (2000). Emotional regulation and display in classroom victims of bullying: Characteristic expression of affect, coping styles and relevant contextual factors. *Social Development, 9,* 226–245.

Mahler, Margaret S., Pine, Fred, & Bergman, A. (1975). *The psychological birth of the human infant: Symbiosis and individuation.* New York: International Universities Press.

Mahowald, Mary B., Verp, Marion S., & Anderson, R.R. (1998). Genetic counseling: Clinical and ethical challenges. *Annual Review of Genetics, 32,* 547–559.

Maier, Susan E., Chen, Wei-Jung A., & West, James R. (1996). The effects of timing and duration of alcohol exposure on development of the fetal brain. In Ernest L. Abel (Ed.), *Fetal alcohol syndrome: From mechanism to prevention.* Boca Raton, FL: CRC Press.

Main, Mary. (1995). Recent studies in attachment. In Susan Goldberg, Roy Muir, & John Kerr (Eds.), *Attachment theory: Social, developmental, and clinical perspectives.* Hillsdale, NJ: Analytic Press.

Mandler, Jean M., & McDonough, Laraine. (1998). On developing a knowledge base in infancy. *Developmental Psychology, 34,* 1274–1288.

Mange, Elaine Johnson, & Mange, Arthur P. (1999). *Basic human genetics.* Sunderland, MA: Sinauer Associates.

Manning, Wendy D., & Smock, Pamela J. (2000). "Swapping" families: Serial parenting and economic support for children. *Journal of Marriage and the Family, 62,* 111–122.

Marcus, Gary F. (2000). *Pabiku* and *Ga Ti Ga*: Two mechanisms infants use to learn about the world. *Current Directions in Psychological Science, 9,* 145–147.

Markman, Ellen M. (1989). *Categorization and naming in children: Problems of induction.* Cambridge, MA: MIT Press.

Markus, Hazel R., & Kitayama, S. (1991). Culture and the self: Implications for cognition, emotion, and motivation. *Psychological Review, 98,* 224–253.

Marsh, Herbert E., Hau, Kit-Tai, & Kong, Chit-Kwong. (2000). Late immersion and language of instruction in Hong Kong high schools: Achievement growth in language and nonlanguage subjects. *Harvard Educational Review, 70,* 302–346.

Marshall, Paul. (2001). *Religious freedom in the world.* Nashville, TN: Broadman and Holman.

Marsiglio, William, Amato, Paul, Day, Randal D., & Lamb, Michael D. (2000). Scholarship on fatherhood in the 1990s and beyond. *Journal of Marriage and the Family, 62,* 1173–1191.

Martin, Carol Lynn, Eisenbud, Lisa, & Rose, Hilary. (1995). Children's gender-based reasoning about toys. *Child Development, 66,* 1453–1471.

Martin, Carol Lynn, & Fabes, Richard. (2001). The stability and consequences of young children's same-sex peer interactions. *Developmental Psychology, 37,* 431–446.

Martin, Joyce A., Hamilton, Brady E., Ventura, Stephanie J., Menacker, Fay, & Park, Melissa M. (2002, February 12). Births: Final data for 2000. *National Vital Statistics Report, 50*(5).

Martin, Sandra L., English, Kathleen T., Clark, Kathryn Andersen, Cilenti, Dorothy, & Kupper, Lawrence L. (1996). Violence and substance use among North Carolina pregnant women. *American Journal of Public Health, 86,* 991–998.

Martin, Sandra L., Kim, Haesook, Kupper, Lawrence I., Meyer, Robert E., & Hays, Melissa. (1997). Is incarceration during pregnancy associated with infant birthweight? *American Journal of Public Health, 87,* 1526–1531.

Marvin, Robert S. (1997). Ethological and general systems perspectives on child-parent attachment during the toddler and preschool years. In Nancy L. Segal, Glenn E. Weisfeld, & Carol C. Weisfeld (Eds.), *Uniting psychology and biology: Integrative perspectives on human development.* Washington, DC: American Psychological Association.

Masataka, Nobuo. (1992). Early ontogeny of vocal behavior of Japanese infants in response to maternal speech. *Child Development, 63,* 1177–1185.

Masoro, Edward J. (1999). *Challenges of biological aging.* New York: Springer.

Masten, Ann S. (2001). Ordinary magic. *American Psychologist, 56,* 227–238.

Masten, Ann S., & Coatsworth, J. Douglas. (1998). The development of competence in favorable and unfavorable environments: Lessons from research on successful children. *American Psychologist, 53,* 205–220.

Masterpasqua, Frank. (1997). Toward a dynamic developmental understanding of disorder. In Frank Masterpasqua & Phyllis A. Perna (Eds.), *The psychological meaning of chaos: Translating theory into practice.* Washington, DC: American Psychological Association.

Masterpasqua, Frank, & Perna, Phyllis A. (1997). *The psychological meaning of chaos: Translating theory into practice.* Washington, DC: American Psychological Association.

Matsuda, Fumiko. (2001). Development of concepts of interrelationships among duration, distance, and speed. *International Journal of Behavioral Development, 25,* 466–480.

Mauro, Christine F., & Harris, Yvette R. (2000). The influence of maternal child-rearing attitudes and teaching behaviors on preschoolers' delay of gratification. *Journal of Genetic Psychology, 161,* 292–306.

Mayberry, Rachel I., & Nicoladis, Elena. (2000). Gesture reflects language development. *Current Directions in Psychological Science, 9,* 192–195.

Mayes, Susan D., Calhoun, Susan L., & Crowell, Errin W. (2000). Learning disabilities and ADHD: Overlapping spectrum disorders. *Journal of Learning Disabilities, 33,* 417–424.

McCarty, Michael E., & Ashmead, Daniel H. (1999). Visual control of reaching and grasping in infants. *Developmental Psychology, 35,* 620–631.

McCloskey, Laura Ann, & Stuewig, Jeffrey. (2001). The quality of peer relationships among children exposed to family violence. *Development and Psychopathology, 13,* 83–96.

McCrae, Robert R., Costa, Paul T. Jr., de Lima, Margarida Pedroso, Simões, António, Ostendorf, Fritz, Angleitner, Alois, et al. (1999). Age differences in personality across the adult life span: Parallels in five cultures. *Developmental Psychology, 35,* 466–477.

McDevitt, Thomas M. (1998). *World population profiles: 1998.* Washington, DC: U. S. Commerce Department.

McDonald, Katrina Bell, & Armstrong, Elizabeth M. (2001). De-romanticizing black intergenerational support: The questionable expectations of welfare reform. *Journal of Marriage and the Family, 63,* 213–223.

McDonough, Laraine, & Mandler, Jean M. (1994). Very long term recall in infants: Infantile amnesia reconsidered. In Robyn Fivush (Ed.), *Long-term retention of infant memories.* Hove, England: Erlbaum.

McGroder, Sharon M. (2000). Parenting among low-income, African-American single mothers with preschool-age children: Patterns, predictors, and developmental correlates. *Child Development, 71,* 752–771.

McGue, Matthew. (1995). Mediators and moderators of alcoholism inheritance. In J.R. Turner, L.R. Cardon, & J. K. Hewitt (Eds.), *Behavior genetic approaches to behavioral medicine.* New York: Plenum Press.

McGuffin, Peter, Riley, Brien, & Plomin, Robert. (2001). Toward behavioral genomics. *Science, 291,* 1232–1249.

McKenzie, Kwame, & Murray, Robin M. (1999). Risk factors for psychosis in the U.K. Afro-Caribbean population. In D. Bhugra &
V. Bahl (Eds.), *Ethnicity: An agenda for mental health* (pp. 48–59). London: Gaskell.

McKusick, Victor A. (1994). *Mendelian inheritance in humans* (10th ed.). Baltimore: Johns Hopkins University Press.

McLanahan, Sara S., & Sandefur, Gary. (1994). *Growing up with a single parent: What hurts, what helps.* Cambridge, MA: Harvard University Press.

McLoyd, Vonnie C. (1998a). Children in poverty: Development, public policy, and practice. In William Damon (Series Ed.), Irving E. Sigel, & K. Ann Renninger (Vol. Eds.), *Handbook of child psychology*: Vol. 4. *Child psychology in practice* (5th ed., pp. 135–210). New York: Wiley.

McLoyd, Vonnie C. (1998b). Socioeconomic disadvantage and child development. *American Psychologist, 2,* 185–204.

McLoyd, Vonnie C., & Smith, Julia. (2002). Physical discipline and behavior problems in African American, European American, and Hispanic children: Emotional support as a moderator. *Journal of Marriage and the Family, 64,* 40–53.

Meadows, Sara. (1993). *The child as thinker: The development and acquisition of cognition in childhood.* London: Routledge.

Medved, Michael. (1995, October). Hollywood's 3 big lies. *Reader's Digest, 147,* 155–158.

Meis, Paul J., Goldenberg, Brian, Mercer, Brian M., Moawad, Atef, Das, Anita, McNellis, et al. (1995). The preterm prediction study: Significance of vaginal infections. *American Journal of Obstetrics and Gynecology, 173,* 1231–1235.

Melhuish, Edward C. (2001). The quest for quality in early day care and preschool experience continues. *International Journal of Behavioral Development, 25,* 1–6.

Merrell, Kenneth W., & Gimpel, Gretchen A. (1998). *Social skills of children and adolescents: Conceptualization, assessment, treatment.* Mahwah, NJ: Erlbaum.

Merriman, William E. (1998). Competition, attention, and young children's lexical processing. In B. MacWhinney (Ed.), *The emergence of language.* Mahwah, NJ: Erlbaum.

Merzenich, Michael M. (2001). Cortical plasticity contributing to child development. In James L. McClelland & Robert S. Siegler (Eds.), *Mechanisms of cognitive develop-*
ment: Behavioral and neural perspectives (pp. 67–96). Mahwah, NJ: Erlbaum.

Messinger, Daniel S., Fogel, Alan, & Dickson, K. Laurie. (1999). What's in a smile? *Developmental Psychology, 35,* 701–708.

Metallinos-Katsaras, Elizabeth & Gorman, Kathleen S. (1999). Effects of undernutrition on growth and development. In Daniel B. Kessler and Peter Dawson (Eds.). *Failure to thrive and pediatric undernutrition* (pp. 375–384). Baltimore: Brooks.

Midanik, Lorraine, & Greenfield, Thomas K. (2000). Trends in social consequences and dependence symptoms in the United States: The national alcohol surveys, 1984–1995. *American Journal of Public Health, 90,* 53–56.

Miller, Alison L., & Olson, Sheryl L. (2000). Emotional expressiveness during peer conflicts: A predictor of social maladjustment among high-risk preschoolers. *Journal of Abnormal Child Psychology, 28,* 339–352.

Miller, Brent C., Fan, Xitao, Christensen, Mathew, Grotevant, Harold D., & van Dulmen, Manfred. (2000). Comparisons of adopted and non-adopted adolescents in a large, nationally representative sample. *Child Development, 71,* 1458–1473.

Miller, Jane E., & Davis, Diane. (1997). Poverty history, marital history, and quality of children's home environments. *Journal of Marriage and the Family, 59,* 996–1007.

Miller, M., Bowen, J. R., Gibson, F. L., Hand, P. J., & Ungerer, Judy A. (2001). Behavior problems in extremely low birth-weight children at 5 and 8 years of age. *Child: Care, Health, and Development, 27,* 569–581.

Miller, Orlando J., & Therman, Eeva. (2001). *Human chromosomes* (4th ed.). New York: Springer.

Miller, Patricia H. (2002). *Theories of developmental psychology* (4th ed.). New York: Worth Publishers.

Mills, James L., McPartlin, Joseph M., Kirke, Peadar N., & Lee, Young J. (1995). Homocysteine metabolism in pregnancies complicated by neural-tube defects. *Lancet, 345,* 149–151.

Min, Pyong Gap. (2000). Korean Americans' language use. In Sandra Lee McKay & Sau-ling Cynthia Wong (Eds.), *New immigrants in the United States* (pp. 306–332). Cambridge, England: Cambridge University Press.

Mitchell, Katherine. (2001). Education for democratic citizenship: Transnationalism, multiculturalism, and the limits of liberalism. *Harvard Educational Review, 71,* 51–78.

Mitchell, Peter, & Kikuno, Haruo. (2000). Belief as construction: Inference and processing bias. In Peter Mitchell & Kevin J. Riggs (Eds.), *Children's reasoning and the mind* (pp. 281–300). Hove, England: Psychology Press.

Mitchell, Peter, & Riggs, Kevin J. (Eds.). (2000). *Children's reasoning and the mind.* Hove, England: Psychology Press.

Moats, Louisa C. (2001). Overcoming the language gap: Invest generously in teacher professional development. *American Educator, 25*(2), 4–9.

Moffitt, Terrie E. (1993b). The neuro-psychology of conduct disorder. *Development and Psychopathology, 5,* 135–151.

Moffitt, Terrie E. (1997b). Helping poor mothers and children. *Journal of the American Medical Association, 278,* 680–682.

Moffitt, Terrie E., & Caspi, Avshalom. (2001). Childhood predictors differentiate life-course persistent and adolescence-limited antisocial pathways among males and females. *Development and Psychopathology, 13,* 355–375.

Moffitt, Terrie E., Caspi, Avshalom, Harrington, Hona Lee, & Milne, Barry J. (2002). Males on the life-source-persistent and adolescent-limited antisocial pathways: Follow-up at 26 years. *Developmental Psychopathology, 59.*

Mohan, Dinesh. (2000). Injury control and safety prevention: Ethics, science, and practice. In Dinesh Mohan & Geetam Tiwari (Eds.), *Injury prevention and control.* London: Taylor & Francis.

Molfese, Victoria J. , & Martin, Tina B. (2002). Intelligence and achievement: measurement and prediction of developmental variations. In Dennis L. Molfese & Virginia J. Molfese. (Eds.). *Developmental variation in learning.* Mahwah, NJ: Erlbaum. 275–308.

Moon, Christine, Cooper, Robin Panneton, & Fifer, William P. (1993). Two-day olds prefer their native language. *Infant Behavior & Development, 16,* 495–500.

Moore, Keith L., & Persaud, T. Vidhya N. (1998). *The developing human: Clinically oriented embryology.* Philadelphia: Saunders.

Morgenstern, Hal, Bingham, Trista, & Reza, Avid. (2000). Effects of pool-fencing ordinances and other factors on childhood drowning in Los Angeles County, 1990–1995. *American Journal of Public Health, 90,* 595–601.

Morita, Yohji, Soeda, Haruo, Soeda, Kumiko, & Taki, Mitsuru. (1999). Japan. In Peter K. Smith, Yohji Morita, Josine Junger-Tas, Dan Olweus, Richard F. Catalano, & Phillip T. Slee (Eds.*), The nature of school bullying: A cross-national perspective.* London: Routledge.

Morrison, Frederick J., Griffith, Elizabeth M., & Alberts, Denise M. (1997). Nature-nurture in the classroom: Entrance age, school readiness, and learning in children. *Developmental Psychology, 33,* 254–262.

Morrongiello, Barbara A., Fenwick, Kimberley D., & Chance, Graham. (1998). Crossmodal learning in newborn infants: Inferences about properties of auditory-visual events. *Infant Behavior & Development, 21,* 543–553.

Mortensen, Preben Bo, Pedersen, Carsten B., Westergaard, Tine, Wohlfahrt, Jan, Ewald, Henrik, Mors, Ole, et al. (1999). Effects of family history and season of birth on the risk of schizophrenia. *New England Journal of Medicine, 340,* 603–608.

Morton, J. Bruce, & Trehub, Sandra E. (2001). Children's understanding of emotion in speech. *Child Development, 72,* 834–843.

Moses, Louis J. (2001). Executive accounts of theory-of-mind development. *Child Development, 72,* 688–690.

Moster, Dag, Lie, Rolv T., Irgens, Lorentz M., Bjerkedal, Tor, & Markestad, Trond. (2001). The association of Apgar score with subsequent death and cerebral palsy: A population-based study in term infants. *Journal of Pediatrics, 138,* 798–803.

Mott, Frank L., Kowaleski-Jones, Lori, & Menaghan, Elizabeth G. (1997). Paternal absence and child behavior: Does a child's gender make a difference? *Journal of Marriage and the Family, 59,* 103–118.

Mpofu, Elias, & van de Vijver, Fons J. R. (2000). Taxonomic structure in early to middle childhood: A longitudinal study with Zimbabwean schoolchildren. *International Journal of Behavioral Development, 24,* 204–212.

Murphy, J. Michael, Wehler, Cheryl A., Pagona, Maria E., Little, Michelle,

Kleinman, Ronald E., & Jellinek, Michael S. (2001). Relation between hunger and psychosocial functioning. In Margaret E. Hertzig & Ellen A. Farber (Eds.). *Annual progress in child psychiatry and child development, 1999* (pp. 215–228). New York: Brunner/Routledge.

Myers, B. J. (1987). Mother-infant bonding as a critical period. In M.H. Bornstein (Ed.), *Sensitive periods in development: Inter-disciplinary perspectives.* Mahwah, NJ: Erlbaum.

Nagin, Daniel S., & Tremblay, Richard E. (1999). Trajectories of boys' physical aggression, opposition, and hyperactivity on the path to physically violent and nonviolent juvenile delinquency. *Child Development, 70,* 1181–1196.

Naito, Mika, & Miura, Hisayoshi. (2001). Japanese children's numerical competencies: Age- and school-related influences on the development of number concepts and addition skills. *Developmental Psychology, 37,* 217–230.

Nakamura, Suad, Wind, Marilyn & Danello, Mary Ann. (1999). Review of hazards associated with children placed in adult beds. *Archives of Pediatrics and Adolescent Medicine, 153,* 1019–1023.

Nantais, Kristin, & Schellenberg, E. Glenn. (1999). The Mozart effect: An artifact of preference. *Psychological Science, 10,* 370–373.

Nation, Kate, & Snowling, Margaret J. (1998). Individual differences in contextual facilitation: Evidence from dyslexia and poor reading comprehension. *Child Development, 69,* 996–1011.

National Academy of Sciences. (1994). *Assessing genetic risks: Implications for health and social policy.* Washington DC: National Academy Press.

National Center for Education Statistics. (2001). *Digest of Education Statistics: 2000.* Washington, DC: U.S. Department of Education.

National Center for Health Statistics. (1999). *Health, United States, 1999: With health and aging chartbook.* Hyattsville, MD: National Center for Health Statistics.

National Center for Health Statistics. (2000). *Health, United States, 2000.* Hyattsville, MD: Centers for Disease Control and Prevention.

National Center on Child Abuse and Neglect. (2001). *Child maltreatment 2000: Reports from the States.* Washington, DC: NCCAN.

National Endowment Goals Panel. (1997). *National endowment goals panel monthly.* Washington DC: National Endowment Goals Panel.

National Research Council and Institute of Medicine. (2000). *From neurons to neighborhoods: The science of early childhood development.* Jack P. Shonkoff & Deborah A. Phillips (Eds.). Washington, DC: National Academy Press.

Nazzi, Thierry, Bertoncini, Josiane, & Mehler, Jacques. (1998). Language discrimination by newborns: Towards an understanding of the role of rhythm. *Journal of Experimental Psychology: Human Perception and Performance, 24,* 756–766.

Nelson, Adie. (2000). The pink dragon is female: Halloween costumes and gender markers. *Psychology of Women Quarterly, 24,* 137–144.

Nelson, Charles A. (1997). The neurobiological basis of early memory development. In Nelson Cowan & Charles Hulme (Eds.), *The development of memory in childhood: Studies in developmental psychology.* Hove, East Sussex, England: Psychology Press.

Nelson, Katherine. (1981). Individual differences in language development: Implications for development and language. *Developmental Psychology, 17,* 171–187.

Nelson, Katherine. (1996). *Language in cognitive development.* New York: Cambridge University Press.

New York Times (1998, November 2). Metropolitan diary, p. B-2.

NICHD Early Child Care Research Network. (1996). Characteristics of infant child care: Factors contributing to positive child caregiving. *Early Childhood Research Quarterly, 11,* 469–306.

NICHD Early Child Care Research Network. (1997). The effects of infant child care on infant-mother attachment security. Results of the NICHD study of early child care. *Child Development, 68,* 860–879.

NICHD Early Child Care Research Network. (1998). Early child care and self-control, compliance, and problem behavior at 24 and 36 months. *Child Development, 69,* 1145–1170.

NICHD Early Child Care Research Network. (1999). Child care and mother-infant interaction in the first three years of life. *Developmental Psychology, 35,* 1399–1413.

NICHD Early Child Care Research Network. (2000). The relation of child care to cognitive and language development. *Child Development, 71,* 960–980.

NICHD Early Child Care Research Network. (2001). Child care and children's peer interaction at 24 and 36 months: The NICHD study of early child care. *Child Development, 72,* 1478–1500.

NICHD Early Child Care Research Network. (2002). Parenting and family influences when children are in child care: Result from the NICHD study of early child care. In John G. Borkowski, Sharon Landesman Ramey, and Marie Bristol-Power (Eds.). *Parenting and the child's world: Influences on academic, intellectual, and social-emotional development.* Mahwah, NJ: Erlbaum.

Nichols, Francine, & Zwelling, Elaine. (1997) *Maternal newborn nursing.* Philadelphia: Saunders.

Nielsen Media Research. (2000). Nielsen Media Research.

Nieto, Sonia. (2000). *Affirming diversity* (3rd ed.). New York: Addison Wesley Longman.

Nixon, James. (2000). Injury prevention and human rights. In Dinesh Mohan & Geetam Tiwari (Eds.), *Injury prevention and control.* London: Taylor & Francis.

Noppe, Ilene C. (2000). Beyond broken bonds and broken hearts: The bonding of theories of attachment and grief. *Developmental Review, 20,* 514–538.

Nunan, David, & Lam, Agnes. (1998). Teacher education for multilingual contexts: Models and issues. In Jasone Cenoz & Fred Genesee (Eds.), *Beyond bilingualism: Multilingualism and multilingual education.* Clevedon, England: Multilingual Matters.

O'Connor, Thomas G. & Croft, Carla M. (2001). A twin study of attachment in preschool children. *Child Development, 72,* 1501–1511.

O'Connor, Thomas G., Rutter, Michael, Beckett, Celia, Keaveney, Lisa, Kreppner, Jana M., & English and Romanian Adoptees Study Team. (2000). The effects of global severe privation on cognitive competence: Extension and longitudinal follow-up. *Child Development, 71,* 376–390.

Offenbacher, Steven, Katz, Vern, Fertik, Gregory, Collins, John, Boyd, Doryck, Maynor, Gayle, McKaig, Rosemary, & Beck, James. (1996). Periodontal infection as a possible risk factor for preterm low birth weight. *Journal of Periodontology, 67,* 1103–1113.

O'Hara, Michael W. (1997). The nature of postpartum depressive disorders. In Lynne Murray & Peter J. Cooper (Eds.), *Postpartum depression and child development.* New York: Guilford.

Ohsako, Toshio. (1999). The developing world. In Peter K. Smith, Yohji Morita, Josine Junger-Tas, Dan Olweus, Richard F. Catalano & Phillip T. Slee (Eds.), *The nature of school bullying: A cross-national perspective.* London: Routledge.

Oliver Ryalls, Brigette. (2000). Dimensional adjectives: Factors affecting children's ability to compare objects using novel words. *Journal of Experimental Child Psychology, 76,* 26–49.

Oliver Ryalls, Brigette, Gul, Robina, & Ryalls, Kenneth R. (2000). Infant imitation of adult and peer models: Evidence for a peer model advantage. *Merrill-Palmer Quarterly, 46,* 188–202.

Olweus, Dan. (1992). Bullying among schoolchildren: Intervention and prevention. In Ray D. Peters, Robert J. McMahon, & Vernon L. Quinsey (Eds.). *Aggression and violence throughout the life span.* Newbury Park, CA: Sage.

Olweus, Dan. (1993a). *Bullying at school: What we know and what we can do.* Oxford, England: Blackwell.

Olweus, Dan. (1993b). Victimization by peers: Antecedents and long-term outcomes. In K.H. Rubin & J.B. Asendorf (Eds.), *Social withdrawal, inhibition, and shyness in childhood.* Mahwah, NJ: Erlbaum.

Olweus, Dan. (1999). Norway. In Peter K. Smith, Yohji Morita, Josine Junger-Tas, Dan Olweus, Richard F. Catalano, & Phillip T. Slee (Eds.), *The nature of school bullying: A cross-national perspective.* London: Routledge.

Olweus, Dan. (2001). Peer harassment: A critical analysis and some important issues. In Jaana Juvonen and Sandra Graham (Eds.). *Peer harassment in school: The plight of the vulnerable and victimized* (pp. 3–20). New York: Guilford Press.

O'Neill, Daniela K., & Chong, Selena C. F. (2001) Preschool children's difficulty understanding the type of information obtained through the five senses. *Child Development, 72*, 803–815.

Ong, Elisa K., & Glantz, Stanton A. (2001). Constructing "sound science" and "good epidemiology": Tobacco, lawyers, and public relations firms. *American Journal of Public Health, 91*, 1749–1757.

Oosterlaan, Jaap, Logan, Gordon D., & Sergeant, Joseph A. (1998). Response inhibition in AD/HD, CD, comorbid AD/HD + CD, anxious, and control children: A meta-analysis of studies with the stop task. *Journal of Child Psychology & Psychiatry & Allied Disciplines, 39*, 411–425.

Opie, Iona. (1993). *The people in the playground.* Oxford, England: Oxford University Press.

Oppenheim, David. (1998). Perspectives on infant mental health from Israel: The case of changes in collective sleeping on the kibbutz. *Infant Mental Health Journal, 19*, 76–86.

Orme, John G., & Buehler, Cheryl. (2001). Foster family characteristics and behavioral and emotional problems of foster children: A narrative review. *Family Relations, 50*, 3–15.

Oswald, Ramona Faith. (2002). Resilience within the family networks of lesbians and gay men: Intentionality and redefinition. *Journal of Marriage and the Family, 64*, 374–383.

Overton, Willis F. (1998). Developmental psychology: Philosophy, concepts, and methodology. In William Damon (Series Ed.) & Richard M. Lerner (Vol. Ed.), *Handbook of child psychology: Vol. 1. Theoretical models of human development* (5th ed., pp. 107–188). New York: Wiley.

Oyserman, Daphna, Coon, Heather, & Kemmelmeier, Markus. (2002). Rethinking individualism and collectivism: Evaluation of theoretical assumptions and meta-analyses. *Psychological Bulletin, 128*, 3–72.

Panksepp, Jaak. (1998). Attention deficit hyperactivity disorders, psychostimulants, and intolerance of childhood playfulness: A tragedy in the making? *Current Directions in Psychological Science, 7*, 91–98.

Parke, Ross D. (1995). Fathers and families. In Marc H. Bornstein (Ed.) *Handbook of parenting: Status and social conditions of parenting.* Mahwah, NJ: Erlbaum.

Parke, Ross D. (1996). *Fatherhood.* Cambridge, MA: Harvard University Press.

Parke, Ross D., & Buriel, Raymond. (1998). Socialization in the family: Ethnic and ecological perspectives. In William Damon & Nancy Eisenberg (Eds.), *Handbook of child psychology: Vol. 3. Social, emotional, and personality development* (5th ed., pp. 463–552). New York: Wiley.

Parke, Ross D., Ornstein, Peter A., Rieser, John J., & Zahn-Waxler, Carolyn. (1994). The past as prologue: An overview of a century of developmental psychology. In Ross D. Parke, Peter A. Ornstein, John J. Rieser, & Carolyn Zahn-Waxler (Eds.), *A century of developmental psychology.* Washington, DC: American Psychological Association.

Parker, Richard. (2002). The global HIV/AIDS pandemic, structural inequalities, and the politics of international health. *American Journal of Public Health, 92*, 347–351.

Parten, Mildred B. (1932). Social participation among preschool children. *Journal of Abnormal and Social Psychology, 27*, 243–269.

Patterson, Charlotte J. (1995). Lesbian mothers, gay fathers, and their fathers. In Anthony R. D'Augelli & Charlotte J. Patterson (Eds.), *Lesbian, gay, and bisexual identities over the lifespan: Psychological perspectives.* New York: Oxford University Press.

Patterson, Charlotte J., & Redding, Richard E. (1996). Lesbian and gay families with children: Implications of social science research for policy. *Journal of Social Issues, 52*(3), 29–50.

Patterson, Gerald R. (1998). Continuities— A search for causal mechanisms: Comment on the special section. *Developmental Psychology, 34*, 1263–1268.

Pecheux, Marie Germaine, & Labrell, Florence. (1994). Parent-infant interactions and early cognitive development. In Andre Vyt, Henriette Bloch, & Marc H. Bornstein (Eds.), *Early child development in the French tradition:* Contributions from current research. Mahwah, NJ: Erlbaum.

Pellegrini, Anthony D., & Smith, Peter K. (1998). Physical activity play: The nature and function of a neglected aspect of play. *Child Development, 69*, 577–598.

Pellegrini, Anthony D., & Smith, Peter K. (2001). Physical activity play: The nature and function of a neglected aspect of play. In Margaret E. Hertizig & Ellen A. Farber (Eds.). *Annual progress in child psychiatry and child development, 1999* (pp. 1–36). New York: Brunner Routledge.

Pennington, Bruce F. (2001). Genetic methods. In Charles A. Nelson & Monica Luciana (Eds.), *Handbook of developmental neuroscience* (pp. 149–158). Cambridge, MA: MIT Press.

Pennisi, Elizabeth, & Roush, Wade. (1997). Developing a new view of evolution. *Science, 277*, 34–37.

Pepler, Debra, Craig, Wendy M., & O'Connell, Paul. (1999). Understanding bullying from a dynamic systems perspective. In Alan Slater & Darwin Muir (Eds.), *The Blackwell reader in developmental psychology.* Oxford, England: Blackwell.

Perner, Josef. (2000). About + belief + counterfactual. In Peter Mitchell & Kevin J. Riggs (Eds.), *Children's reasoning and the mind* (pp. 367–401). Hove, England: Psychology Press.

Peterson, Carole, & Rideout, Regina. (1998). Memory for medical emergencies experienced by one- and two-year-olds. *Developmental Psychology, 34*, 1059–1072.

Petitto, Anne, & Marentette, Paula F. (1991). Babbling in the manual mode: Evidence for the ontogeny of language. *Science, 251*, 1493–1496.

Pew Environmental Health Commission. (2000). Attack asthma: Why American needs a public health defense system to battle environmental threats. Baltimore, MD: Johns Hopkins School of Public Health.

Piaget, Jean. (1952a). *The child's conception of number.* London: Routledge & Kegan Paul.

Piaget, Jean. (1952b). *The origins of intelligence in children* (Margaret Cook, Trans.). New York: International Universities Press.

Piaget, Jean. (1962). *Play, dreams, and imitation in childhood.* New York: Norton.

Piaget, Jean. (1970a). *The child's conception of movement and speed.* (G.E.T. Holloway & M.J. Mackenzie, Trans.). New York: Basic Books.

Piaget, Jean. (1970b). *The child's conception of time.* (A.J. Pomerans, Trans.). New York: Basic Books.

Pinderhughes, Ellen E., Nix, Robert, Foster, E. Michael, Jones, Damon, & The Conduct Problems Prevention Research Group. (2001). Parenting in context: Impact of neighborhood poverty, residential stability, public services, social networks, and danger on parental behaviors. *Journal of Marriage and the Family, 63,* 941–953.

Pinker, Steven. (1994). *The language instinct.* New York: Harper-Collins.

Pipe, Margaret-Ellen, Gee, Susan, Wilson, J. Clare, & Egerton, Janice M. (1999). *Developmental Psychology, 35,* 781–789.

Pipp-Siegel, Sandra, Siegel, Clifford J., & Dean, Janet. (1999). Neurological aspects of the disorganized/disoriented attachment classification system: Differentiating quality of the attachment relationship from neurological impairment. In Joan I. Vondra & Douglas Barnett (Eds.), Atypical attachment in infancy and early childhood among children at developmental risk. *Monographs of the Society for Research in Child Development, 64*(Serial No. 258), 25–44.

Pisecco, Stewart, Baker, David B., Silva, Phil A., & Brooke, Mark. (2001). Boys with reading disabilities and/or ADHD: Distinctions in early childhood. *Journal of Learning Disabilities, 34,* 98–106.

Plomin, Robert, DeFreis, John C., McClearn, Gerald E., & McGuffin, Peter. (2001). *Behavioral genetics* (4th ed.). New York: Worth Publishers.

Plunkett, Kim. (1997). Theories of early language acquisition. *Trends in Cognitive Sciences, 1,* 146–153.

Poehlmann, Julie, & Fiese, Barbara. (2001). The interaction of maternal and infant vulnerabilities on developing attachment relationships. *Development and Psychopathology, 13,* 1–11.

Pollack, Harold A., & Frohna, John G. (2001). A competing risk model of sudden infant death syndrome in two US birth cohorts. *Journal of Pediatrics, 138,* 661–667.

Pollak, Seth D., Cicchetti, Dante, Hornung, Katherine, & Reed, Alex. (2000). Recognizing emotion in faces: Developmental effects of child abuse and neglect. *Developmental Psychology, 36,* 679–688.

Pollitt, Ernesto, Golub, Mari, Gorman, Kathleen, Levitsky, David, Schurch, Beat, Strupp, Barbara, & Wachs, Theodora. (1996). A reconceptualization of the effects of undernutrition on children's biological, psychological and behavioral development.

Social Policy Report of the Society for Research in Child Development, 10, (5), 1–32.

Ponsoby, Anne-Louise, Dwyer, Terence, Gibbins, Laura E., Cochrane, Jennifer A., & Wang, Yon-Gan. (1993). Factors potentiating the risk of sudden infant death syndrome associated with the prone position. *New England Journal of Medicine, 329,* 377–382.

Pool, Robert. (1993). Evidence for the homosexuality gene. *Science, 261,* 291–292.

Popper, Karl R. (1965). *The logic of scientific discovery.* New York: Harper.

Porter, Richard, Varendi, H., Christensson, K., Porter, R. H. and Winberg, J. (1998). Soothing effect of amniotic fluid smell in newborn infants. *Early Human Development, 51,* 47–55.

Posada, German, Gao, Yuan, Wu, Fang, Posada, Roberto, Tascon, Margarita, Schöelmerich, Axel, et al. (1995). The secure-base phenomenon across cultures: Children's behavior, mothers' preferences, and experts' concepts. In Everett Waters, Brian E. Vaughn, German Posada, & Kiyomi Kondo-Ikemura (Eds.), *Caregivng, cultural and cognitive perspectives on secure-base behavior and working models: New growing points of attachment theory and research. Monographs of the Society for Research in Child Development, 60*(Serial No. 244), 27–48.

Posner, Michael I. & Rothbart, Mary K. (2000). Developing mechanisms of self-regulation. *Development and Psychopathology, 12,* 427–441.

Poulin, François, & Boivin, Michel. (2000). The role of proactive and reactive aggression in the formation and development of boys' friendships. *Developmental Psychology, 30,* 233–240.

Pufall, Peter B. (1997). Framing a developmental psychology of art. *Human Development, 40,* 169–180.

Pyke, Karen. (1999). The micropolitics of care in relationships between aging parents and adult chidlren: Individualism, collectivism, and power. *Journal of Marriage and the Family, 61,* 661–672.

Quinn, Paul C., Cummins, Maggie, Kase, Jennifer, Martin, Erin, & Weissman, Sheri. (1996). Development of categorical representations for above and below spatial relations in 3- to 7-month-old infants. *Developmental Psychology, 32,* 942–950.

Rall, Jaime, & Harris, Paul L. (2000). In Cinderella's slippers? Story comprehension

from the protagonist's point of view. *Developmental Psychology, 36,* 202–208.

Ramey, Craig T., Bryant, Donna B., Wasik, Barbara H., Sparling, Joseph J., Fendt, K.H., & Levange, L.M. (1992). The Infant Health and Development Program for low birth weight, premature infants: Program elements, family participation, and child intelligence. *Pediatrics, 89,* 454–465.

Ramey, Craig T. & Ramey, Sharon L. (1998). Early intervention and early experience. *American Psychologist, 53,* 109–120.

Ramey, Craig T., Ramey, Sharon Landesman, Lanzi, Robin Gaines, & Cotton, Janice N. (2002). Early educational intervention for high-risk children: How center-based treatment can augment and improve parenting effectiveness. In John G. Borkowski, Sharon Landesman Ramey, and Marie Bristol-Power (Eds.). *Parenting and the child's world: Influences on academic, intellectual, and social-emotional development.* Mahwah, NJ: Erlbaum.

Ramey, Sharon Landesman, & Ramey, Craig T. (2000). Early childhood experiences and developmental competence. In Sheldon Danziger & Jane Waldfogel (Eds.), *Securing the future* (pp. 122–150). New York: Russell Sage Foundation.

Ramey, Sharon Landesman. (2002). The science and art of parenting. In John G. Borkowski, Sharon Landesman Ramey, & Marie Bristol-Power (Eds.), *Parenting and the child's world: Influences on academic, intellectual and social-emotional development.* Mahwah, NJ: Erlbaum.

Ranyard, Rob, Crozier, W. Ray, & Svenson, Ola. (Eds.). (1997). *Decision making: Cognitive model and explanations.* New York: Routledge.

Rao, Raghavendra, & Georgieff, Michael K. (2000). Early nutrition and brain development. In Charles A. Nelson (Ed.), *The Minnesota Symposia on Child Psychology: Vol. 31. The effects of early adversity on neurobehavioral development.* Mahwah, NJ: Erlbaum.

Ratner, Hilary Horn, Foley, Mary Ann, & Gimpert, Nicole. (2000). Person perspective on children's memory and learning: What do source monitoring failures reveal? In Kim P. Roberts & Mark Blades (Eds.), *Children's source monitoring.* Mahwah, NJ: Erlbaum.

Rauscher, Frances H., & Shaw, Gordon L. (1998). Key components of the Mozart effect. *Perceptual and Motor Skills, 86,* 835–841.

Rauscher, Frances H., Shaw, Gordon L., & Ky, Katherine N. (1993). Music and spatial task performance. *Nature, 365,* 611.

Rayner, Keith, Foorman, Barbara R., Perfetti, Charles A., Pesetsky, David, & Seidenberg, Mark S. (2001). How psychological science informs the teaching of reading. *Psychological Science in the Public Interest, 2,* 31–74.

Reed, Edward S. (1993). The intention to use a specific affordance: A conceptual framework for psychology. In Robert H. Wozniak & Kurt W. Fischer (Eds.), *Development in context: Acting and thinking in specific environments.* Mahwah, NJ: Erlbaum.

Reese, Elaine, Haden, Catherine A., & Fivush, Robyn. (1993). Mother-child conversations about the past: Relationships of style and memory over time. *Cognitive Development, 8,* 403–430.

Reid, John B., Patterson, Gerald R., & Snyder, James J. (2002). *Antisocial behavior in children and adolescents.* Washington, DC: American Psychological Association.

Reiss, David. (1997). Mechanisms linking genetic and social influences in adolescent development: Beginning a collaborative search. *Current Directions in Psychological Science, 6,* 100–105.

Reiss, David, & Neiderhiser, Jenae M. (2000). The interplay of genetic influences and social processes in developmental theory: Specific mechanisms are coming into view. *Development and Psychopathology, 12,* 357–374.

Renninger, K. Ann, & Amsel, Eric. (1997). Change and development: An introduction. In Eric Amsel & K. Ann Renninger (Eds.), *Change and development: Issues of theory, method, & application.* Mahwah, NJ: Erlbaum.

Rest, James R. (1983). Morality. In Paul H. Mussen (Ed.), *Handbook of child psychology: Vol. 3. Cognitive development.* New York: Wiley.

Rest, James R., Narvaez, Darcia, Bebeau, Muriel J., & Thoma, Stephen J. (1999a). A neo-Kohlbergian approach: The DIT and scheme theory. *Educational Psychology Review, 11,* 291–324.

Rest, James R., Narvaez, Darcia, Bebeau, Murel J., & Thoma, Stephen J. (1999b). *Postconventional moral thinking: A neo-Kohlbergian approach.* Mahwah, NJ: Erlbaum.

Reynolds, Arthur J. (2000). *Success in early intervention: The Chicago child-parent centers.* Lincoln: University of Nebraska.

Reznick, J. Steven, Chawarska, Katarzyna, & Betts, Stephanie. (2000). The development of visual expectation in the first year. *Child Development, 71,* 1191–1204.

Rice, Amy L., Sacco, Lisa, Hyder, Adnan, & Black, Robert E. (2000). Malnutrition as an underlying cause of childhood deaths associated with infectious diseases in developing countries. *Bulletin of the World Health Organization, 78,* 1207–1221.

Rice, George, Anderson, Carol, Risch, Neil, & Ebers, George. (1999). Male homosexuality: Absence of linkage to microsatellite markers at Xq28. *Science, 284,* 665–667.

Richardson, Gale A. (1998). Prenatal cocaine exposure: A longitudinal study of development. *Annals of the New York Academy of Science, 846,* 144–152.

Ridley, Matt. (1999). *Genome.* London: Fourth Estate Limited.

Rigby, Ken, & Slee, Phillip T. (1999). Australia. In Peter K. Smith, Yohji Morita, Josine Junger-Tas, Dan Olweus, Richard F. Catalano, & Phillip T. Slee (Eds.), *The nature of school bullying: A cross-national perspective.* London: Routledge.

Riley, Lisa A., & Glass, Jennifer L. (2002). You can't always get what you want—infant care preferences and use among employed mothers. *Journal of Marriage and the Family, 64,* 2–15.

Rind, Bruce, Tromovitch, Philip, & Bauserman, Robert. (1998) A meta-analytical examination of assumed properties of child sexual abuse using college students. *Psychological Bulletin, 124,* 22–53.

Riordan, Jan, & Auerbach, Kathleen. (1998). *Breast feeding and human lactation* (2nd ed.). Boston: Jones and Bartlett.

Rios-Ellis, Britt, Bellamy, Laura, & Shoji, Junichi. (2000). An examination of specific types of Ijime within Japanese schools. *School Psychology International, 21,* 227–241.

Rivara, Fred P. (1994). Unintentional injuries. In Ivan Barry Pless (Ed.), *The epidemiology of childhood disorders.* New York: Oxford University Press.

Robert, Elizabeth. (1996). Treating depression in pregnancy, editorial. *New England Journal of Medicine, 335,* 1056–1058.

Roberts, Kenneth. (1988). Retrieval of a basic-level category in prelinguistic infants. *Developmental Psychology, 24,* 21–27.

Roberts, Kim P. (2000). An overview of theory and research on children's source monitoring. In Kim P. Roberts & Mark Blades (Eds.), *Children's source monitoring.* Mahwah, NJ: Erlbaum.

Robin, Daniel J., Berthier, Neil E., & Clifton, Rachel K. (1996). Infants' predictive reaching for moving objects in the dark. *Developmental Psychology, 32,* 824–835.

Robinson, Thomas N., & Killen, Joel D. (2001). Obesity prevention for children and adolescents. In J. Kevin Thompson & Linda Smolak (Eds.), *Body image, eating disorders, and obesity in youth* (pp. 261–292). Washington, DC: American Psychological Association.

Rochat, Philippe. (2001). *The infant's world.* Cambridge, MA: Harvard University Press.

Rodier, Patricia H. (2000). The early origins of autism. *Scientific American, 282* (2). 56–63.

Roehlkepartain, Eugene, Benson, Peter L., & Sharman, Anu. (1994). *Growing up adopted.* Minneapolis: Search Institute.

Rogoff, Barbara. (1990). *Apprenticeship in thinking: Cognitive development in social context.* New York: Oxford University Press.

Rogoff, Barbara. (1997). Evaluating development in the process of participation: Theory, methods, and practice building on each other. In Eric Amsel & K. Ann Renninger (Eds.), *Change and development: Issues of theory, method, & application.* Mahwah, NJ: Erlbaum.

Rogoff, Barbara. (1998). Cognition as a collaborative process. In William Damon (Series Ed.), Deanna Kuhn & Robert S. Siegler (Vol. Eds.), *Handbook of child psychology: Vol. 2. Cognition, perception, and language* (5th ed., pp. 679–744). New York: Wiley.

Rohlen, Thomas P., & LeTendre, Gerald K. (1996). *Teaching and learning in Japan.* Cambridge, England: Cambridge University Press.

Rolls, Edmund T. (2000). Memory systems in the brain. *Annual Review of Psychology, 51,* 599–630.

Romaine, Suzanne. (1999). Bilingual language development. In M. Barrett (Ed.), *The development of language* (pp. 251–275). Hove, England: Psychology Press.

Romo, Harriett D., & Falbo, Toni. (1996). *Latino high school graduation: Defying the odds.* Austin: University of Texas Press.

Rose, Amanda J., & Asher, Steven R. (1999). Children's goals and strategies in response to conflicts within a friendship. *Developmental Psychology, 35,* 69–79.

Rose, Susan A., & Feldman, Judith F. (2000). The relation of very low birth weight to basic cognitive skills in infancy. In Charles A. Nelson (Ed.), *The Minnesota Symposia on Child Psychology: Vol. 31. The effects of early adversity on neurobehavioral development.* Mahwah, NJ: Erlbaum.

Rose, Susan A., Feldman, Judith F., & Jankowski, Jeffrey J. (2001a). Attention and recognition memory in the first year of life: A longitudinal study of preterm and full-term infants. *Developmental Psychology, 37,* 135–151.

Rose, Susan A., Feldman, Judith F., & Jankowski, Jeffrey J. (2001b). Visual short-term memory in the first year of life: Capacity and recency effects. *Developmental Psychology, 37,* 539–549.

Rosenblith, Judy F. (1992). *In the beginning: Development from conception to age two* (2nd ed.). Newbury Park, CA: Sage.

Rosenthal, M. Sara. (1996). *The fertility sourcebook.* Lincolnwood, Illinois: Lowell House.

Rosser, Pearl L., & Randolph, Suzanne M. (1989). Black American infants: The Howard University normative study. In J. Kevin Nuegent, Barry M. Lester, & T. Berry Brazelton (Eds.), *The cultural context of infancy: Vol 1. Biology, culture, and infant development.* Norwood, NJ: Ablex.

Rothbart, Mary K., & Bates, John E. (1998). Temperament. In William Damon (Series Ed.), Nancy Eisenberg (Vol. Ed.), *Handbook of child psychology: Vol. 3. Social, emotional, and personality development* (5th ed., pp. 105–176). New York: Wiley.

Rothbaum, Fred, Pott, Martha, Azuma, Hiroshi, Miyake, Kazuo, & Weisz, John. (2000). The development of close relationships in Japan and the United States: Paths of symbolic harmony and generative tension. *Child Development, 71,* 1121–1142.

Rovee-Collier, Carolyn K. (1987). Learning and memory in infancy. In J. Doniger Osofsky (Ed.), *Handbook of infant development* (2nd ed.). New York: Wiley.

Rovee-Collier, Carolyn K. (1990). The "memory system" of prelinguistic infants. In

A. Diamond (Ed.), *The development and neural bases of higher cognitive functions.* New York: New York Academy of Sciences.

Rovee-Collier, Carolyn K. (2001). Information pick-up by infants: What is it, and how can we tell. *Journal of Experimental Child Psychology, 78,* 35–49.

Rovee-Collier, Carolyn K., & Gerhardstein, Peter. (1997). The development of infant memory. In Nelson Cowan & Charles Hulme (Eds.), *The development of memory in childhood: Studies in developmental psychology.* Hove, East Sussex, England: Psychology Press.

Rovee-Collier, Carolyn K., & Hayne, Harlene. (1987). Reactivation of infant memory: Implications for cognitive development. In H.W. Reese (Ed.), *Advances in child development and behavior* (Vol. 20). New York: Academic Press.

Rovee-Collier, Carolyn K., Hayne, Harlene, & Colombo, Michael. (2001). *The development of implicit and explicit memory.* Amsterdam: John Benjamins.

Rowe, David C., & Jacobson, Kristen C. (1999). In the mainstream: Research in behavioral genetics. In Ronald A. Carson & Mark A. Rothstein (Eds.), *Behavioral genetics: The clash of culture and biology* (pp. 12–34). Baltimore: Johns Hopkins Press.

Rubenstein, Adam J., Kalakanis, Lisa, & Langlois, Judith H. (1999). Infant preferences for attractive faces: A cognitive explanation. *Developmental Psychology, 35,* 848–855.

Rubin, Glenna B., Fagen, Jeffrey W., & Carroll, Marjorie H. (1998). Olfactory context and memory retrieval in 3-month-old infants. *Infant Behavior & Development, 21,* 641–658.

Rubin, Kenneth H., Bukowski, William, & Parker, Jeffrey G. (1998). Peer interactions, relationships, and groups. In William Damon (Series Ed.) & Nancy Eisenberg (Vol. Ed.), *Handbook of child psychology: Vol. 3. Social, emotional, and personality development* (5th ed., pp. 619–700). New York: Wiley.

Ruble, Diane N., & Martin, Carol Lynn. (1998). Gender development. In William Damon & Nancy Eisenberg (Eds.), *Handbook of child psychology,* Vol. 3. *Social, emotional and personality development* (5th ed., pp. 933–1016). New York: Wiley.

Rumbert, Ruben, & Portes, Alejandro. (2001). *Ethnicities: Children of immigrants in*

America. University of California Press/ Russell Sage Foundation.

Russell, Mark. (2002). Institute helps spread use of vaccines in Asia. *Science, 295,* 611–612.

Rust, John, Golombok, Susan, Hines, Melissa, Johnson, Katie, Golding, Jean, & ALSPAC Study Team. (2000). The role of brothers and sisters in the gender development of preschool children. *Journal of Experimental Child Psychology, 77,* 292–303.

Rutstein, Shea O. (2000). Factors associated with trends in infant and child morality in developing countries during the 1990s. *Bulletin of the World Health Organization, 78,* 1256–1270.

Rutter, Michael. (1998). Some research considerations on intergenerational continuities and discontinuities: Comment on the special section. *Developmental Psychology, 34,* 1269–1273.

Rutter, Michael. (2002). Nature, nurture, and development: From evangelism through science toward policy and practice. *Child Development, 73,* 1–12.

Rutter, Michael, Giller, Henry & Hagell, Anne. (1998). *Antisocial behavior by young people.* Cambridge, England: Cambridge University Press.

Rutter, Michael, & Rutter, Marjorie. (1993). *Developing minds: Challenge and continuity across the life span.* New York: Basic Books.

Rutter, Michael, & Sroufe, L. Alan. (2000). Developmental psychopathology: Concepts and challenges. *Development and Psychopathology, 12,* 265–296.

Rutter, Michael, Thorpe, K., & Golding, J. (2000). *Twins as a natural experiment to study the causes of language delay.* Report to the Mental Health Foundation, London.

Sabbagh, Mark A., & Baldwin, Dare A. (2001). Learning words from knowledgeable versus ignorant speakers: Links between preschoolers' theory of mind and semantic development. *Child Development, 72,* 1054–1070.

Sacks, Oliver. (1995). *An anthropologist on Mars: Paradoxical tales.* New York: Random House.

Sadeh, Avi, Raviv, Amiram, & Gruber, Reut. (2000). Sleep patterns and sleep disruptions in school-age children. *Developmental Psychology, 36,* 291–301.

Saffran, Jenny R., Aslin, Richard N., & Newport, Elissa L. (1996). Statistical learning by 8-month-old infants. *Science, 274,* 1926–1928.

Salzarulo, Piero, & Fagioli, Igino. (1999). Changes of sleep states and physiological activities across the first year of life. In A. F. Kalverboer, Maria Luisa Genta, & J. B. Hopkins (Eds.), *Current issues in developmental psychology.* Dordrecht, Netherlands: Kluwer.

Sampaio, Ricardo C., & Truwit, Charles L. (2001). Myelination in the developing human brain. In Charles A. Nelson & Monica Luciana (Eds.), *Handbook of developmental neuroscience* (pp. 35–44). Cambridge, MA: MIT Press.

Sampson, Paul D., Streissguth, Ann P., Bookstein, Fred L., Little, Ruth E., Clarren, Sterling K., Dehaene, Philippe, et al. (1997). Incidence of fetal alcohol syndrome and prevalence of alcohol-related neurodevelopmental disorder. *Teratology, 56,* 317–326.

Sampson, Robert J., Raudenbush, Stephen W., & Earls, Felton. (1997). Neighborhoods and violent crime: A multilevel study of collective efficacy. *Science, 277,* 918–924.

Sanchez, Maria del Mar, Ladd, Charlotte O., & Plotsky, Paul M. (2001). Early adverse experience as a developmental risk factor for later psychopathology: Evidence from rodent and primate models. *Development and Psychopathology, 13,* 419–450.

Sandelowski, Margarete. (1993). *With child in mind: Studies of the personal encounter with infertility.* Philadelphia: University of Pennsylvania Press.

Sapolsky, Robert M. (1997). The importance of a well-groomed child. *Science, 277,* 1620–1621.

Sapp, Felicity, Lee, Kang, & Muir, Darwin. (2000). Three-year-olds' difficulty with the appearance-reality distinction: Is it real or is it apparent? *Developmental Psychology, 36,* 547–560.

Sargent, James D., Stukel, Therese A., Dalton, Madeline A., Freeman, Jean L., & Brown, Mary Jean. (1996). Iron deficiency in Massachusetts communities: Socioeconomic and demographic risk factors among children. *American Journal of Public Health, 86,* 544–550.

Savin-Williams, Ritch C., & Diamond, Lisa M. (1997). Sexual orientation as a developmental context for lesbians, gays, and bisexuals: Biological perspectives. In Nancy L. Segal, Glenn E. Weisfeld, & Carol C. Weisfeld (Eds.), *Uniting psychology and biology: Integrative perspectives on human development.* Washington, DC: American Psychological Association.

Saxe, Geoffrey B. (1999). Sources of concepts: A cultural-developmental perspective. In Ellen Kofsky Scholnick, Katherine Nelson, Susan A. Gelman, & Patricia H. Miller (Eds.), *Conceptual development: Piaget's legacy* (pp. 253–268). Mahwah, NJ: Erlbaum.

Saxe, Geoffrey, Guberman, Steven R., & Gearhart, Maryl. (1987). Social processes in early number development. *Monographs of the Society for Research in Child Development, 52* (Serial No. 216).

Schacter, Daniel L., & Badgaiyan, Rajendra D. (2001). Neuroimaging of priming: New perspectives on implicit and explicit memory. *Current Directions in Psychological Science, 10,* 1–4.

Schaffer, Rudolph H. (2000). The early experience assumption: Past, present, and future. *International Journal of Behavioral Development, 24,* 5–14.

Schaffner, Kenneth F. (1999). Complexity and research strategies in behavioral genetics. In Ronald A. Carson & Mark A. Rothstein (Eds.), *Behavioral genetics: The clash of culture and biology* (pp. 61–88). Baltimore: Johns Hopkins Press.

Schaie, K. Warner. (1996). *Intellectual development in adulthood: The Seattle Longitudinal Study.* Cambridge, England: Cambridge University Press.

Scharf, Miri. (2001). A "natural experiment" in childrearing ecologies and adolescents' attachment and separation representation. *Child Development, 72,* 236–251.

Scheuffgen, Kristina, Happe, Francesca, Anderson, Mike, & Firth, Uta. (2000). High "intelligence," low "IQ"? Speed of processing and measured IQ in children with autism. *Development and Psychopathology, 12,* 83–90.

Schirmer, Barbara R. (2000). *Language and literacy development in children who are deaf* (2nd ed.). Boston: Allyn and Bacon.

Schlegel, Alice, & Barry, Herbert. (1991). *Adolescence: An anthropological inquiry.* New York: Free Press.

Schneider, Wolfgang. (1998). The development of procedural metamemory in childhood and adolescence. In Guiliana Mazzoni & Thomas O. Nelson (Eds.), *Monitoring and control processes in metacognition and cognitive neuropsychology* (pp. 1–21). Mahwah, NJ: Erlbaum.

Schneider, Wolfgang, & Bjorklund, David F. (1998). Memory. In William Damon (Series Ed.), Deanna Kuhn, & Robert S. Siegler (Vol. Eds.), *Handbook of child psychology: Vol. 2. Cognition, perception, and language* (5th ed., pp. 467–522). New York: Wiley.

Schneider, Wolfgang, Bjorklund, David F., & Maier-Bruckner, Wolfgang. (1996). The effects of expertise and IQ on children's memory: When knowledge is, and when it is not enough. *International Journal of Behavioral Development, 19,* 773–796.

Schneider, Wolfgang, & Pressley, Michael. (1997). *Memory development: Between two and twenty.* Mahwah, NJ: Erlbaum.

Schwartz, David, Chang, Lei, & Farver, JoAnn M. (2001). Correlates of victimization in Chinese children's peer groups. *Developmental Psychology, 37,* 520–532.

Schweder, Richard A., Goodnow, Jacqueline, Hatano, Giyooo, LeVine, Robert A., Markus, Hazel, & Miller, Peggy. (1998). The cultural psychology of development: One mind, many mentalities. In William Damon (Series Ed.) & Richard M. Lerner (Vol. Ed.), *Handbook of child psychology: Vol. 1. Theoretical models of human development* (5th ed., pp. 865–937). New York: Wiley.

Schweinhart, Lawrence J., & Weikart, David P. (1997). *Lasting differences: The High/Scope preschool curriculum comparison study through age 27.* Ypsilanti, MI: High/Scope Educational Research Foundation.

Scott, Fiona J., & Baron-Cohen, Simon. (1996) Logical, analogical, and psychological reasoning in autism: A test of the Cosmides theory. *Development and Psychopathology, 8,* 235–245.

Scott, Stephen, Spender, Quentin, Doolan, Moira, Jacobs, Brian, Aspland, Helen, & Webster-Stratton, Carolyn. (2001). Multicentre controlled trial of parenting groups for childhood antisocial behavior in clinical practice. *British Medical Journal, 323,* 194–197.

Scovel, Thomas. (1988). *A time to speak: A psycholinguistic inquiry into the critical period for human speech.* New York: Newbury.

Sedlak, Andrea J., & Broadhurst, Diane D. (1996). *Third national study of child abuse and neglect: *Final report.* Washington DC: U.S. Department of Health and Human Services.

Sena, Rhonda, & Smith, Linda B. (1990). New evidence on the development of the word Big. *Child Development, 61,* 1034–1052.

Sénéchal, Monique, & LeFevre, Jo-Anne. (2002). Parental involvement in the development of children's reading skill: A five-year longitudinal study. *Child Development, 73,* 445–460.

Senghas, Ann, & Coppola, Marie. (2001). Children creating language: How Nicaraguan Sign Language acquired a spatial grammar. *Psychological Science, 12,* 323–328.

Shahin, Hashem, Walsh, Tom, Sobe, Tama, Lynch, Eric, King, Marie-Claire, Avraham, Karen B., & Kanaan, Moien. (2002). Genetics of congenital deafness in the Palestine population. *Human Genetics, 110,* 284–289.

Shatz, Marilyn. (1994). *A toddler's life.* New York: Oxford University Press.

Shaw, Daniel S., Vondra, Joan I., Hommerding, Katherine Dowdell, Keenan, Kate, & Dunn, Marija. (1994). Chronic family adversity and early child behavior problems. A longitudinal study of low income families. *Journal of Child Psychology and Psychiatry, 35,* 1109–1122.

Sherman, Stephanie L. & Waldman, Irwin D. (1999). Identifying the molecular genetic basis of behavioral traits. In Ronald A. Carson & Mark A. Rothstein (Eds.), *Behavioral genetics: The clash of culture and biology* (pp. 35–60). Baltimore: Johns Hopkins Press.

Shi, Rushen, Werker, Janet F., & Morgan, James L. (1999). Newborn infants' sensitivity to perceptual cues to lexical and grammatical words. *Cognition, 72,* B-11—B-21.

Shiono, Patricia H., Rauh, Virginia A., Park, Mikyung, Lederman, Sally A., & Zuskar, Deborah. (1997). Ethnic differences in birthweight: The role of lifestyle and other factors. *American Journal of Public Health, 87,* 787–793.

Shirley, Mary M. (1933). *The first two years: A study of twenty-five babies.* (Institute of Child Welfare Monograph No. 8.) Minneapolis: University of Minnesota Press.

Shneidman, Edwin S. (2001). *Contemplating suicide: Landmarks in 20th century psychology.* Washington DC: American Psychological Association.

Shonkoff, Jack P. (2000). Science, policy, and practice: Three cultures in search of a shared mission. *Child Development, 71,* 181–187.

Shore, R. Jerald, & Hayslip, Bert, Jr. (1994). Custodial grandparenting: Implications for children's development. In Adele Eskeles Gottfried & Allen W. Gottfried (Eds.), *Redefining families: Implications for children's development.* New York: Plenum Press.

Shrebman, Laura. (2000). Intensive behavioral/psychoeducational treatment for autism: Research needs and future directions. *Journal of Autism and Pervasive Developmental Disorders, 30,* 373–378.

Shute, Nancy, Locy, Toni, & Pasternak, Douglas. (2000, March 6). The perils of pills. *U.S. News and World Report,* 45–49.

Siegler, Robert S., & Jenkins, E. A. (1989). *How children discover new strategies.* Hillsdale, NJ: Erlbaum.

Silk, Jennifer S., Nath, Sanjay R., Siegel, Lori R., & Kendall, Philip C. (2000). Conceptualizing mental disorders in children: Where have we been and where are we going? *Development and Psychopathology, 12,* 713–735.

Silva, Phil A. (1996). Health and development in the early years. In Phil A. Silva & Warren R. Stanton (Eds.), *From child to adult: The Dunedin multidisciplinary health and development study.* New Zealand: Oxford University Press.

Silver, Rawley. (2001). *Art as language.* Philadelphia: Psychology Press.

Simmons, Roberta G., & Blyth, Dale A. (1987). *Moving into adolescence: The impact of pubertal change and school context.* New York: de Gruyter.

Simon, Herbert A. (2001). Learning to research about learning. In Sharon M. Carver & David Klahr (Eds.), *Cognition and instruction* (pp. 205–226). Mahwah, NJ: Erlbaum.

Simons, Ronald L. (1996). *Understanding differences between divorced and intact families.* Thousand Oaks, CA: Sage.

Simpson, Joe Leigh, Grito, Jamie A., Handyside, Alan, & Verlinsky, Yury. (1999). Preimplantation genetic diagnosis: The new frontier. *Contemporary Ob/Gyn, 44,* 55–78.

Siperstein, Gary N., Leffert, James S., & Wenz-Gross, Melodie. (1997). The quality of friendships between children with and

without learning problems. *American Journal on Mental Retardation, 102,* 111–125.

Skinner, Burrhus Frederic. (1953). *Science and human behavior.* New York: Macmillan.

Skinner, Burrhus Frederic. (1957). *Verbal behavior.* New York: Appleton-Century-Crofts.

Slobin, Dan I. (2001). Form-function relations: How do children find out what they are? In Melissa Bowerman & Stephen C. Levinson (Eds.), *Language acquisition and conceptual development* (pp. 406–449). Cambridge, England: Cambridge University Press.

Smetana, Judith G., Killen, Melanie, & Turiel, Elliot. (1991). Children's reasoning about interpersonal and moral conflicts. *Child Development, 62,* 629–644.

Smith, George Davey. (2000). Learning to live with complexity: Ethnicity, socioeconomic position, and health in Britain and the United States. *American Journal of Public Health, 90,* 1694–1698.

Smith, Jacqui, & Baltes, Paul B. (1999). Trends and profiles of psychological functioning in very old age. In P. B. Baltes & K. U. Mayer (Eds.), *The Berlin aging study: Aging from 70 to 100.* New York: Cambridge University Press.

Smith, Linda. (1995). Self-organizing processes in learning to learn words. In C.A. Nelson (Ed.), *Basic and applied perspectives on learning, cognition, and development* (Minnesota Symposium on Child Psychology, Vol. 28). Mahwah, NJ: Erlbaum.

Smith, Peter K., Morita, Yohji, Junger-Tas, Josine, Olweus, Dan, Catalano Richard, & Slee, Phillip. (1999). *The nature of school bullying: A cross-national perspective.* London: Routledge.

Smith, Peter K., Shu, Shu, & Madsen, Kirsten. (2001). Characteristics of victims of school bullying: Developmental changes in coping strategies and skills. In Jaana Juvonen and Sandra Graham (Eds.). *Peer harassment in school: The plight of the vulnerable and victimized* (pp. 332–351). New York: Guilford Press.

Snarey, John R. (1993). *How fathers care for the next generation: A four-decade study.* Cambridge, MA: Harvard University Press.

Snijders, R.J.M., & Nicolaides, K.H. (1996). *Ultrasound markers for fetal chromosomal defects.* New York: Parthenon.

Snow, Catherine E. (1984). Parent-child interaction and the development of communicative ability. In Richard L. Schiefelbusch & Joanne Pickar (Eds.), *The acquisition of communicative competence*. Baltimore: University Park Press.

Society for Research in Child Development (SRCD). (1996). Ethical standards for research with children. *SCRD Directory of Members*, 337–339.

Soken, Nelson H., & Pick, Anne D. (1999). Infants' perception of dynamic affective expressions: Do infants distinguish specific expressions? *Child Development, 70*, 1275–1282.

Sonnenschein, S., Brody, G., & Munsterman, K. (1996). The influence of family beliefs and practices on children's early reading development. In L. Baker & P. Afflerbach (Eds.), *Developing engaged readers in school and home communities* (pp. 3–20). Mahwah, NJ: Erlbaum.

Soussignan, Robert, & Tremblay, Richard. (1996). Other disorders of conduct. In Seija Sandberg (Ed.). *Hyperactivity disorders of childhood* (pp. 195–245). Cambridge, England: Cambridge University Press.

Spelke, Elizabeth S. (1993). Physical knowledge in infancy: reflections on Piaget's theory. In Susan Carey & Rochel Gelman (Eds.), *The epigenesis of mind: essay on biology and cognition*. Hillsdale, NJ: Erlbaum.

Spelke, Elizabeth S., & Tsivkin, Sanna. (2001). Initial knowledge and conceptual change: space and number. In Melissa Bowerman & Stephen C. Levinson (Eds.), *Language acquisition and conceptual development* (pp. 70–97). Cambridge, England: Cambridge University Press.

Spieker, Susan J., Larson, Nancy C., Lewis, Steven M., Keller, Thomas E., & Gilchrist, Lewayne. (1999). Developmental trajectories of disruptive behavior problems in preschool children of adolescent mothers. *Child Development, 70*, 443–458.

Spock, Benjamin. (1976). *Baby and child care*. New York: Pocket Books.

Springer, Sally P., & Deutsch, Georg. (1997). *Left brain, right brain: Perspectives from cognitive neuroscience* (5th ed.). New York: Freeman.

Sridher, Dheepa, & Vaughn, Sharon. (2001). Social functioning of students with learning disabilities. In Daniel P. Hallahan and Barbara K. Keogh (Eds.), *Research and global perspectives in learning disabilities* (pp. 65–91). Mahwah, NJ: Erlbaum.

Sroufe, L. Alan. (1996). *Emotional development: The organization of emotional lie in the early years*. Cambridge, England: Cambridge University Press.

Sroufe, L. Alan. (2002). From infant attachment to promotion of adolescent autonomy: Prospective, longitudinal data on the role of parents in development. In John G. Borkowski, Sharon Landesman Ramey, and Marie Bristol-Power (Eds.). *Parenting and the child's world: Influences on academic, intellectual, and social-emotional development*. Mahwah, NJ: Erlbaum. 187–202.

Stanovich, Keith E. (1999). *Who is rational? Studies of individual differences in reasoning*. Mahwah, NJ: Erlbaum.

Stanovich, Keith E. (2000). Progress in understanding reading: Scientific foundations and new frontiers. New York: Guilford.

Staples, Robert, & Johnson, Leanor B. (1993). *Black families at the crossroads*. San Francisco: Jossey-Bass.

Stassen, David. (2002, January 15). Conversation between David Stassen and the author.

Stecher, B. M., & Bohrnstedt, G. W. (2000). *Class size reductions in California: The 1998–99 evaluation findings*. Sacramento, CA: California Department of Education.

Steele, Kenneth M., Bass, Karen E., & Crook, Melissa D. (1999). The Mozart effect: An artifact of preference. *Psychological Science, 10*, 370–373.

Stern, Daniel N. (1985). *The interpersonal world of the infant*. New York: Basic Books.

Sternberg, Robert J. (1996). *Successful intelligence*. New York: Simon & Schuster.

Sternberg, Robert J. (2002). Everything you need to know to understand the current controversies you learned from psychological research. *American Psychologist, 57*, 193–197.

Sternberg, Robert J., Grigorenko, Elena Y., & Bundy, Donald A. (2001). The predictive value of IQ. *Merrill-Palmer Quarterly, 47*, 1–41.

Stigler, James W., & Hiebert, James. (1999). *The teaching gap*. New York: The Free Press.

Stiles, Joan. (1998). The effects of early focal brain injury on lateralization of cognitive function. *Current Directions in Psychological Science, 7*, 21–26.

Stipek, Deborah. (2001). Pathways to constructive lives: The importance of early school success. In Arthur C. Bohart & Deborah J. Stipek (Eds.), *Constructive and destructive behavior: Implications for family, school & society* (pp. 291–316). Washington, DC: American Psychological Society.

Stipek, Deborah J., Feiler, Rachell, Daniels, Denise, & Milburn, Sharon. (1995). Effects of different instructional approaches on young children's achievement and motivation. *Child Development, 66*, 209–223.

Stormshak, Elizabeth, Bierman, Karen, & The Conduct Problems Prevention Research Group. (1998). The implications of different developmental patterns of disruptive behavior problems for school adjustment. *Development and Psychopathology, 10*, 451–468.

St. Pierre, Robert G., Layzer, Jean I., Goodson, Barbara D., & Bernstein, Lawrence S. (1997). *The effectiveness of comprehensive, case management interventions: Findings from the national evaluation of the comprehensive child development program*. Cambridge, MA: Abt Associates.

Strassberg, Zvi, Dodge, Kenneth A., Pettit, Gregory S., & Bates, John E. (1994). Spanking in the home and children's subsequent aggression toward kindergarten peers. *Development and Psychopathology, 6*, 445–462.

Straus, Murray A. (1994). *Beating the devil out of them: Corporal punishment in American families*. Lexington, MA: Lexington Books.

Strauss, David, & Eyman, Richard K. (1996). Mortality of people with mental retardation in California with and without Down syndrome, 1986–1991. *American Journal on Mental Retardation, 100*, 643–653.

Streissguth, Ann P., & Connor, Paul D. (2001). Fetal alcohol effects and other effects of prenatal alcohol: Developmental cognitive neuroscience implications. In Charles A. Nelson & Monica Luciana (Eds.), *Handbook of developmental neuroscience*. Cambridge, MA: MIT Press.

Suarez-Orozco, Carola, & Suarez-Orozco, Marcelo M. (2001). *Children of immigration*. Cambridge, MA: Harvard University Press.

Sun, Yongmin, & Li, Yu. (2001). Marital disruption, parental investment and children's academic achievement: A prospective analysis. *Journal of Family Issues, 22*, 27–62.

Suomi, Stephen. (2002). Parents, peers, and the process of socialization in primates. In John G. Borkowski, Sharon Landesman Ramey, & Marie Bristol-Power (Eds.), *Parenting and the child's world: Influences on academic, intellectual, and social-emotional development.* Mahwah, NJ: Erlbaum.

Susman, Elizabeth J., Schmeelk, Karen H., Ponirakis, Angelo, & Gariepy, Jean Louis. (2001). Maternal prenatal, postpartum, and concurrent stressors and temperament in 3-year-olds: A person and variable analysis. *Development and Psychopathology, 13,* 629–652.

Sutton-Smith, Brian. (1997). *The ambiguity of play.* Cambridge, MA: Harvard University Press.

Swain, Merrill, & Johnson, Robert K. (1997). Introduction. In Robert K. Johnson & Merrill Swain (Eds.), *Immersion Education: International Perspectives.* Cambridge, England: Cambridge University.

Swanson, H. Lee. (1999). *Interventions for students with learning disabilities: A meta-analysis of treatment outcomes.* New York: Guilford.

Swenson, Nora C. (2000). Comparing traditional and collaborative settings for language intervention. *Communication Disorders Quarterly, 22,* 12–18.

Szatmari, Peter. (2001, Spring). Thinking about autism, Asperger disorder, and PDD-NOS. *Newsletter of the Centre for Studies of Children at Risk, 4.*

Szkrybalo, Joel, & Ruble, Diane N. (1999). "God made me a girl": Sex-category constancy judgments and explanations revisited. *Developmental Psychology, 35,* 392–402.

Takahashi, T., Nowakowski, Richard S., & Caviness, Verne S., Jr. (2001). Neocortical neurogenesis: Regulation, control points, and a strategy of structural variation. In Charles A. Nelson & Monica Luciana (Eds.), *Handbook of developmental neuroscience.* Cambridge, MA: MIT Press.

Talukder, M. Q.-K. (2000). The importance of breastfeeding and strategies to sustain high breastfeeding rates. In Anthony Costello & Dharma Manandhar (Eds.), *Improving newborn infant health in developing countries.* London: Imperial College Press.

Tamis-LeMonda, Catherine S., Bornstein, Marc H., & Baumwell, Lisa. (2001). Maternal responsiveness and children's achievement of language milestones. *Child Development, 72,* 748–767.

Tangney, June Price. (2001). Constructive and destructive aspects of shame and guilt. In Arthur C. Bohart & Deborah J. Stipek (Eds.). *Constructive and destructive behavior: Implications for family, school and society* (pp. 249–270). Washington, DC: American Psychological Society.

Tanner, James M. (1978). Fetus into Man: Physical growth from conception to maturity. Cambridge, MA: Harvard University Press.

Tanner, James M. (1991b). Menarche, secular trend in age of. In Richard M. Lerner, Ann C. Petersen, & Jeanne Brooks-Gunn (Eds.), *Encyclopedia of adolescence* (Vol. 2). New York: Garland.

Tarter, Ralph, Vanyukov, Michael, Giancola, Peter, Dawes, Michael, Blackson, Timothy, Mezzich, Ada, & Clark, Duncan B. (1999). Etiology of early age onset substance use disorder: A maturational perspective. *Development and Psychopathology, 11,* 657–683.

Tatz, Colin. (2001). *Aboriginal suicide is different.* Canberra: Aboriginal Studies Press.

Taylor, H. Gerry, Klein, Nancy, & Hack, Maureen. (2000). School-age consequences of birth weight less than 750 grams: A review and an update. *Developmental Neuropsychology, 17,* 289–321.

Taylor, H. Gerry, Klein, Nancy, Schatschneider, Christopher, & Hack, Maureen. (1998). Predictors of early school age outcomes in very low birth weight children. *Journal of Developmental and Behavioral Pediatrics, 19,* 235–243.

Taylor, Marjorie. (1999). *Imaginary companions and the children who create them.* Oxford, England: Oxford University Press.

Teicher, Martin H. (2002). Scars that won't heal: The neurobiology of child abuse. *Scientific American, 286,* (3), 68–75.

Teitelbaum, Philip, Teitelbaum, Osnat, Nye, Jennifer, Fryman, Joshua, & Maurer, Ralph G. (1998). Movement analysis in infancy may be useful for early diagnosis of autism. *Proceedings of the National Academy of Sciences, 23,* 13982–13987.

Terrell, J., & Modell, J. (1994). Anthropology and adoption. *American Anthropologist, 96,* 155–161.

Terwogt, Mark Meerum, & Stegge, Hedy. (1998). Children's perspective on the emotional process. In Anne Campbell & Steven Muncer (Eds.), *The social child.* East Sussex, England: Psychology Press.

Thapar, Anita, Holmes, J., Poulton, K., & Harrington, R. (1999). Genetic basis of attention deficit and hyperactivity. *British Journal of Psychiatry, 174,* 105–111.

Theimer, Christine E., Killen, Melanie, & Stangor, Charles. (2001). Young children's evaluation of exclusion in gender-stereotypic peer contexts. *Developmental Psychology, 37,* 18–27.

Thelen, Esther, Corbetta, Daniela, Kamm, Kathi, Spencer, John P., Schneider, K., & Zernicke, R.F. (1993). The transition to reaching: Mapping intention and intrinsic dynamics. *Child Development, 64,* 1058–1098.

Thomas, Alexander, & Chess, Stella. (1977). *Temperament and development.* New York: Brunner/Mazel.

Thomas, Alexander, Chess, Stella, & Birch, Herbert G. (1963). *Behavioral individuality in early childhood.* New York: New York University Press.

Thomas, Jeanne L., Sperry, Len, & Yarbrough, M. Sue. (2000). Grandparents as parents: Research findings and policy recommendations. *Child Psychiatry and Human Development, 31,* 3–22.

Thompson, Frances E., & Dennison, Barbara. (1994). Dietary sources of fats and cholesterol in U.S. children aged 2 through 5 years. *American Journal of Public Health, 84,* 799–806.

Thompson, Richard F. (2000). *The Brain* (3rd ed.). New York: Worth.

Thompson, Ron A., & Sherman, Roberta. (1993). *Helping athletes with eating disorders.* Bloomington, IN: Human Kinetics Books.

Thompson, Ross A. (1992). Developmental changes in research risk and benefit: A changing calculus of concerns. In B. Stanley & J.E. Sieber (Eds.), *Social research on children and adolescents: Ethical issues.* Newbury Park, CA: Sage.

Thompson, Ross A. (1998). Early sociopersonality development. In William Damon & Nancy Eisenberg (Eds.), *Handbook of child psychology:* Vol. 3. *Social, emotional, and personality development* (5th ed., pp. 25–65). New York: Wiley.

Thompson, Ross A. (2000). The legacy of early attachments. *Child Development, 71,* 145–152.

Thompson, Ross A. (2001). Panel discussion of *From neurons to neighborhoods*. Biennial meeting of Society for Research in Child Development, Minneapolis, Minnesota.

Thompson, Ross A., & Nelson, Charles A. (2001). Developmental science and the media: Early brain development. *American Psychologist, 56,* 5–15.

Tobin, Allan J. (1999). Amazing grace: Sources of phenotypic variation in genetic boosterism. In Ronald A. Carson & Mark A. Rothstein (Eds.), *Behavioral genetics: The clash of culture and biology.* (pp. 1–11). Baltimore: Johns Hopkins Press.

Tomasello, Michael. (2000). Culture and cognitive development. *Current Directions in Psychological Science, 2,* 37–45.

Tomasello, Michael. (2001). Perceiving intentions and learning words in the second year of life. In Melissa Bowerman & Stephen C. Levinson (Eds.), *Language acquisition and conceptual development* (pp. 132–158). Cambridge, England: Cambridge University Press.

Torff, Bruce, & Gardner, Howard. (1999). The vertical mind: The case for multiple intelligences. In M. Anderson (Ed.), *The development of intelligence.* London: University College Press.

Tremblay, Richard E. (2000). Quoted in Constance Holden. The violence of the lambs. *Science, 298,* 580–581.

Triandis, H. C. (1989). The self and social behavior in differing cultural contexts. *Psychological Review, 96,* 506–520.

Tronick, Edward S. (1989). Emotions and emotional communication. *American Psychologist, 44,* 112–119.

Tronick, Edward S., Als, Heidelise, Adamson, Lauren, Wise, S., & Brazelton, T. Berry. (1978). The infant response to entrapment between contradictory messages in face-to-face interaction. *Journal of the American Academy of Child Psychiatry, 17,* 1–13.

True, Mary McMahan, Pisani, Lelia, & Oumar, Fadimata. (2001). Infant-mother attachment among the Dogon of Mali. *Child Development, 72,* 1451–1466.

Tsui, Amy O., Waserheit, Judith N., & Haaga, John G. (Eds.; Panel on Reproductive Health, National Research Council). (1997). *Reproductive health in developing countries: Expanding dimensions, building solutions.* Washington, D.C.: National Academy Press.

Tucker, G. Richard. (1998). A global perspective on multilingualism and multilingual education. In Jasone Cenoz & Fred Genesee (Eds.), *Beyond bilingualism: Multilingualism and multilingual education.* Clevedon, England: Multilingual Matters.

Turiel, Elliot, Smetana, Judith G., & Killen, Melanie. (1991). Social context in social cognitive development. In William M. Kurtines & Jacob L. Gewirtz (Eds.), *Handbook of moral behavior and development: Vol. 2. Research.* Mahwah, NJ: Erlbaum.

Uhlenberg, Peter. (1996). Mutual attraction: Demography and life-course analysis. *Gerontologist, 36,* 226–229.

Umilta, Carlo, & Stablum, Franca. (1998). Control processes explored by the study of closed head injury patients. In Giuliana Mazzoni & Thomas O. Nelson (Eds.), *Metacognition and cognitive neuropsychology: Monitoring and control processes.* Mahwah, NJ: Erlbaum.

United Nations Development Program. (2001). *Human Development Report.* New York: Oxford University Press.

Updegraff, Kimberly A., Madden-Derdich, Debra A., Estrada, Ana Ulloa, Sales, Lara J., & Leonard, Stacie A. (2002). Young adolescents' experiences with parents and friends: Exploring the connections. *Family relations, 51,* 72–80.

U. S. Bureau of the Census. (1972). *Statistical abstract of the United States, 1972* (92nd ed.). Washington, DC: U.S. Department of Commerce.

U. S. Bureau of the Census. (1986). *Statistical abstract of the United States.* Washington, DC: U. S. Department of Commerce.

U. S. Bureau of the Census. (1999). *Statistical abstract of the United States, 1999* (119th ed.). Washington, DC: U.S. Department of Commerce.

U. S. Bureau of the Census. (2000). *Statistical abstract of the United States, 2000* (120th ed.). Washington, DC: U.S. Department of Commerce.

U. S. Bureau of the Census. (2001). *Statistical abstract of the United States, 2001* (121th ed.). Washington, DC: U.S. Department of Commerce.

U. S. Congress. (2000, July 26). Joint statement on the impact of entertainment violence on children, presented at the Public Health Summit, Washington, DC.

U. S. Department of Education. (2001). *Digest of education statistics, 2000* (NCES 2001-034). Washington, DC: Office of Educational Research and Improvement, U.S. Department of Education.

U. S. Department of Health and Human Services. (2000). *Trends in the well-being of America's children and youth.* Washington, DC: U.S. Government Printing Office.

U. S. Department of Health and Human Services. (2001). *Child maltreatment 1999: Reports from the States.* Washington, DC: U. S. Government Printing Office.

U. S. Department of Health and Human Services. (2002, February 14). Annual update of HHS poverty guidelines. *Federal Register, 67,* 6931–6933.

U. S. Department of Justice. (2002). *Source book of Criminal Justice Statistics.* Washington DC.

Uttal, William R. (2000). *The war between mentalism and behaviorism.* Mahwah, NJ: Erlbaum.

Valsiner, Jaan. (1997). Constructing the personal through the cultural redundant organization of psychological development. In Eric Amsel & K. Ann Renninger (Eds.), *Change and development: Issues of theory, method, & application.* Mahwah, NJ: Erlbaum.

van IJzendoorn, Marinus H., & Hubbard, Frans O. A. (2000). Are infant crying and maternal responsiveness during the first year related to infant-mother attachment at 15 months? *Attachment and Human Development, 2,* 371–391.

van IJzendoorn, Marinus H., & Kroonenberg, P. (1988). Cross-cultural patterns of attachment: A meta-analysis of the Strange Situation. *Child Development, 59,* 3–9.

van IJzendoorn, Marinus H., Moran, Greg, Belsky, Jay, & Pederson, David. (2000). The similarity of siblings' attachments to their mother. *Child Development, 71,* 1086–1098.

Van Tuijl, Cathy, Leseman, Paul P. M., & Rispens, Jan. (2001). Efficacy of an intensive home-based educational intervention programme for 4–6 year-old ethnic minority children in the Netherlands. *International Journal of Behavioral Development, 25,* 148–159.

Vandell, Deborah L., Hyde, Janet S., Plant, E. Ashby, & Essex, Marilyn J. (1997). Fathers and "others" as infant care providers: Predictors of parents' emotional well-being and marital satisfaction. *Merrill-Palmer Quarterly, 43,* 361–385.

Varendi, Heili, Christensson, Kyllike, Porter, Richard H., & Winberg, Jan. (1998). Soothing effect of amniotic fluid smell in newborn infants. *Early Human Development, 51,* 47–55.

Varnhagen, Connie. (2002). *Making sense of psychology on the Web.* New York: Worth.

Verschueren, Karine, Buyck, Petra, & Marcoen, Alfons. (2001). Self-representations and socioemotional competence in young children: A 3-year longitudinal study. *Developmental Psychology, 37,* 126–134.

Vickers, James C., Dickson, Tracey C., Adlard, Paul A., Saunders, Helen L., King, Carolyn E., & McCormack, Graeme. (2000). The causes of neural degeneration in Alzheimer's disease. *Neurobiology, 60,* 139–165.

Victora, Cesar; Bryce, Jennifer; Fontaine, Liver, & Monasch, Roeland. (2000). Reducing deaths from diarrhea through oral rehydration therapy. *Bulletin of the World Health Organization, 78,* 1246–1255.

Vinden, Penelope. (1996). Junin Quechua Children's understanding of the mind. *Child Development, 67,* 1707–1716.

Volker, Susanne, Keller, Heidi, Lohaus, Arnold, & Cappenberg, Martina. (1999). Maternal interactive behaviour in early infancy and later attachment. *International Journal of Behavioral Development, 23,* 921–936.

Vondra, Joan I., & Barnett, Douglas (Eds.) (1999). *Atypical attachment in infancy and early childhood among children at developmental risk. Monographs of the Society for Research in Child Development, 64* (Serial No. 258), 145–171.

Vygotsky, Lev S. (1925/1994). Principles of social education for deaf and dumb children in Russia. In Rene van der Veer & Jaan Valsiner (Eds., 1994), *The Vygotsky Reader.* Oxford, U.K.: Blackwell.

Vygotsky, Lev S. (1934/1986). *Thought and language.* Cambridge, MA: MIT Press.

Vygotsky, Lev S. (1934/1994). The development of academic concepts in school aged children. In Rene van der Veer & Jaan Valsiner (Eds.), *The Vygotsky Reader,* Blackwell.

Vygotsky, Lev S. (1978). *Mind in society: The development of higher psychological processes.* Cambridge, MA: Harvard University Press.

Vygotsky, Lev S. (1987). *Thinking and speech* (N. Minick, Trans.). New York: Plenum Press.

Wachs, Theodore D. (1999). Celebrating complexity: Conceptualization and assessment of the environment. In S. Freidman & T.D. Wachs (Eds.), *Measuring environment across the lifespan: Emerging methods and concepts.* Washington, DC: American Psychological Association.

Wachs, Theodore D. (2000). *Necessary but not sufficient.* Washington, DC: American Psychological Association.

Wainryb, Cecilia, Shaw, Leigh A., Laupa, Marta, & Smith, Ken R. (2001). Children's, adolescents' and young adult thinking about different types of disagreements. *Developmental Psychology, 37,* 373–386.

Wainryb, Cecilia, & Turiel, Elliot. (1995). Diversity in social development: Between or within cultures? In Melanie Killen & Daniel Hart (Eds.), *Morality in everyday life: Developmental perspectives.* Cambridge, England: Cambridge University Press.

Waldfogel, Jane. (1998). Rethinking the paradigm for child protection. *The Future of Children: Protecting Children from Abuse and Neglect, 8,* 4–22.

Waldron, Nancy L. & McLeskey, James. (1998). The effects of an inclusive school program on students with mild and severe learning disabilities. *Exceptional Children, 64,* 395–405.

Walker, Lawrence J. (1988). The development of moral reasoning. *Annals of Child Development, 55,* 677–691.

Walker, Lawrence J., Gustafson, Paul, & Hennig, Karl H. (2001). The consolidation/transition model in moral reasoning development. *Developmental Psychology, 37,* 187–197.

Walker, Lawrence J., Hennig, Karl H., & Krettenauer, Tobias. (2000). Parent and peer contexts for children's moral reasoning development. *Child Development, 71,* 1033–1048.

Walker, Lawrence J., Pitts, Russell C., Hennig, Karl H., & Matsuba, M. Kyle. (1995). Reasoning about morality and real-life moral problems. In Melanie Killen & Daniel Hart (Eds.), *Morality in everyday life:*

Developmental perspectives. Cambridge, England: Cambridge University Press.

Walsh, Froma. (2002). A family resilience framework: Innovative practice applications. *Family Relations, 51,* 130–137.

Walton, Irene, & Hamilton, Mary. (1998). *Midwives and changing childbirth.* Cheshire, England: Books for Midwives Press.

Warash, Bobbie Gibson, & Markstrom-Adams, Carol. (1995). Preschool experiences of advantaged children. *Psychological Reports, 77,* 89–90.

Wartella, Ellen A., & Jennings, Nancy. (2000). Children and computers: New technology—old concerns. *The Future of Children, 10,* (2), 31–43.

Waters, Mary C. (2000). *Black identities: West Indian immigrant dreams and American realities.* Cambridge, MA: Harvard University Press.

Watson, John B. (1924). *Behaviorism.* Chicago: University of Chicago Press.

Watson, John B. (1928). *Psychological care of the infant and child.* New York: Norton.

Watson, John B. (1998). *Behaviorism.* New Brunswick, NJ: Transaction.

Wegar, Katarina. (2000). Adoption, family ideology and social stigma: Bias in community attitudes, adoption research, and practice. *Family Relations, 49,* 363–370.

Weinberg, M. Katherine, Tronick, Edward Z., Cohn, Jeffrey F., & Olson, Karen L. (1999). Gender differences in emotional expressivity and self-regulation during early infancy. *Developmental Psychology, 35,* 175–188.

Weissbluth, Marc. (1999). *Healthy sleep habits, happy child* (Rev. ed.). New York: Fawcett.

Weizman, Zehave Oz, & Snow, Catherine E. (2001). Lexical input as related to children's vocabulary acquisition: Effects of sophisticated exposure and support for meaning. *Developmental Psychology, 37,* 265–279.

Wellman, Henry M., Cross, David, & Watson, Julanne. (2001). Meta-analysis of theory-of-mind development: The truth about false belief. *Child Development, 72,* 655–684.

Wendland-Carro, Jaqueline, Piccinini, Cesar A., & Millar, W. Stuart. (1999). The role of an early intervention on enhancing the quality of mother-infant interaction. *Child Development, 70,* 713–721.

Wentworth, Naomi, Benson, Janette B., & Haith, Marshall M. (2000). The development of infants' reaches for stationary and moving targets. *Child Development, 71,* 576–601.

Werner, Emmy E. (1994). Overcoming the odds. *Journal of Developmental and Behavioral Pediatrics, 2,* 131–136.

Werner, Emmy E., & Smith, Ruth S. (1992). *Overcoming the odds: High risk children from birth to adulthood.* Ithaca, NY: Cornell University Press.

Wertsch, James V. (1985). *Vygotsky and the social formation of mind.* Cambridge, MA: Harvard University Press.

Wertsch, James V., & Tulviste, Peeter. (1992). L.S. Vygotsky and contemporary developmental psychology. *Developmental Psychology, 28,* 548–557.

Whitaker, Daniel J., Miller, Kim S., & Clark, Leslie F. (2000). Reconceptualizing adolescent sexual behavior: Beyond did they or didn't they? *Family Planning Perspectives, 32,* 111–117.

Whitam, Frederick L., Diamond, Milton, & Martin, James. (1993). Homosexual orientation in twins: A report on 61 pairs and three triplet sets. *Archives of Sexual Behavior, 22,* 187–206.

White, Lynn, & Rogers, Stacy J. (2000). Economic circumstances and family outcomes: A review of the 1990s. *Journal of Marriage and the Family, 62,* 1035–1051.

Whiting, Beatrice Blyth, & Edwards, Carolyn Pope. (1988). *Children of different worlds: The formation of social behavior.* Cambridge, MA: Harvard University Press.

Willatts, Peter. (1999). Development of means-end behavior in young infants: Pulling a support to retrieve a distant object. *Developmental Psychology, 35,* 651–667.

Williams, Benjamin R., Ponesse, Jonathan S., Schachar, Russell J., Logan, Gordon D., & Tannock, Rosemary. (1999). Development of inhibitory control across the life span. *Developmental Psychology, 35,* 205–213.

Wingerson, Lois. (1998). *Unnatural selection: The promise and the power of human gene research.* New York: Bantam Doubleday Dell.

Winsler, Adam, Carlton, Martha, & Barry, Maryann J. (2000). Age-related change in preschool children's systematic use of private speech in a natural setting. *Journal of Child Language, 27,* 665–687.

Winsler, Adam, Díaz, Rafael M., Espinosa, Linda, & Rodríguez, James L. (1999). When learning a second language does not mean losing the first: Bilingual language development in low-income, Spanish-speaking children attending bilingual preschool. *Child Development, 70,* 349–362.

Wishart, Jennifer G. (1999). Learning and development in children with Down's syndrome. In Alan Slater and Darwin Muir (Eds.) *The Blackwell reader in developmental psychology.* Oxford, England: Blackwell.

Wolfe, David A., Wekerle, Christine, Reitzel-Jaffe, Degborah, & Lefebvre, Lorrie. (1998). Factors associated with abusive relationships among maltreated and nonmaltreated youth. *Development and Psychopathology, 10,* 61–85.

Wollons, Roberta Lynn. (2000). *Kindergartens and cultures: The global diffusion of an idea.* New Haven, CT: Yale University Press.

Wolraich, Mark L., Hannah, Jane N., Baumgaertel, Anna, & Feurer, Irene D. (1998). Examination of DSM-IV criteria for attention deficit hyperactivity disorder in a county-side sample. *Journal of Developmental & Behavioral Pediatrics, 19,* 162–168.

Wong, Sau-ling C., & Lopez, Miguel G. (2000). English language learners of Chinese background: A portrait of diversity. In Sandra Lee McKay & Sau-ling Cynthia Wong (Eds.), *New immigrants in the United States* (pp. 263–305). Cambridge, England: Cambridge University Press.

Wong, Siu Kwong. (1999). Acculturation, peer relations, and delinquent behavior of Chinese-Canadian youth. *Adolescence, 34,* 108–119.

Woodward, Amanda L., & Markman, Ellen M. (1998). Early word learning. In William Damon (Series Ed.), Deanna Kuhn, & Robert S. Siegler (Vol. Eds.), *Handbook of child psychology:* Vol. 2. *Cognition, perception and language* (5th ed., pp. 371–420). New York: Wiley.

Woolley, Jacqueline D., Phelps, Katrina E., Davis, Debra L., & Mandell, Dorothy J. (1999). Where theories of mind meet magic: The development of children's beliefs about wishing. *Child Development, 70,* 571–587.

World Health Organization (WHO). (1990). *The Innocenti declaration on the protection, promotion, and support of breastfeeding.* Adopted by the WHO and UNICEF. Florence, Italy, August 1.

World Health Organization. (1998). *Obesity: Preventing and managing the global epidemic: Report of a WHO consultation on obesity.* Geneva: World Health Organization.

Wright, Charlotte M., & Talbot, E. (1996). Screening for failure to thrive: What are we looking for? *Child: Care, Health & Development, 22,* 223–234.

Wright, William. (1998). *Born that way.* New York: Knopf.

Wyman, Peter A., Cowen, Emory L., Work, William C., Hoyt-Meyers, Lynne, Magnus, Keith B., & Fagen, Douglas B. (1999). Caregiving and developmental factors differentiating young at-risk urban children showing resilient versus stress-affected outcome: A replication and extension. *Child Development, 70,* 645–659.

Yoos, H. Lorrie, Kitzman, Harriet, & Cole, Robert. (1999). Family routines and the feeding process. In Daniel B. Kessler & Peter Dawson (Eds.), *Failure to thrive and pediatric undernutrition* (pp. 375–384). Baltimore: Brooks.

Yoshikawa, Hirokazu. (1994). Prevention as cumulative protection: Effects of early family support and education on chronic delinquency and its risks. *Psychological Bulletin, 115,* 28–54.

Yoshikawa, Hirokazu, & Hsueh, JoAnn. (2001). Child development and public policy: Toward a dynamic systems perspective. *Child Development, 72,* 1887–1903.

Zahn-Waxler, Carolyn, Schmitz, Stephanie, Fulker, David, Robinson, Joann, & Emde, Robert. (1996). Behavior problems in 5-year-old monozygotic and dyzygotic twins: Genetic and environmental influences, patterns of regulation, and internalization of control. *Development and Psychopathology, 8,* 103–122.

Zarbatany, Lynne, Hartmann, Donald P., & Rankin, D. Bruce. (1990). The psychological functions of preadolescent peer activities. *Child Development, 61,* 1067–1080.

Zeifman, Debra, Delaney, Sarah, & Blass, Elliott. (1996). Sweet taste, looking, and calm in two- and four-week-old infants: The eyes have it. *Developmental Psychology, 32,* 1090–1099.

Zeskind, Philip Sanford, & Barr, Ronald G. (1997). Acoustic characteristics of naturally occurring cries of infants with "colic." *Child Development, 68,* 394–403.

Ziatas, Kathryn, Durkin, Kevin, & Pratt, Chris. (1998). Belief term development in children with autism, Asperger syndrome, specific language impairment, and normal development: Links to theory of mind development. *Journal of Child Psychology & Psychiatry & Allied Disciplines, 39,* 755–763.

Zigler, Edward. (1998). School should begin at age 3 years for American children. *Journal of Developmental and Behavioral Pediatrics, 19,* 37–38.

Zigler, Edward, & Muenchow, Susan. (1992). *Head Start: The inside story of America's most successful educational experiment.* New York: Basic Books.

Zigler, Edward, & Styfco, Sally J. (Eds.). (1993). *Head Start and beyond: A national plan for extended childhood intervention.* New Haven, CT: Yale University Press.

Zigler, Edward, & Styfco, Sally J. (2001). Can early chidhood intervention prevent deliquency? A real possibility. In Arthur C. Bohar & Deborah J. Stipek (Eds.). *Constructive and destructive behavior: Implications for family, school and society* (pp. 231–248). Washington, DC: American Psychological Association.